LAST TSAR

S. S. OLDENBURG

LAST TSAR

Nicholas II, His Reign & His Russia

⟨⟨✧⟩⟩

Volume 4

THE WORLD WAR, 1914-1918

Translated by Leonid I. Mihalap and Patrick J. Rollins
Edited by Patrick J. Rollins

⟨⟨✧⟩⟩

ACADEMIC INTERNATIONAL PRESS

1978

THE RUSSIAN SERIES / Volume 25-4

Sergei S. Oldenburg **Last Tsar! Nicholas II, His Reign
and His Russia.** Volume 4: **The World War, 1914-1917.**
Translation of *Tsarstvovanie Imperatora Nikolaia II*,
Volume 2 (Munich, 1949), Part IV, Chapters XVIII-XXI.

ISBN: 0-87569-074-2

Maps by Richard D. Kelly, Jr.
Composition by Jean MacNeil and Jeanette Rawlinson
Title page by King & Queen Press

Illustrations from Count Paul Vassili (pseud.), *Behind the Veil
at the Russian Court* (London, 1914); *Literary Digest History
of the World War.* Volume 7. (New York, 1919); S.S. Oldenburg,
Tsarstvovanie Imperatora Nikolaia II. Volume 2; Anon., *Russian
Court Memoirs, 1914-16* (London, 1917); Paul Milyoukov,
Russia and its Crisis (Chicago, 1905); Princess Catherine Radziwell,
Rasputin and the Russian Revolution (New York, 1918); A.J.
Sacks, *The Birth of the Russian Democracy* (New York, 1918);
A. Elchaninov, *The Tsar and His People* (London, c. 1917).

Printed in the United States of America

ACADEMIC INTERNATIONAL PRESS
POB 555 Gulf Breeze FL 32561

CONTENTS

CONVERSION TABLE

Linear Measure
    1 *versta* (plur., *verst*) = 0.663 mile
    1 *arshin* = 28 inches

Land Area
    1 *desiatina* (plur., *desiatin*) = 2.7 acres
    1 *kvadratnaia versta* = 0.43957 square miles

Weight
    1 *pud* = 36.113 pounds
    1 *berkovets* (10 puds) = 361.13 pounds

Volume, Dry Measure
    1 *chetvert* = 6 bushels (approx.)

Volume, Liquid Measure
    1 *vedro* (plur., *vedra*) = 3.25 gallons
    1 *bochka* (40 *vedra*) = 131.5 gallons

Currency
    1 *rubl* (gold ruble, 1896-1914) = $ 0.50 (approx.)
        (The "Witte" or gold-standard ruble of 1896-97 was equal to
        two-thirds the value of the old silver ruble.)
    1 *kopeika* (kopeck) = 1/100th ruble

THE   EMPIRE

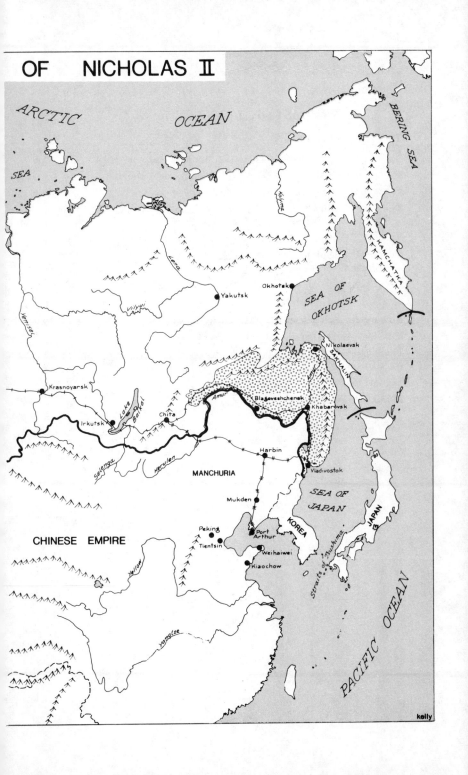

ARCTIC   OCEAN

SEA

BERING SEA

Lena

Yakutsk

Okhotsk

SEA OF OKHOTSK

Kolyma

KAMCHATKA

Vilyui

Nikolaevsk

SAKHALIN

Yenisei

Krasnoyarsk

Lake Baikal

Chita

Amur

Blagoveshchensk

Khabarovsk

Irkutsk

Selenga

Kerulen

Harbin

MANCHURIA

Vladivostok

SEA OF JAPAN

Mukden

Peking

Port Arthur

KOREA

JAPAN

CHINESE   EMPIRE

Tientsin

Weihaiwei

Kiaochow

Straits of Tsushima

Yangtze

Yellow

PACIFIC OCEAN

kelly

LIST OF ILLUSTRATIONS

CHAPTER EIGHTEEN

AUSTRIA'S ULTIMATUM, RUSSIA'S RESPONSE

Foreign minister Sazonov learned of the Austrian ultimatum around 10 a.m. on 11/24 July, when he was handed a cable from the Russian charge d'affaires in Belgrade. His reaction was instantaneous: *"C'est la guerre europienne!"*, and that generally was the initial reaction to Austria's demands.[1] That feeling became even more pronounced when the Austro-Hungarian embassy communicated the text of Vienna's note to Serbia. The emperor, who was at Tsarskoe Selo, was notified by phone. "This is outrageous!" he exclaimed and promptly summoned the council of ministers to an emergency session. The meeting convened at 3 p.m. The government decided to contact the other powers and to advise Serbia to avoid any resistance so as not to aggravate the crisis. At the same time, in order to avoid the impression that Russia contemplated the possibility of standing aside, the government issued a brief statement which appeared on the following morning (12/25 July) in the semi-official military journal *Russkii invalid*: "The government is gravely concerned over recent events and the ultimatum presented to Serbia by Austria-Hungary. The government is vigilantly following the development of the Austro-Serbian conflict, toward which Russia cannot remain indifferent." With this terse and moderate notice the Russian government clearly proclaimed that it did not intend to remain passive if Austria-Hungary attempted to impose its will on Serbia by force. In essence the Austrian ultimatum and the Russian response made war inevitable.

Austria—and Germany, which was forewarned of its ally's action—possibly counted on achieving a bloodless diplomatic coup on the assumption that Russia would pay any price to avoid war. They counted on the emperor's well-known disposition toward peace, but former Chancellor Bülow at least should have recalled the warning that the emperor personally had delivered to him fifteen years earlier.[2]

Historic traditions prevented Russia's retreat, especially under alien pressure. For centuries Russia had looked upon itself as the successor to the Byzantine Empire and the champion of all other Slavic peoples. Only Russia itself could reverse that policy and deliberately refocus its attention on the East. The government moved toward that reorientation ahead of the public, which never really grasped the scope of the emperor's Asian policy. "Avant-garde" public opinion remained far more closely attached to the policies of the mid-nineteenth century. Especially in the years following the Bosnian crisis, a broad segment of the intelligentsia had developed an interest in the Near East and the Balkan Slavs. Moreover, in recent years Russia and Serbia had forged a bond of mutual obligations, even though their ties had not been sealed by a formal treaty. During the Bosnian crisis (1909), on the question of Serbian access to the sea (1912), and in the Scutari question (1913) Serbia followed Russia's advice. As a result the Serbs had avoided international complications. For that reason Russia was obliged to defend Serbia against any act of violence. All Russian statesmen acknowledged that obligation, even those who preferred friendship with Germany over the rapprochement with England. That was the point of Durnovo's memorandum, which directly asserted that in order to improve the tone of their relations, Germany had to be responsive to Russia's desires and check the "excessive intrigues of Austria-Hungary in the Balkans."[3]

In a wire to the emperor on 11/24 July Prince Alexander of Serbia pleaded: "We cannot defend ourselves. Therefore we beg Your Majesty to render us assistance as soon as possible. . . . We firmly trust that this appeal will find a response in Your Majesty's Slavic and noble heart." The emperor replied on 14/27 July: "As long as the slightest hope of avoiding bloodshed exists, all of our efforts must be directed to that end. But if, contrary to our sincerest desire, we are not successful in that, Your Highness can rest assured that in no case will Russia remain indifferent to the fate of Serbia." That telegram was received in Belgrade on the very day of the Austrian declaration of war on Serbia, and the tsar's message deeply moved the Serbs. Nicholas Pasić (Pashich), chairman of the council of ministers, was so touched that he could speak only in phrases—"Sire, gracious Russian tsar! What a consolation!"—and he was unable to hold back his tears.[4] In his reply to the tsar on 16/29 July Prince Alexander declared: "Times of trial cannot but strengthen the deep bonds which unite Serbia with Holy Slavic Russia. Your Majesty's assistance and protection inspire a sense of eternal gratitude to be held as sacred in the hearts of all Serbs."

Nicholas II could take no other position, and the whole of Russian public opinion supported him. But the Dual Monarchy also found itself in a situation from which its government could not retreat, since to do so would destroy the prestige of the monarchy in the eyes of its multinational subjects. Russia could not abandon Serbia to the mercies of the Austrians, but Vienna raised the issue in such a way that any interference in the dispute would be regarded as an affront to the honor of the Dual Monarchy.

Austria went too far at the very outset by closing off any possibility of a negotiated agreement. From then on the international situation was essentially hopeless, even though negotiations dragged on for several more days. There was, perhaps, one point at which Vienna might have drawn back while simultaneously claiming victory: The Serbian response of 13/26 July went much farther than expected toward satisfying Austria's demands. The only stipulation rejected by the Serbs would have allowed Austro-Hungarian authorities to conduct an investigation [into the assassination of Franz Ferdinand] on Serbian soil. But the Serbs were even willing to negotiate that point. Thus, having read Serbia's reply, the kaiser expressed his satisfaction. Austria, however, was not satisfied. Vienna severed diplomatic relations with Belgrade on that same day and on 15/28 July the Austrians declared war on the Serbs.

Official circles in Russia initially entertained the hope that Germany would exert a moderating influence on Austria. With that in mind the tsar sent Emperor William several telegrams. But the Germans saw no way of denying support to Austria-Hungary, their only ally. In any case, they had all but completely accepted the inevitability of war. Even so radical a paper as the *Frankfurter Zeitung* made the following comment immediately upon learning of the Austrian ultimatum (11/24 July): "If a European war is somehow avoided now, then unfortunately there is still the danger that in a few years Russian nationalism will try to efface today's humiliation."

A similar sense of inevitability reigned in France and England. For the French the situation was quite clear: with no direct interest in the conflict France would adhere strictly to its obligations as an ally. Those Frenchmen who accepted the inevitability of a Franco-German war were just as content that the conflict at hand originated with Russia, which consequently could no longer exert a restraining influence as it had during the Moroccan crisis. Likewise the British, who had seen German propaganda interpret every event of recent years in the light of the Anglo-German rivalry, saw little harm in a development that drew Russia and then France into an open conflict with Germany.

Russian opinion reacted almost unanimously to the Austrian ultimatum. Only *Rech* initially found cause to censure the Russian government. "It seems unlikely that Serbia, especially after Russian encouragement, will respond with a very satisfactory reply," wrote the Kadet paper on 12 July. "We already have encouraged Serbia and already have accepted a certain share of the responsibility for the consequences. Therefore, it appears already beyond our power to stem the course of events." Within two days, however, even *Rech* acknowledged the more than satisfactory character of the Serbian response.

Street demonstrations took place in St. Petersburg on Sunday, the 13th of July, with crowds chanting: "Long live the army! Long live the war!" On the following day *Novoe vremia* wrote: "It was an unusual night—a night of national jubilation and national enthusiasm in anticipation of a war, the only popular war since the war of liberation against the Turks [1877-78] and the only one to be ennobled as such."

RUSSIAN MOBILIZATION

Since Russia had decided not to remain "indifferent to the fate of Serbia," preparatory military measures had to be taken. On 15/28 July Austria declared war on Serbia, and the Russian government decided to proceed with the mobilization of four military districts, a move that entailed approximately half of the army. Hopeful of not breaking with Germany until

For the members of the Entente the war began under very favorable conditions. England and its ally, Japan, immediately joined Russia, France, and Serbia, but Germany and Austria-Hungary got no support from Italy or from Rumania (where contrary to the attitude of King Carol I the royal council urged a neutral policy). Sweden, in whom Germany placed great hope, also remained neutral.

PATRIOTISM AND UNITY

The Great War came as a surprise to Russian society, but from the beginning of the crisis (from the 11th to the 19th of July) society's response was completely unanimous. The government's position met with general approval, and when Germany delivered its ultimatum and then its declaration of war, everyone considered it an unwarranted attack and no one questioned the need to answer it. As in the Russo-Japanese War, Russia was only responding to aggression (in 1904 the enemy was even more cunning than in 1914), but this time Russian society viewed the war as something more than a direct response to an enemy attack. This war in particular was the logical consequence of a policy supported by the liberal circles of the intelligentsia: the alliance with France, the rapprochement with England, and the activist policy in the Balkans. The patriotic urge to repel the enemy converged with the conviction that this war was attuned ideologically to the "progressive" avant-garde ideals of society. Those who favored a rapprochement with Germany were coerced into unwilling silence by the obvious Austro-German attack on Russia.

Nearly every city witnessed huge patriotic demonstrations. The masses, especially in the villages, did not show any genuine enthusiasm for the war but answered the call to service as the fulfillment of a natural obligation to tsar and fatherland. The mobilization proceeded successfully and much more rapidly than anticipated. Moreover there were none of the frequent drunken orgies that normally occurred on such occasions, since by imperial decree the sale of alcoholic beverages was suspended throughout the mobilization period.

For Russia's intelligentsia the outbreak of the war marked a great spiritual change for the better. The vague yearning to be of service to the nation, which had been growing for some years and gradually overcoming the earlier faith in the revolution, suddenly found an outlet. The desire to participate in a common cause even overwhelmed those who had remained hostilely aloof during the war against Japan. "Something indescribable is happening everywhere," wrote V.V. Rozanov about the first days of the war. "You feel it within yourself and all around you. It is something like an infusion of youth. People in the streets seem younger. People in trains seem younger." The words of a poetess, one of the "decadents" [symbolists], neatly described the basic mood of the intelligentsia during the first months of the war: "The unemployed have been waiting, and now that they have received big important jobs their grimy faces are as cheerful and bright as a clear harvest day."

When the two legislative chambers convened in extraordinary session on 26 July, the unity of the legislature and government was complete. The emperor held a reception for the members of the two chambers and told them: "The great swell of patriotism, love of country, and loyalty to the throne which has blown across our land like a tornado serves in my eyes, and I think also in yours, as a guarantee that our great Mother Russia will wage to a victorious end this war, which has been given to us by the Lord. I am convinced that all of you, each in turn, will assist me in surmounting the challenge that has been thrust upon me, and that all of us, beginning with myself, will fulfill our duty to the end. Great is the God of the Russian Land!"

The State Duma unanimously approved all credits and legislation associated with the conduct of the war. Even the Trudoviks through their spokesman A.F. Kerensky announced their affiliation with the majority.[12] The Social Democrats did not vote for the war credits but chose instead to abstain.[13]

At a special session which began on 25 July the Moscow zemstvo assembly voted to enlist all zemstvos into a cooperative effort to assist the army, beginning first of all with assistance to the sick and wounded. A convention summoned for that purpose warmly approved the idea, except that the original sponsors of the resolution did not become the leaders of the All-Russian Union of Zemstvos. Instead, leaders of the old semi-legal national zemstvo organization [of 1904-1905] were elected, including Prince George Lvov who became chairman.[14] At that time, however, the turnabout created no problem.

Public representatives without party labels announced their unity with the government for the duration of the struggle with the foreign enemy. For its part the government met its recent opponents halfway. It immediately approved the formation of the Union of Zemstvos and also the All-Russian Union of Municipalities and furnished them state funds in considerable sums, despite their Kadet leadership.[15] The government cancelled prosecutions in old matters,[16] and it approved the prominent Kadet, M.V. Chelnokov, as mayor of Moscow. The newspaper *Rech*, suspended by order of the supreme commander, was allowed to publish again after two or three days, when the editors assured the government of their earnest desire to lend all their strength to the national effort.

The patriotic enthusiasm of the Russian intelligentsia was a new and indisputable phenomenon. As if embarrassed by those unaccustomed sentiments, the leftists rationalized their patriotism by contending that the defeat of Germany would produce socialism on the ruins of the Hohenzollern dynasty and that the central issue of the war was the struggle of democracy against "feudal militarism." There were no audible protests. Lenin, who was in Cracow when the war broke out, took a nearly unique position when in August 1914 he wrote his *Theses on the War*: "From the point of view of the working class and the toiling masses of all the peoples of Russia, by far the lesser evil would be the defeat of the tsarist armies and the tsarist autocracy." At that point in the war Lenin's old comrade George Plekhanov was avidly promoting the war against German militarism, and even the former chairman of the St. Petersburg Soviet, Leon Trotsky, wrote (in the emigre paper *Nashe slovo* [Our Word]) that a Russian defeat was undesirable because it would mean a victory for reactionary Germany.

AN APPEAL TO THE POLES

About two weeks were required to mobilize and deploy the European armies, and the first reports of battle came from

the Western Front. The timely redeployment of troop concentrations into areas more remote from the frontiers gave
the Russian high command considerable leeway in choosing
the objectives for its operations. From France, however, came
urgent requests for Russia to focus the brunt of its attack not
on Austria but on Germany. The Germans, meanwhile, were
on the defensive on the Eastern Front, except for the occupation of a few unprotected towns in the western part of the
Polish salient. The Austrians, who were preparing an offensive from Galicia in the direction of Lublin and Kholm, were
counting to some extent on an uprising in the Kingdom of
Poland. The Austrian army included Polish volunteer units in
special uniforms, and their leader was the experienced revolutionary, Joseph Pilsudski.

Russia frustrated those hopes with an appeal to the Polish
people, issued on 1 August in the name of the supreme commander, Grand Duke Nicholas Nikolaevich:

The hour has struck when the cherished dreams of your fathers and
grandfathers are to be realized. A century and a half ago, the living
body of Poland was torn asunder, but her soul did not die . . . . Let
the boundaries which have separated the Polish nation be obliterated.
Let the Poles be reunited as one people under the scepter of the Russian Tsar. Let Poland be reborn under that scepter—free in its faith,
language, and self-government. Russia expects only one thing of you—
an equal regard for the rights of those nationalities to whom you are
bound by history. Great Russia greets you with an open heart and
outstretched hand. She trusts that the sword that struck down the foe
at Grünwald has not rusted.

This appeal combined with old Franco-Polish ties to cause
prominent public figures in Russian Poland openly to announce their loyalty to the allies. The Pilsudski legions found
scant support in the Polish kingdom. The Entente was able
to promise more than its enemies, because Austria could not
give the Poles Poznan and the Baltic coast which the Germans
so assiduously had colonized.

All of the Russian Empire's other nationalities remained
loyal in this hour of trial, and in the early stages of the war
national rivalries created no problem. The one exception was
Finland where the people still smouldered with resentment
over the recent laws dealing with imperial legislation. The
Finns, who had not been conscripted for service since 1899,

took no part in the war, although several thousand young
Finns fled abroad through Sweden and formed volunteer chas-
seur battalions in the German army. But in Finland itself
there were no attempted uprisings since a great number of
Russian troops were stationed there.

SOBER SPIRITS FOR A SACRED CAUSE

During the first days of the war, the most intractable domestic problems seemed amenable to easy solutions. The emperor,
therefore, seized the opportunity to inaugurate a bold reform
which in past years had been especially dear to his heart,
namely the prohibition of the sale of alcoholic beverages.
Prohibition first was introduced as a normal provision of the
mobilization, but then on 22 August the government announced that it would remain in effect for the duration of
the war. The measure, applied first to the sale of vodka,
gradually expanded to include wine and beer. Early in September during an interview with Grand Duke Constantine
Konstantinovich in his capacity as chairman of the Temperance League, the emperor declared that he "already had decided to prohibit the state sale of vodka in Russia forever."
At that time the emperor's intention corresponded fully to
the general popular mood which regarded prohibition as a
means of purging Russia of sin. Consequently no one suspected that legislation to that effect, determined in advance
by the tsar, would run into resistance in the legislative chambers.

Only wartime conditions, which upset all normal budgetary
considerations, made it possible to adopt a measure that
amounted to a renunciation of the state's largest source of
income. Before 1914 no other nation had adopted such a
radical measure to combat alcoholism. It was a grandiose
scheme, quite unheard of. Naturally within a short time boot-
leggers began to operate, and all sorts of alcoholic substitutes
became available. Nevertheless, mainly because of the lack of
imports from abroad, the Russian consumption of alcohol
decreased several times over during the first year of the war.

PRECIPITATE DISASTERS IN EAST PRUSSIA

The first great battles on the Eastern Front began on the
4/17th of August. Russian forces were advancing into German

territory from the east along the Petersburg-Berlin railways. The Austrians were mounting an offensive from Galicia toward Lublin and Kholm, while Russia was preparing to strike the Austrian flank from Volynia. In the West the failure of the French offensive in Alsace-Lorraine had become apparent. The Belgian "dam" had burst, and the German armies were pouring into northern France.

French ambassador Paleologue met personally with the emperor and urgently appealed for help. Westerners held an exaggerated opinion of the capabilities of the Russian army, which they envisioned as a "steam roller" that flattened everything that stood in its way. No one considered Russia's relative lack of mobility, due to the inferior development of its railway system, or Germany's superiority in artillery, particularly in heavy guns. While it was true that the Russian army, including reservists and home guards of the first class, numbered some five million men, only about three and a half million formed the actual army in the field. Moreover, the total force could be concentrated in the war zone no sooner than two months after the start of mobilization.

But the Allies overestimated Russia's military capacity. The French war minister spoke quite seriously with the Russian military attache about a possible Russian invasion of Germany and a drive from Warsaw to Berlin. The West asked for even more direct help than that: At the height of the East Prussian and Galician campaigns on 17/30 August the British embassy approached Sazonov about the possibility of sending three or four Russian corps to the Western Front, for which the British offered to send the requisite number of vessels to Arkhangel. N.A. de Basily, director of the diplomatic chancellery at the army headquarters, wrote: "In view of the impatience with which the French government treats our offensive in Germany, the chief of staff of the supreme commander has asked that I pass on the information that the offensive against Germany is being carried out by great masses and is being undertaken with all possible speed consistent with the demands of prudence." However, Russia's desire to assist its allies at their moment of peril forced the high command to depart from "the demands of prudence" and launch a hasty offensive against strongly fortified German positions in East Prussia. The desire to help the allies triumphed over all other considerations.

In addition to General Rennenkampf's army which was advancing into East Prussia from the east a second army under General Samsonov was moving into Prussia from the south.[17] As the Germans retreated, the Russians occupied vast areas. However, a strongly fortified zone covered with a thick railroad network separated the two advancing Russian armies. The Germans took advantage of the rail system and threw the entire bulk of their forces against Samsonov in the south, leaving only a cavalry screen in the fortified positions in front of Rennenkampf. A great battle ensured. In Russia it was known as the battle of Soldau, but the Germans called it Tannenberg, as if to efface the memory of the defeat of the Teutonic Knights which took place there in the middle ages.[18] Samsonov's army was routed, tens of thousands of his troops were taken prisoner, and he himself committed suicide. The battle established the reputations of the German Generals Hindenburg and Ludendorf.[19]

The Germans then hurled their unopposed army against Rennenkampf and drove him back to the frontier [in the First Battle of the Masurian Lakes].[20] Thus Russia's first forced offensive against Germany ended in failure, although it achieved the goal sought by the French ambassador: as a result of the battles in East Prussia, the Germans transferred two army corps from the Western Front to the east and they held up four other corps that were on their way to France. The German army was weakened at the most decisive moment of its drive into France. General Joffre gained the opportunity to fight the battle of the Marne and to spoil the plans of the German high command to end the war in the West in one swift blow.

ALLIED UNITY AND WAR AIMS

The war was about a month old when the members of the Entente formally pledged not to conclude a separate peace. The suggestion for the treaty came (several days after the Russian misfortune at Soldau) from Lord Grey, the British foreign minister. The Franco-Russian Alliance already created that obligation for the two allies. The agreement of 23 August/5 September declared: "The Russian, British, and French governments mutually agree not to conclude a separate peace in

Russian Prisoners and Guns after Tannenberg

the course of the present war. The three governments agree
that when the time has come to discuss peace terms, none of
the Allied Powers will offer conditions of peace without previous agreement with each of the other Allies."[21]

The allies previously had coordinated their policies toward
the Balkans and Turkey, and the need then arose to exchange
views on the terms of peace. The Allied war aims developed
slowly and without benefit of a preconceived plan. Except
for French insistence on the return of Alsace and Lorraine,
the remainder of the war aims emerged gradually and changed
frequently. Since Turkey had remained neutral to that point,
the Allies proposed to guarantee its territory. Russia was in-
terested in the annexation of Galicia and Poznan (in order to
fulfill its promise to the Poles). France and England frequently
expressed a desire to preserve the Austro-Hungarian Empire
in order to tear the Austrians away from the Germans. Russia,
however, favored a more radical partition of the Danubian
Monarchy.[22]

EARLY VICTORIES IN GALICIA

As the debacles in East Prussia were unfolding, Russia received
entirely different news from the Austrian front. After initial
successes, the Austrians were forced to retreat. On 21 Au-
gust/3 September Russian troops captured Lvov [Lemberg],
the capital of Eastern Galicia, and the ancient Russian town
of Galich [Halicz]. The Austrian army was utterly defeated.
The Russians captured over a hundred thousand prisoners,
pressed on across the River San, and laid siege to the fortress
of Przemysl. As far as the Russian public was concerned, the
September victories in Galicia completely overshadowed the
disaster at Soldau, all the more since the Russian army renewed its offensive against the Germans, though on a reduced
scale. Meanwhile in France the battle zone was sliding to the
north and leaving in its wake a fixed and fortified front.

The Austrians' position became so perilous that the Germans decided to come to their rescue. A massive Austro-German offensive drove across Poland toward the mid-course of
the Vistula and rolled to within a few miles of Warsaw. After
a series of battles that raged for about a week (1-7/14-20 October), the Russians checked the offensive, and the Germans

and Austrians began to fall back. Once again the Russian armies began to push forward. Their offensive carried far beyond the first and eventually threatened to take the city of Cracow. Russian troops stood on the western frontier of Poland, and columns of cavalry probed the province of Poznan [Posen]. The Russian communique of 24 October/6 November announced: "During the past eighteen days we have expanded our successes along the entire 500 verst [300 mile] front; everywhere we have broken the resistance of the enemy who is now in full retreat."

Early in November, however, the Germans launched another counter-offensive between the Vistula and the Warta. Advance units of the Russian army began to retreat. The Germans under the command of General Mackenson broke through the front but soon found themselves in danger of being surrounded. On 13/26 November the Petersburg evening reported that several trains had been dispatched to the front to evacuate the tens of thousands of prisoners. But with heavy losses Mackensen's divisions fought their way out of the encirclement around Brzeziny.[23] The Russians repulsed the German counter attack but did not resume the offensive. Winter was setting in; by the end of November the heavy fighting ground to a halt, and the troops dug into an uninterrupted front that stretched from the Baltic Sea to the Rumanian frontier. It became obvious that an early end to the war could not be expected. In the West too the armies were frozen into a continuous front from the North Sea to Switzerland.

THE WAR AT SEA: THE TURKISH ATTACK

Russia's Baltic Fleet, commanded by Admiral Essen,[24] was so numerically inferior to the German fleet that offensive operations were out of the question. Still, the German fleet, which was considerably weaker than the British, made no attempt to enter Russian waters for fear of losing some of its capital ships. Both sides, therefore, limited their offensive operations to skirmishes between their smaller vessels. The sinking of the German cruiser *Magdeburg* by a mine was an event of very special significance, for the Russians recovered from her wreckage and passed on to their allies the secret German naval code. Possession of the code proved a valuable asset in combatting German espionage. The Russian cruiser *Pallada* also blew up on a mine and went to the bottom with her entire crew.

Quite a different situation prevailed in the Black Sea. At the outset of the war two of Germany's newest ships, the dreadnought-cruiser *Goeben* and the light cruiser *Breslau*, were cruising in the Mediterranean. They eluded the pursuit of the French and British squadrons and reached the safety of the Dardanelles. The Turks quite properly interned the vessels, but soon afterward the German government announced that it had sold the ships to Turkey. The evasive nature of the sale was obvious, if only because their German crews continued to man the ships.

Russia had three dreadnoughts under construction in the Black Sea, but only aged vessels made up the Black Sea Fleet. Turkish naval superiority, however temporary, and the possibility of Muslim uprisings in the Caucasus prompted Turkey's military leaders to risk an attack on Russia.[25] First the Turks closed the Dardanelles to Russian commerce. Then on 16/29 October without warning the *Goeben* and *Breslau* [and other Turkish warships] appeared off the ports of Odessa and Feodosia and began to bombard them. The grand vizir alleged that the naval actions were "precipitated by the Russian fleet." The Russian government immediately severed diplomatic relations with Turkey—with some pleasure, it should be added, since a victorious conclusion of the war held out the coveted "bonus" of annexing the Straits and Armenia. Thus a new front opened in the Caucasus. The tsar appointed as its commander Adjutant-General Count I.I. Vorontsov-Dashkov, the viceroy of the Caucasus. His chief of staff, General A.Z. Myshlaevsky, soon was succeeded by General N.N. Yudenich.[26]

Offensive action began on the Caucasus Front when the Russians seized the mountain fortress of Sayazet, but with the arrival of Turkish reinforcements Enver Pasha, the war minister, launched his own offensive. In the middle of December the Turks in a swift move penetrated deep into Russian territory. Panic swept through the Georgian districts. Despite the enemy's numerical superiority, the Russians broke the Turkish assault at Sarikamish and then drove the invaders back across the frontier.

THE TWO FACES OF THE HOME FRONT

One might say that Russia had no domestic policy during the first months of the war, for the country was ruled by a universal desire for victory. Russians expectantly awaited the conflict's speedy resolution and naturally deferred controversial issues until the end of the war. The army and its leaders were immensely popular. The war had relatively little effect on the home front, especially in comparison to France or Germany. Studies went on in the higher schools and universities; the theaters and cinemas were packed. Industry and commerce adjusted in one way or another to the new environment in which every vital frontier was sealed.

Especially after the closing of the Dardanelles, the outside world was accessible only through remote Vladivostok or Arkhangel, which was frozen for more than half of the year. Growing restrictions governed commerce through neutral Sweden and Rumania. There was, of course, not even the whisper of a food shortage. Concurrently the prohibition of alcohol and the extensive assistance rendered to the families of reservists called to the colors produced a sharp increase in savings deposits.[27] The improved well-being of the people was quite evident. When the war broke out, it was feared that the disruption of the export of grain and other foodstuffs (butter, eggs, poultry) would cause a catastrophic decline in prices and that producers would be ruined. The fears proved groundless: increasing domestic demand, especially to satisfy the requirements of the army, quickly took up the slack from the closed foreign markets.

From the start of the war Empress Alexandra Feodorovna and Grand Duchesses Olga Nikolaevna and Tatiana Nikolaevna, having completed nurse's training, worked in that capacity in the empress's hospital at Tsarskoe Selo. The empress also set aside part of the Winter Palace as a warehouse for clothing to be distributed to troops at the front. Officials of the ministry of interior established at their own expense another similar warehouse in the name of the empress. Grand Duchess Olga became the head of a committee to assist the families of reservists. In 1915 in response to the swelling number of refugees an imperial decree created a special committee to care for them and named Grand Duchess Tatiana to direct it.

"Throughout the first six months of the year just ended, the oppositionist mood of society increased steadily," recalled *Vestnik evropy* on 1 January 1915 in its annual review. "Then the war erupted and every trace of mounting opposition and dissatisfaction suddenly vanished. Like a magic knife the war severed the first half of the year from the second . . . . The war sobered the people. What was impossible to accomplish under conditions of peace was accomplished . . . . In the sixth month of the cruelest of cruel wars the nation enters the new year without the slightest sign of fatigue."

There was, of course, a negative side. The war gave rise in Russia, as in all the warring countries, to a plethora of provocative literature. The movement began with the Germans' cruel treatment of foreigners who remained in Germany. Then came evidence of German cruelty in Kalisz and other towns that they occupied in Russian Poland. As large-scale military operations expanded, tales of "German atrocities" multiplied. Russia also experienced riots, as in the sacking of the German embassy in Petersburg. In its written report to the emperor the foreign ministry labelled the incident a "terrifying and regrettable event." Generally, however, Russia witnessed fewer cases of violence than other countries. But even the intelligentsia succumbed to an indiscriminate rejection of everything German. Various scholarly and scientific societies expelled their German and Austrian members, and some philosophers even went to the trouble to prove that there was essentially no difference between Kant and Krupp.

Before long the denunciation of everything Germanic began to focus on the Germans within Russia. The Baltic nobility as well as German colonists, including the Mennonites who had settled along the Volga during the reign of Catherine the Great, became the objects of suspicion and accusation. No matter that in the Duma's session of 26 July the representatives of the Russian Germans, Barons Felkersham and Lutz, had delivered patriotic declarations like everyone else.[28] Within a few months the empire's entire German population became suspect. Every German newspaper was closed—one of them, the *St. Petersburg Zeitung*, had been published since the time of Peter the Great. Some Russian newspapers, most notably the *Vechernee vremia* [Evening Times], busied themselves by scouring the rosters of government departments for

German names. This anti-German witch hunt became the first sign of domestic discord during the Great War. Since the leftists always regarded the Germans as a conservative element, they raised no particular objection.

At first the government applied repressive measures only against the citizens of enemy states, except for Austrian Slavs and Alsatians. However, on 2 February 1915 in accord with Article 87 the government ordered the compulsory alienation of all land owned within 75 miles of the border region by persons of German or Austro-Hungarian extraction. Such persons were allowed from ten to sixteen months to liquidate their holdings voluntarily.

The Senate ruled by a vote of 56-32 that citizens of enemy states did not enjoy legal protection. That paved the way for anyone in debt to a German or Austrian citizen to refuse payment. Many persons and even firms took advantage of that ruling. The extension of the rules of war to private contracts represented something of a precedent in international relations. During the Crimean War, for example, Russia considered itself obligated to pay interest to Englishmen for their loans even though the empire was at war with England.

Like a great earthquake the Great War distorted men's minds and overturned their concepts of justice and the good—ideas which once had seemed immutable. Next to heroism and sacrifice the war begat the mentality that "the good is what leads to success." That mentality of war formed the threshold of revolutionary change. It appeared equally on both sides of the front, but few anywhere were alert to the danger. One of the few was the Empress Alexandra Feodorovna. At the first report that the conduct of Russian soldiers had provoked unfavorable comment in occupied territory, she wrote to the tsar: The war "has lifted up spirits and cleansed the many stagnant minds . . . .   Only one thing, I long that that our troops should behave exemplarily in every sense, and do not rob and pillage—leave that horror to the Prussian troops . . . . Everything has its ugly and its beautiful sides, and so it is here. Such a war ought to cleanse the spirits and not defile them, is it not so? . . . I want the name of our russian troops to be remembered hereafter in the countries with awe and respect—and admiration."[29]

DEFEATISM AND WAR WEARINESS

By the end of 1914 when it became evident that the war would drag on, old antagonisms began to revive. Whenever local authorities took repressive measures against revolutionary agitators, oppositionist circles immediately accused the government of misunderstanding the new conditions. During the trial of five Bolshevik deputies charged with promoting Lenin's defeatist theses, some of the public contended that the Social Democrats merely wanted to protest "the intrigues of the extreme right."[30]

Little by little rumors spread that reactionary elements at court desired a separate peace; the tales originated in circles hostile to the supreme authority. Meanwhile only Count Witte, who was rather far removed from rightist as well as court circles, came out openly for an end to the war and predicted major disasters if it continued. Although Witte's statement did not reach the press, it alarmed the Allied diplomats. When Witte died (27 February/11 March 1915), the French ambassador noted with satisfaction in his diary that "a great hearth of intrigue has been extinguished." But, in fact, the former prime minister was quite without influence, especially at court.

Besides his carefree optimism the ordinary citizen began to give some signs of war weariness. Despite the military censorship, some indications of that fatigue slipped into the press.

The outbreak of war inspired Russia's poets to pour forth volumes of poems, which for the most part lacked both power and originality. Feodor Sologub prophesied: "Before the spring descends on the moist laps of the valleys, our troops will seize haughty Berlin." Igor Severianin was even less restrained: "Have you forgotten, Germany—wasn't it Bismarck who built you? All the same, your stern grandeur is simply a place for the Russian soldier to blow his nose." Zinaida Hippius, perhaps the only one to urge restraint, warned: "Do not be too hasty, poets: Victory is still in God's hand; today the wounds still are burning, and words are unnecessary." By the middle of the winter, however, the mood had changed. Then Severianin, for example, pleaded that "one is not a traitor for being joyous and youthful, for not inflicting pain on a prisoner of war, or for not rushing into shrapnel and smoke." (That poem brought the editors of *Birzhevie vedo-mosti* a flurry of letters of protest.)

At that point the average citizen placed less hope in a military victory than in the imminence of famine in Germany. The introduction of bread rationing in Germany in January 1915 was taken as an indication that the enemy was about to collapse. The Russian press enumerated the varieties of buns, rolls, and breads available to city dwellers and contrasted Russian abundance with German deprivation: "How poor are they in their silks and velvets; how rich are we in our rags."

EMPTY ARSENALS, SILENT GUNS

If it was conceivable to predict an inevitable shortage of food in Germany—the Germans were importing foodstuffs, including 15 percent of their bread grains—it was equally if not more evident that Russia could expect a different type of "famine" even more desperate in wartime—the shortage of military supplies. According to General Danilov, Russian requirements "immediately exceeded the most fantastic expectations." For the short war that everyone expected at the outset Russian war supplies were reasonably adequate. The output of Russian war industries was known to be relatively low, but by the summer of 1914 Russia had accumulated tolerably large stockpiles.

The war ministry and the war minister failed without question to be adequately attentive to the need to expand Russian war production. They, too, were victims of the short-war illusion. Moreover it appeared useless to squander money on the construction of factories that could begin production only in 18-24 months at best. In Russia it was true that war industries did not have to close because their workers were mobilized, as was the case in France where too few exemptions were granted to war production workers. Nevertheless, Russian rifle manufacturers sometimes turned out fewer rather than more weapons than in peacetime, because they were too busy repairing rifles that had been returned by the army. In 1914 Russian arsenals contained about five million rifles, but even that supply was inadequate to arm the six and a half million men who were mobilized. Eventually production rose to 600-700,000 rifles per year.

The situation was even worse with respect to artillery and shells. By 8/21 September 1914 Grand Duke Nicholas Nikolaevich already was reporting that the shortage of artillery ammunition was holding up operations on several fronts. Although production rose to 100,000 shells per month, the army expended shells at the rate of 1,000,000 per month. The tragedy was that with only a short time until the spring campaign and almost completely cut off from the outside world Russia found it physically impossible to make up the deficiency.[31] The only recourse was to hide the problem from the enemy and hope that a German famine or some political development—the surrender of Hungary or perhaps Italian intervention—would end the war before the "shell famine" struck with full force. In order to conceal that weakness from the enemy, officials of the war ministry also had to conceal it from the Russian public. As a result they opened themselves to heavy criticism which eventually turned into charges of treason.

Only a handful of Russians were aware of the completely hopeless situation that loomed ahead, and on those who knew, it weighed like a nightmare. Early in 1915 General Yanushkevich, the chief of staff, described his agony to war minister Sukhomlinov: "If recruits could be rushed up immediately and if we could get twelve more motorized units, we could seize the initiative from the Germans. But it is already too late now, and it breaks my heart. At night I seem to hear a voice repeating, 'You've sold out, you've sold out, you've overslept . . . .' "

The lack and distance of communications hampered Russia's ability to obtain supplies abroad. It was no joke to compare Russia to a house that could be entered only through the chimney and the drainpipes. In addition, Allied and neutral factories alike were swamped with orders from the Western Front, which the Allies invariably regarded as the crucial arena.

Thus the shortage of shells and rifles was a major factor in reducing combat operations on the Eastern Front between the end of November 1914 and the beginning of March 1915. Russia and its allies had every reason to fear that those shortages would place the summer campaign of 1915 in even greater jeopardy.

A REPEAT PERFORMANCE BY THE DUMA

The Duma met for three days in January 1915, although its budget commission already had been at work for two weeks. The budget and all appropriations passed without opposition; this time, however, the Social Democrats voted against the budget, while the Trudoviks abstained. The deputies gave foreign minister Sazonov an overwhelming ovation. Rodzianko, the chairman of the Duma, paid respect to the emperor: "Accept, Great Sovereign, the humble obeisance of your subjects. Your people firmly believe that all sorrow is about to be laid to rest."

Michael Alekseenko, the chairman of the budget commission, praised the emperor's prohibition on the sale of liquor: "The legislative chambers set out to deal with this matter by devious means, but the question was decided differently: it was decided the right way—radically . . . . The solution went right to the heart of the problem, and it met with approval everywhere in the land."

Goremykin openly mentioned Constantinople for the first time: "The entire world historical future of Russia looms clearly before us on the shores of the sea before the walls of Tsargrad." Various nationalist representatives among the deputies made patriotic speeches, but this time no one was present to represent the empire's Germanic peoples. Otherwise the January session was much like the assembly of the previous July.

PAWN, KNIGHT, KING, ROOK

At the end of February 1915 the Allies launched an operation that might have paved the way for "caravans" of shells and thereby eliminated the danger that threatened the Eastern Front. An Anglo-French fleet began by shelling the Dardanelles forts, and they quickly levelled the outlying fortifications. On 5 March, however, the fleet attempted to force the Straits, and several large ships were sunk by floating mines. After that the British decided not to risk their dreadnoughts, and they abandoned the attempt to drive through the Dardanelles. As it turned out, that unsuccessful operation called the Turks' attention to the danger in that area. Therefore, when the Allies finally landed on the Gallipoli Peninsula, they ran into a well-entrenched enemy.

On 9/22 March the Austrian fortress of Przemysl and its garrison of about 117,000 men capitulated after a four-month Russian siege. The fall of the fortress on the San caused jubilant demonstrations all across Russia. Control of Eastern Galicia finally seemed secure. The territory was reorganized into provinces and a governor, Count G.A. Bobrinsky, was appointed. The authorities then stepped up the campaign against the region's pro-Austrian "Ukrainian" element.[32]

THE MIASOEDOV AFFAIR

In March Russians were treated to the alleged discovery of a large spy organization headed by a gendarme colonel, S.N. Miasoedov. An official announcement disclosed that a court-martial had sentenced him to death and that he had been hanged. Beyond that the matter was cloaked in military secrecy and remains so today.[33] Some recalled that Guchkov had accused this same officer of treason several years before and that war minister Sukhomlinov had protected him. The "Miasoedov affair," the details of which were unknown, provided fodder for critics of the regime and, incidentally, also underlined the perspicacity of Guchkov.

PREMATURE FESTIVITIES IN GALICIA

By the first of April the military situation looked quite promising. Russian forces had occupied more than two-thirds of Galicia and Bukovina. They were entrenched for a considerable distance along the ridge of the Carpathian Mountains and thus poised for a descent into the Danubian basin. It was believed that an invasion of Hungary would prompt the Magyars to secede from the empire and that their defection would precipitate the collapse of the Danubian Monarchy. The Polish Front meanwhile had remained stable for more than four months. A German attempt to mount a winter offensive had been smashed at Prasnysz north of the Bobr-Narev line.[34] Russian troops held positions on the Prussian border and early in March launched successful raids against the cities of Memel and Tauroggen [which had been lost in February].

Following their unsuccessful effort to break through the Dardanelles, the Allies landed on the Gallipoli Peninsula in

April. Negotiations to bring Italy into the war on the Allied side were drawing to a close. To achieve that Italy was promised extensive territory along the Adriatic coast, a region heavily populated by Slavs.[35]

Such was the situation when at the invitation of the supreme commander the emperor arrived in Galicia to inspect the territory whose incorporation into the Russian Empire seemed unquestionable. He visited Lvov on 9 April, received the new municipal authorities, and was greeted by a large crowd of local inhabitants. He spent the 10th and 11th in recently reconquered Przemysl and inspected the battered but formidable fortifications at great length.

On 17 April an explosion was set off at the large military works at Okhta in the factory that produced shell fuses. The shock of the blast was felt for miles around Petersburg. The destruction of that factory, the work of enemy agents, dealt a serious blow to the army's supplies.

On the night of 18 April/1 May the Austro-German armies launched a huge offensive on the Galician front. For the first time the enemy employed the "hurricane of fire," a tactic that proved most effective against an army suffering from lack of ammunition. General Golovin has provided a graphic description of the tactic:

Creeping like some huge beast, the German army would move its advanced units close to the Russian trenches, just near enough to hold the attention of its enemy and to be ready to occupy the trenches immediately after their evacuation. Next, that gigantic beast would draw its tail, the heavy artillery, toward the trenches. That heavy artillery would take up positions in places which were almost or entirely beyond the range of the Russian field artillery, and the heavy guns would start to shower their shells on the Russian trenches, doing it methodically, as was characteristic of the Germans. That hammering would go on until nothing of the trenches remained, and their defenders would be destroyed. Then the beast would cautiously stretch out its paws, the infantry units, which would seize the demolished trenches. In the meantime the Russian artillery and the Russian rear would be subjected to a fierce fire from the German heavy guns, while the German field artillery and machine guns would protect the advancing infantry from Russian counterattacks . . . . Having gained full possession of the Russian trenches the 'beast' would draw up its tail again, and its heavy guns would start their methodical hammering of the next Russian line of defense.[36]

The "hurricane of fire" instantly and sharply revealed the unequal strength of the two armies: one Russian army corps, holding the center of the front on the Dunajec River between Gorlice and Tarnow, had only four heavy guns to oppose the 200 guns concentrated by the Germans. The Russians could reply to the "hurricane of fire" only with rifles and five or ten shells per gun per day. An official communique on 23 April eloquently reported that "owing to the enemy's superiority in heavy artillery, our troops suffered heavy losses. However, during his attacks the enemy also suffered fiercely from our shrapnel and rifle fire." The press noted that in the fighting on the Dunajec mentioned above the Germans fired 700,000 shells in a few hours, whereas it took Russian factories six months to produce the same amount. The discrepancy could not fail to make itself felt.

THE GORLICE–TARNOW BREAKTHROUGH

The Germans broke through the Russian front between the Vistula and the Carpathians. General Mackensen's German "phalanx" advanced almost unhindered. The Russian forces occupying the spine of the Carpathians had to retreat in haste. So rapid was the enemy's advance through the Galician plain that several units found their path of retreat blocked. General Lavr Kornilov[37] distinguished himself for bravery but was captured with the remnants of his division.

Simultaneously the Germans unleashed another offensive in the northern sector of the front. Advanced units captured Libau even before the breakthrough around Gorlice. Although the Germans held the Kingdom of Poland in a vise, the northern defensive line along the Rivers Nieman, Bobr, and Narev was not easily surmounted, and the Germans failed to close the jaws on the Russian army.

Meanwhile the "phalanx" steadily developed the breakthrough in Galicia. Early in May the Russians fell back across the San, but they were able to hold even that line for only two or three weeks. On the night of 21 May/3 June Przemysl, its conquest still fresh in everyone's memory, had to be abandoned. On 9/22 June Austro-Hungarian forces occupied Lvov, the Galician capital, which only two months before had celebrated the emperor's arrival. One month's fighting had wiped out the fruits of nine months of struggle. Reports from the front, each more tragic than its predecessor, spread through the capitals. A wave of refugees fleeing the Northern Front from the provinces of Kovno, Grodno, and Kurland poured into the interior.

THE MADDING CROWD

The shortage of artillery shells and rifles struck home with full effect at the moment the Germans and Austrians launched their offensive. The troops were demoralized. There was talk of treason, allegations that the army purposely had been deprived of ammunition, that rifles deliberately had been withheld from the troops, and that the traitors were the generals, the ministers . . . .[38]

The impact of those events on Russian society was easily understandable given society's customary disposition to blame the government for every untoward development. The fall of Przemysl in particular made a profound impression on a broad segment of the population. On 27-29 May/9-11 June serious disorders broke out in Moscow as revolutionary and pogromist passions mixed with patriotic indignation. The riot began with groups of citizens setting out to make the rounds of shops, factories, stores, and private residences in order to "check" for German and Austrian subjects. For a time the police stood by passively. Soon, however, the groups swelled into crowds and the "checking" turned into the indiscriminate destruction of businesses which "fell into the hands" of mobs gone berserk. At its height the riot degenerated into mass looting. As the government's report stated: "In the streets one could observe even well-dressed people laden with stolen property." In sum, mobs looted 475 commercial and industrial enterprises and 207 apartments. Among the victims were 113 enemy aliens, 489 Russians with foreign surnames, as well as allied and neutral nationals and even Russians with foreign surnames, as well as allied and neutral nationals and even Russians with Russian surnames. The government estimated the losses sustained during the three-day pogrom at 40,000,000 rubles.

The most ominous aspect of that explosion of popular passions was the obvious distrust of the authorities, who were

accused of "indulgence toward Germans." To most of the
nation the sudden turn in the fortunes of war could be explained only by treachery.

The same spirit took a different form in the conference of
representatives of commerce and industry which convened in
Moscow [on 26 May] just about the time of the pogrom.
The industrialists expressed their readiness to fight the foreign
enemy to the very end, but they demanded a reorganization
of the government. The industrialists immediately formed the
Central War Industry Committee as a voluntary organization
to "mobilize industry" for war.[39] Guchkov, whose attitude
toward the government was sufficiently well-established, was
elected chairman.[40]

DEMAND FOR A "MINISTRY OF PUBLIC CONFIDENCE"

The Kadets convened a party conference on 6 June, and their
proceedings reflected the same sense of alarm. Deputies who
had toured the front attested to the army's bitterness and
also to its patriotism. The same charges of treason were repeated, although Miliukov's position was rather moderate.
"It was hardly a question of treason," he said. The disaster
was due to "the inability of foreign manufacturers to fill on
schedule the orders that had been placed with them."

The Kadets resolved to insist on the immediate convocation of the State Duma, and they put forth the demand for a
"ministry of public confidence." In a very revealing speech
Miliukov explained why that formula was most acceptable to
the opposition. The idea of a responsible ministry, presumably more liberal than the present government, actually would
be less advantageous, he declared. "It is sufficient simply to
imagine the problems of a responsible ministry with a right-
wing majority in the Fourth Duma . . . . To a conciliatory
cabinet we would not say: Here are the men who will replace
you. On the contrary, we say: Here is what you must do.
To those who, out of bitter experience or political conviction,
cannot and will not accept that, we say: Leave us. And let
those who replace them earn the trust of the public through
their labors."

A "ministry of public confidence" meant in other words
a power that would accept direction from the "party" and

the "public" as expressed through the press and the so-called "public [voluntary] organizations." The party, however, would assume no burden of responsibility. It is not difficult to understand why the leftists would prefer that type of government to a government directly responsible to a majority of the Duma. Moreover the formula "ministry of public confidence" seemed to be "less offensive" and more acceptable to a wider audience. Thus it was that the Kadet conference of 7-9 June 1915 first proclaimed the slogan destined to become a nationwide focus of agitation.[41]

STAVKA AND THE GOVERNMENT

In appointing Grand Duke Nicholas Nikolaevich to command the Russian armies at the beginning of the war, the emperor conscientiously refrained from direct interference in military operations so as to avoid even a hint of divided authority. Nevertheless he frequently visited Stavka [General Headquarters] in order to familiarize himself firsthand with the situation at the front. He also reviewed the troops who were on their way to the war zone and personally inspected various sections of the front, as for example the fortress of Osovets which had repelled several enemy assaults. Nevertheless, the direction of combat operations remained in the hands of the grand duke, who was greatly admired by both the army and the country. His popularity gave rise to rumor that his position was creating a "Bonapartist sentiment." Grand Duke Nicholas Mikhailovich, for example, wrote that "his popularity is not good either for the country or the dynasty." The empress, too became rather "jealous" and her letters frequently reminded the emperor that the tone of the grand duke's appeals to the army and the public were becoming only to a monarch.

The emperor, however, retained his confidence in the loyalty of the supreme commander, and as long as the front was not imperiled he spurned any suggestion that he should assume a more active role in the conduct of the war. However, when the enemy broke through the Galician Front, the emperor rushed to Stavka, arriving on 5 May and remaining for more than a week. To the empress he wrote: "You can judge for yourself whether I could go away from here in such difficult circumstances. It would have been understood as meaning that I avoided staying with the army at critical moments. Poor N. [Nicholas Nikolaevich], while telling me this, wept in my private room, and even asked me whether I thought of replacing him by a more capable man . . . . He kept on thanking me for staying here, because my presence here supported *him personally*."[42] The emperor's calm resolution in that time lent moral support to the supreme commander.

Still, the situation at the front and in the rear required prompt measures that went beyond purely military considerations. Many Stavka decisions created problems on the home front. General Yanushkevich, the chief of staff, ordered the mass "evacuation" of Jews from Galician and Russian territory along the frontier. The army staff had discovered that it was the Jewish population that harbored the greatest number of enemy spies. They transmitted information across the front either with signals or by greeting the advancing foe with ready information on the number and weapons of the Russian troops. In Galicia in particular it was quite likely that the Jews were more sympathetic to the Austrians than the Russians. In an article in the Spring 1915 issue of the journal *Novoe zveno* Count M.M. Perovsky-Petrovo-Solovovo explained the Jewish attitude by an Aesopian tale set in South America: Columbia and Venezuela were allegedly at war; in one of those countries lived an Indian tribe, the "Itskasru-leibas," who enjoyed full civil liberties, while in the other country the same tribesmen were limited in their rights. Therefore it was not difficult to figure out which country that tribe favored. (Although the censors allowed the article to pass, that issue later was confiscated and *Novoe zveno* was closed.)

The indiscriminate condemnation of the entire Jewish population for espionage was unfounded, of course, and Stavka's actions were ill-advised. Tens and then hundreds of thousands of Jews from Galicia and the western provinces were ordered to move within 24 hours under penalty of death. They were driven into the interior far from the theater of war. Ignorant of the Russian language and yet forcibly uprooted and driven deep into Russia, that great mass of Jewish humanity became a breeding ground first of panic and plague and then of a smoldering hatred for the state.

Other Stavka decrees, less categoric and more compassion-ate than brute force, applied to the evacuation of other na-tional minorities. Guided by the thought that the enemy entering a devastated area would find it difficult to obtain food and shelter for his troops, the Russian command as-sisted the mass exodus of people eastward. In the process both villages and fields were burned; livestock was slaughtered on the spot or died on the road. The goal was to allow nothing to fall into enemy hands. The council of ministers was highly critical of this "strategy of 1812," but since the supreme commander ruled the entire theater of war, the cabinet was powerless to do anything about it.[43]

CONCESSIONS

Talk of treason in connection with the shortage of shells became so common that finally at the end of May the emperor formed a commission headed by the war minister and includ-ing the chairman of the Duma and several deputies to acquaint the representatives of the public with the true situation. Mean-while from the army came reports of the officer corps' in-credible fury. Responsibility for the ammunition shortage was heaped on the war ministry, and in order to quiet the situation the emperor decided to dismiss Sukhomlinov. Con-vinced that Sukhomlinov was a scapegoat for shortcomings that were impossible to prevent, the emperor addressed him warmly at their parting.

Next came the task of reorganizing the government. Through the first year of the war, the emperor's policy was to avoid domestic conflict without making any basic changes. Therefore, when the education minister, Kasso—ardently de-tested by the entire left—died, the tsar chose as his successor Count P.N. Ignatiev,[44] who had gained the confidence of the Duma as assistant minister of agriculture. The public wel-comed the appointment.

Then when the demand arose for a special war supply board, for the "mobilization of industry," and also for the prompt convocation of the Duma, the emperor decided to meet the public halfway while simultaneously reserving full power to himself. He successively dismissed all the ministers whose actions had provoked heavy criticism in the Duma:

interior minister Maklakov (6 June), Sukhomlinov (12 June), Sabler, the director-general of the holy synod (5 July), and justice minister Shcheglovitov (6 July). In their places he appointed: Prince N.B. Shcherbatov,[45] a member of the State Council's right wing, as minister of interior; A.A. Khvostov[46] as minister of justice; and A.D. Samarin,[47] the marshal of the nobility of Moscow and a man who once had the reputation as a confirmed supporter of unlimited autocracy, as director of the synod. Only the vacancy in the war ministry went to a "liberal"—A.A. Polivanov,[48] the former assistant war minister whom the military regarded as an able "technician." Polivanov's close ties with Guchkov biased the emperor against him, but after a lengthy interview with the candidate at Stavka, Nicholas decided to overlook that fault.

Finally, at Stavka on 14 June the council of ministers convened under the presidency of the tsar and with the Grand Duke Nicholas Nikolaevich and his closest advisors in attendance. The outcome of the conference was a decision to demonstrate confidence in the public by convening the State Duma at the earliest possible moment and by relaxing the censorship on the press.

THE LONG RETREAT

The military situation remained serious. Wherever the Germans launched a determined offensive the Russian front disintegrated. By the end of June nearly all of Galicia had been abandoned. In the north the Germans drove deep into Kurland; the Polish salient was outflanked on both sides. Meanwhile the Russian soldiers' steadiness under fire and the high command's strategic skill averted a "Sedan" or a "new Tannenberg." The entire front rolled back slowly. The Germans failed to achieve any more breakthroughs or any major encirclement of Russian forces. Russia had to abandon a vast area in order to save the bulk of the army. Because of the great disparity in artillery, Russian casualties were very high and the number of prisoners rose alarmingly.[49] In many cases entire units were forced to surrender after using up all their ammunition. Demoralization, expressed especially in allegations of treason in high places, was widespread, and yet the retreat remained orderly and nowhere did it deteriorate into panicked flight.

RETURN OF THE DUMA

The change of ministers and the convocation of the Duma, scheduled for 19 July—the anniversary of the declaration of war, cut two ways. These measures undoubtedly met with public approval and at the same time raised hopes in the army of a change for the better. But if these concessions pacified the opposition, they also whetted its appetite for even greater changes. The opposition formed the conviction that the war had made it possible to win concessions that the government could have refused in peacetime.

Between the emperor and the public was developing a serious misunderstanding: He believed that power had to be concentrated in his own hands in order to win the war. He had to be able to govern through people whom he could rely on implicitly. *Whether those people were popular or not with the public* was to him an important but nevertheless secondary consideration. Society, on the other hand, had concluded that it now had the opportunity not only to "depose" but also to "appoint" the ministers. The almost simultaneous resignations of Maklakov, Sabler, and Shcheglovitov played a critical role in creating that misunderstanding. Sukhomlinov's dismissal, however, was a genuinely unavoidable if "symbolic gesture" that implied a radical improvement of the system of war supply.

Foreigners also misinterpreted the tsar's reorganization of the government. David Lloyd George, the British minister of munitions, commented openly on Russian political affairs. He expressed his personal satisfaction that the Germans "with their monster artillery . . . are shattering the rusty bars that fettered the strength of the Russian people." He hoped, he said, that now the Russian people would pull together and resist the enemy.

The Duma opened on 19 July/1 August 1915 and again the speeches of the deputies resounded with determination to prosecute the war to a victorious conclusion. But the public contrarily suspected the government and the rightists of desiring peace with Germany, and separate peace at that. Unlike the previous wartime sessions, the government's policies came under vigorous attack. The measures against Jews and Germans, as well as the failure to take sufficient precautions against "German domination," the demand for amnesty for political prisoners and the demand for a ministry of public confidence—all were openly debated in the Duma and in the columns of the newspapers. Only occasionally did the military censors prohibit even the most unrestrained attacks, and then a blank space would appear on the page of a newspaper.

Meanwhile, the situation at the front continued to deteriorate. Warsaw was abandoned on 22 July/4 August. Rumor had it that the army would dig in along a line from Kovno to Brest-Litovsk, but the Germans attacked and seized Kovno (General Grigoriev, the commandant, was court-martialled for total incompetence)[50] and the Brest forts were blown up even before the Germans arrived. Huge stocks of supplies that could not be evacuated were destroyed. The enemy was advancing on the Western Dvina River, and the high command ordered a hasty evacuation of Riga, an important industrial center. Stavka anticipated an Austro-German offensive out of Galicia in the direction of Kiev but had no idea of where the army could check the advance.

The country, though not the press, buzzed with talk of the inactivity of the Allies. There had been no action on the Western Front since April. During that time the full weight of enemy pressure had fallen on the Eastern Front. Buchanan, the British ambassador, finally felt compelled to make some statement, and in August *Novoe vremia* carried a long interview in which the ambassador explained the Allies' inaction. The Western Front, he said, had become a chain of small fortresses which could be attacked only with a clear superiority of war material. The Allies were accumulating the necessary guns and ammunition, and once they had achieved the necessary advantage they would go over to the offensive.

Italy, the focus of so many hopes, finally entered the war on 11/24 May, just as the Galician debacle was beginning to unfold. However, the Italian army faced heavily fortified mountain strongholds both in the Tyrol and on the route to Trieste. Consequently Italy could not divert Austrian troops in sufficient numbers to affect the situation on the Russian front.

THE EMPEROR TAKES COMMAND

In this time of trial for Russia the emperor decided to place himself at the head of his troops. He recalled the decisive moment in a letter to the empress: "I remember very clearly that I was standing before the large icon of Our Saviour in the big church (at Tsarskoe Selo) and it seemed that some inner voice was urging me to reach a definite decision and to write immediately to Nicholas and inform him."

As the war zone spread into western Russia the division of authority between Stavka and the council of ministers became intolerable. The cabinet was highly critical of the policies of the high command. In that regard the newer ministers, Polivanov and Shcherbatov, were not be be outdone by Krivoshein or Rukhlov.[51] At the council's meeting of 16 July[52] Krivoshein declared that "in any case this bedlam must be brought to an end. No nation, not even long-suffering Russia, can exist under two governments." Khvostov demanded to know "what is going on in those areas that we are evacuating? The various activities are neither planned nor coordinated. Everything is done by chance in haste, and without any system." Rukhlov contended that "we, the ministers, have gotten ourselves into a terrible mess with Stavka. That organization is charged with directing our military operations and fighting the enemy, but in the meantime it is meddling in every facet of the country's life and trying to take charge of everything."

As if to prove the point, Yanushkevich, the chief of staff, apparently did assume that responsibility, for general policy indeed had devolved upon him. He sent Krivoshein, the minister of agriculture, a comprehensive plan for allocating land to soldiers [who performed their duty] and confiscating the holdings of those who deserted or surrendered. His proposal generated the scorn and wrath of the council of ministers. "From Yanushkevich one can expect anything," declared Sazonov.[53] "The horrible thing is that the grand duke is a prisoner of such a gentleman. It is no secret to anyone that he is hypnotized by Yanushkevich and Danilov; he is in their pockets."

The army held the same opinion. The grand duke's popularity among the rank and file was untarnished; his courage was legendary, and he was respected for his stern treatment of "incompetent generals." But Stavka itself had lost all prestige. In the officer corps the names of the grand duke's closest assistants aroused the same hostility as did the name of Sukhomlinov before his dismissal. Those same persons, and especially General Yanushkevich, also were detested by the public, primarily because of the brutal policy of expulsion that they directed against the Jews.

The dual authority of Stavka and the council of ministers had to be eliminated, and Stavka itself had to be reorganized. Grand Duke Nicholas Nikolaevich, however, was not disposed to sacrifice his closest aides, whom he continued to trust. And yet to replace the grand duke with someone of "inferior" social standing would have seemed an insult and a disgrace. The emperor had no desire either to humiliate or discredit the grand duke, nor did the public want such a solution.

Under the circumstances the only possible solution seemed to be for the emperor himself to assume the command. That would eliminate the division of authority. Moreover, as Krivoshein emphasized to the council of ministers, it was not without reason that the rules for administering the war zone had been drawn up on "the assumption that the emperor himself would become the supreme commander-in-chief. In that way there could have been no misunderstanding, and all questions would have been solved in a simple way: all power would have been in the hands of one man."[54] By yielding his position to the tsar the grand duke, who earlier had suggested that possibility, was able to retire with honor and without any loss of prestige. Furthermore, it was only natural that the most intimate members of his staff should depart with him. New leaders—including General Michael Alekseev,[55] chief of staff of the Northern Front, who had the finest reputation and whom the tsar referred to as "my cross-eyed friend"—were appointed to replace Yanushkevich and his staff.

When the emperor first confided his intention to his war minister, Polivanov felt obliged to reveal that confidence to the cabinet, which immediately raised a series of objections. The ministers discussed the emperor's decision with great excitement in several meetings, even though it seemed the logical conclusion to be drawn from all the discussion of the relationship between Stavka and the government.[56] The

Grand Duke Nicholas Nikolaevich

arguments began with the contention that if further defeats befell the country, the emperor himself would be held responsible.

Polivanov warned: "It is horrible to think what effect it would have on the country if His Majesty the Emperor were to give the order for the evacuation of Petrograd[57] or, God help us, Moscow, in his own name." Prince Shcherbatov raised a rather bizarre point: "The Tsar's automobile could not even move quickly through the mass of refugees along the crowded roads. And how is the Emperor to be protected from the thousands of deserters—hungry, angry men wandering in the forests?" Krivoshein observed that "for a long time now, since Khodynka and the Japanese campaign, the people have considered His Majesty an unlucky and unfortunate Tsar."

Prime minister Goremykin explained the emperor's position: "I must say to the council of ministers that all attempts to dissuade the Emperor will be useless, in any event. His conviction was formed a long time ago. He has told me more than once that he will never forgive himself for not leading the army at the front during the Japanese war. In his own words, the duty of the Tsar dictates that the monarch be with his troops in moments of danger, sharing both their joy and their sorrow . . . . Now, when there is virtually a catastrophe at the front, His Majesty considers it the sacred duty of the Russian Tsar to be with his troops, to conquer with them or to perish." Later, Goremykin added: "I repeat that his decision is unshakable. Various influences have nothing to do with it. All rumors to that effect are nonsense which the government can ignore."[58]

As it turned out, Goremykin was correct. All the individual appeals of the ministers and of the chairman of the Duma and finally even a collective letter signed by all the ministers except Goremykin and Khvostov, the minister of justice—all failed to shake the tsar from his deliberate decision. Those various efforts merely showed the emperor which ministers he could rely on unconditionally and which were not so steadfast.

It was on 21 August, the eve of his departure for Stavka, that the ministers sent the tsar their collective written appeal, urging him not to dismiss the grand duke and drawing attention to their "basic disagreement" with the chairman of the council of ministers. "Finding ourselves in such circumstances," the letter concluded, "we are losing our faith in the possibility of serving You and our Motherland with any real sense of usefulness."

Goremykin took the following position toward his associates in the cabinet: "I am not interfering with your individual declarations. Report to His Majesty everything that your reason and conscience dictate. To my mind His Majesty the Emperor is the Anointed of God, the Hereditary Bearer of Supreme Power. He personifies Russia. He is forty-seven years old. He has not been reigning over and disposing the fate of the Russian people since yesterday. When the will of such a man is determined and his course of action irrevocably taken, loyal subjects must submit, no matter what the consequences. Beyond that there is only the will of God.

So I think, and in this knowledge will I die."[59]

August 22 marked the formal inauguration of several special councils, new advisory organizations made up of members of both legislative chambers and representatives of the voluntary organizations.[60] Each special council functioned under the chairmanship of the appropriate minister, and their function was to resolve various problems associated with the war effort. The emperor himself opened the councils and expressed the conviction that all the participants would work harmoniously for the victory of Russia. "Let us set aside for the time being all other concerns about affairs of state which, though important, are not urgent at this moment," he urged. "Nothing must distract our thoughts, our will, and our strength from what is now our sole aim—to drive the enemy from our land."

Then on that same day, 22 August, the emperor set out for Stavka, which recently had been transferred from Baranovichi to Mogilev, there to assume command over all the armed forces of Russia.

CHAPTER NINETEEN

"We have learned that our valiant army, bloodied by the loss of over 4,000,000 men killed, wounded, and captured, is not only in retreat but may continue to retreat . . . . With heavy hearts we have learned, Sire, that more than 1,200,000 Russian soldiers are in enemy captivity." Thus read a memorandum prepared by the Duma's naval commission in August 1915. The figures were not exaggerated. At the moment the emperor assumed command the total losses of the Russian army indeed exceeded four million men, and the number of prisoners in fact had reached 1,600,000. During the four months of retreat from May to August, the army was losing men at the monthly rate of about 200,000 killed and 300,000 captured. Despite the fact that over ten million men had been placed under arms since the beginning of the war, the effective army was smaller than at the outbreak of hostilities.

More than 1,500,000 men drafted in August were just beginning their training, but beside the western front the empire had to man a second front in the Caucasus. Worse, less than a million rifles were available to equip the troops in training. In addition to the sheer numbers lost during the first six months of offensives that had saved France from the German onslaught was the merciless slaughter that decimated the officer corps and took a heavy toll of the army's veteran cadres.

The front had been pushed back inside the borders of Russia. Battles raged along the line of the Western Dvina from the outskirts of Riga to Dvinsk. On the Northwestern Front the Germans had overcome the obstacle of the Belovezhsky Forest and were pressing on into the Pripet Marshes. To the south Austro-German forces, having driven across Poland, were deep inside Volynia, while in Galicia they were forcing the Russians back to their western frontiers.

Russian citizens who followed the enemy's movements on maps began to calculate the distance from the front to the capitals. The authorities already had appointed a committee for the evacuation of Kiev, and the council of ministers considered whether to remove the relics and other holy artifacts from the Pechersky Monastery. The naval commission's memorandum noted that "the ancient city of Pskov is being fortified in confusion and haste amid general disorder and turmoil."

The emperor inherited a bitter legacy when he arrived at Stavka on 23 August/5 September 1915. "As of this date," declared his general order, "I have assumed command of all land and naval forces located within the war zone. With steadfast belief in God's help and unshakable confidence in final victory, we shall fulfill our sacred obligation to defend our homeland to the end, and we shall not bring shame upon our Russian land."

For his closest assistant as chief of staff the tsar chose General M.V. Alekseev. The war zone was redivided into three rather than two sectors. General Ruzsky commanded the Northern Front along the Dvina, General Evert[1] the Western Front from Dvinsk to the Pripet Marshes, and General Ivanov remained in charge of the Southwestern Front. Grand Duke Nicholas Nikolaevich, the newly-appointed viceroy of the Caucasus, departed for a rest in the Crimea after more than a year of exhausting, uninterrupted work at Stavka. The emperor hoped to devote all his efforts to the war, but even as he was taking command, political developments were afoot—developments that would alter fundamentally the course of Russian history.

ZIMMERWALD

On 23 August/5 September 1915 representatives of the radical socialist parties gathered for a meeting in the Swiss village of Zimmerwald. Their conference marked the first attempt to re-establish the Second International, which had been wrecked by the war. After a year of hostilities, the mood among socialists had changed drastically. Gone was the spontaneous patriotism that originally swept the leaders along with the masses. Those leaders bound by certain declarations could

not retreat from their positions, but among the rank-and-file
anti-war protests grew louder, and a new leadership was emerg-
ing. Russian socialists also were affected by that movement.
Revolutionists like Lenin, who had opposed the war from
the outset, suddenly began to acquire greater influence.

Italian and Swiss socialists took the initiative in summon-
ing the Zimmerwald conference, and the call was answered
by 33 delegates from ten countries—Germany, Italy, Russia,[2]
France, Holland, and others. The conference, which lasted
four days, adopted a resolution condemning the "imperialist
war." It rebuked all socialists who had used "defense of the
fatherland" as an excuse to collaborate with the bourgeoisie,
to join their governments, or to vote for war credits. It declared the proletarian objective to be immediate peace. About
a third of the delegates, led by Lenin, maintained that the
resolution was too weak. Lenin argued that the "imperialist
war" had to be turned into a "civil war." The arming of
millions of "proletarians" provided the opportunity, he contended, to seize power in order to carry out a social revolution. For the moment, however, the Leninists contended
themselves with the Zimmerwald resolution.

The Zimmerwald program was enormously influential. All
socialists and generally everyone grown weary of the war
eagerly awaited the word, "arbitrary" as it was, as proclaimed
by the international socialist center. Though suppressed in
every belligerent country, copies of the Zimmerwald program
rapidly spread far and wide. In Russia the resolution gave a
strong impetus to anti-war sentiments among workers and the
semi-intelligentsia. Individual Social Democratic leaders like
Plekhanov and Aleksinsky, a former member of the Second
Duma, strenuously objected to "Zimmerwald," but the party
masses immediately rallied behind the resolution on peace.
The only distinction was between those who supported the
"majority" and those who backed the "left" [the Leninists].

FORMATION OF THE PROGRESSIVE BLOC

The program of the so-called Progressive Bloc was adopted
on 25 August 1915. Since the opening of the Duma's summer
session, members of the Kadet and Progressist parties had negotiated regularly with Duma moderates—the Left-Octobrists,

Peace for a Russian Peasant

Zemstvo-Octobrists, and centrists. They even made overtures to the Nationalists, but a majority of that group opposed cooperation with the left. Nevertheless, the Nationalist left led by V.V. Shulgin and A.I. Savenko formed a special fraction which took the name Progressive Nationalists and continued to discuss the formation of a left-center majority.

Dissatisfaction with the government formed the basis of the coalition in which moderates joined the opposition in order to bring about a change of government. The leftists urged adoption of a general program, and representatives of the various fractions worked on one for two or three weeks. All members of the Bloc agreed on two basic propositions: that the war had to be brought to a victorious conclusion and that to achieve that end it was necessary to unite the government and the public. From that generally accepted position the leaders of the coalition concluded that the government had to be made to conform to the demands of the public. That was the start of an inclined plane: the leaders equated the liberal intelligentsia with "the public" and insisted that its will was reflected in the voluntary organizations which arose during the war—the All-Russian Union of Zemstvos, the Union of Municipalities, and the war industry committees. Those organizations, originally founded to deal with non-partisan matters related to the war effort, suddenly were accorded the stature of tribunes that expressed the political will of the nation.

When the unions first came into existence, no one cared particularly that Kadet elements dominated the leadership as long as they effectively tended the sick and wounded. But then that one-sided political leadership began to show its other face. Guchkov, for example, was elected chairman of the Central War Industry Committee. No one questioned either his energetic leadership or his patriotic stand on the war, but it also was common knowledge that he was an irreconcilable foe of the government and moreover that he was hostile personally to the bearer of the supreme power.

The basic aim of the Progressive Bloc was to transfer power into other hands. Its program had no real significance but was drafted primarily to justify to the leftist public the Kadets' alliance with such recently "odious" elements as the Octobrists or Nationalists such as Shulgin. Indeed, the first articles

of the Bloc's program represented concessions to the extreme
left, which had refused to join the coalition. The program demanded a general political amnesty and the release of all
persons exiled administratively. Such measures coupled with
the new militancy of the socialists could serve only to inten-
sify the anti-war protests. No one could believe seriously that
the Kamenevs and Stalins released from exile would be so
filled with gratitude that they would switch immediately to
a patriotic stance.

Other points of the program called for Polish autonomy,
reconciliation with Finland, the abolition of repressive measures against self-styled "Ukrainians," and "a start toward the
abolition of the limitations on the civil rights of the Jews."
(The last point was particularly difficult for the right wing
of the Bloc to swallow.) Finally, the program urged the Duma
to take up legislation concerning equal rights for the peasantry
(the government used Article 87 to establish that law in 1906,
but the Duma had not yet considered it), the volost zemstvo,
zemstvo and municipal government reform, the cooperatives,
and other similar questions.[3] All of those matters, the emperor
had declared, though "important and of concern to the state,"
were nevertheless "not vital at this time."

Even before the Progressive Bloc program had been signed,
the country began to clamor for a ministry of public confidence, the demand formulated by the Kadets at their party
conference in June. On behalf of the Central War Industry
Committee Guchkov sent a letter to Goremykin bluntly demanding the resignation of the cabinet.[4] Then on 18 August
the Moscow municipal duma unanimously approved a resolution calling for "a government invested with the country's
trust." Other dumas and zemstvo assemblies endorsed the
Moscow resolution. The program of the Progressive Bloc referred to a government "composed of individuals who enjoy
the confidence of the country and who have agreed with the
legislative establishments upon the implementation, at the
earliest date, of a definite program."

Six Duma fractions numbering some 300 of the 420 deputies joined the Progressive Bloc, and three groups (left, center,
and non-party) within the State Council also joined it. On
25 August N.E. Markov, the leader of the Duma rightists,
asked whether he might "be permitted to say that this Bloc

is not red, for the Reds with their distinctly bloody hue have not joined it . . . . It would be more appropriate to call it a yellow bloc." "Not yellow," retorted Shulgin, "but tricolored!" The prominent Kadet, Prince D.I. Shakhovskoy, declared: "It is unthinkable to include everyone in the Bloc. There always will be someone to the right, and to the left is the ocean."

The Progressive Bloc was a weapon in the struggle for power. With its solid majority in the State Duma the Bloc was able to deliver telling blows against the government. The groups that joined it actually submitted to the leaders of the Kadet fraction, which was politically more experienced and which knew more clearly than the others exactly what it wanted. The Kadets often restrained their more "moderate" colleagues when the others in anger were prepared to follow an extreme, precipitate course. Indeed, Kadet restraint preserved the Bloc.

When the Bloc was formed, some members of the cabinet considered it necessary to negotiate; some even were inclined to accept an agreement in which some ministers would resign and be replaced by "public figures." The emperor emphatically spurned the idea. He believed that power had to be concentrated and that it was unthinkable, especially in wartime, that ministers could "serve two masters"—the monarch who bore all responsibility and "the public" with its fleeting and shifting moods. The Duma having concluded its consideration of all legislation pertaining to the conduct of the war, Goremykin went to Stavka to report to the emperor. At that time Nicholas charged his prime minister to prorogue the Duma. That action served as his answer to the demand to transfer power into other hands.

THE MOSCOW CONGRESSES

The Duma was prorogued on the 3rd of September. Some deputies wanted to "stage a scandal" on the spot and to resign demonstratively from all the special conferences. The majority, however, decided to submit in strict correctness. In place of the Duma, the oppositionists found the opportunity to vent their emotions in the congresses of the zemstvos and municipalities, which convened in Moscow on 6

September. V.I. Gurko resurrected the legend of Rasputin by proclaiming: "We need a power that rules over the Khlyst, not one that succumbs to the Khlyst." Guchkov praised the Duma, "the sickly child of the Sablers and Kharuzins," which had risen to national importance. A.I. Shingarev declared that "Russian slavery fell after the thunder of Sevastopol, the first shoots of the Russian constitution appeared after the Japanese war, and this conflict will produce the birth pangs of national freedom and our liberation from the old forms and institutions of power . . . ." Although that was not Shingarev's intention, his reference to the "beneficial consequences" of lost wars coincided with the attitude of the defeatists.

Both congresses elected delegations to call upon the emperor in order to present their resolutions demanding a change of government.[5] Naturally he refused to receive them. Meanwhile on 15 September the cabinet met at Stavka, and the tsar clearly informed his ministers of his determination to dedicate his total energies to the conduct of the war and of his resolve not to tolerate political strife until victory had been won. One by one those ministers who favored concessions to the Progressive Bloc had to leave the cabinet. (A.D. Samarin and Prince N.B. Shcherbatov were the first to be dismissed; A.V. Krivoshein and P.A. Kharitonov followed soon afterward.)

THE GERMAN ADVANCE CHECKED

As the struggle for a ministry of public confidence developed on the home front major changes took place in the war zone. Russian troops had great success on the Western Front in the vicinity of Tarnopol and Trembovl. They captured several thousand prisoners and reoccupied a large area of Galicia. Only a shortage of shells prevented the further development of that victory and an advance in the direction of Lvov.

On the Northern Front the Russians repulsed enemy attacks on their bridgeheads all along the Dvina River. The Germans delivered one more strong blow against the Western Front in early September and managed to break the Russian line near Novo-Sventsiany on the Warsaw railroad. German cavalry made a deep eastward penetration into the Modedechno district, and a mounted patrol even reached the Moscow-Brest railway. The Russian army had to withdraw from Vilna, but part of the German units that broke through the Russian line were wiped out and the rest were pushed back. Russian forces completely liquidated the wedge that the Germans had driven into their front. "Great losses were inflicted on the enemy forces which penetrated deeply," reported the communique of 19 September.

At that point the German offensive ended. Once again the front began to "settle down"—along the Dvina, along the chain of lakes a short distance west of Minsk, through the Pripet Marshes to a point south of the Rivers Gorynia and Styr. The threat to Riga, Pskov, and Kiev, to say nothing of the capitals themselves, had passed. The autumn rains began to fall. Germany's technical superiority diminished as the distance of its armies from their bases increased. Their first victories over the Germans raised the morale of the Russian troops. The great retreat finally had ended.

In contrast to the cries of panic in the capitals, the army accepted the change of the supreme command as a matter of course. The mass of troops shared the tsar's conviction that the proper course was to take command at such a perilous time. And, according to the British General Sir Alfred Knox who was assigned to Stavka, the officers "were readily prepared to pay the price of the grand duke's retirement in order to obtain dismissals as desirable as those of Yanushkevich and Danilov."[6]

The 1915 campaign on the Eastern Front was over. "Russia has made her contribution for the present, and what a heroic contribution it was to the cause of European freedom," wrote Lloyd George. "For the next several months, as far as the Russian army is concerned, we shall not be able to count on the kind of energetic support that we have enjoyed thus far . . . . Who will take Russia's place while her armies are being rearmed?" "How can we repay Russia for everything she has done for Europe?" asked *The Times* (11/24 September 1915). In 1915 Russia did indeed bear the major burden of the war. By the fall of the year 137 Austro-German infantry and 24 cavalry divisions were concentrated on the Eastern Front, while 85 infantry divisions and one cavalry division manned the Western Front. No military action by the British and French relieved the pressure on Russia in the summer of 1915 as the Russian army had relieved the Allies during the first months of the war.[7] The reason usually given was that the strongly fortified Western Front made it extremely difficult to mount an offensive. During 12-25 September 1915, however, the Allies finally launched strong attacks simultaneously around Arras and in Champagne. They smashed the first German line and took about 25,000 prisoners. *Novoe vremia* observed that "the apparent inactivity of the Allies was a period of preparing the blow." But that was the end of the offensive, and the fighting cost the Allies nearly twice the casualties of the Germans. Nevertheless, the sudden activity on the Western Front apparently played some role in ending the German offensive in Russia.

FIRST SIGNS OF INFLATION

Events at the front strongly affected the life of the country. The retreat of 1915 frightened and disturbed the broad masses who normally remained quite indifferent to politics. A person no less than former interior minister N.A. Maklakov later testified that "everyone was depressed, that was inevitable. I myself felt the same during the time of the military failures." The tension produced by the fighting was separate from the oppositionists' campaign against the government, although they tried to exploit that mood. While the agitation of the Progressive Bloc swept across the surface, the Zimmerwald program was sinking deeper roots into the country as weariness with the war increased.

As the front stabilized and millions of war refugees were relocated in the rear,[8] rail communications more or less returned to normal, and quiet suddenly descended over the country. Economic activity remained comparatively untouched by the war, although at the end of August the lack of coinage produced something of a crisis. The supply of silver and then of copper coins dwindled practically from day to day. The government issued substitute marks to replace them. At first the people grumbled about the "money that flies away," but they quickly accepted it.

Price increases were relatively moderate: by the end of 1915 bread had increased 40 percent over prewar levels, butter

45 percent, meat 24 percent, and sugar 33 percent. The abundance of money in circulation and rising wages insulated most of the population against rising prices, but there were complaints about the high cost of goods. Provincial governors fought inflation by resorting to price fixing, a measure that sometimes interrupted the supply of goods. The capitals occasionally experienced sugar and meat shortages. The reason was that sugar and meat consumption increased during the war. Because of prohibition, increased rations for the army, and the abundance of money in the villages, during the first years of the war the Russian people ate better than before the war. Sugar consumption, for example, rose to 24.4 pounds per person in 1915 as compared to the prewar average of 18 pounds.

The war production industry was developing rapidly. Huge new government works were under construction, and older factories were being modernized. The government concluded an agreement with the Allies to finance the purchase of large orders mainly in America and England.

HELP FROM THE DISTAFF SIDE

The emperor lived at Stavka, but about once a month he returned to Tsarskoe Selo for a few days. Most of the time the tsarevich remained with his father. The emperor continued to make all the responsible decisions, but at the same time he relied on the empress to maintain constant contact with the ministers and to keep him informed of developments in the capital.

Empress Alexandra Feodorovna was the person closest to the emperor, and she alone was privy to his plans. She completely shared her husband's outlook, and he could depend on her without fail. Nevertheless, when he departed for Stavka, he did not entrust her with any formal responsibilities or obligations (as for example did Peter the Great with Catherine, or Napoleon I with Maria Louisa, or Napoleon III with Eugenie). The best explanation was that the empress was personally unpopular in most circles and was distrusted because of her German background or her blind faith in Rasputin. As for the emperor himself, he trusted her absolutely. Everyday she wrote him detailed letters—"reports"—a fact well known

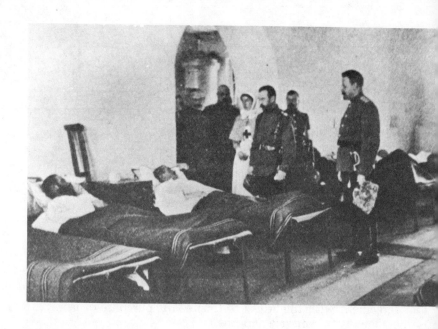

The Tsar Visiting Wounded Soldiers. Quarters of the
Tsar and Tsarevich at Stavka

to the ministers, who often reported their views to the emperor through the empress.

The dismissal of the ministers who advocated compromise with the Duma bloc gave the cabinet a more, though not completely, homogeneous character. A.F. Trepov,[9] an energetic rightist official, became minister of communications. The post of minister of interior went to A.N. Khvostov, the former governor of Nizhni Novgorod and chairman of the faction of rightists in the State Council. The emperor had had Khvostov in mind for the post earlier (in 1911) after the assassination of Stolypin. A.N. Volzhin,[10] a politically colorless figure, became director-general of the holy synod, and A.N. Naumov, elected to the State Council by the Samara zemstvo, was named minister of agriculture. The appointment of Naumov, who was known to hold moderately liberal views, was intended to soften the effect of the other appointments. The post of state comptroller was filled by N.N. Pokrovsky.[11]

Khvostov launched a vigorous though somewhat demagogic campaign against high prices and German dominance, both popular causes among the non-party milieu. The recess of the State Duma was scheduled to last until November 1915, but on Goremykin's recommendation its reopening was postponed until the budget commission completed its work. Khvostov denied the voluntary organizations permission to hold their scheduled December conferences. No pressing business warranted their convention every three months, and meeting without purpose they would serve merely as centers of agitation. The country accepted the postponement of the Duma and the cancellation of the conferences with little comment. Overall the Duma remained in recess for about five months, from 3 September 1915 to 9 February 1916.

OPPOSITIONISTS AND MONARCHISTS TAKE STOCK

The bureau of the Progressive Bloc soon sensed that a change was taking place. At its meeting of 19 October Miliukov announced that he sensed "a collapse," that public reaction had become "languid." N.I. Astrov[12] acknowledged that "the mood of the very core of society has changed. The policy of the frisky minister (Khvostov) has succeeded." A.I. Shingarev, too, noticed "a perceptible shift in the attitude of the bulk of the population," and V.A. Maklakov even suggested the reason for the change: "We then claimed that we were being led to defeat . . . . If we achieve total victory, we will not be able to revive the ill-will toward Goremykin. We will be left without a response." The chairman of the Union of Municipalities, M.V. Chelnokov, urged as a general policy that the Bloc postpone its aim of settling scores with the government until after the war.

"We blundered badly over the change of command," declared Count D.A. Olsufiev during the meeting of 28 October. "All of us were wrong. The emperor was more farsighted. The change was for the better . . . . We urged a reorganization of the cabinet for the sake of the war. The least desirable minister (Goremykin) remained, but the military situation improved. The influx of refugees has ended, Moscow will not fall, and that is infinitely more important than who will become minister and when the Duma will be reconvened." Count V.A. Bobrinsky agreed that "the situation is improving. The shells arrived and we stopped the enemy."

The fact was that the improved situation at the front and the calm at home represented defeats for the Duma bloc which had forecast a catastrophe. Nevertheless, the Bloc decided to continue its "merciless struggle" against the government. Speaking in that connection, Guchkov declared: "An appeal to the street? Perhaps, but only in an extreme case."[13] Guchkov even favored the rejection of the budget, but the Duma refused to go along.

At the end of November 1915 a congress of rightist organizations convened in Petrograd under the chairmanship of Ivan Shcheglovitov. The congress unanimously endorsed the policy of carrying the war to a victorious conclusion, and it censured the demands of the Progressive Bloc. "A monarchist who associates himself with the demand for a ministry of public confidence is no monarchist," declared Shcheglovitov, and Professor Levashov denounced the "bacchanalia of lies." The congress of monarchists angered the left-wing press, but the emperor telegraphed his gratitude for its resolutions. N.A. Pavlov, a prominent nobleman, wrote an article—"Do Not Interfere"—for *Moskovskie vedomosti* in which he contended that the voluntary organizations and political parties were not supporters but rather impediments to the government's conduct of the war.

THE ANNIHILATION OF SERBIA

The halt of the Russian armies to reconstruct the front and rebuild their strength gave the Austro-German alliance the chance to deliver a fatal blow to Serbia. The government of Basil Radoslavov, then in power in Bulgaria, maintained an Austrian orientation but meanwhile also negotiated with the Allies for a pledge to cede Macedonia, which Serbia had acquired at the end of the Balkan wars. However, the promises of the belligerents had less influence on Tsar Ferdinand and Radoslavov than the actual military situation. Thus in Russia's weakness Bulgaria's politicians saw an opportunity to "avenge the year 1913."

When Bulgarian preparations for an attack on Serbia became apparent, the Russian government attempted to forestall that event through diplomacy but its efforts were unavailing. On 23 September 1915 Russia severed its diplomatic relations with Bulgaria.[14] On that same day Austro-German forces launched an offensive against Serbia along the Danubian front, and simultaneously Bulgaria attacked the Serbs in the rear. Despite the difficult straits of his own forces, the tsar ordered five army corps to concentrate in Bessarabia in order to be in a position to cross Rumania and attack the Bulgarians. Unfortunately there were not enough rifles to equip that army. The Allies, who had promised the immediate delivery of 500,000 rifles, subsequently reported that they could provide only 300,000 and those no earlier than December. Rumania, citing the threat of the Austro-German armies, refused to allow Russian forces to pass through its territory. The Greek government declared that its alliance with Serbia obligated it to intervene only in a Serbo-Bulgarian war and did not require its participation in a world struggle involving the great powers.

An Allied landing at Saloniki proved too little and too late. The enemy overran Serbia in October and November and Montenegro in December. The Serbian army had to retreat to the sea through the mountain passes of Albania. The emperor instructed the Russian ambassador, Prince G.N. Trubetskoy, to accompany the Serbian government during its retreat and to share its fate. Russia demanded that the Allies transport the Serbian army to the Aegean island of Corfu where it could rest and recover its combat strength.

By the end of the year the Allies had evacuated the Gallipoli Peninsula where they had failed to capture the main
Turkish positions. The British also wanted to pull out of
Saloniki. However, the Russian government, backed by the
new French premier Aristide Briand,[15] insisted and the British finally agreed to hold that bastion in the Balkans in order
to prevent the Central Powers from occupying the entire
peninsula.

THE SEPARATE PEACE: A FABRICATION AND ITS CONSEQUENCES

The year 1915 was one of great disappointments for the
Allies: stalemate on the Western Front, German victories in
the East, and the fall of Serbia. Yet nowhere among the
Entente countries was there evidence of any inclination to
sue for peace. The Russian Emperor certainly did not waver
in his resolve. Nevertheless the Progressive Bloc consistently
suspected the government and the Russian right of a desire
to conclude a separate peace. Rumors to that effect spread to
the western press. At the end of 1915 the *Revue de France*
alleged that I.G. Shcheglovitov, N.A. Maklakov, and other
reactionaries were "intriguing to end the war." Although such
allegations were denied emphatically, the notion that certain
"reactionaries" were conspiring to conclude a separate peace
became one of the cliches in western propaganda. Perhaps
the assertion was employed for its psychological effect: the
Allies may have counted on the alleged "intrigues of the
reactionaries" to squelch any thought of a possible separate
peace among the leftist and liberal parties. If so, the credence
given to those rumors produced a false perspective on Russian
affairs and ensured that the real danger from the left was
concealed and ignored.[16]

Among the masses in general and the workers in particular
the idea of peace—the "Zimmerwald" peace—sunk its roots
deeper and deeper. In September 1915 the election of workers'
delegates to choose representatives of 219,000 Petrograd
workers to the Central War Industry Committee produced an
unexpected Bolshevik victory. When the electors met, they
simply refused to elect any representatives and instead adopted
a resolution, which declared in part: "The slogan 'defense of
the fatherland' and its variations—defense of freedom, culture,

national interests, rights, morals, and so on—are only a subter-
fuge to mask the rapacious claims of the ruling classes and a
lure to help mold the worker into a blind tool of their imperialist ambitions."

Only two months later, aided by a combination of repressive measures and hand-picked electors, was it possible to
elect delegates from the worker group. The labor representatives, however, quite aware of their tenuous position among
their comrades, tried to subordinate the workers' hostility to
the war by a firm defense of the workers' extreme economic
demands and by more intensive opposition to the government.
The leader of the Labor Group, K.A. Gvozdev,[17] declared at a
meeting of the group on 19 November 1915 that unity was
necessary "for the struggle against the German attackers and
for the struggle with our dreaded internal enemy, the autocratic regime. Active participation in the work of the Central
War Industry Committee is essential to achieve those two
goals."

The Zimmerwald mentality also extended to the students.
A great number of them volunteered for military service, but
the attitude of those who remained behind was quite different.
When early in 1916 a decree extended conscription into the
active army to students, they staged protests in many of the
higher institutions. Their spokesmen declared that if they did
enter the army, it would be solely to disseminate revolutionary propaganda.

The journal *Letopis* [Chronicle], edited by Maxim Gorky,
first appeared in December 1915. It like other leftist journals
reflected a definite Zimmerwald tendency. Deprived of the
possibility of attacking the government openly, radical journalists heaped ridicule on the leaders of the Progressive Bloc
and those socialists who adhered to the cause of "war to a
victorious conclusion."

Disillusionment with the Allies began to be evident among
the citizenry in general and to some degree even within the
army. It became a rather common expression that "England
and France are determined to fight right down to the last
Russian soldier." General Knox recorded that in October 1915
even General Lebedev, the quartermaster-general of the Western Front, told him that "history will judge the British and
French with contempt, for they sit month after month like

rabbits in their holes and leave the whole burden of the war to fall on Russia." The French apparently felt the same way, but in their own behalf. In December 1915 General Joffre told General Zhilinsky: "France alone fights the war; the others only beg for her assistance."[18]

Paul Doumer, a prominent politician who later became president of the French Republic, visited Stavka during the fall of 1915. He insisted that Russia contribute 40,000 men a month to the Western Front. France, he promised, would arrange their transportation and provide their equipment. Alexandre Ribot later pleaded with A.I. Shingarev to "help us with what you have in abundance, help us with men." The emperor, however, declined to send large units of troops to France but consented to "token" detachments, the first consisting of 8,000 men. That gesture underlined the solidarity of the Allies without simultaneously weakening the long-suffering Eastern Front.

THE EMPEROR'S EFFORTS AT RECONCILIATION AND UNITY

By the beginning of 1916 the question of what policy to adopt toward the Duma confronted the emperor. The government was in a far stronger position than in the previous fall and without great risk he could have deferred the convocation of the Duma until the end of the war. (The Austrian parliament, for example, did not meet between 1914 and 1917.) The extraordinary circumstances imposed by war on an unprecedented scale furnished the necessary justification to depart from established legal norms. The tenure of the Fourth Duma was due to expire in half a year. No business required the Duma as then constituted to be reconvened, and moreover the election of its successor would depend entirely on the course of the war.

But the emperor was not inclined toward such a drastic solution. He preferred instead to follow a middle course. The transfer of power to the majority of the Duma was equally out of the question. Agreeing completely with the assessment of "the public" as expressed in Durnovo's memorandum, the tsar had no confidence in the Duma as a vital force that might assist the government. All the same, he had no desire to aggravate the situation or to provoke some new basis for agitation across the country. The chief target of the "public campaign" was Goremykin, the prime minister. ("If the old man comes, we cannot guarantee peace," Shingarev told the bureau of the Progressive Bloc.) Goremykin himself thought that the Duma's session, if permitted at all, should be limited to a few days and restricted to consideration of the budget. The emperor decided, however, to meet the Duma halfway and to "smooth the rough edges" without essentially changing his policy.

On 20 January 1916 a warm and gracious decree announced Goremykin's retirement and elevated him to the rank of "personnage of the first class." In his place the tsar appointed Boris Stürmer, a member of the rightist group of the State Council.[19] Cultured and well-bred, Stürmer was less fixed in his views than Goremykin but no less ready to carry out his sovereign's instructions. His first statement proclaimed his good will toward the Duma and the voluntary organizations and expressed his willingness to take into account their "methods, expertise, and traditions." He also announced that the Duma would convene at the beginning of February and that it would continue to sit as long as the deputies themselves deemed it necessary.

The change of prime ministers relieved the tension and threw the leaders of the Duma bloc into a quandry. At its meeting of 28 January a majority of the bureau spoke favorably of the possibility of cooperation with the government. Goremykin's retirement was regarded as a victory for the Duma. "If a hand is stretched out to us, we should work together," said Baron Meller-Zakomelsky, a member of the State Council. "It will be easier to negotiate initially than it was with Goremykin," said Shidlovsky. "We cannot come out on the first day and say that we do not trust the government," declared Basil Maklakov. "Since Goremykin is gone, that is impossible." Miliukov's advice was for the deputies to bide their time until the new prime minister revealed whether or not he could get along with the Duma. Shulgin concluded that "we must be more forthcoming than Stürmer."

The emperor went beyond the appointment of a new prime minister. He left the front and came to the capital to attend the opening of the Duma. On 9 February he attended a *Te Deum* celebrated in the Tauride Palace and then, for the first time since the convening of the First State Duma in 1906, he delivered a welcoming address to the deputies:

I am happy to be among you and among my people, whose chosen representatives you are. Invoking God's blessing on the work that lies ahead of you, especially in such a difficult hour, I trust that each and every one of you will apply your full knowledge of local conditions and your complete devotion to your fatherland in order to accomplish all that is required by the vital interests of our country and your responsibilities to me, and that your work will be guided solely by those considerations. Your devotion will always aid you and serve as your guiding star in the fulfillment of your duty to our motherland and to me. With all my soul I wish the State Duma a productive session and every success.

In his memoirs Rodzianko alleged that after the speech he said to the emperor: "Do make the most of this joyous occasion and proclaim here, at once, your will to grant a responsible ministry." After a brief silence the emperor replied: "I will think it over." Judging by all circumstances, such a request was simply out of place.

The country was happily stirred by the emperor's visit to the Duma, Goremykin's retirement, and the news of a great victory on the Caucasus Front—the capture of the mighty fortress of Erzerum on 4 February. Those events created an environment ill-suited to attacks by the opposition. Nevertheless, S.I. Shidlovsky announced a resolution of the Progressive Bloc, composed beforehand, which again called for "the formation of a government composed of persons who are capable and knowledgeable, who are strong because they enjoy the confidence of the country, who are prepared to change decisively the methods of government employed until now, and who can work in harmony with the people's representatives."

The debates of the Duma, however, did not generate interest as they had in 1915. To be sure, the Kadet newspapers defended the maneuvers of the Bloc, but the leftists ridiculed them and the moderate rightists, who once had welcomed the emergence of the Bloc, spoke scornfully of the struggle that constituted "a rerun of the fall session." *Moskovskie vedomosti* observed that the liberals "have all grown stiff in their old frames—everything they say is so familiar, so old, and so hopelessly trite!" The organs of the extreme right—*Zemshchina, Russkoe znamia*—were of course even more caustic.

VOLUNTARY ORGANIZATIONS: MYTH AND REALITY

The Duma's right wing of about one hundred deputies conducted a running battle with the Progressive Bloc. The leading spokesmen on the right were N.E. Markov, G.G. Zamyslovsky, P.A. Safonov, and Professor Levashov. The Duma majority had little patience with them and constantly interrupted their speeches. On 11 February Markov sharply attacked the voluntary organizations. "So far," he said, "all those war industry committees have done nothing for the army: not one single rifle, not a solitary gun. You provided no shells, you provided no guns, you provided no rifles—and all your shouting cannot conceal those facts!"

On the following day Rodzianko, Konovalov, and N.V. Nekrasov took the rostrum to deliver detailed speeches in defense of the voluntary organizations. The Duma debates afforded an opportunity to get at the truth of the matter, for if the right was disposed to minimize the contributions of the voluntary organizations, the liberal press supporting the Bloc exaggerated them to excess. The Kadet organ *Rech*, for example, contended that "the Central War Industry Committee has girded the nation and caused it to resound with the clang and roar of machines and tools producing war equipment."

The Union of Zemstvos as well as the Union of Municipalities ran extensive programs to assist the sick and wounded. In some areas, such as the transportation of wounded from the front to hospitals in the rear or in the organization of feeding stations, their contributions were substantial. The All-Russian Union of Zemstvos took the responsibility for the delivery of some supplies (leather, for instance), and it acquitted itself very well. But as for strictly military supplies the achievements of the unions were quite modest. T.I. Polner,[20] one of Prince George Lvov's closest assistants, admitted openly that the Zemgor[21] actually accomplished very little. Most of the Zemgor committees lacked the equipment and the expertise to meet the army's technical requirements. Local committees were even more helpless than the central organization, and usually their deliveries arrived late and were as much as 50 percent defective.

In response to Markov's charge that "you provided no shells," Miliukov shouted: "But we forced them to provide!"

That, in Polner's view, was the chief contribution of the Zemgor—not its own efforts but the fact that it compelled the war ministry to become "less careless." As a result, in 1916 "the quantity of military supplies nearly reached sufficiency."

The extent of the unions' activities were best reflected statistically. The Union of Zemstvos was made up of about 8,000 organizations with several hundred thousand employees, who were exempted from military service. (Rightists referred to them as "zem-hussars.") Like the Union of Municipalities, it existed on subsidies provided by the state treasury. In the first 25 months of the war (to 1 September 1916) the Union of Zemstvos received government subventions totaling 464 million rubles. In addition, local zemstvos and municipalities appropriated about nine million rubles for its use. By that time, however, Russia's total military expenditure amounted to about 20 billion rubles, and it is apparent that the voluntary organizations' role in war supply was far more modest than commonly believed during the war.[22]

As for the war industry committees, their central concerns were the placing of orders and the preparation of various administrative forms pertaining to the needs of the army, the productive forces of the country, and similar matters. The war department frequently complained that the committees were lax in determining that deliveries were made at prices advantageous to the treasury.[23] That, however, was a minor consideration at a time of rapid general inflation.

On the other hand, the voluntary organizations played a very prominent political role. The Progressive Bloc tended to look on them as its cadres, although actually most of the employees of those organizations held far more radical views. The central committees of the zemstvo and municipal unions maintained that they were well-informed as to the attitude of the army, and therefore they even attempted to speak for the army. The bureau of the Progressive Bloc, for example, held a meeting on 2 November 1916 during which it discussed a memorandum first alleged to have come "from the army." It later turned out that the document had been prepared by the Zemgor committee of the Southwestern Front. The report portrayed the condition of the army in the most depressing terms. A.I. Shingarev, who as chairman of the Duma's naval committee was better informed on the situation, protested

exerted a powerful influence over the course of state policy. The letters reveal that though the empress sincerely regarded Rasputin as a "man of God" and was prepared to follow his advice, the emperor completely disregarded that advice. Here are examples of the "advice" that Rasputin gave the empress and that she passed on to the emperor:[24]

6 April 1915—Rasputin advised the emperor not to go to Galicia until the end of the war. The trip was made.

17 June 1915—Rasputin advised against convening the State Duma. The Duma was convened.

15 November 1915—Rasputin advised the tsar "to launch an offensive around Riga." Needless to say, no offensive took place.

15 and 29 November 1915—Rasputin changed his mind and then urged the convocation of the Duma—"Now that everyone wants to work, you should show that you trust them." The opening of the Duma was postponed until February.

12 October 1916—Rasputin begged the tsar "to stop the senseless bloodshed" in the attacks around Kovel; many others, including members of the Progressive Bloc, took the same position. Those pleas had no effect on military operations.

19 December 1915—Rasputin "recommended" Count S.S. Tatishchev for minister of finance; 29 January 1916—General Ivanov as minister of war; 10 November 1916—Engineer Valuev as minister of communications. The emperor simply ignored these "recommendations" and did not even respond to the empress. At about that time, incidentally, General Ivanov was relieved of command of the Southwestern Front.

16 April 1915—Rasputin requested the tsar not to appoint Samarin; 23 May 1916—he asked the tsar not to appoint Makarov. Both appointments were made.

16 October 1916—Rasputin suggested the appointment of Prince Obolensky as Protopopov's assistant and "doesn't care very much for Kurlov." Kurlov was appointed.

All these pieces of "advice" the emperor rejected quietly so as not to hurt the empress's feelings. Occasionally, however, he became irritated: "Our Friend's opinions of people are sometimes very strange, as you know yourself." (9 September 1916) or "I beg, do not drag Our Friend into this" [10 November 1916].

These examples taken from correspondence over a period of two years reveal the absurdity of any insistence on a "reign of Rasputin." Of course, some decisions accorded with Rasputin's wishes: obviously the emperor could not reject every decision or appointment simply because Rasputin favored it. In 1915, for example, Rasputin spoke against drafting recruits of the second class, and the draft was postponed until September but only for good reasons: 1) there were not enough rifles to equip even the field army; 2) the Council of Ministers concluded that the Duma should pass the appropriate legislation; and 3) the conclusion was to institute the draft at the end of the harvest season. Rasputin was "in sympathy" with the appointments of Khvostov, Stürmer, and Protopopov, but there were also good political reasons, completely independent of the wishes of the "monk," for each of these appointments.

Finally, Rasputin himself wanted to maintain and support the rumors of his influence (since they gave him "weight" as well as many lesser advantages). Having no definite views of his own, he generally tried to follow the lead of the emperor and empress and he adjusted his position to their views and wishes. If he managed to find out about some as yet unpublished decision of the emperor, he quickly ascribed it to his influence. Thus he "spoke out" for prohibition, against a "ministry of public confidence," and for the emperor's assumption of command. Nothing, however, suggests that Rasputin's opinions had any effect on the emperor's decisions in those matters. Concerning the supreme command, the tsar's letter of 8 August 1916 contained a direct rebuke to the empress. Again, without foundation the emperor's visit to the Duma on 9 February 1916 was attributed to Rasputin, and yet the emperor made that decision at Stavka and no mention of it appeared in his letters to the empress.[25]

Since he never wished to be wrong, Rasputin's position on the war was typical. On 16 July 1914 he sent through Anna Vyrubova the following telegram with its double meaning: "Do not worry too much about war. When the time comes, an end will have to be put to it, but that time is not yet and your suffering will be crowned."[26] That telegram later was used to indicate that Rasputin "begged" the tsar not to declare war. In fact, since he had no idea of what was in the emperor's mind at the time, he simply was afraid to take a definite position.

Another side to the legend of Rasputin was its paralyzing effect on individuals. Those who came under its influence began to suspect the motives of the tsar. They thought they detected in his words the echo of "alien influences" and thus began to go against his will, suspecting that it was not the tsar but Rasputin whom they heard. Despite their honest mistakes, such people no longer could serve the crown loyally, and they had to be dismissed. The best known instance of that kind was the dismissal of A.D. Samarin, whose personal integrity and disinterest were beyond reproach.

Rasputin's political influence, therefore, was a myth, but a harmful one which spread sedition among the people and sowed confusion among monarchists.

KHVOSTOV'S PLOT

Discovering no other way to combat the legend, Khvostov tried to be rid of the person around whom it was created. He suggested to some officials in his ministry that they take upon themselves the "removal" of Rasputin. Though embarrassed by such a suggestion, at first they were too timid to object. To plot a murder ran counter to the morals and manners of the Russian police. As assistant interior minister S.P. Beletsky later declared, officials of the government could not turn "into some kind of Mafia." Certain officials therefore saddled others with the unpleasant task.[27] The latter, in their search for an executioner, went so far as to contact the notorious Iliodor, who was living abroad. The plot was delayed, and eventually Khvostov's scheme became known to Rasputin, and through him the empress learned of it. Counter-intelligence agents, who were under the jurisdiction of the war department, were assigned to shadow Khovstov and his agents. The emperor learned of the plot when he visited Tsarskoe Selo. Indignant at such conduct on the part of his minister, he immediately dismissed Khvostov and delegated the management of the ministry of interior to the chairman of the council of ministers, B.V. Stürmer.

The public learned the reason for Khvostov's dismissal and that only enhanced the Rasputin legend. Meanwhile, any minister or assistant minister who disdained Rasputin, who refused to receive him, or who ignored his "little notes" with their requests and recommendations continued to enjoy the emperor's confidence. Those who believed in the power of Rasputin's influence and groveled for his favor in no way improved their situation. During that difficult time, the ministers who acquitted themselves honorably were those who found the courage to ignore not so much Rasputin himself—that was comparatively easy—but the legend of Rasputin. Those ministers, therefore, served the emperor as though Rasputin did not exist. To the honor of the Russian military and administrative services, a majority of the officials conducted themselves in that manner. But that did not prevent the enemies of the regime from hanging the label of *"Rasputinets"* on almost every official that they did not like.

SUKHOMLINOV'S ARREST

The emperor tried to accomodate the public mood on another matter that he found personally painful when he agreed to an investigation into the conduct of former war minister V.A. Sukhomlinov. The emperor himself had no doubt of Sukhomlinov's innocence.[28] But attacks on the former minister became so persistent that even the conservative Nationalist L.B. Polovtsov denounced him as a "scoundrel" to the Duma and demanded that he be put on trial. Having agreed to an investigation, the emperor considered it inappropriate to interfere with the legal process. Nevertheless he felt a great injustice had been done when the first department of the State Council [Senate?] recommended that Sukhomlinov be brought to trial and when on 20 April 1916 he was arrested and confined in the Fortress of Peter and Paul. Sukhomlinov may have been guilty of lacking administrative skill and of negligence, but nothing justified a charge of treason. Finally in the fall, after a long period of hesitation, the emperor instructed the appropriate ministers to alter the regime of confinement and transfer Sukhomlinov from the fortress to house arrest.[29]

The Allies did not know what to make of Russia's behavior: the prosecution for treason of a former war minister, who had held that post for the entire first year of the war—and, as the trial revealed, on clearly insufficient evidence—and even worse, the official admission that such conduct was possible.

The trial shattered the morale of the country by destroying confidence in the highest wielders of power and giving rise to rumors of more "treason." This concession to "public opinion" had only the most harmful consequences.

THE POLITICIANS "AT WORK"

The session of the Duma dragged on from 9 February to 20 June 1916 with only a one-month recess. Interest in its proceedings slackened even among the deputies, who frequently failed to provide a quorum. The Progressive Bloc, as N.N. Shchepkin explained at one of the meetings of the bureau, regarded it "necessary at least to maintain the appearance of work for the sake of an unrestricted rostrum." The Duma considered only the ordinary budget (it had no jurisdiction over military expenditures), and those debates took about two months. It approved several interpellations—on a ministerial circular dealing with Jews, on a bill to introduce preliminary censorship, and other matters. It carefully examined the bill on peasant liberties, which Stolypin had put into effect in 1906 under Article 87. The debates produced some excitement when the Kadets attempted to amend the peasant bill with a provision granting full equality to Jews. Objections arose not only among other factions of the Bloc but even from one of the Kadets scheduled to speak on the bill, V.A. Maklakov. Consequently the amendment was rejected.

Rightists insisted that the question of German domination be added to the agenda, since they knew that the Bloc was sharply divided on that issue. The Duma, however, voted to defer the question until the fall. All in all the sessions of the Duma were as dull as the Moscow congresses.

In April a delegation consisting of prominent figures from both chambers visited England, France, and Italy. Led by the vice-chairman of the State Duma, A.D. Protopopov, the legislators remained abroad until nearly the end of the session. The delegation was received everywhere with great ceremony. A large meeting in Paris on 12/25 May 1916 featured speeches by Protopopov, Paul Doumer, and Édouard Herriot.[30] Herriot praised the Russian Emperor who "always has embodied the spirit of the people from within and without; he has defended them with an unflinching loyalty that demands admiration

General V.A. Sukhomlinov

General A.A. Brusilov

and inspires respect." Protopopov heralded the inviolability
of the Franco-Russian Alliance and declared that "in this
dreadful war to any Russian any Frenchman is a brother."

The Petrograd municipal elections of early 1916 were a re-
flection of the prevailing mood. In 1913 a substantial majority
of Progressists dominated the municipal duma which, following Guchkov's lead, frequently adopted political resolutions.
In the elections of February 1916, however, the Progressists
were routed: 27 "old-thinkers" [*starodumtsy*] or conservatives were elected in the first curia and in the second the Progressists were outnumbered 35 to 19. Combined with the older
membership (only half of the duma was up for re-election),
the conservatives claimed a majority of 93 of the 160 representatives. The Petrograd city duma ceased to be one of the
strongholds of the Progressive Bloc. A non-party member,
Lelianov, who once had been mayor, was re-elected to that
position.

1916: THE BRUSILOV OFFENSIVE

Soon after the emperor assumed supreme command, the Allies
made a serious effort to coordinate military activities on the
various fronts. The Russian chief of staff, General Alekseev,
developed a bold strategic plan which General S.G. Zhilinsky
presented to an inter-allied staff meeting at Chantilly in December 1915. Alekseev's plan proposed a general offensive
against Hungary in 1916—a Russian drive through Carpathia
and an Anglo-French (and Serbian) offensive from Saloniki
with the armies converging on Budapest. The blow was intended to deprive the Germans of all their allies and cut off
their sources of supply. The French and British, however, adhered to the belief that France was the decisive front and all
others were secondary, and they rejected the plan. Instead the
Allies decided that, after a build-up of strength, they would
launch simultaneous offensives on the Western and Eastern
Fronts.

Unfortunately the Germans beat them to the punch and
unleashed a major assault against Verdun in February 1916.
At the height of the battle of Verdun the Russian army resumed the offensive for the first time since the great retreat of
1915. The Russian attack concentrated on the area around

Lakes Naroch and Vishnevskoe south of Dvinsk. The battle raged for two weeks from 5/18 to 17/30 March. The reawakening of the Russian army alarmed the Germans to such an extent that they halted their attack on Verdun for about a week until they were satisfied that the Russian attack was only a tactical move.

While the relentless struggle at Verdun bled both sides of their reserves, the Austrian commander, Conrad von Hötzendorf, opened a boldly conceived campaign against Italy. Striking from the South Tyrol, Austrian forces drove toward the Po valley and threatened to cut off from their bases all major Italian forces operating in the Carnic Alps and on the route to Trieste.

Then, just as in 1914, the Allies turned to Russia and once again the Russian army, replenished and considerably stronger numerically if not qualitatively, moved to the attack ahead of schedule. On 22 May/4 June the armies of the Southwestern Front under General A.A. Brusilov[31] (who recently had succeeded Ivanov) broke through the enemy front at several points in Volynia and Galicia. Advancing rapidly the Russians captured the cities of Lutsk and Dubno and took over a hundred thousand prisoners.

The brilliant victory over the Austrians doomed Conrad's Italian campaign. Moreover, he was held negligent in not anticipating the Russian offensive and relieved of command. Italy was saved from a perilous threat. The Brusilov offensive also affected the western campaign, for it forced the Germans to hasten reinforcements to the East and thus depleted the reserves needed to continue the battle of attrition around Verdun. The Russian victory in Volynia was the Allies' first major success after a string of defeats. The morale of the Allied nations soared, and the neutrals, who had decided that the war would end in a draw, began to have second thoughts.

The offensive on the Southwestern Front continued to go well and soon spread from Volynia to Galicia and Bukovina. During the first three weeks of the campaign, the number of prisoners (mainly Austrians) exceeded 200,000. The attack on Verdun came to a halt, and the British and French launched an offensive on the Somme River. They advanced at a crawl with heavy losses—"like Germans at Verdun"—but they did advance.[32] Although the Germans had managed to preempt the Allies' coordinated general offensive, by midsummer they had failed nevertheless to prevent their opponents from seizing the initiative. The Germans were forced onto the defensive on both fronts.

THE ENTENTE AND THE JEWISH QUESTION

The iron necessity of victory bound Russia and its allies in a common cause. The agreement that committed the Allies not to conclude a separate peace accorded fully with the emperor's determination to see the war end under no condition but general victory. He was prepared to make great sacrifices for the victory of the Entente and thus felt justified in expecting the same commitment from the Allies. Negotiations between Russia, France, and England dealt mainly with the allocation of war material, the coordination of military operations, and the war aims of each ally. From Russia the Allies sought soldiers and gold.[33] The imperial government looked to the Allies for war supplies and credits for purchases in neutral countries.

The British and French governments both understood that the tsar would permit no interference in Russian domestic affairs and they scrupulously avoided any hint of meddling. On two issues—Poland and Russian Jewry—Russian policy probably failed to satisfy the Allies, but tact and loyalty restrained them from attempting to influence Russian domestic affairs. Just as it would not have occurred to the Russian government to suggest that England introduce home rule into Ireland or that France revoke its laws against monastic orders, so the Allied governments did not consider it proper to pressure Russia for reforms.

Unofficial pressure was another matter, however. At the beginning of the war certain British financial circles headed by Baron Rothschild approached Count Benckendorff, the Russian ambassador to London, in an effort to obtain a revision of the laws on Jews. The emperor categorically forbade any promises of that kind to be made in the fall of 1914, and he subsequently repeated those instructions. During the Russian parliamentary delegation's visit to London, its chairman A.D. Protopopov rather boldly assured Rothschild that Jewish equality soon would become a fact in Russia. On returning to Petrograd, A.I. Shingarev informed the naval committee on 19

June that Jewish reforms would be necessary to facilitate Allied loans in the United States. The prominent American financier, Jacob Schiff,[34] though generally regarded as pro-German, promised under those circumstances to take it upon himself to float a Russian government loan. Miliukov cited statements by the French financier Victor Bache to confirm Shingarev's observations.

N.E. Markov, the leader of the rightists, angrily protested such interference: "The issue is quite clear: His Jewish Majesty, His Majesty Jacob Schiff, orders the Allies to compel Russia to introduce within its borders reforms which His Jewish Majesty desires. Those are our orders. Hopefully we will like the reforms, but they give the order whether we like it or not. You do not argue that Jacob Schiff is right—all you say is that without him you will not get the money. In other words, if you are ordered and refuse, you will be forced! That those conditions are intolerable should be clear not only to supporters of the autocracy but even to constitutional monarchists, even to republicans!"

A stormy debate ensued. Kerensky rather provocatively predicted that the Allies would demand even more. Then he argued that "since dignity and pride do not permit the Markovs to yield to a blow of the fist what they could not grant by their own free will," it was necessary to remove "the confederates of Markov" from power. Shingarev found it necessary to emphasize that his report was merely a statement of the facts and not a recommendation: "I cannot endorse the position that Russia must give in to demands under pressure."

The emperor held to the view that domestic reforms had to be postponed until the end of the war.[35] He was certain that the Allies' stake in Russia's security was too great to allow the Jewish question to halt the delivery of war material. In the end J.P. Morgan rather than Jacob Schiff handled the Allied loans in America.[36]

THE POLES, THE ENTENTE, AND SAZONOV'S DISMISSAL

The Polish question was more complex. Since the outbreak of the war, the Poles had sought an international guarantee for the broad autonomous status promised by the Russian Tsar. The reunification of Poland depended on a general Allied victory, and therefore the Allies had some basis for an interest in the Polish question. But there again the emperor viewed the issue from the standpoint of Russia's unlimited sovereignty. He was quite prepared to grant the Kingdom of Poland rather broad rights, but he considered it inadmissable that foreign powers should involve themselves in the relationship between Russians and Poles.

Foreign minister Sazonov advanced the Polish question in the spring of 1916. He believed that it was in the Allied interest to announce his plan for Polish autonomy as an appeal for Polish sympathies and to prevent Germany and Austria from recruiting Polish troops. (It was widely rumored at the time that Vienna was about to begin recruiting Poles for military service.)[37]

The emperor, on the other hand, was convinced that the status of the future Kingdom of Poland should not be determined while the territory was totally under enemy control: generous promises would be interpreted as a sign of weakness. Moreover, an autonomous status acceptable to Russia might be considered inadequate by the Poles. Disagreement over the Polish question became the decisive factor in Sazonov's resignation.[38] Sazonov's earlier position on domestic policies—the ministerial letter concerning the supreme command and the government's relations with the Progressive Bloc—had displeased the tsar. On the Polish question it appeared that the foreign minister defended Allied views before the Russian government more vigorously than he defended the Russian government's views before the Allies. Consequently on 10/23 July 1916 Sazonov was dismissed. At the time the emperor could find no suitable replacement for him, and therefore he delegated the direction of the foreign ministry to the prime minister, Stürmer. (Stürmer yielded his duties as interior minister to the minister of justice, A.A. Khvostov [the Uncle], who in turn was succeeded by former interior minister A.A. Makarov.)[39]

STÜRMER AS FOREIGN MINISTER

Stürmer's appointment introduced no change into Russian foreign policy—it could not be otherwise since the emperor himself was the source of Russian policy. That was true with

Stürmer just as it had been with Sazonov. Still, the dismissal of a minister who had held office for six years and was well known to foreign ambassadors had to be a cause of some misgivings in Allied diplomatic circles.[40] Among the Russian newspapers only the Kadet press indicated displeasure at Sazonov's departure. *Novoe vremia* sharply criticized the departed minister and in particular rebuked him for his failure to foresee and prevent the collapse of Serbia.

An uncommon incident occurred during Stürmer's first month as foreign minister. The British prime minister Lord Asquith made a speech in which he raised the possibility of prosecuting the leaders of the Central Powers. Part of the British press (*The Economist*, for example) took exception to his remark, and in Russia the right-wing journalist Paul Bulatsel, writing in the limited editions of *Russkii grazhdanin* [The Russian Citizen], angrily attacked the statement: "And so Asquith promises to realize the dream of the Freemasons to create an international tribunal of parliamentarians, power brokers, and lawyers and to give up to their judgment the crowned head of the German Empire himself . . . . The English, who have advanced their front only a few hundred meters during two years of war, cannot do that by themselves . . . . We have an obligation to fight not only until our stubborn, brave, and powerful German enemies admit that they have been crushed and agree to a peace that is honorable and advantageous to Russia but also to fight on until Russian bayonets have dethroned the reigning German dynasty of the Hohenzollerns."

The British ambassador perceived the article to imply some shift in Stürmer's foreign policy.[41] He sounded the alarm and sent a protest to the foreign ministry. Stürmer immediately gave Buchanan complete satisfaction: he ordered Bulatsel to deliver an apology to the British embassy and to submit meekly to a stern reprimand by the ambassador. *Russkii grazhdanin* was forced to undergo preliminary censorship.

ALEKSEEV'S PLAN FOR A MILITARY DICTATORSHIP

The emperor worried a great deal about the coordination of the various departments of government. The matter also concerned the chief of staff, General Alekseev, who suggested a

plan for the establishment of a "military dictatorship"—the
subordination of the ministers to Stavka. In March 1916 the
Duma bloc was angered to learn that General Polivanov had
been replaced as war minister by General Dmitry Shuvaev,
who had run the ministry's quartermaster and supply department effectively [since 1909].[42] A conference to consider the
question of a "dictatorship" was held at Stavka on 28 June.
The emperor, however, was reluctant to initiate a major revision of the existing system. Therefore he settled the issue by
resolving some of the conflicts between individual departments
and by broadening the authority of the prime minister, Stürmer.

At about the same time the minister of agriculture, A.I.
Naumov, retired. The reason for his departure was a conflict
with A.F. Trepov, the minister of communications, and Stürmer over whether to make explanations of problems of food
supply to the State Council. The rest of the ministers considered it unnecessary. The empress's letter of 23 June 1916,
repeating Sturmer's words, indicated more substantial reasons:
"He does not agree with the Government, looks at things quite
fr. another point of view. Tho' being a loyal and charming
man, he is obstinate and sticks to the ideas of Duma, Zemstvo
etc. and trusts their work better than the Governments; this is
not famous for a minister and makes work with him very difficult." To succeed Naumov on 22 July the tsar selected Count
Alexis A. Bobrinsky, the former chairman of the rightist faction in the Third Duma. The cabinet gradually was acquiring a
more homogeneous rightist character.

RUMANIA'S BID FOR GLORY

The success of Russian arms and the occupation of nearly all
of Bukovina finally convinced wavering Rumania to enter the
war on the side of the Entente. During preliminary negotiations, the emperor promised to support Rumanian claims to
Transylvania, but he flatly refused to cede any part of Russian
territory, especially in southwestern Bukovina. Russia did not
particularly encourage Rumania to enter the war. The military
had little confidence in the strength of the Rumanian army
and did not relish an extension of the front. However, the

intervention of a country so long undecided was considered a major psychological victory as a clear indication that the "by-standers" felt the German cause lost.

Having underestimated the Central Powers' resistance, Rumania declared war on Austria-Hungary on 14/27 August 1916. Then, disregarding the advice of the Russian high command, the Rumanians attacked into Transylvania on a broad front. (The Russian staff recommended a defensive stance in Transylvania and an offensive into Bulgaria toward the Allied forces at Saloniki.) The German alliance summoned its last ounce of strength. Hindenburg was made supreme commander-in-chief over all fronts. Germany, Bulgaria, and Turkey declared war on Rumania, and a combined German-Bulgarian-Turkish force under General Mackensen pushed into the Dobrudja and drove a wedge between Rumania and the Black Sea. The Rumanian army, which had swept 150 kilometers into Transylvania, soon was forced to retreat to the border under the blows of Austro-German counterattacks.

Rumania's decision for war came too late. By August the momentum of the Russian offensive was nearly spent. Germany had managed to concentrate formidable forces on the Eastern Front, and stubbornly repeated Russian attacks in the direction of Kovel and Vladimir-Volynsk produced great losses without success. The imperial guards suffered such heavy casualties that the emperor found it necessary to relieve General V.M. Bezobrazov of his command. The autumn rains were beginning to fall, and the flood plains of the Pripet depression were becoming morasses. On several occasions entire regiments refused to attack—the first such occurrences in the Russian army. Nevertheless the bloody fighting went on. But just as in the western offensive on the Somme, it became impossible to detect any progress on a map. A decisive victory obviously was not to be expected in 1916.

THE INCREASING STRAIN OF WAR

By the fall of 1916 all sections of the Russian population had begun to feel the burden of war. Mobilization "scraped up" 15 million male adults,[43] not counting about 2.5 million engaged in defense work in factories, mines, railways, and public organizations. Agriculture began to feel a manpower shortage.[44] In July 1916 Turkestan experienced a bloody revolt as a result of efforts to recruit non-Slavic minorities in Central Asia—groups that formerly had been promised exemption from military service. The seriousness of the situation led to the introduction of martial law, the appointment of General A.N. Kuropatkin (an expert on local conditions) as governor-general, and the cancellation of the draft in some localities.

The food situation was tolerable. The army did not encounter even a day's lack of supplies, nor did the home front experience a food shortage, although price increases accelerated and the people began to fear that winter might bring famine. By July-August 1916 wholesale prices in comparison to prewar levels were: bread, up 91 percent; sugar, up 48 percent; butter, 145 percent; and salt, 256 percent. In some areas retail prices increased even more substantially. Part of the cause was the increase in paper money, but the principal factor was in effect a strike in the villages. The peasants, who produced seven-eights of all Russian bread grains, were less and less willing to sell their products. In fear of requisitioning they began to hide their grain and bury it in the ground.

That "producer's strike" had no political motivation. It simply reflected the shortage of consumer goods in the country. Peasants were unable to satisfy their needs in return for their produce. Cloth, footwear, and iron goods were in short supply, and the prices on all those items had increased far out of proportion to the prices of agricultural commodities. "We used to pay 1.5 puds of grain for a pud of iron, but now it is 6 puds. We used to be able to buy 10 arshins of cotton for one pud of wheat, but now we get only two," reported a member of the Kiev zemstvo board at a conference on food in Petrograd in late August. The cost of iron goods, nails for example, increased eight-fold.

The problem of food and supplies, not only for the front but also for the home market, prompted lively discussion. Some economists demanded decisive government intervention: establishment of an official grain monopoly, rationing of agricultural commodities, and price-fixing to combat inflation. That was the position of representatives of the Union of Municipalities headed by V.G. Groman. Leftists displayed great admiration for Germany's "war socialism." Others maintained that a free market economy was necessary lest all products disappear from the marketplace, and they also insisted that fixed prices should be applied only to government purchases. Some economists like Peter Struve believed that price fixing was necessary in all commercial transactions but that prices should not be lowered artificially—that the fixed price had to take account of the costs of production.

Another area of complaint was the "chaotic state of the railroads." By the fall of 1916, transportation evidently had become a weakness everywhere. The French parliament, for instance, also spent several closed sessions on the "transportation crisis."

THE STRANGE CAREER OF ALEXANDER PROTOPOPOV

When the chairman of the Russian parliamentary delegation, Alexander Protopopov, returned from abroad, he made a detailed report of his tour to Sazonov, who was still foreign minister. His report included impressions gathered in England and France as well as his conversation with the counselor of the German embassy in Stockholm, Fritz Warburg. The meeting took place in the private apartment of a Swedish official. Warburg's statements seemed to indicate that the Germans were far from confident of victory and that their best hope was a rupture between Russia and England. Sazonov found those observations interesting enough to arrange to have Protopopov invited to Stavka in order to repeat them to the tsar. Nicholas took a liking to Protopopov who in turn was completely "charmed" by the emperor. Therefore, when in early September A.A. Khvostov indicated his desire to leave the post of minister of interior, the emperor decided to take a bold step—to offer the post to Protopopov—and he instructed Stürmer to talk it over with the candidate.

Protopopov, an industrialist, was a prominent member of the Progressive Bloc, vice-chairman of the State Duma, and a member of the Central War Industry Committee. He was the marshal of the nobility of Simbirsk and also was active in zemstvo affairs. During the summer of 1916 when Rodzianko was pressing the emperor to create a "ministry of public confidence," the chairman of the Duma had recommended Protopopov to head the ministry of commerce and industry.

B.V. Stürmer

A.D. Protopopov

Protopopov's appointment represented a continuation of the emperor's policy of "smoothing the rough edges" without introducing any substantial changes. He assumed that it would be easier for Protopopov, as a prominent member of the Duma, to convince his confederates of the need to defer their political demands until the end of the war. According to his own account, Protopopov for his part counted on obtaining the emperor's agreement to new reforms "desired by the Bloc": improved status for Jews, legislation establishing the legal responsibilities of ministers, broader rights for the zemstvos, and regular salaries for the clergy.

But the Duma bloc, too, had decided on a definite goal: the transfer of power to persons responsible to "the public" and independent of the crown. The Bloc had in mind candidates for nearly every post, with either Prince G.E. Lvov or Rodzianko on tap for the position of prime minister. Except for marking the transfer of some power from the hands of the bureaucracy, the appointment of a member of the Bloc to the head of a ministry was regarded not as a concession but, on the contrary, as a trick, a maneuver to divide the Bloc. Therefore against Protopopov the opposition applied the tactics that Miliukov, writing in *Osvobozhdenie* in 1904, had threatened to use against any public figure who agreed to cooperate with the government during "the spring of Sviatopolk-Mirsky": "If anyone among us tells you [the government] that he can open credit for you, don't believe him. He either deceived you or he deceives himself. You might if you can manage it, win him over, but understand this—that from the moment he becomes yours, he will cease to be ours, and therefore he also will cease to be of use to you."

A well-known journalist named Doroshevich warned Protopopov: "You are being driven into a corner, and they will hound you to death." At first Protopopov did not believe it, but he soon found out how easy it was for the "Bloc," with its control of the press and voluntary organizations to mobilize a campaign of slander and to hypnotize public opinion. The new interior minister was a member of the Duma presidium, head of the parliamentary delegation abroad, and one of the Progressive Bloc's candidates for a ministerial position, not to mention his other "civic" responsibilities. Yet within a few weeks before the very eyes of Russia, he was transformed into a deranged man who suffered from progressive [syphlitic] paralysis, into a personally dishonest figure, into a Germanophile, and even into an outright traitor (because of his meeting with Warburg).[45] One could only wonder whatever led the Bloc to consider him a potential minister and why the Duma had elected him to be its vice-chairman.

The purpose of those extraordinary measures was to ensure that no one else crossed over from the camp of the Bloc to the camp of the government. ("How many other Protopopovs are sitting here in our midst?" asked Shulgin at one of the meetings of the bureau.) The malicious campaign took its toll of Protopopov himself. He lost his presence of mind and his self-confidence. He became nervous and began to flit from left to right.

The government at that point was considering whether to transfer food administration from the ministry of agriculture to the ministry of interior. The move was expedient in case it became necessary to limit food consumption through the use of ration cards, since only the ministry of interior had the means to administer the program through its widely dispersed police apparatus. The emperor signed the ukaz ordering the transfer, but Protopopov, fearful of censure, dared not publish it on the eve of the Duma's return. For his assistant Protopopov chose P.G. Kurlov, a police expert. But the Duma was uncompromisingly hostile to Kurlov, whom many held responsible for Stolypin's assassination. Protopopov did not have the courage to announce Kurlov's appointment and thus he left him in an awkward and impossible position. In short, although undoubtedly well intentioned, Protopopov easily allowed himself to be "driven into a corner," and he was not capable of the mission entrusted to him. He probably was no more and no less fit for the difficult problems of administration than the rest of his colleagues in the Progressive Bloc and the voluntary organizations.

RUSSIAN ACHIEVEMENTS IN 1915-1916

Looking back over a year of hard work, the imperial government was able to take pride in its accomplishments. Not only had it averted the cession of a single inch of Russian territory, but it even had managed to recover substantial areas of

Volynia, Galicia, and Bukovina (with its area of about 30,000 square kilometers). In the Caucasus the Russian army had driven deep into Turkey's Anatolian plateau. Nearly all of Armenia was in Russian hands. About a million prisoners, mostly Austrians, had been captured, raising the total to about two million.[46]

By the opening of the 1916 campaign, the supply of war material was satisfactory. By the end of the year the increase of war production was striking. The production of rifles had doubled in comparison to 1914 (110,000 per month as compared to 55,000); the production of machine guns increased sixfold (from 160 per month in 1914 to 900 per month); the output of light artillery increased tenfold (665 per month over 70 in 1914); and the production of 3-inch shells increased sixteen times over (from 100,000 per month to 1,600,000).[47] The manufacture of heavy artillery increased fourfold, and aircraft production tripled (from 263 planes to 716).

But that was not all. At the end of 1915 Russia began to receive war material from abroad at an accelerating rate. In 1915, for example, Russia obtained 1,057 machine guns, but in 1916 it received 9,428; in 1915 about one million 3-inch shells, in 1916 about eight million; 129,000 4- and 6-inch shells in 1915, 1,692,000 in 1916. During 1916 Russia also imported 446 heavy (siege) guns and 46,000 rounds of explosives for them. Churchill wrote: "Few episodes of the Great War are more impressive than the resuscitation, re-equipment and renewed giant effort of Russia in 1916. It was the last glorious exertion of the Czar and the Russian people for victory . . . . By the summer of 1916 Russia, who eighteen months before had been almost disarmed, who during 1915 had sustained an unbroken series of frightful defeats, had actually managed, by her own efforts and the resources of her Allies, to place in the field—organized, armed and equipped—sixty Army Corps in place of the thirty-five with which she had begun the war."[48]

The massive importation of foreign supplies and equipment required prodigious efforts to improve the transportation system. At the start of the war the government began construction of about 16,000 kilometers of railroad; by the end of 1917 about 12,000 kilometers [7,500 miles] had been completed. Moreover, within the war zone itself a completely new

strategic rail network was built to facilitate the rapid movement of troops from one sector of the front to another. Only
Vladivostok and Arkhangel afforded Russia access to the outside world. Construction began on a second track of the Great
Siberian Railway. The narrow guage line connecting Vologda
and Arkhangel was replaced by the wider standard guage,
which then opened the route to through traffic. However, ice
closed the port of Arkhangel for almost six months each year.
In order to overcome that liability, in May 1915 the government began to construct the Murmansk route. Covering a distance of 1,050 kilometers [652 miles],[49] the Murmansk railway crossed tundra. swamps, and the rocky mountains of the
Kola Peninsula in its course through the zone of permafrost
and into the polar night far beyond the Arctic Circle. (The
world's most northerly railroad, the Murmansk line extends
beyond 69° North Latitude.) Enormous construction problems were overcome in the space of twenty months. To speed
construction track was laid simultaneously in ten different sections, and on 15 November 1916 A.F. Trepov, the minister of
communications, opened the route to local traffic. The railway
was completed in record time, and Russia had a new "window"
on the outside world.

Through great effort and careful management Russia not
only maintained but even increased its output of fuel. Coal
production, which stood at 35,138,000 tons in 1914, rose to
37,774,000 tons in 1916. Oil output climbed from 9,931,000
tons in 1914 to 10,870,000 tons in 1916 (the highest level
since the Baku fires of 1905). The sown area of cotton in Turkestan increased from 430,000 [desiatins] to 534,000 [or
from 1,161,000 acres to 1,442,000].

Four cruisers of the superdreadnought type were nearing
completion. By the fall of 1917 the Baltic Fleet was scheduled
to have eight first-class combat units. In addition, three dreadnoughts were scheduled for completion in the Black Sea. (One
of them, the *Imperatritsa Mariia*, sank in the harbor of Sevastopol as the result of an accident, but efforts to raise the
ship already were underway.)

In the realm of foreign affairs the imperial government, after lengthy negotiations, finally [in April 1915] secured Allied
recognition to Russia's rights to Constantinople and the Straits,
including both the Bosporus and the Dardanelles.[50]

Despite the incredible difficulties involved in financing history's most costly war, Russia's financial administration managed brilliantly. By the end of 1916 the war had cost Russia 25 billion rubles. Foreign and domestic loans covered about two-thirds of that sum,[51] and only the other third, about 8 billion rubles, was charged to inflation, that is, to paper currency.

Nevertheless, the Russian government never achieved distinction in touting its own achievements, a failing never more true than in the fall of 1916. Most citizens simply were unaware of the government's enormous accomplishments in 1916. Much of the information, of course, fell under military secrecy. The people clearly did not understand that plows and nails were scarce because most iron production went into war material. They did not know that the army, which had grown to eight million men including reserve units, consumed from two-thirds to three-fourths of all Russian-made textiles. While the people applauded the watchword "everything for the war," they were not fully aware of the severe domestic implications of that slogan.

THE LIBERALS MAKE THE MOST OF WAR WEARINESS

The autumn of the third year of the war was a period of sagging spirits. As usual, news from the front played a major role. Memories of the victories of early summer rapidly faded. Again the front became immobile, and battles even more bloody than those of 1915 raged on. Russia lost two million men in 1916, and only 10 percent were prisoners as compared to 40 percent during the great retreat. Reports from the Western Front also spoke of "marking time" and atrocious losses.

The war seemed endless. The Germans appeared to have solved the problems of food supply on which the Allies had counted so heavily in the spring of 1915. Workers, students, and the semi-intelligentsia succumbed increasingly to the Zimmerwald appeal, which told them that the struggle was an imperialist war that had to be stopped. There arose a new formula—"defensism"—which fused the new surge of patriotism with the Zimmerwald program: "Yes, we are prepared to defend our motherland, but we seek no conquests. We stand for 'peace without annexations or indemnities' and therefore we oppose the government which prolongs the war for the sake of imperialist aims." Variations of this theme also took hold of the leftist groups of the Duma: Kerensky's Trudoviks, Chkeidze's Mensheviks, and the workers' group in the Central War Industry Committee. The newspaper *Den* and the journals *Russkoe bogatstvo*, *Letopis*, *Severnye zapiski*, and others followed a similar line.

No propaganda could overcome the war weariness of the Russians. Only iron discipline and strict consorship could defeat it temporarily. Only the tsar's power, only firm authority could stem or contain the signs of collapse. The Duma bloc was linked inseparably with "defensist" elements through the voluntary organizations, which harbored a substantial number of left extremists. The "defensists" in turn were indistinguishable from the moderate Zimmerwaldists. Thus the Bloc's answer to "defeatism" was not repression but amnesty and relaxed censorship.

Russians were sick of war. To one degree or another that malady afflicted every belligerent nation.[52] But the Russian public, oblivious to the true causes of failure, was convinced that the government was responsible. Functionaries of the Duma bloc who were members of the special conferences knew very well what the average citizen could not. They knew what the government had accomplished. Nevertheless, they continued to insist that the regime was "incompetent." To admit otherwise would have required them to acknowledge their own mistakes, and political parties do not like and do not know how to do that.

In August 1916 Guchkov wrote to General Alekseev: "The government is rotting on the stalk . . . . But it is impossible to expect the transport system to be in good repair under the management of Mr. Trepov, or reliable output from industry under the care of Prince Shakhovskoy,[53] or prospering agriculture and proper administration of the food supply under Count Bobrinsky . . . . At the head of the entire government stands Mr. Stürmer who has the reputation (both in the army and among the people) if not of a traitor already then of one who is prepared to commit treason." Guchkov could not possibly have been ignorant of the great achievements of 1916. Yet in slandering the government before the very head of the army he had little concern for "objectivity." In that he was at one with the voluntary organizations with their purported memoranda "from the army."

The bureau of the Bloc resumed its work early in October. At the meeting of 3 October Count V.A. Bobrinsky declared that "our position was more dangerous last year. But if we had much to endure then, now we can press hard. The enemy's invasion has been stopped: now the time has come to take on the government." But Paul Miliukov, a more experienced tactician, recommended that they "concentrate our pressure on Stürmer." The chairman of the council of ministers, a rather colorless person who passively executed his sovereign's will, actually offered little to attack. He was, however, the formal head of the cabinet, and if the government was to be changed, he had to be overthrown first. Therefore the Bloc attacked Stürmer on two fronts: they used his German name[54] to label him an advocate of a separate peace; simultaneously they charged that he was "a protege of Rasputin" who followed the evil one's instructions in every matter.

Members of the Bloc had less than total confidence in themselves. Some bureau members like Shulgin even doubted their capacities: "It is all well and good to criticize Stürmer, but we also must indicate an alternate course." Unfortunately the Bloc had no workable program, especially with regard to the burning issue of food. Nor did the mood of the country evoke any great confidence, although the Bloc was fully aware of the nation's war weariness. "I do not believe that a separate peace would bring forth a revolution," said Shingarev. "The mass of exhausted people would say, let us sleep, wash, and eat our fill. They already are saying that in the villages and in the army and at court (?)." Count Kapnist agreed: "The villages will welcome peace, and they won't be choosy over what kind it is."

The Duma was scheduled to reconvene on 1 November, and as that date approached the bureau began to work out its declaration. Miliukov and Shulgin each drafted a statement. Miliukov's text was antagonistic. It directly charged that the choice of ministers pointed to "a guiding hand" whose activities increasingly appeared to be "a direct extension of the activities of our enemies . . . . Belief in the treasonable actions of Russia's official leaders has grown stronger and is becoming universal . . . . With grieving heart the State Duma witnessed the aimless waste of war material amassed as a result of its initiative and, even more depressing, it watched the useless shedding of the people's blood." Such was Miliukov's verdict on the 1916 campaign which had saved Italy, relieved the pressure on Verdun, and inspired Rumania to attack the Central Powers. Shulgin's draft was more restrained and did not mention the word "treason."

Even the Bloc disagreed as to whether the government could be accused of treason with no evidence but their own dissatisfaction with its policy. The Progressive-Nationalists and Zemstvo-Octobrists objected. "The government is trash and we must oppose it," declared Shulgin, "but since we ourselves are not planning to take to the barricades, we cannot incite others to do it." The Octobrist Stempkovsky agreed: "We do not wish to summon anyone to the barricades, and we must not speak now in a manner that will excite the crowd." (However, Stempkovsky also observed: "But what if nothing more stormy than the Petrograd weather follows our act? What if the public bears every humiliation and then the war ends happily? . . . They [the reactionaries] will say: We won without the Duma.")

In the end the Bloc excluded any reference to treason from the declaration. (That action followed the Progressists' threat to leave the Bloc.) The Bloc agreed, however, to focus its attack on Stürmer and secondly on Protopopov and generally to follow an uncompromisingly denunciatory line. Only Paul Krupensky apparently tried to restrain the Bloc from embarkon an open assault against the government.

The functionaries of the Bloc scarcely realized the responsibility they were taking upon themselves. The country's nerves were strained to the limit. No one could judge the response to irresponsible but authoritative statements. Those whose aim was to wage the war to a victorious conclusion, and who knew in fact how much had been accomplished toward that end, should have silenced their lips against public criticism with a triple seal. Instead, they decided to do just the opposite.

An editorial in *Novoe vremia* on 31 October 1916 noted that "it is as difficult to judge the mood of the country as it is to make out what goes on in a darkened apartment through the window . . . . The typical signs of the time are a poorly defined sense of purpose and the absence of responsible attitudes toward the problems we face."

On 30 October the empress wrote to the tsar: "It will be a rotten Duma."

CHAPTER TWENTY

THE WAGES OF WAR

Deep anxiety gripped Russia in the fall of 1916. A major cause and probably the determining factor behind the uneasiness was the war weariness that had overcome the masses. Fear of famine, grief over Russia's enormous losses, and the hopeless feeling that "this war has no end" created among people remote from the center of power a growing resentment against the authorities who directed the war. Hostility toward the government grew more intense especially among workers and the semi-intelligentsia, who even before the war had been influenced strongly by socialist ideas. In the shops and factories of the capital the Bolsheviks became the dominant political force.

The army, its prewar cadres practically annihilated, clung only to the memory of its former traditions. Most of the junior officers had received their commissions during the war. They were younger men recruited from the intelligentsia and semi-intelligentsia and rushed through officer-training schools. Nevertheless, the spirit of the military code—the spirit of the old imperial army—remained vigorous, so that even the shadow of tradition was sufficient to maintain discipline in an army eight million strong. Alarming rumors to the contrary, the number of deserters remained insignificant; cases of insubordination at the front were exceedingly uncommon. Among the masses and within the army the prestige of the tsar's authority still prevailed amid signs of disintegration. In the third year of the Great War Russia still obeyed "the tsar's command." But that prestige barely survived among the workers of the capital. Meanwhile the public, including its most prominent representatives, were working with suicidal fervor to destroy all confidence in the tsar's government. They magnified its shortcomings, maligned and slandered and paraded their contempt for it. The bitter truth of Konstantin Leontiev's description of Russia's elite became all too apparent: "Our sense of self-preservation is weak. Our society is more inclined to follow the course of others."

Those elements that always were the most active politically succumbed to a passionate desire to change the system. Society blended the aspirations of the earlier intelligentsia and the patriotism of the early war years into the rationalization that "victory requires it." They waged a struggle for power under the banner of patriotism and, since their efforts were sincere, the contestants were genuinely nobler than the defeatists of 1904-1905. But that made them even more dangerous. By the winter of 1916-1917 any distinction between the patriots—the "defensists"—and the "defeatists" was wiped out. A change of government became the basic item on their agenda. The war became a secondary objective even though the opposition used it constantly to abuse the government: even for the defeatists the basic goal was not the defeat of Russia but the overthrow of the tsarist regime. Others naively imagined that a political transformation of that kind could be achieved merely by casting aside the old trappings of power—that it was possible to wrest power from the hands of the monarch by an appeal to "the union of tsar and people."

Russian society entered the fall of 1916 beguiled by two phantoms, each equally lacking in substance. One was the "ministry of public confidence," which could not be realized. The other was the belief in "dark forces," which did not exist. Everyone interpreted a "ministry of public confidence" in a different light. To liberal "bureaucrats" it meant a cabinet headed by an authoritative and popular official. To functionaries of the Progressive Bloc it signified a government composed of members of their bureau, an idea that more radical politicians found preposterous. What was authoritative to some was vacuous to others. In short, the ministry of public confidence, the object of public clamor, would have produced a government that enjoyed neither the confidence of the tsar nor the confidence of the masses.

As for "dark forces," there were none. During that difficult period of the country's history, the emperor alone ruled Russia. No one "whispered" to him. No one influenced him. The "dark forces" were the figments of slander and sick imaginations. People high and low discussed them endlessly, but when called upon to name precisely who made up those "dark forces," the answer was either Rasputin or the name of some person, casually mentioned, who was without influence altogether. (Guchkov later even tossed out the idea of some "dark stock exchange hacks"!)

Nevertheless, the appearance of those apparitions was no accident. They were instruments of struggle employed by certain circles. In the "revolutionary conditions" of 1916, beside natural developments there also existed a struggle between two determined wills.

On one side was the Sovereign Emperor Nicholas Aleksandrovich. He firmly believed that Russia required the strong authority of the tsar, for he was convinced that only that authority could lead Russia to victory. In that conviction he stood almost alone. His faithful friend and helpmate was the empress who, like the tsar himself, was imbued with faith in the historic mission of the tsar's power, a faith instilled by her consort. The emperor considered concessions beyond a certain point impossible. He felt that he had no right to transfer the helm of state to others in time of war. He did not believe that others were capable.

On the other side stood a group of people who knew that as long as Nicholas II retained power Russia would remain essentially an autocratic monarchy, though with partially limited powers. Those people made it their objective to replace the tsar. They used the war as a convenient pretense to mask a struggle that they had been waging for some time.

"I decided on the need for the sovereign's abdication long before the time of the actual overthrow," Guchkov testified. "Months before the revolution when I and some of my friends were seeking a way out of the situation, we assumed that under certain logical conditions—a change in the composition of the government and its renewal by public figures who enjoyed the confidence of the nation—that even then no solution would be found. Therefore, it became necessary to act decisively and quickly, to join forces with those who sought to replace the supreme power. So much guilt before Russia had accumulated on the hands of both the emperor and empress and those continuously associated with them that the quality of their characters gave absolutely no hope of including them in any viable political combination. All that made it clear to me that the emperor had to relinquish the throne."[1]

"THE MAD CHAUFFEUR"

The legend of Rasputin, the malicious campaign against the
"German woman," the slanderous "hurricane of fire" against
individual ministers all concealed the true aim of their perpe-
trators—the overthrow of the monarchy itself. Only a few, of
course, settled on that goal as early and as openly as Guchkov
and "his friends." Not even the Kadets and Miliukov pursued
that end so determinedly. (However, judging by some of Prince
Lvov's statements, he was close to Guchkov's position.)

In September 1915 Vasily Maklakov published in *Russkie
vedomosti* an allegory about "The Mad Chauffeur": "Imagine
that you are in a car that is racing headlong down a steep narrow road; one wrong turn and you will be gone forever. The
people in the car are dear to you, one is your own mother.
Suddenly you realize that the chauffeur cannot drive. Either
he does not know how to handle the car on steep hills, or he
is tired and no longer understands what needs to be done? In
any event he is carrying you and himself to destruction."
Later Maklakov asked how it was possible to remove the chauffeur from behind the wheel when he refused to yield? "Could
it be done during the breakneck descent down a mountain
road . . . when with one false turn the car would be demolished?"

Maklakov's riddle was repeated frequently in those days,
but it should have been restated: "The chauffeur" was certain
that he alone was experienced and capable of saving the "automobile." He saw the road more clearly than the others, he was
more aware of its hazards than the passengers, he alone had
the skill to maneuver the car along the "steep narrow road"
between two abysses. The passengers, having gone beserk, had
only one thing in common: an urge to take the wheel themselves. Therefore, they demanded that "the chauffeur" give
his seat to them. Would he be right in yielding to them, even
when he knew that they might throw him out?

In his history of the war on the Eastern Front Churchill
recorded that "Nicholas II, distressed, remained immovable.
He saw as clearly as they did the increasing peril" but he saw
no way to avert it. He knew only that the historic power of
autocracy had steeled the Russians to endure as much as they
had. No people, no nation, no state had ever been tested like

Russia and managed to survive intact. "The vast machine creaked and groaned. But it still worked. One more effort and victory would come. To change the system, to open the gate to intruders, to part with any portion of the despotic power, was in the eyes of the Czar to bring about a total collapse." Critics who never experienced such ordeals found it easy to cite "lost opportunities." They spoke "lightly of changing the fundamental principles of the Russian State in the stress of the War from absolute monarchy to some British or French parliamentary system . . . . The very rigidity of the system gave it its strength and, once broken, forbade all recovery. The absolute Czar in spite of all his lamentable deficiencies commanded Russia. It can never be proved that a three-quarters Czar or half-Czar and the rest a Parliament, could in such a period have commanded anything at all. In fact, once the Czar was gone, no Russian ever commanded again."[2]

Other forces were at work in Russia too. German agents undoubtedly did their best to undermine the regime and foment disorder in any way possible. Right-wing elements came to believe rumors that British agents were backing a revolution. Allegations also circulated about the activities of international Freemasons and American Jewry (Jacob Schiff). Jewish circles, as in 1905, very possibly did what they could to assist the revolutionary movement against the tsarist regime. Moreover, some prominent figures in the Progressive Bloc were known to have been Masons.[3] It is quite improbable, however, that England would have run the terrible risk of ruining a great ally while the outcome of the war remained uncertain.

The actual significance of all these hidden traces of subversion cannot be estimated. It is sufficient to recall that prohibition, which drastically reduced the consumption of alcohol, also had some effect on the psychology of the masses by upsetting their traditional habits. At any rate enough obvious problems were available to judge that conditions in Russia were extremely ominous.

MILIUKOV'S SALVO

The State Duma, which reconvened on 1 November, opened in its customary manner with a speech by the chairman, who discussed the army and the Allies and reaffirmed the Duma's support of war to a victorious end. Knowing that violent attacks were to follow, the ministers followed Stürmer out of the chamber immediately after Rodzianko's speech. The diplomatic corps followed their example. The Menshevik Chkeidze delivered a speech that was directed mainly against the Bloc. Then the rightist Levashov spoke on the food problem and the struggle against German domination. After Kerensky made a statement, the Octobrist Sergei Shidlovsky mounted the rostrum and read the Bloc's declaration. The more controversial issues were omitted, but he reproached the ministers for their "lack of information, incompetence in the responsibilities entrusted to them, and hostility toward the public." He reminded the government that Sukhomlinov had not been brought to trial and charged that "the press has been squeezed between a vise." He also rebuked the new foreign minister. Shidlovsky then recommended that the government "give way to people who are prepared to be responsive to the majority of the State Duma and to realize its program." It was a dull session. Vasily Maklakov passed the press section and remarked: "Alas, there is no real enthusiasm."

But everything changed the moment Paul Miliukov began to speak. By all accounts he "outdid himself" as an orator on that day. The Kadet leader faced the task not only of making the usual attack on the government but also of saving the Bloc from disintegration and reinforcing his own position of leadership which had been shaken by the left. "It is not serious," he told the French ambassador two days before the session, "but something will have to be said from the rostrum. Otherwise we will lose influence with our electors, and they will desert to the extreme left."

Following the tactic that he himself had outlined, Miliukov concentrated his attack on Stürmer He discussed the suspicious characters around the prime minister.[4] He cited an array of German and Austrian newspapers which ironically noted that the "German" Stürmer had been called to direct the policy of "Pan-Slavism." Speaking in German,[5] Miliukov observed that on 25 July 1916 the *Neue Freie Presse* [Vienna] had added Stürmer to "the peace party said to be forming around the young empress." Recalling his own conversations with foreign statesmen, he hinted at a certain "pro-German salon" which had "migrated from Florence to Montreux"

[and on to Petrograd]. By mentioning officials who allegedly
attended those soirees in behalf of Stürmer, Miliukov skilfully
implied that he knew far more than he actually was revealing.
Only once, when he referred to "a memorandum of the extreme right" which advocated a separate peace and allegedly
upset the Allies, was he interrupted by shouts from the right:
"Slanderer!" "Let us have the signatures!" His response was
that he had seen the note mentioned in the foreign press,
which had attributed it to "Moscow newspapers."

Miliukov's speech was heard with avid interest and excitement. His listeners seemed to believe that he was drawing
aside the curtain that concealed the innermost secrets of government policy. "We shall fight you . . . until you go!" he
declared. "It is said that a member of the council of ministers,
on learning that on this occasion the Duma would speak of
treason, excitedly exclaimed: 'I may be a fool, but I am not a
traitor.'[6] . . . But gentlemen, does it matter as a practical
question whether we are, in the present instance, dealing with
stupidity or treason? When the Duma perpetually insists that
the rear must be organized for a victorious struggle, the government persists in its claim that to organize the country
means to organize the revolution, and it deliberately prefers
chaos and disintegration.[7] I ask you: Is this stupidity or
treason?"

Continuously interrupted by stormy applause, Miliukov
concluded: "It is only in wartime that they [the ministers]
are a menace. They are a menace to the war, and it is precisely for that reason, in time of war and in the name of war,
for the sake of that very thing which induced us to unite,
that we are fighting them now . . . . All the various arguments
boil down to this one overriding consideration: the incapacity
of the government as presently composed. (Applause) That is
our main evil, and to overcome it would be tantamount to
winning the entire campaign."

The session ended as a majority of the deputies gave Miliukov a great ovation. With that speech Miliukov achieved what
he had set out to do: he reinvigorated the Bloc, strengthened
his own position as a leader, and struck a heavy blow against
Stürmer's government. Nevertheless, the impact of the speech
may have exceeded the orator's ambitions.

Paul Miliukov

The vagueness of Miliukov's accusations and his vicious tone were typical of oppositionist tactics. The Bloc had only one serious accusation to bring against the government—its unwillingness to step aside for the Bloc's candidates. Its weightiest charge against the conduct of Russian foreign policy was that the government failed to beat Germany in publishing its project for Polish autonomy. (The German proclamation appeared on 23 October/5 November 1916.) The matter was of no practical consequence, however, since the Poles paid far more attention to the military situation than to promises. The opposition also attacked Russian diplomacy for its support of Greek King Constantine. The emperor himself believed it unjust and unwise to force the Greeks into the war, but the Russian ambassador nevertheless supported Allied efforts to form an army at Saloniki.[8]

As for domestic policy the opposition objected to the transfer of Sukhomlinov, a sick old man, from the fortress to house arrest. They condemned the "ruinous state of the food supply," and yet a majority of the Duma (the right wing of the Bloc and the extreme right) endorsed the policies of the ministry of agriculture. They complained about the censorship, but ignored the even stricter censorship in the Allied countries, especially in France.[9] But specific issues were of no concern. No one considered them. From the rostrum of the Duma the charge of treason was hurled at the government and bandied about the country.

Miliukov's speech seemed to confirm the malicious suspicions that circulated through the population. It seemed to be the word that everyone was waiting for. The government prohibited the publication of the speeches of Miliukov, Chkeidze, and Kerensky; and newspaper reports on the activities of the Duma appeared as blank spaces. The prohibited speeches spread in huge quantities throughout the country. Sometimes the speeches were "expanded" and "reinforced." The people and the army were introduced to an elementary lie: Duma member Miliukov has *proven* that the empress and Stürmer are betraying Russia to Kaiser William.

Miliukov, of course, had not claimed that at all. His carefully contrived speech only inquired, implied, and expressed puzzlement. It neither accused nor slandered: it did nothing more than string together a series of innuendoes. V.L. Burtsev later said that "it was an historic speech, but it was all built on lies." The author himself in a subsequent explanation[10] admitted that he had no real evidence. He said no less but much more than he actually knew.

The government quickly dispatched a circular to its allies denying Miliukov's allegations of a separate peace. It continued to forbid newspapers to print vicious speeches made in the Duma. However, the speeches that Shulgin and V.A. Maklakov made on 3 November were distributed by the same primitive method. Local organs of the Zemgor distributed "illegal" Duma speeches throughout the army.

On 4 November the war and naval ministers, Shuvaev and Grigorovich, (presumably on the advice of Count P.N. Ignatiev, the minister of education) took the rostrum to declare that by the will of the emperor the war would be pursued to victory. General Shuvaev presented data that illustrated an astonishing surge of war production: "Compared to January 1915, the production of 3-inch guns has increased by a factor of eight, howitzers by a factor of four, rifles four times, heavy shells nine times, 3-inch shells 19.7 times, detonating fuses nineteen times, bombs sixteen times, explosives forty times, and gases 69 times over . . . . We must bow low before our artillerymen . . . . Gentlemen, the enemy is subdued and beaten down. . . . There is no power which can overcome the Russian Tsardom."

The deputies welcomed both ministers warmly and attached a special significance to their speeches. Miliukov declared that "the ministers of war and the navy are on the side of the State Duma and the people." *Rech* wrote that General Shuvaev approached Miliukov and said, "I thank you." More likely the war minister simply thanked all the deputies who flocked to extend greetings.

STÜRMER FAILS THE TEST

Writing about Stürmer on 4 November, the empress said: "Poor old man may die fr. the vile way his spoken to & of at the Duma," but on the 7th she added: "being the red flag for that madhause, its better he should disappear a bitt . . . ." The emperor at Stavka did not learn immediately of the proceedings of the Duma. Although the war and naval ministers

had spoken without his authorization, he did not reprove
them. He believed, however, that Stürmer clearly was not in a
position to handle the situation. On 8 November he wrote to
the empress: "I reproach him for his excessive prudence . . . .
I am afraid that with him things will not go smoothly . . . .
I do not understand how it is, but nobody has confidence in
him!"[11] Stürmer, a well-bred but by no means determined
man, came to power as a sign of goodwill toward the Duma
and the voluntary organizations, but he proved unable to give
a proper rebuff to the onslaught of the Duma bloc. The emperor decided to replace him with A.F. Trepov, a firmer and
more energetic person.

The Duma meanwhile recessed and waited to see what the
government would do in the wake of the speeches of the
ministers of war and the navy. The Bloc already had decided
to boycott Stürmer's cabinet. At that point Alexander Trepov
wanted to report to the naval commission on the Murmansk
railway. Shingarev convened the commission, which then debated for two hours whether it would hear the minister. A
majority finally agreed to admit him, but nearly half of the
members walked out.

The ukaz announcing Stürmer's dismissal was published on
11 November. The Duma's reaction was that although the
first victory had been won, the representatives could not rest
on their laurels. "What has happened threatens to overshadow
the meaning of what is taking place," warned *Rech*. The
Kadet paper then outlined new conditions—Protopopov's dismissal and Sazonov's return to the cabinet. *Rech* gave Trepov
to understand that the naval commission clearly expressed
the Duma's attitude toward him. In the *Moskovskie vedomosti*
of 11 November Lev Tikhomirov predicted that "the matter
will not end with the departure of ministers undesirable to
the Duma opposition. Even fiercer agitation will be generated
to see that portfolios are offered to no one but the generals
of the revolution. In no way will they settle for anything
less."

The bureau of the Progressive Bloc, however, argued over
tactics. The Progressive-Nationalists were satisfied with the
recent accomplishment, but representatives of the voluntary
organizations insisted on continuing the struggle. "The very
fact of the Duma's victory is a source of great satisfaction,"

declared Prince Lvov on 16 November—but "not full satisfaction," added Alexander Konovalov of the Central War Industry Committee: "The government must rest on public support, but Trepov is one of Stürmer's associates." Ivan Godnev announced that "we are not satisfied with anything—[Trepov is] another Stürmer, only more polite." Miliukov expressed satisfaction and recommended a wait-and-see policy: "The first of November marked a new era. Now even the workers see that the Duma plays the leading role."

The emperor was informed of those attitudes and discussions. He summoned Trepov and Protopopov to Stavka, and on 13 November the empress also arrived there, as did Rodzianko, the chairman of the Duma. The emperor's first impulse was to replace the minister of interior. But with things as they were, he decided that everyone would take such a move as a total capitulation to the demands of the Bloc—a move that would only lead to a stepped-up attack on the government. Consequently he instructed Trepov, who urged Protopopov's dismissal, to work with the ministers whom he, the tsar, had chosen.

THE ONSLAUGHT GOES ON

Trepov made his inaugural statement to the Duma on 19 November. Like Stürmer in his first speech to the Duma, the new prime minister spoke of his desire to cooperate with the Duma and the voluntary organizations. He also announced for the first time that the Allies had agreed to award Constantinople and the Straits to Russia.[12] Unfortunately by then nearly everyone was completely indifferent to the historic legacies and national interests of Russia.

Radical leftists began the session by attempting to organize a demonstration against Trepov; eight deputies were expelled under vigorous protest. "We remain at our posts as loyal servants of the people," exclaimed Kerensky, "and we say: The country is perishing, and there is no salvation in the Duma!" Chkeidze likewise declared: "The people, who are not to be seen here, have their own opinion about current events, and I warn you, their opinion is not only against the government but against you as well!"

The Nationalist leader, Count V.A. Bobrinsky, devoted his speech to Stürmer's replacement as the next target of the Bloc. The sensation of the day, however, was the speech of V.M. Purishkevich. That prominent representative of the far right, long recognized as an unbalanced character, had been collecting all sorts of rumors and gossip at the front and in the capital. He intended to speak for the rightists against the government but, after acquainting themselves with his speech, they secretly and unanimously voted not to recognize him as their spokesman. As a result he withdrew from the rightist group, but one of the fractions in the Bloc offered him a place in its roster of speakers. Nevertheless, a broad segment of the public still considered Purishkevich "a representative of the extreme right."[13]

Purishkevich's passionate and muddled speech leveled accusations against the most diverse persons. Some he accused of acting out of self-interest, others of conspiracy, and still others of indulging Germans. He concluded by calling on the ministers to go to Stavka, prostrate themselves at the feet of the tsar, and beg him to deliver Russia from Rasputin. "These nights I cannot sleep, you may take my word of honor for it. I lie with open eyes and see visions of countless telegrams, reports, and notes addressed [by Rasputin] now to one and then another minister."

Even the journalist Menshikov, who generally supported the Bloc's campaign, ridiculed the speech and pointed out that Purishkevich lacked "political literacy" and committed "obvious school-boy mistakes." He then supported his criticism with a series of factual rebuttals. Despite that, the Bloc's followers understandably exploited the charges of a universally recognized reactionary. Leftists, on the other hand, scorned their demagoguery. Kerensky wrote that "the sense of proportion became dull; the bounds between the tolerable and the intolerable were wiped out. The public began to confuse Rodichev and Purishkevich, as long as it served to intimidate the enemy."[14]

Three days later Markov took the floor to speak for the right in answer to the oratory of the Bloc. The seated deputies continually interrupted him with their shouts. Rodzianko admonished him and finally withdrew his right to speak. At that point the indignant Markov addressed some well-chosen remarks to the chairman of the Duma.[15] The Duma voted to expel Markov for fifteen sessions, and the deputies only regretted that their rules did not allow a longer period of suspension.

The Duma spurned Trepov's offer of cooperation, and the campaign against the government mounted to new heights. On 22 November the chamber resolved that "the influence of dark irresponsible forces must be eliminated" and that all means had to be employed to form a cabinet "prepared to be responsive to the State Duma and to realize the program of its majority." Stürmer's dismissal gave many the feeling that power already was passing into other hands.

DEFECTION OF THE STATE COUNCIL AND UNITED NOBILITY

The State Council followed the course of the State Duma. Prince Eugene Trubetskoy recalled that in 1812 Alexander I had listened to the voice of the people and appointed Kutuzov, though he himself favored Barclay de Tolly.[16] "But, you say, there are no heroes like that. On the contrary, gentlemen, they do exist. We know their names. The emperor will find it possible to appoint them, and they will lead us to victory." V.I. Karpov vigorously denounced Protopov, and the distinguished jurist, N.S. Tagantsev, exclaimed that "the fatherland is in danger!" Only Count A.A. Bobrinsky, recently retired as minister of agriculture, found the courage to speak out against the allegations of "dark forces." "Freedom of speech," he declared, "is a fine thing. But when the podium is used as an armored platform for false and unfounded accusations and for attacks aimed at promoting lawlessness, then the country's reasonable elements have an obligation to shout: Enough! Recognize your limits. It is a dangerous game you play, and it will bring both you and Russia to misfortune." But in the end by a majority of 94 to 34 the State Council approved a resolution which basically reiterated the Bloc's terminology of "irresponsible forces" and "a government which rests on the country's trust."

Nicholas Maklakov joined the debate on 24 November. His remarks are of special interest since his outlook was similar to the emperor's: "A fine, clever effort, well concealed by pious phrases got underway at the very outset of the war. The

Russian people were inculcated and made to believe that what
in reality would lead us to disintegration and collapse was
essential to the war and to victory . . . . That was a lie,
gentlemen, an unintentional lie for most, but for the few who
sought to take over the leadership of the country's political
life it was a deliberate lie and almost a criminal one . . . . It
was all done for the sake of the war, in the name of victory;
and the government humbly lowered its eyes." The devasta-
tion of Russian life deepened just as the public was organizing. "The outlines of the staff of Russia's militant public
were forged" in the Moscow congresses. The center dispatched
its orders, the localities returned their answers, and a sense of
unity was created. The struggle for power—for the people's
rights—was underway. "Without pausing to consider the war,
the public consistently ignores the war's importance. It does
everything for the war, but its war is a war against law and
order. It does everything for victory, but its victory is a victory over the government."

Maklakov castigated the policy of concessions: "Day-by-
day the government was humiliated, defamed, dethroned, covered with shame, until finally it went away . . . . We extinguished the light, and now we curse the darkness . . . .
Now we can see that surrendering individual forts is a very
poor way to save the fortress itself." He emphatically denied
the allegation that rightists desired peace: "That is a lie. For
us, the members of the right, Great Russia's world status is
the highest consideration, for it affords Russia the right to
live her own distinctive Russian life."

"The fatherland is in danger. That is true, but the danger
will evaporate like smoke, it will vanish like an illusion if
only the government—the lawful government—will use its
power convincingly and consistently, if all of us, each in turn,
will remember our duty before the tsar and our motherland.
. . . With this faith we will fight, and with this faith we will
die."[17]

On 25 November the emperor returned to the capital to be
with the empress for the feast of St. George. He remained at
Tsarskoe Selo for about ten days. During that period the
United Nobility joined the Progressive Bloc. The Duma elections of the previous year had indicated that the nobility was
retreating from the attitude that prevailed during the 1905

revolution and was returning to its more customary tradition of moderate liberalism. The chairman of the association, A.P. Strukov, had opposed a responsible ministry in August 1915, and he again expressed his opposition when the congress assembled in late November 1916. But on 30 November the congress adopted a resolution which echoed the Duma's denunciation of "dark forces" and called for "a ministry that enjoys the confidence of the country." The nobility's formula differed only in its stipulation that the ministry be "responsible to the monarch alone."[18] Twenty-five delegates (about one-fifth of the congress) refused to endorse the resolution and sent the emperor a separate telegram expressing their loyalty. The attitude that spread from the Duma to the State Council also spread from the congress of nobles to society and the court, up to and including members of the imperial family. Everyone discussed "dark forces" and a "ministry of confidence."

Though "distressed," the tsar remained "immovable." The preceding year and a half had convinced him that concessions only inspired fresh demands. He had become fully aware of the real aims of the instigators of the assault on the government. He had dismissed the ministers who antagonized the public—Maklakov, Sukhomlinov, Sabler, and Shcheglovitov in the summer of 1915; Goremykin in January 1916; Stürmer and Bobrinsky in November 1916. He had convened the Duma in November 1916 for an extended session even though the deputies merely went through the motions of legislation for the sake of an unfettered rostrum. Against his best judgment he had agreed to the trial of Sukhomlinov. He frequently had appointed ministers "acceptable" to the Bloc only to see them become fodder for further demands or to be "anathematized" as in the case of Protopopov.

In his appointment of ministers the tsar generally sought to avoid controversy and gladly nominated "neutral" candidates. Early in December 1916, for example, he named A.A. Rittikh to head the ministry of agriculture in place of Count A.A. Bobrinsky, and he selected N.N. Pokrovsky as foreign minister with S.G. Feodosiev assuming the latter's vacated post as state comptroller. No one objected to any of those nominees, but at the same time the emperor decided that he had reached the limit on concessions. Therefore, when Trepov insisted on

Protopopov's dismissal, the emperor thought better of it, at least until the Duma recessed. Otherwise the Bloc would claim Protopopov's departure as a new victory and immediately begin to pummel its next victim. And the next target was slated to be Trepov himself.[19]

THE GERMAN PEACE OFFENSIVE

The fighting subsided on both the Eastern and Western Fronts, and only in Rumania were great battles in progress. However, the Rumanian Front collapsed under heavy blows from three sides. Bucharest fell on 22 November, and by the end of the month over half of the country was in enemy hands. The Russian army formed a new Rumanian Front [August 1916] under the command of General V.V. Sakharov. A lack of communications seriously impeded the movement of Russian troops to Rumania since, before 1914, Rumania had been regarded as part of the enemy coalition. Then after the war broke out, Bucharest's hesitation prevented any early cooperation. But by the winter of 1916-1917 Russians were paying little attention to the detailed episodes of the war. The war weighed on Russia oppressively, like a dull pain. "The early dreams have grown dim, the early fears have vanished. No one expects to reach Constantinople or Berlin in the near future, nor does anyone anticipate the enemy's arrival in Petrograd or Moscow"—thus wrote the Populist journal *Russkie zapiski* [Russian Notes] at the end of November 1916.

The war suddenly came to life with the report that on 29 November the German chancellor had informed the Reichstag of Germany's willingness to begin peace negotiations.[20] The news appeared in the Russian press a day later than in other countries, and the report was accompanied by a firm declaration that peace following a German victory (the capture of Bucharest) was unacceptable. On 2 December Nicholas Pokrovsky, the newly appointed foreign minister, unequivocally advised the Duma that peace without victory was out of the question. The Duma unanimously endorsed the "categorical refusal of the Allied governments to enter into any negotiation whatsoever under the present circumstances."

The Duma's majority, which began the session by attacking a government that allegedly favored a separate peace, of course could give no other response. Nevertheless the reports of peace raised some hope among the people. Newspapers carrying stories of the German offer and later of American mediation sold out the moment they hit the streets. But both the government and its critics flatly rejected peace, and their agreement on that issue gave the impression of unanimity.

No organized political force in Russia desired peace at that point. Even the Zimmerwaldists, the "defeatists," did not want to lose the opportunity to overthrow the government. Although in principle they stood for an end to the war, their goal was peace on the day after the fall of the monarchy. Rightist circles knew full well that the emperor's intention was to see the war through to total victory. A few, perhaps, believed that peace alone could preserve Russia from revolution and disintegration but, persistent rumors notwithstanding and as far as can be determined, no "reactionaries" submitted "memoranda" urging peace to the emperor.

The emperor had more information than the politicians and had a much clearer view of the general situation than they. He knew that the material balance was tipping increasingly toward the side of the Entente, and he believed that Germany stood little chance of surviving the 1917 campaign. Under the circumstances any ally that faltered and thus spoiled the victory of all would have failed the test of history. Since the beginning of the war, the emperor had maintained without exception that he would not lay down his arms as long as even one enemy soldier stood on Russian soil. Even if Germany conceivably might have offered to evacuate all Russian territory and promised Constantinople at the expense of its Turkish ally (German agents spread such rumors, and the government's enemies eagerly repeated them), the tsar remained true to his word, and indeed even overly scrupulous in its observance. Never did the thought cross his mind of concluding a separate peace or of violating either the Franco-Russian treaty or the Allied pact of 23 August 1914.

To appeal to the Allies for peace because of Russian internal conditions not only would have been humiliating but also would have deprived Russia of any hope of obtaining its share of the fruits of victory. It probably would have been useless as well, since neither the British nor French governments displayed any inclination for peace. At the end of

November Lloyd George, calling for a more energetic prosecution of the war, succeeded Lord Asquith as head of the British government. Any Russian indication of a predisposition for peace probably would have prompted the Allies to recite the Duma's declarations on a struggle to the end and to advise the government to introduce domestic reforms.

THE TSAR'S ANSWER

The tsar's foes feared as early as 1905 that he would redistribute the lands of the nobility to the peasants and thereby "crush" the rise of constitutionalism. But the tsar considered such a step unjust and economically ruinous, and he did not resort to it. In 1916 the enemies of monarchy trembled at the possibility that, having concluded a separate peace, the tsar would retain power with the support of the war-weary masses. But again no such thought entered his mind. It was inconceivable to him to follow a course that he considered dishonest and inappropriate to Russia's dignity as a great power in order to retain his own power.

As things then stood, the emperor believed that the only alternative was to continue the war until victory had been won. He knew that victory was possible and perhaps even imminent. He recognized that the main danger to Russia came from within, but still he rejected the idea of a peace dictated by fear of revolution. That was a risk, he believed, that had to be taken. Russian military strength would peak in 1917. Russia could not stand the strain for too long; a fourth winter of war might be too much. He was certain, however, that Russia was strong enough to endure the third winter and last out the summer campaign of 1917.[21] Russia had to hold on for a few more months.

The tsar's order of the day, read to the armed forces on 12/25 December 1916, declared that the time for peace had not yet come:

The enemy has not yet been expelled from the provinces that he has seized; Russia has not yet attained the aim created by this war—the possession of Constantinople and the Straits; and we still have not assured the formation of a whole and independent Poland out of its three existing but as yet separate parts. To conclude a peace with Germany now would be to render less than full honor to the heroic efforts of the Russian Army and Fleet. Those efforts and the sacred memory of those gallant sons of Russia who have perished on the field of battle forbid us even to consider peace before achieving a final and complete victory over an enemy who dares to think that, since he could begin the war, he can end it whenever he pleases . . . .

Then let us remain firm and unflinching in our confidence in victory, and the Almighty will bless our banners. He will cover them once more with undying glory and will grant us a peace worthy of your heroic deeds, my glorious troops—a peace for which future generations will bless you and which will render your memory forever sacred to them.[22]

During the summer of 1916, Grand Duke Nicholas Mikhailovich headed a commission to determine Russian aims at a future peace conference. It was assumed that Russia would annex Constantinople, the Straits, and Turkish Armenia. Poland was to be reunited as a kingdom bound to Russia by a personal union. At the end of December the emperor told Count S.I. Velopolsky that he regarded free Poland as a country with a separate constitution, separate legislative chambers, and its own army (an arrangement similar to the status of the Kingdom of Poland under Alexander I). Russia would incorporate Eastern Galicia, Northern Bukovina, and the Carpathian Rus. The commission contemplated the creation of a Czechoslovakian kingdom, and regiments of Czech and Slovak prisoners already were being formed on Russian territory. The emperor apparently favored the idea of weakening Prussia and of strengthening the other German states at Prussia's expense. Finally, Russia would support French demands for the reorganization of the territory along the Rhine.

The aged Emperor Franz Joseph died on 9/22 November 1916. His successor, Charles I, was married to a princess of French blood [the House of Bourbon-Parma], and her brothers were serving in the Belgian army. Consequently a change in Austro-Hungarian policy could be expected and with it the fact that France and England would be more receptive to an Austrian reorientation than Russia, Italy, or Serbia.

The emperor returned to Stavka on 4 December. "Those days spent together were difficult,"[23] he wrote to the empress, "but only thanks to you have I spent them more or less calmly. You were so strong and steadfast—I admire you more than I can say." The tsar rejected the demands of the Bloc and its supporters and made arrangements with Trepov to prorogue the Duma, if, when it reassembled, it resumed its attacks on the government. (The term of the Fourth Duma expired in about six months.) That "dirty business," as the emperor called it, he left to Trepov, although the empress indicated that she did not trust him.[24] On 13 December the emperor informed her that Trepov "was quiet and submissive and did not touch upon the name of Protopopov."

The voluntary organizations convened again in Moscow, but the authorities took the necessary preventive measures. The police quickly broke up their unauthorized attempts to meet on the 9th and 11th of December. A resolution distributed by the Union of Municipalities referred to a responsible ministry and declared: "The State Duma with unfailing energy and vigor must carry out to the end its struggle with the shameful regime. All of Russia stands with it in this struggle!"

The Duma responded to the call and scheduled an inquiry into the prohibition of the Moscow congresses. The interior minister invoked Article 44 of the Duma's regulations and demanded that the public be excluded from that session. The deputies then preferred to postpone the matter. However, on 16 December, the day the Duma was scheduled to recess, it suddenly brought the issue before the house. Miliukov observed that after the first of November "the thrust that began here spread in a broad wave across the country." Now "in public meetings some of the most radical proposals are offered by the most conservative elements . . . . The political movement in Russia has recovered the united front that it possessed before 17 October [1905] . . . . The atmosphere is saturated with electricity—one can feel the approach of a thunderstorm. No one knows, gentlemen, when or where the lightning will strike."

The Duma's rightists rose to the defense of the government. P.A. Safonov warned: "If a restless home front gave us an inglorious peace in 1905, then this restless home front is preparing the ruin of the country!" G.G. Zamyslovsky added: "When you are busying yourselves with revolutionary meetings during wartime, the government should ask you: Is this stupidity or treason?" Censure of the government for prohibiting the congresses carried by a vote of 123-47 with 6 abstentions. Had the rightists left the chamber instead of remaining to vote against the motion, the Duma would have been left without a quorum.

THE MURDER OF RASPUTIN

On the night of 16-17 December, following the recess of the
Duma, there occurred an event comparable in its consequences
to the Duma speeches of the first of November. In the private
residence of Prince Felix Yusupov[25] Rasputin was murdered.
Lured there as a guest, he was poisoned unsuccessfully and
finally shot. His body was taken to one of the Neva islands
and thrown from a bridge into an open patch of water in the
middle of the icebound river. Purishkevich, whose speech had
incited a few young socialites to commit the crime, was among
the assassins. Convinced of the legend of Rasputin, the mur-
derers believed that by eliminating the source of evil they were
saving both Russia and the dynasty.

In fact, they only stained the legend with blood and
strengthened its hold over the masses. The popular reaction
quite often differed from the reaction in higher places. Paleologue, the French ambassador, recorded how some peasants
maintained that at the tsar's court there was a man of the
people, who protected the people from the courtiers, and so
they killed him. Similarly, Ivan Skvortsov, the editor of *Kolokol*, reported that the people regarded Rasputin's murder as a
"bad omen."

Rasputin's assassination also revealed that his "influence"
was strictly a myth. The government's policy remained un-
changed; rumors of "dark forces" continued, but the search
moved to a higher level. On 20 December *Den* observed that
"dark forces had become a euphemism for Rasputin. Actually
Rasputin was a negligible quantity among the dark forces, and
the dark forces remain as they were. Rasputin made us fail to
notice them." To the enemies of imperial power the emperor,
who embodied and wielded that power, was the principal
"dark force."

If Rasputin was as important as he was alleged to be, passions should have subsided with his murder. Instead, just the
reverse occurred. Suddenly everyone "discovered" that "the
monk" had not been the problem after all, and the struggle
erupted with renewed vigor. From then on tales began to mul-
tiply of conspiracies involving the most illustrious members of
society or members of the imperial guards. Finally the slanderous barrage descended directly on the imperial couple. At last

the mask had been removed. If Miliukov's speech produced unexpected results, it was even more certain that the reaction to Rasputin's murder was hardly what the assassins had hoped for.

BOLSTERING THE INNER DEFENSES

On 19 December the emperor returned to Petrograd to assume personal direction over affairs in general. (On that morning Rasputin's corpse was fished from the Neva.)[26] His first concern was to reconstitute the government with persons whom he could trust personally. The danger was real. Rasputin's murder was proof of how seditious chatter led to rebellious acts. Regrettably, the emperor had to judge people in a different light. Capable and talented people might, nevertheless, prove unreliable and wind up in the wrong positions. The government had to be reorganized in order to prevent a palace coup or terrorist assaults on the highest officials. Those considerations made Protopopov, though technically a weak man, indispensable, since his personal loyalty was beyond question.[27] Therefore he was promoted from director of the ministry of interior to minister. Protopopov also had one decisive advantage over his colleagues: he had a superior knowledge of the enemy with whom he had to deal, and he was difficult to deceive. "He is our obvious and implacable enemy," said Guchkov, who was himself an obvious and implacable enemy of the emperor.

To succeed A.A. Makarov in the ministry of justice the tsar chose N.A. Dobrovolsky, a rightist serving in the Senate and an associate of Shcheglovitov. The new circumstances led Trepov to repeat his request to be retired, and the emperor agreed. The new prime minister was Prince N.D. Golitsyn. An elderly official who never had held any high position, Golitsyn offered one invaluable quality: both the emperor and empress knew him personally and were absolutely certain of his loyalty to them.[28] General Shuvaev gave way to his assistant, General M.A. Beliaev, European-educated (an essential consideration in anticipation of the approaching Inter-Allied conference) and personally devoted to the imperial couple.

The liberal minister of public education, Count P.N. Ignatiev, who had retained his post for two years despite the bitter attacks of rightists, begged to be relieved of "the unbearable burden of serving against the dictates of my conscience." Not long before the emperor had appealed to Ignatiev's patriotism to convince him to remain at his post, but in December he granted the count's request. One of Kasso's former assistants, N.K. Kulchitsky, replaced Ignatiev. The emperor had no desire to compel anyone to serve him in those menacing circumstances. The remainder of the government consisted of several outstanding experts in their fields who served loyally to the end.[29]

In response to the vacillation that he witnessed in the State Council, the emperor's publication of the list of active members for 1917 contained eighteen new names and retired sixteen serving members to inactive status. All the new appointees were rightists, and they replaced eight members of the center, four unaligned councilors, and four rightists, including Stürmer. I.G. Shcheglovitov was appointed chairman of the State Council. Members of the right and right-center once again acquired a majority in the upper chamber. Two prominent officials excluded from the active list protested by resigning from the Council.

THE SCENT OF PALACE REVOLUTION

The spread of discontent to his closest circle of associates embittered the emperor. The upper strata of Russian society, which normally ignored politics, grew concerned for the future but found no response except to parrot the Bloc's demands. The grand dukes individually advised him to appoint "more popular" ministers and to cooperate with the Duma. Persons suspected of complicity in the murder of Rasputin first were placed under house arrest and then exiled to their estates; Grand Duke Dmitry Pavlovich[29] was sent to the Persian Front.

Those measures prompted several members of the imperial family to compose a collective appeal to the tsar, urging him to "change your decision and replace anger with mercy." Indignation and bitterness filled the tsar's reply: "No one has the right to commit murder. I know that not many derive peace from conscientious conduct. I am astonished that you address yourselves thus to me." Grand Duke Nicholas Mikhailovich was ordered to leave for Grushevka, his estate in

Kherson province. The tsar sent Grand Duke Cyril Vladimiro-vich[31] [on an inspection tour] to Murmansk and Grand Duke Boris Vladimirovich to the Caucasus. The tsar took those steps to break the feverish politicking that peaked during the New Year holidays.

Part of the intriguing included a visit by A.I. Khatisov, the mayor of Tiflis, to Grand Duke Nicholas Nikolaevich. Acting in behalf of the Union of Municipalities, Khatisov suggested that the grand duke lead a coup to place himself on the throne. The former supreme commander spurned the offer because of the monarchist sympathies of the army.[32] Other members of the imperial family openly discussed the desirability of a pal-ace revolution with the French ambassador.

The mood of society, to say nothing of the broad masses, did not favor a palace coup. In January 1917 the chairman of the Kadet central committee, Prince Peter Dolgorukov, wrote that "a palace revolution not only is undesirable but would be disastrous for Russia since no member of the house of Romanov could replace our sovereign. A palace revolution could not produce anyone who could win general recognition as successor to the monarchic power of the Russian throne." Therefore, although treason surrounded the throne—treason rationalized as patriotism—it did not give birth to a coup thanks to the honor of the highest members of society and to the officers of the imperial guards. Some residual monarchist loyalties apparently restrained the stupified actors from cross-ing the threshhold to ciminality.

As it turned out, only the group already dedicated to over-throw Emperor Nicholas II continued to develop its plans for a palace or military coup. Guchkov himself later revealed those plans: "Not only was I ideally motivated to that course, but I also took active steps . . . . Technically it was a difficult problem . . . . I will not mention names,[33] but the plan was to seize the imperial train somewhere between Tsarskoe Selo and Stavka, to force the abdication, and then with the assist-ance of all reliable military units in Petrograd to arrest the present government and simultaneously announce the revolu-tion and the persons who would head the new government . . . . The problem was to identify the unit assigned to guard the railway, and that was hard to do." But as Guchkov indicated, the problems were not entirely technical: "Many held certain

principles, beliefs, and loyalties; to many it spelled disaster . . .
a certain caution on our part was essential."[34]

THE EMPEROR'S LONELY STRUGGLE

Gentle and amiable by nature, the emperor, when necessary,
could be sharp and caustic. During one of his last reports,
Rodzianko began to repeat the gossip about "intrigues sur-
rounding the empress" and "dark forces," but the emperor
interrupted and asked him bluntly: "Then, in your opinion,
am I the foremost traitor?" The chairman of the Duma could
only babble, "Your Majesty—God-annointed . . . ." The foreign ambassadors also tried to sway him to make concessions
to the Bloc. During an interview on 25 December 1916, Maurice Paleologue tried several times to turn their conversation
to domestic affairs and mentioned the doubts that plagued
"the best minds." The emperor replied: "I know that the
Petrograd salons are full of great agitation," and without al-
lowing the ambassador to go on he casually asked: "And how
are things with our friend Ferdinand of Bulgaria?" giving the
ambassador to understand that he had no desire for any more
discussion of Russian affairs.

In a private audience on 30 December the British ambassador Sir George Buchanan asked the emperor to listen to
him. "I am listening," replied Nicholas drily. Buchanan then
launched into a discussion of "German intrigues," "Protopopov's harmful influence," and the need to "earn the trust
of the people." That was at a time when conspiracies were
rampant everywhere, and the tsar answered: "But isn't it
rather my people who ought to earn my trust?" The tsar then
turned to the matter of "influences" and said: "You apparently think that I follow someone's advice in my choice of
ministers. You are completely mistaken. I choose them myself without any assistance from outside. Good day, Mr. Ambassador."

The Duma was scheduled to remain in recess until 12 January, but an ukaz of 5 January postponed its opening until
14 February. At the same time in an imperial rescript to
Prince Golitsyn the emperor noted that the basic problems
that faced the government were the organization of the food
supply and the transportation system. "I wish to believe that

the actions of the council of ministers will meet with the assistance of the State Council and the State Duma in a unanimous and fervent desire to pursue this war to victory. I charge those whom I have called into government service with a direct responsibility to adopt a benevolent, straightforward, and dignified attitude toward the legislative establishments."

Several congresses of the nobility took place in January 1917, and most associated themselves with the United Nobility's resolution of 30 November. One exception was the Kursk nobility, which on 18 January adopted by a vote of 119-6 the following declaration to the emperor: "Faint hearts are confused, passions rage, and gullible minds seek to place the burden of failure on members of the government whom you have appointed; in ministerial changes they see a guarantee of future success . . . . Should we, in these dark days, add our voice to theirs . . . should we forget the lessons of history and the examples of the recent past? No, Sire . . . the people called to lofty government service must be invested with your confidence and no one else's, unknown and unstable . . . ."[35]   In his reply the emperor said that the address had "touched him deeply."

Monarchist organizations in many cities sent the emperor petitions and appeals to dissolve the Duma and impose strict control over the voluntary organizations. The Russian Assembly expelled Purishkevich, who indeed found himself rejected by all of his former confederates. *Zemshchina* referred to him as "a squeezed-out lemon." Rightist circles, however, did not have much influence in the country, but then neither did the Progressive Bloc. Elemental forces were at work in the country. Speeches in the Duma denouncing "treason" and the murder of Rasputin spread wide circles, and those events had a deep psychological effect on the people.

An imperial ukaz issued at the end of 1916 appointed a commission of the Senate to investigate the deferments granted to persons called to military service. Temporary deferments were awarded regularly not only to officials whose jobs were essential to the effective operation of the administration but also to many others who worked in the various voluntary organizations. The military quickly dubbed the latter "zemhussars," and they frequently engaged in anti-government activities at the front and became purveyors of malicious rumors.

The emperor decided to put an end to that activity. The first step was to determine on what basis those persons were granted privileges and actually who was being excused from fulfilling his military obligations at the front. The tsar selected Senator Prince A.A. Shirinsky-Shikhmatov, a prominent member of the State Council, to head the commission, and he appointed Senators A.V. Stepanov and V.A. Brune de St. Hippolyte as his deputies.

THE INTER-ALLIED CONFERENCE: MILNER'S NOTE

The war ground on. At the end of December the Russians attacked around Riga—"the only offensive that took us by surprise," according to the German commander, Max von Hoffmann. In the deep cold Russian forces advanced across frozen swamps toward Mitava (Mitau), but after a week of fighting the offensive halted. It was rumored that again some units had refused to attack. Military analysts explained that the Riga offensive was a "limited offensive" to relieve German pressure on the Rumanian Front and that it was partially successful. It was, however, the final offensive of the imperial army.

The Inter-Allied Conference began in Petrograd on 19 January. England was represented by Lords Milner and Revelstoke [John Baring] and France by Gaston Doumerge and General Castelnau. The ambassadors also attended the meeting. The Russian delegation consisted of N.N. Pokrovsky, Generals M.A. Beliaev and Vasily Gurko (Alekseev's replacement as chief of staff during his illness), P.L. Bark, and E.B. Voinovsky-Krieger. The purpose of the conference, which lasted until 7/20 February, was to develop a common strategy for the 1917 campaign.

Russian society, which by then viewed everything in terms of domestic affairs, entertained the most incredible rumors. The Allies, one learned, had decided to take the Russian government "under their direction," to name their own appointees to the general staff, and to demand "a responsible ministry." The Allied delegates were treated especially well. Muscovites staged several formal banquets in their honor, and their speeches, allegedly pregnant with meaning, were widely discussed.

Lord Milner humorously punctured those expectations at a banquet in Petrograd on 30 November. Russian hospitality, he observed, tested the mettle of foreign visitors but he hoped that "our mental capacities will also brilliantly pass the test. In this land of truly astonishing rumors a person as trusting as I could almost be driven to madness. I often recall the anecdote related about Bismarck, who told a friend that every morning upon waking he would say, 'No, no, no!' because, being a man of weak character, he feared that during the day he would agree to something detrimental to himself. I have a similar feeling about your rumors." Milner assured his audience that "there is nothing dramatic about our conference." In fact the Allies did not dare advise the emperor directly on domestic affairs, all the more since they were in no position to make demands. Nevertheless some basis for exaggerated expectations apparently was furnished by a secret letter that Lord Milner delivered to the emperor on 4 February.

Touching on the distribution of war material among the Allies, Milner wrote that "we are all in the same boat, and we will sink or swim together. Any separate interests of the Allies are out of the question." The capacities of the Allies are limited, he continued, and there are some things that Russia itself could produce and not draw on the Allies for.[36] "To that end a better organization is needed." Milner praised the work of the Zemgor and, using England as an example, pointed out the desirability of employing the most competent experts and appointing them "without regard to official traditions to the highest executive positions." Milner then suggested that any [special] equipment delivered by the Allies should be accompanied by skilled technicians [to ensure their proper delivery and use at the front]. "There can be no question of interference in the affairs of the Russian military authorities;" our only request is to satisfy ourselves "that we are giving Russia not only the equipment but also our experience in handling it." Milner did not explain in detail what form this technical cooperation was to take, and in the end nothing was done to put his proposal into effect.

The French in particular were insistent on a coordinated spring offensive to begin as early as possible. The date of 2/15 April was proposed. General Gurko argued, however, that the Russian army was in a process of reorganization—60 new divisions were being created by reforming regiments on the basis of three rather than four battalions—and that more time

Alexander Kerensky in 1917

was needed. The French delegation did secure Russia's formal pledge to support French claims to Germany's Rhine frontier. When the Allied delegations returned home around the 20th of February, their spokesmen informed the press that Russians were unanimous in their attitude toward the war. "The disputes only involve administrative matters of the kind that are witnessed also in England," said Lord Milner.

The Germans' concerns over the 1917 campaign led them to the desperate policy of unrestricted submarine warfare. Their goal was to starve the British into submission and to interrupt communications between England and the continent before the Allies could launch a decisive offensive. Germany announced its policy on 31 January 1917 and [on 3 February] the United States severed relations with the German government. As American intervention grew imminent, prospects of an Allied victory rose accordingly.[37]

AT THE EDGE OF THE ABYSS

At the end of January the government arrested the workers' group of the Central War Industry Committee. That element formed the connecting link between the revolutionary labor organizations (which often branded the group as "compromisers" and yet used their services) and the oppositionist "bourgeois" forces.[38] The action provoked an immediate public protest. Guchkov appealed to Prince Golitsyn and was able to obtain relief for some of the arrested delegates. Seized documents, however, left no doubt as to the revolutionary nature of the group's activities.

Early in February the emperor received N.A. Maklakov and instructed him to prepare a manifesto for the possible dissolution of the Duma. This confirmed his decision, arrived at while Trepov was prime minister, to dispatch the Fourth Duma if it adhered to its course of determined and open struggle with the government.

The Duma reconvened on 14 February. The government expected demonstrations, since a march on the Tauride Palace was rumored. The opening day passed quietly, however. Alexander Rittikh, the minister of agriculture, followed Rodzianko to the rostrum and gave a detailed report on the food problem. The public's expectation of a sensational session proved false. Toward the end of the opening session Purishke-vich spoke without notable success, and after him the Progressive Party's leader, I.N. Efremov, averred that "a responsible ministry would do wonders." The Progressive Bloc stood perplexed on the threshhold of great events. The best Miliukov could do was to repeat his speech of 16 December.

During the session of 15 February; attention centered on Kerensky's speech in which he called for an open struggle with the government. The issue, he said, was not "the ill-intentioned motives of individuals . . . . The greatest mistake is the tendency to search everywhere for traitors, to look for German agents or for individual Stürmers under the influence of dark forces or Germans. We have an enemy much more powerful than German influence, and that is the system . . . ."[39] Kerensky addressed the Bloc in the name of the revolutionary forces: "If you gentlemen have no will to act, then you should refrain from uttering words that are irresponsible and too weighty for your intentions. You think your job ends because you have diagnosed the country's ills. But you forget the simple masses who take seriously your words about the condition of the country, who want to respond to the actions of one side in solidarity with the actions of the other side, who in their naive misjudgment want to help you, the majority of the State Duma."

Kerensky rejected the Bloc's position on the war: "Gentlemen, you are at one with the government on the idea of imperialist conquest, and just like the government you are all megalomaniacs. We maintain that the war must be liquidated. I maintain that a declaration of unlimited aggression cannot meet with support." (From his seat Shingarev shouted "That is not so!" and there was commotion in the chamber.) "You want to listen to no one but yourselves, but you must listen, because if you refuse to hear the voice of warning now, you will find yourselves face to face with facts—not warnings."

The government demanded that the chairman of the Duma turn over a stenographic transcript of Kerensky's speech, but Rodzianko refused. The possibility of prosecuting Kerensky for making a revolutionary appeal remained open. The Duma then followed its normal course. It staged an inquiry into the arrest of the workers' group. The food supply problem gave rise to disputes within the Bloc. Savich and Shulgin broke with

Miliukov and supported Rittikh's policy which sought if possible to avoid compulsion in obtaining foodstuffs. Shulgin went so far as to declare that if Rittikh could deliver Russia from hunger, he would be forgiven his "sin" of having served in the same government as Protopopov.

The trial of Manasevich-Manuilov, a former official who had served as Stürmer's private assistant, took place on 13-16 February. He was sentenced to serve eighteen months on a labor gang. In the preceding fall Manuilov's ability to avoid prosecution had been one of the opposition's chief complaints against the government.[40]

The new chairman of the State Council, I.G. Shcheglovitov, squelched every effort to invoke the rule on "extraordinary declarations" in order to raise political issues.

Artistic, cultural, and social events went on as usual. Olenina-d'Alheim opened the 1917 season at the House of Song in Petrograd. The January edition of *Russkie mysli* [Russian Thoughts] introduced the first part of Alexander Bloch's new poem, "Retribution." On 22 February Meyerhold's presentation of Lermontov's *Masquerade* made its premier before a packed house at the Aleksandrinsky Theater.

CHAPTER TWENTY-ONE

THE PETROGRAD POWDER KEG

The Russian people, restrained by the unwritten rules of behavior in wartime, seldom demonstrated during the war. Since the fighting began, only two major disturbances had occurred: the anti-German pogrom in Moscow in May 1915 and the native revolt in Turkestan in the summer of 1916. During a demonstration in the Petrograd factory district in the fall of 1916, troops of a reserve battalion fired on cossacks sent to disperse the crowd. The incident attracted little attention, however, and the censors kept it out of the newspapers.

By 1917 some 200,000 soldiers were stationed in Petrograd and its environs. They were mainly new recruits who had yet to see combat and veterans recovering from their wounds. The army intended to send most of those troops to the front for the spring offensive scheduled to begin around the end of March. The units included reserve battalions of the guards regiments, but except for their designations and two or three officers they had nothing in common with the valiant regiments serving on the Southwestern Front. The troops were jammed into barracks under incredible conditions; they slept on plank bunks three tiers deep and drilled in the streets and squares of the capital. They were fed a daily diet of the rumors that swept the city and were exposed constantly to the defeatism that infected the working class. In the newspapers they read the speeches and resolutions aimed at the government. Rasputin's murder introduced them to all the vicious gossip that surrounded his name. Veterans discharged from hospitals described the "hurricane of fire," the poison gas, and the frightful bloodletting at the front. Most of the garrison was driven by a single fervent hope—that some miracle would deliver them from the necessity of "going to the slaughter." Only iron discipline maintained obedience among that mass that scarcely knew its officers. A grim joke expressed the soldiers' mood: "What is more dreadful than a German bullet?—Only one of our own!"

Neither the Petrograd police chief, General A.P. Balk, nor the military district commander, Lieutenant General S.S. Khabalov, considered the situation dangerous. Only interior minister A.D. Protopopov, whom the Okhrana kept well informed, was concerned about the mood of the capital. When he inquired about the size of the forces available to maintain order, he was told that the police, mounted units, and training cadres of the regimental commands numbered about 10,000 men—hardly sufficient to control a city whose wartime population had swelled to 2.5 million let alone a potentially mutinous garrison.

Protopopov advised the emperor of the situation in the middle of January. The tsar ordered General Gurko to reinforce the Petrograd garrison by withdrawing units of the imperial guard from the front and sending them to the capital for a rest. The first units designated for transfer were the 1st Guards Cavalry Division and an armored car detachment. However, General Khabalov protested Gurko's order: the barracks, he warned, were absolutely full and there were no facilities to house the reserve battalions. Thereupon Gurko, who apparently did not consider the matter one of major importance, relented. As a result the cavalry was not sent to the capital. Instead, Gurko transferred some officers and crews of the naval guard, who were easier to quarter. According to Protopopov, the emperor was greatly upset by the failure to station the guards cavalry in Petrograd.[2]

RETURN TO STAVKA

Having prolonged his stay in the capital for more than two months, the emperor decided that it was time to return to Stavka. The empress and Protopopov urged him not to depart. (The tsarevich had fallen ill with measles, and before long the grand duchesses also were infected.) The emperor promised to return as soon as possible, and on the 22nd of February he left Tsarskoe Selo. General Alekseev, who for several months had been undergoing medical treatment in the Crimea, returned to Stavka three days before the emperor. The chief of staff's return surprised the high command, since it was obvious that he still was a sick man.

The Duma seemed intent on its usual parliamentary struggle and proceeded to reject a bill authorizing the new department of public health which had been established [in September 1916] under Article 87. The purpose of the new state health administration, directed by Professor G.E. Rein, was to unify and coordinate measures to combat epidemics and unsanitary conditions. The emperor insisted on its creation over the objections of Stürmer's cabinet, which hoped to avoid a new battle with the Duma. When the Duma's commission rejected the bill, Rein withdrew it. A special resolution of the Duma then interpreted his retraction to signify that the agency had been abolished.[3]

The emperor's departure seemed to be the signal for the enemies of order, for on the following day, 23 February, serious street demonstrations erupted.

THE BREAD RIOTS

By the middle of February heavy snow drifts slowed the movement of trains. On the 20th Guchkov addressed the State Council and warned that a breakdown of the transport system threatened the capital's food supply. Quickly the word spread throughout the city that before long no bread would be available. The residents of the city began to stock up on food and to bake hard biscuits and bread against the future. As a result many bakers and confectioners could not meet the demand. Those at the tail end of the lines who failed to get bread formed angry groups and moved along the streets shouting for bread. Isolated groups swelled into crowds. Since at first they consisted mainly of women and children, they caused no particular concern. However, by 23 February 90,000 workers were on strike, and the Vyborg section of the Bolshevik city committee decided to exploit the people's movement and transform it into a general strike. The demonstrations quickly acquired a political character. Red banners burgeoned among the crowds together with placards urging "Down with the Autocracy!" and "Down with the War!"

On 24 February an official announcement in the newspapers assured the city that "bread is available" and that supplies of flour were quite sufficient; the war department had appropriated part of the quartermaster's reserve to feed the civilian population, and any shortage was eliminated. But the mass movement did not subside; the crowds grew larger. Cossacks and other mounted troops were called in to help the police clear the streets, but the people scattered only to come together again in a nearby street. The authorities were lenient with the demonstrators—"They're only asking for bread," were the reports—but the incidents in which mobs set upon the police grew more frequent. On the 23rd and 24th of February some 28 policemen were beaten up.

A COMPLACENT CABINET

The Duma saw the disorders as only one more indication of the folly of the government's policy, but the council of ministers attached no special significance to the demonstrations, and they were not even mentioned during the council's meeting of 24 February. The ministers were wholly occupied by the conflict with the Duma. A few were convinced that some changes had to be made in the cabinet and some compromise reached with the Duma's bloc.

On 25 February the disturbances spilled onto the Nevsky Prospekt and through the entire central district. Znamensky Square opposite the Nikolaevsky [Moscow] Station became the scene of one continuous rally.[4] From the base of the monument to Alexander III resounded revolutionary speeches, the thrust of which was "Down with the War!" Individual deeds proved decisive. On Znamensky Square a policeman named Krylov tried to wrest a red flag from a demonstrator and was killed with a revolver; the rally went on without interruption. At the Trubochny Works, however, a Lieutenant Gosse shot and killed a rioter who had threatened him with his fist, and the mob immediately dispersed, leaving behind its flags and banners.

The cabinet met again later that evening. Again the discussion centered on whether to advise the emperor to appoint new ministers—the attitude of the Duma still seemed more dangerous than the temper of the rioters. The ministers knew that the Duma was preparing a new assault on the government for the 28th, when a resolution denouncing Rittikh's food policy was to be debated. The cabinet was of two opinions: Protopopov, Dobrovolsky, and others argued that the

Duma should be dissolved as soon as it attacked the government, as Trepov earlier had recommended; others contended
that the government should be prepared to compromise and
negotiate with the Duma's majority. Both sides agreed, however, that the Duma should be prorogued for a few weeks,
and that was the decision unanimously agreed upon on the
25th.

Adjournment until no later than April became the compromise solution, aimed at avoiding a bitter conflict that only
could result in dissolution. The agreement was reached by
Rittikh and Pokrovsky who negotiated with representatives
of the Bloc. Those who hoped for a compromise—and apparently they were numerous—counted on reaching some agreement during the break, and they assumed that when the Duma
reconvened there would be a new cabinet. Prince Golitsyn
wired the emperor to that effect.

Reports of the spreading disturbances reached the emperor
at Stavka only on the 25th. He immediately understood the
need for the most energetic measures and telegraphed General
Khabalov: "I command you to put an end to the disturbances
in the capital which are inadmissible during this difficult time
of war against Germany and Austria." When the council of
ministers received this message, some of them doubted whether
the disorders were serious enough to warrant forceful action.
Every minister admitted, however, that once the rioters began to kill policemen in the streets and to shoot at the cossacks, stern measures had to be taken.

The popular movement, incited by the most disparate elements, was developing without any apparent plan. German
agents undoubtedly were hard at work, and agitators of the
extreme left seized the opportunity to deliver incendiary
speeches. Through the factories spread a call for a "Soviet of
Workers Deputies." The Philistines gloated at the government's inability to control "small groups," and they applauded
the Cossacks for their half-hearted efforts in breaking up demonstrations. Members of the Duma clung to the hope that the
disorders would compel the government to compromise.

BLOODY CLASHES

February 26th was a Sunday. The demonstrations began somewhat later than usual. (Khabalov already had reported to

Stavka that some abatement of the movement had been detected during the morning.) During the afternoon, however, events took a bloody turn as crowds clashed with the police, the Cossacks, and the regimental cadres summoned to assist them. Firing could be heard in several parts of the city. Although the number of casualties could not be determined, the violence resulted in dead and wounded. By evening the morale of the activists was failing. The radicals who assembled in Kerensky's apartment were on the verge of concluding that "the government has won." Since the newspapers ceased publication on 26 February, the public was in the grip of the most outlandish rumors.

Around 4 p.m. on the 26th, however, an event of some consequence occurred. The fourth company of the reserve battalion of the Pavlovsky Regiment (about 1,500 men) had crowded into the street in front of its barracks. Suddenly the troops began to fire at random on other soldiers who were dispersing a crowd. Then the two units began to exchange fire, and several companies from regiments billeted nearby were rushed to the scene. They established a cordon around the area, and the regimental commander and regimental priests arrived to "reason" with the mutineers. Somewhat later, because they were persuaded but also because they were surrounded, they retired to their barracks and surrendered their weapons. (Twenty-one rifles were missing, however.) Nineteen leaders were arrested and imprisoned in the fortress.

That evening Rodzianko sent a long cable to General Alekseev in which he asked the chief of staff to inform the emperor that the disorders were caused by "complete distrust of the government." He insisted on the formation of "a government that enjoys the confidence of all the people" and maintained that "there is no other access to a bright road."[5] The Duma chairman still assumed, apparently, that only a Duma ministry could pacify the revolutionary workers and the mutinous soldiers.

Not all the members of the Bloc shared Rodzianko's optimism. "I understood them, my comrades in the Bloc," Shulgin later reminisced about that day. "We were born to praise or to censure from under the wing [i.e. from a secure position]. In an extremity we were capable of painfully trading our deputy's chairs for the ministerial benches . . . on condition

Mutineers in Petrograd

that the imperial guard would protect us. But our heads spun and our hearts froze before the possible collapse of the government, before the bottomless abyss of that avalanche. Impotence stared at me from behind the white pillars of the Tauride Palace. So disdainful was its visage that I was brought to the point of terror . . . ."[6]

The emperor, always noted for his exceptional self-control, maintained his outward calm, but he had a foreboding sense of impending disaster. For the first time since the defeat at Soldau and the many times during the great retreat of 1915, he could feel "the old heart," as he called it in his letters to the empress. And so it was in those days. On 26 February he wrote: "This morning, during the service, I felt an excruciating pain in the chest, which lasted for a quarter of an hour. I could hardly stand the service out, and my forehead was covered with drops of perspiration."

DESERTION OF THE PETROGRAD GARRISON

All during the night of 26-27 February the troop commander, General Khabalov, and the war minister, General Beliaev, received alarming reports from the barracks. Rumors were investigated and turned out to be false. Then as soon as they stopped believing them, the dreadful confirmations began to arrive: At 7 a.m. one of the battalions of the Volynsky Regiment rebelled; a non-commissioned officer, Timofei Kirpichnikov (the son of a professor, a student drafted in 1915), assembled the soldiers during the night and talked them into revolting against "the autocracy." When the commander of the training cadre, Captain Lashkevich, entered the barracks in the morning, the soldiers refused to obey, murdered him, and rushed in a body into the streets.[7]

Defection—"coming out"—was far more terrifying to the soldiers than to the workers. "You can go back to your houses, but for us it's the firing squad," they told the worker-agitators who called on them to join the demonstrations. "Coming out" armed into the streets, the soldiers knew, was a crime. They also knew that they would escape punishment only if they won.

Besides the Volynsky Regiment, the Pavolvsky Regiment also mutinied on the morning of the 27th—they were urged to save their comrades—as did the Litovsky Regiment. By then the entire Vyborg district was in the hands of the workers. Revolutionary mobs crossed over to the left bank of the Neva by way of the Liteiny Bridge. There they met and merged with the rebellious regiments to form a revolutionary mass.

Khabalov and Beliaev hastily began to summon all reliable units for the defense of the center of the city. A detachment of about a thousand men commanded by Colonel A.P. Kutepov of the Preobrazhensky Regiment moved toward the center of the uprising but could advance no farther than Kirochnaia Street.[8] The great majority of troops were considered unreliable and were ordered to remain in their barracks. By midday rebellious mobs occupied almost the entire right bank of the city [mainly the worker quarters] as well as the Liteiny and Rozhdestvenskaia districts [the eastern third of the center]. The southern working class district was also in the hands of the rebels. The Tauride Palace, which housed the State Duma, was well within the area occupied by the mob.[9]

THE FALL OF THE DUMA

A sizable number of deputies assembled in the Duma chambers on the morning of 27 February, since without newspapers most of the legislators did not know that the Duma had been prorogued. Several private meetings took place. No one knew exactly what was happening, but there was much discussion of the mutinies. The atmosphere was depressing. "The battle of words had come to an end," wrote Shulgin. "It had not prevented the revolution . . . and perhaps it speeded it along."

The deputies recognized that the Duma could not convene legally, but despite the recess, they decided to remain and await the course of events. Meantime they elected representatives of the Bloc and the extreme left as the Temporary Committee of the Duma.[10] At that point the mob, which had reached the palace, burst into the courtyard and then into the building. "Disgust filled my soul from the first moment of that flood," Shulgin recalled. "Machine guns—that's what I wanted, for I felt that the chatter of machine guns was the

only language that the mob could understand." And, he
added: "From that moment the State Duma, to put it bluntly,
ceased to exist."

But if the Duma ceased to exist in fact, its name became a
powerful instrument in the hands of the revolutionary forces.
The country was blanketed with telegrams, signed by the
Temporary Committee of the Duma, and their messages gave
a totally distorted picture of the situation.

The workers' group of the Central War Industry Committee, liberated by the mob from the Kresty Prison, proceeded
at once to the Tauride Palace. There they joined with socialist deputies and representatives of the revolutionary parties
to form the first Executive Committee of the Soviet of Workers Deputies. "Reliable persons" were dispatched to the factories to urge the workers to move at once to elect their representatives (one deputy for each thousand workers) to the
Soviet, whose first meeting was scheduled for 7 p.m. that
evening. Meanwhile, the Soviet's "illegal" Executive Committee made a very important decision. Recognizing that the
mutinous troops soon would be hungry and thirsty, the committee promptly began to requisition food for the "army of
the revolution." Thus the Tauride Palace became not only a
combat headquarters but also a feeding station. That action
immediately established a practical connection between the
"Soviet" and the mass of troops.

As darkness fell, government forces still held the Neva
bridges (except the Liteiny) but had no continuous perimeter
on the left bank. Mobs therefore continued to surge from the
outskirts toward the center. Rifle and machine gun fire punc-
tuated the cold night air.

THE CABINET'S FINAL GESTURE

The council of ministers convened at 6 p.m. in the Mariinsky
Palace. With no apparent comprehension of the true nature
of the popular movement, the ministers assumed that it was
a continuation of the Duma's campaign against Protopopov.
Thus they urged him to "feign illness." To this suggestion
Protopopov, by then completely overwhelmed by events,
readily agreed.[11] Thereupon the government announced that
"due to illness" Protopopov had turned over his duties to his

N.I. Ivanov

M.V. Alekseev

A.E. Evert

N.V. Ruzsky

senior assistant. The *Bulletin of the Petrograd Journalists*[12] quite rightly labeled the order ridiculous. When the emperor learned of it, he wired Golitsyn: "I consider changes in personnel under existing conditions inadmissible." The dismissal of the minister of interior against a backdrop of mutiny by undisciplined soldiers could only produce an utterly useless humiliation of the government.

REBIRTH OF THE SOVIET

The Petrograd Soviet of Workers Deputies met for the first time in the evening of 27 February in the Assembly hall of the State Duma. Several hundred delegates appeared and elected as their chairman Nicholas Chkeidze. One after another representatives of defected regiments mounted the rostrum to pledge to "defend the revolution." The delegates elected an executive committee (composed mainly of experienced Zimmerwaldists) and a publications commission, which immediately set to work to compose a "manifesto" and to prepare for the publication of the *Izvestiia* of the Petrograd Soviet.[13] The early leaders of the Soviet were P.A. Aleksandrovich, a Left SR; N.N. Sukhanov (Gimmer) [a Menshevik]; and Yu.M. Steklov [a Bolshevik].[14]

THE LOCAL MILITARY AUTHORITIES ABDICATE

Loyal troops assembled in front of the Winter Palace during the evening. Using the building as their headquarters were Generals Beliaev, Khabalov, and M.I. Zankevich, who was given command of the units. However, the tsar's brother, Grand Duke Michael Aleksandrovich, requested them to move to the Admiralty in order to ensure that the priceless art treasures of the Hermitage and Winter Palace not come under fire.[15] By morning the entire city except for the Admiralty was in the hands of the revolution. About 1,500 government troops lingered around the Admiralty until noon. Then Grigorovich, the naval minister, requested that the troops be withdrawn so as not to expose irreplaceable ships' blueprints to gunfire. Accordingly, the troops were ordered to lay down their arms and return in small groups to their quarters.

Trucks flying red flags and overloaded with soldiers and armed workers raced about the capital. Bands of troops roamed the streets firing into the air and shouting: "Enough! We're through fighting!" (The indiscriminate shooting created the false impression that supporters of "the old regime" were sniping from rooftops.) Gangs broke into the private residences of the ministers and other high officials and led them away. Everyone was herded to the Tauride Palace which, in addition to its other functions, was becoming a revolutionary police station.[16]

THE DUMA COMMITTEE: CATSPAW OF THE REVOLUTION

The Temporary Committee of the Duma was unable to promote or prevent anything, so it devoted itself to propaganda. Alongside *Izvestiia* of the Petrograd Soviet appeared another news bulletin carrying the Duma's version of events. In that interpretation everything allegedly flowed from an ukaz ordering the "dissolution" of the Duma: the Duma refused to obey, "the people" supported it, the regiments came over to the people and placed themselves at the disposal of the State Duma.[17] When that was written, the Duma could not possibly have been convened, and an illegal "parliament" already was "squatting" on its premises.

By means of the railroad telegraph network Deputy A.A. Bublikov, a Progressist, on 28 February sent to all points in Russia a message which began: "By authority of the Committee of the State Duma I have on this date assumed direction of the ministry of communications," and further that under the leadership of Rodzianko "the State Duma has taken upon itself the responsibility to form a new government."

By 28 February the movement had reached the outskirts of Petrograd. Kronstadt was overwhelmed in a bloodbath. Mutinous sailors murdered Admiral R.N. Wiren, slaughtered several dozen officers, and locked the rest in subterranean casemates. They then ransacked every storehouse in search of liquor. Meanwhile, the military detachments that guarded the imperial residence at Tsarskoe Selo declared their "neutrality." Without their officers the mass of the Petrograd garrison turned into an armed mob, vicious and cowardly, equally prepared to tear apart an "enemy" as to scatter in all directions at the first volley.

GENERAL IVANOV: ROD OF THE EMPEROR'S ANGER

At the first reports of the Petrograd mutinies the emperor ordered General Nicholas Ivanov, an old officer respected by the army and the country, to proceed to Petrograd with emergency powers to restore order. Until Ivanov's arrival, the reins of power—by then purely nominal—remained in the hands of Prince Golitsyn. To enable Ivanov to fulfill his mission the tsar ordered withdrawn from the three major fronts for service in Petrograd two cavalry divisions, two infantry regiments, and a few machine gun detachments. In each case he sought the most reliable units.[18] Stavka informed General Beliaev in Petrograd of the movement at 10:25 p.m. on 27 February.

Meanwhile Grand Duke Michael Aleksandrovich phoned General Alekseev from Petrograd and asked him to inform the emperor that the dismissal of the council of ministers and the appointment of a new prime minister was necessary in order to restore calm. "Personally," he said, "I assume that Prince Lvov could be that person." The emperor instructed Alekseev to reply that troops were being sent to Petrograd and that he would make any other decisions after he reached Tsarskoe Selo. He knew full well that when troops were rebelling and killing their officers "concessions" would only add fuel to the fire, create an impression of irresolution, and condone further lawlessness. After the grand duke's call, Alekseev advised the emperor of a wire from General Ruzsky. The Northern Front commander made essentially the same recommendation—"under existing conditions repressive measures can only complicate the situation." According to Alekseev, the emperor "did not even want to talk to him [Ruzsky]."[19]

After some delay, at around 1 p.m. on 28 February, General Ivanov set out from Mogilev with the St. George Battalion (about 700 men who had won the Cross of St. George). He proceeded by way of the Moscow-Vindavo-Rybinsk railway. Units from the Northern Front that had been placed under his command reached the vicinity of the capital in advance of Ruzsky's train.

The emperor, having issued all the orders for the transfer of troops to Petrograd, then decided to go himself to Tsarskoe Selo. He was motivated apparently by concern for his family or perhaps by the desire to be at the center of events when prompt decisions were required. In any case his departure from Stavka proved to be a fatal mistake.

STAVKA'S FATAL ILLUSION

By 28 February anarchy reigned over the capital, Kronstadt was becoming a slaughter house, and the Petrograd Soviet held the only semblance of power. Someone, however, sent Stavka an entirely different picture, and Alekseev apparently was taken in by it: "Private information indicates that on 28 February complete calm returned again to Petrograd. The garrison is fully behind the Provisional Government, and discipline is being restored. The Provisional Government under the chairmanship of Rodzianko is meeting in the State Duma and has invited the commanders of local military units to come and receive instructions for maintaining order. An appeal to the population, issued by the Provisional Government, speaks of the necessity of the monarchic principle in Russia and of the necessity of new elections for the selection and appointment of a government."[20]

This clearly false information received by Stavka had an important effect on subsequent events. Under the impression that the situation in the capital was developing satisfactorily, Alekseev relayed that information to each commander in the military hierarchy. Between 1 and 2 p.m. on the first of March the front commanders all received the infamous telegram number 1833, advising them that the capital was returning to normal. The message to Ruzsky contained a request to "inform His Majesty of all this and also our conviction that this affair can be brought peacefully to an acceptable conclusion that will strengthen Russia."[21]

Pskov, however, was getting different reports from Petrograd, and after receiving Alekseev's telegram, General Davydov asked Stavka:[22] "Where did the chief of staff obtain the information contained in 1833?" At 5 p.m. on 1 March he received the vague response that the information "was received from Petrograd from various sources considered to be reliable."

THE LAST JOURNEY

The emperor spent the remainder of 28 February on the train and received no fresh news. His train followed the circuitous route Smolensk-Viazma-Likhoslavl in order to leave the direct route through Dno free for military traffic. It spent the night of 28 February-1 March at Malaia Vishera, about 100 miles from Petrograd. There the commander of the train learned that the next major station, Liuban, was in the hands of "revolutionary troops." Since the imperial guard was considered too small to fight its way through, the decision was made to go on to Tsarskoe Selo by way of the Moscow-Vindavo-Rybinsk line. Unfortunately the train was unable to move beyond Dno. At that point, however, a message from Petrograd informed the tsar that Rodzianko was coming to meet him at Dno. Still later it was learned that Rodzianko was not coming to meet him after all. Therefore the imperial train proceeded to Pskov and the headquarters of General Ruzsky, the commander of the Northern Front. The emperor arrived on the night of 1-2 March after 40 hours on the road.

During that period the revolutionary elements in Petrograd had managed to organize themselves. Into the title of Soviet of Workers Deputies were inserted the words "and Soldiers." Individual units marched under red banners to the Tauride Palace where they were welcomed by spokesmen for the Soviet and the Committee of the Duma. At 4 p.m. on 1 March Grand Duke Cyril Vladimirovich also went there to declare that he and his Marine Guard were placing themselves at the disposal of the Committee of the Duma. That event, interpreted by everyone as an indication that the grand dukes were deserting to the revolution, made a tremendous impression. The grand duke later explained that his intention was to demonstrate his support for the moderate elements against the extremists. On that same day four other grand dukes composed a manifesto which, in the name of the sovereign, promised a responsible ministry. However, they were unable to have their document published.[23]

ORDER NO. 1

Power in fact belonged to the radical left: Sukhanov and Steklov overshadowed Rodzianko. The Duma's military commission called upon all soldiers to obey their officers. The ominous reaction of the suspicious rank and file of the garrison compelled the commission chairman, Colonel B.A.

Engelhardt, to execute an about-face and rush out a new order: anyone who attempted to deprive the soldiers of their weapons was to be shot by a firing squad. But that was not the end of the matter. On 1 March the Petrograd Soviet decided to take steps to safeguard the interests of "the soldiers of the revolution." On the spot the Soviet composed a resolution which achieved wide notoriety as "Order No. 1."[24]

The "order" consisted of seven points. All soldiers were ordered: 1) to elect regimental, battalion, and company committees; 2) to elect deputies to the Soviet; 3) in political matters to heed only the Soviet and their own committees; 4) to obey the orders of the Duma only when they were not in conflict with decrees of the Soviet; 5) to keep their weapons available to their committees and "under no circumstances to issue them to officers, even if ordered." The two final points proclaimed "the equality of soldiers and officers when not in formation" and the abolition of the salute, titles, and other perquisites of rank.

Order No. 1, issued during the evening of 1 March and published in the *Izvestiia* of the Petrograd Soviet on the following morning, took effect immediately throughout the entire Petrograd garrison.

Meanwhile the Executive Committee of the Soviet and the Committee of the Duma were negotiating the formation of a Provisional Government. "The socialist party actually gained control of the Petrograd garrison on 27 February and by reason of that became master of the situation; however, it was content to conceal its cards for the time being," wrote Rodzianko in his memoirs.[25] Nevertheless, on 1 March the Duma chairman telegraphed General Ruzsky that "governmental power presently rests with the Temporary Committee of the State Duma."

The Soviet did all it could to promote that illusion. The socialists were almost without direction since their most prominent leaders were either in emigration or in exile. The revolutionaries, moreover, had great fear of "a punitive expedition against Petrograd," and they were gravely concerned about the attitude that prevailed at the front. Consequently they tried to operate behind the facade of the Duma. That was the reason that the leaders of the Soviet urged the Temporary Committee of the Duma to seize power—to cross openly to the side of illegality.

Order No. 1 terrified those with close ties to the army. Guchkov, for example, declared that he never would agree to join the government under those conditions. His resolve was all the greater since "the masters of the situation" already had refused to print his appeal for "war to a victorious conclusion."

ISOLATED REBELLION IN THE PROVINCES

Mass demonstrations under red banners erupted in Moscow on 28 February. The demonstrators converged on the municipal duma where by nightfall the Moscow Soviet of Workers Deputies and the committee of the voluntary organizations were formed and working. After some feeble resistance around the arsenal and the riding school, the entire Moscow garrison went over to the revolution. General J.I. Mrozovsky, the commandant of the Moscow Military District, remained loyal to his duty and was placed under house arrest.

Two or three of the larger cities, including Kharkov and Nizhni Novgorod, experienced similar upheavals. In Tver rioters murdered the governor, N.G. Bunting. (When he saw the mob approaching, he telephoned the bishop and made his last confession.) Most of the provinces, however, remained calm. In many cases local authorities squelched telegraphed reports of the disturbances in the capital. In Rostov-on-Don the local right-wing newspaper, *Rostovskii listok* [Rostov Flyer], reported on 2 March, on the basis of stories gleaned from travelers recently arrived from Petrograd, that events had culminated in the "rout of the Bloc." The Duma, it reported, was dissolved, and the rightist spokesmen, Markov and Zamyslovsky, had joined the government.

THE LOYALIST ADVANCE ON PETROGRAD

General Ivanov's detachment, after a slow journey from Mogiilev, reached Tsarskoe Selo on the night of 1 March. Railway workers had tried to stop his train, but the threat of a court-martial convinced them to let it pass. At one point "revolutionary" soldiers blocked the route, but Ivanov forced them to kneel before him [and he then disarmed them] without a struggle. The 67th Infantry Regiment reached the Aleksandrovskaia [Warsaw] Station several miles from Tsarskoe Selo, but the 68th was held up at Luga. The Luga garrison had mutinied, and the infected troops of the 68th soon lost their desire to continue on to Petrograd. The other units, however, continued their movement from the front.

The situation in Petrograd left no doubt that political measures or concessions would have no success in suppressing the garrison's anarchical revolt against the war. Only force could crush the mutiny, stop the spreading disintegration, and enable Russia to continue the war.

Unquestionably loyal troops still were to be found at the front. Count F.A. Keller, commander of the III Cavalry Corps, and officers of the Guards Cavalry sent the emperor telegrams assuring him of their willingness to die for him. Officers of the Household Guard of the Preobrazhensky Regiment, commanded by Colonel Oznobishin, notified Mogilev that their troops were steadfast. They eagerly boarded the train when the 1st Guard Division received orders to proceed to Petrograd to crush the uprising. Many other units, of course, also remained loyal to their duty.

Fear held the rebel camp in its grip. In his memoirs[26] Bublikov wrote: "One disciplined division from the front was all it would have taken to crush the mutiny. It also could have been suppressed by the simple expedient of cutting off Petrograd's rail communications, for in three days hunger would have forced the city to capitulate. Even in March it still was possible for the tsar to return, and everyone knew it: there was good reason for the panic that repeatedly ran through the Tauride Palace."

But only the emperor at the head of loyal troops could have overcome the anarchy. The "responsible" committee of Duma politicians, controlled by the Soviet of Workers and Soldiers Deputies, was incapable of restoring order. Any government formed in turbulent Petrograd, whether led by a grand duke, Rodzianko, Lvov, or Kerensky, would have become a prisoner of the disaffected garrison. A fire cannot be extinguished from inside the burning building.

Meantime, the two military commanders, Alekseev and Ruzsky, had a completely inaccurate impression of what was going on in the capital. They believed that the Duma had formed a government and that it was supported by disciplined regiments. In order to conduct the foreign war, they desired

above all to avoid a civil war. Unaware that the entire movement was taking place under a red flag, they operated under
the illusion that there was someone in Petrograd to negotiate
with.

PSKOV: THE LAST STOP

At the very hour that Ivanov's detachment was approaching
Tsarskoe Selo and the Petrograd Soviet was adopting Order
No. 1, the imperial train arrived at Pskov. The Northern Front
commander, General Ruzsky, relying on information received
from Stavka, believed that order had been restored in Petrograd and that a pro-monarchist Provisional Government had
been formed and was functioning under Rodzianko's leadership.[27] Ruzsky also had received more recent information
from Alekseev that Moscow and the Baltic Fleet had revolted
and gone over to the side of "the provisional committee."
Included in the messages from Alekseev was a manifesto,
drafted at Stavka for the tsar's signature, which instructed
Rodzianko to form a ministry responsible to the Duma. To
members of the emperor's retinue Ruzsky quite frankly stated
his personal opinion that it was necessary "to throw ourselves
upon the mercies of the victors." He assumed, however, that
"the victors" were the Progressive Bloc of the Duma.

On the evening of his arrival at Pskov the tsar discussed the
situation with Ruzsky for several hours. The substance of their
private meeting is known only through the account of it that
Ruzsky later gave to S.N. Vilchkovsky.[28] Ruzsky "passion-
ately" argued that a responsible ministry was essential. The
emperor replied "calmly, with composure, and from deep conviction: I am responsible before God and Russia for all that
has happened or will happen. Whether the ministers are responsible to the Duma and State Council makes no difference.
I could never watch the ministers act without regard for the
interests of Russia and take consolation from the fact that
the matter is out of my hands." The report continued: "With
extraordinary accuracy the emperor reviewed in his mind the
views of all those who soon might govern Russia . . . and said
that in his opinion the public figures who undoubtedly would
make up the first government were all inexperienced in matters of administration and, once burdened with power, would

be unable to manage." (The reader should bear in mind that at that time the emperor was unaware of the extent of the anarchy in the capital.)

General Ruzsky did not disclose the reasons he adduced during this long conversation to persuade the tsar to agree to a "ministry responsible to the Duma."[29] At any rate, while their meeting still was in progress, a telegram was sent in the tsar's name to Ivanov: "I request you to take no measures whatsoever before my arrival and before reporting to me. (12:20 a.m., 2 March 1917)." At the same time and on his own authority Ruzsky ordered that no more troops were to be sent to Ivanov and that the troop trains that had been sent from the Northern Front were to return to the Dvina sector. During the night Stavka over the emperor's signature also ordered troops already dispatched from the Western Front to stop at the next major terminal and instructed the commander to halt the embarkation of any others. Earlier, on 1 March, Stavka had ordered General Bruilov on the Southwestern Front not to send any troops without "special notification." As a result of the meeting at Pskov, Stavka was informed that the tsar had agreed to empower Rodzianko to form a government "composed of people who enjoy the confidence of all Russia."

RODZIANKO'S BOMBSHELL

By then, however, Rodzianko himself was under the vigilant surveillance of the leaders of the Soviet. He had wanted to meet the emperor at Dno, but had been denied transportation.[30] The revolutionaries were concerned about the movement of counterrevolutionary troops from the front, and they feared that once Rodzianko slipped from their grasp he "would go over to the side of the enemy." The chairman of the Duma's committee then requested to speak to Ruzsky by direct line, but the radicals were reluctant. "Let Messieurs the Workers and Soldiers Deputies give me a guard or accompany me," demanded Rodzianko, "or else I shall be arrested there, at the telegraph office." Finally at 3:30 a.m. on 2 March he was allowed to go to contact Ruzsky.[31]

Ruzsky informed Rodzianko of the results of his conference with the emperor and of the fact that the chairman of the Duma had been entrusted with the responsibility of forming

Michael Rodzianko

a ministry of confidence.[32] To Rodzianko those words rang
with irony. He then explained that the first move was to call
off the movement of troops from the front—"the troops are
disobeying their officers and cannot be controlled." He went
on to assert that "hatred toward the dynasty has reached extreme limits" and finally announced "a very definite demand
for abdication in favor of the son, under the regency of Michael Aleksandrovich."

Ruzsky then apparently began to understand how badly he
had misjudged the situation in Petrograd.[33] "During this day
I did everything that my heart prompted to find a way out,
to secure tranquillity for the present and future . . . . Spring
is approaching and we must concentrate our efforts to prepare
for offensive operations." Rodzianko assured him that "the
entire nation" desired victory and that by meeting the demands "of the people" everything would turn out for the best:
"Our valorous army will not want for anything . . . railway
communications will not be hampered . . . the peasants and all
the populace will provide bread, ammunition, and other necessary equipment."

"God grant that your assumptions regarding the army will
be realized," answered Ruzsky, "but bear in mind that no
violent change can take place without leaving its mark. What
if the anarchy spreads to the army and its leaders lose the
power of their authority? What then will become of our Russia?" Rodzianko replied that the transformation would be
"voluntary and painless for all concerned."

THE HIGH COMMAND CONDONES THE REVOLUTION

Ruzsky immediately sent Alekseev a copy of the conversation,
and at 10:15 a.m. on 2 March the chief of staff relayed Rodzianko's advice on the necessity of abdication to all front commanders.[34] Alekseev added his own opinion that "apparently
the situation does not permit another solution . . . [the existence of the army and the work of the railroads are actually
in the hands of the Petrograd Provisional Government.] We
must save the active army from disintegration, carry on the
struggle against the external enemy, and preserve the independence of Russia and the future of the dynasty."[35] General
Alekseev requested the front commanders, if they shared his

views, to wire their advice immediately to the emperor at Pskov [and inform Stavka of their replies]. By 2:30 p.m. the chief of staff had transmitted the commanders' responses to General Ruzsky.

Grand Duke Nicholas Nikolaevich telegraphed that "extraordinary measures" were necessary and that he as a faithful subject "fall on my knees and implore Your Imperial Majesty to save Russia and your heir . . . . Making the sign of the cross, transmit to him your heritage. There is no other solution." General Brusilov advised that "the only solution . . . without which Russia will perish, is the abdication of the throne . . . ." General Evert noted that "the army in its present state cannot be relied upon for the suppression of internal disorders." Therefore, as "an infinitely loyal subject," he "implored" the emperor to make the only decision "which apparently can stop the revolution and thus save Russia from the horrors of anarchy." General Alekseev, seconding those petitions, also implored the emperor to act without delay out of his "boundless love for Russia, for the sake of her integrity and independence, and in the interests of victory."

General Sakharov, however, began by deploring the "criminal and shocking reply" given to the emperor by the chairman of the Duma—"a small band of plunderers . . . which has treacherously availed itself of an opportune moment to carry out its criminal design." But in conclusion he was "compelled tearfully to state that perhaps the least painful solution for the country . . . would be to meet the conditions as stated."[36]

A WEB OF "TREASON, COWARDICE, AND DECEPTION"

There is no exact record of what the emperor went through and what he felt in those fateful days from 28 February to the 2nd of March. What is definite is that on the morning of the 28th he ordered the Petrograd authorities to suppress the mutiny of the garrison. Then, during his long circuitous journey to Pskov, he spoke only with General V.N. Voeikov, whose memoirs disclose that General Ivanov's slow progress upset the tsar and that on the 1st of March he was prepared to agree to a "responsible ministry" (?) and expected to meet Rodzianko at Dno.[37] Presumably the emperor intended to appoint him prime minister. That, however, was not entirely consistent with what Ruzsky told Rodzianko during their late-night conversation on the direct line: "His Majesty at first wanted to suggest that you should form a cabinet responsible to His Majesty, but later on . . . to meet the general desire of the legislative bodies and the people . . . he has decided to grant a ministry responsible to the legislature . . . ."

On the morning of 2 March the chief of staff of the Northern Front, General Yuri Danilov, reported to Stavka from Pskov: "It took all evening until late into the night to convince the emperor to give in to a responsible ministry. The decision was reached at 2 a.m."[38] Later, when Shulgin arrived in Pskov, Ruzsky confided to him that "yesterday was a difficult day—there was a storm."

The emperor's long meeting with Ruzsky at Pskov marked the turning point. Measures to combat the revolution were cancelled, and the deployment of troops against rebellious Petrograd was stopped in the name of the emperor, apart from (if not contrary to) his will.

Having learned that the tsar's train had been detained at Pskov, the empress on 2 March wrote that the emperor was "in a trap." That probably became a certain fact as soon as Generals Ruzsky and Alekseev accepted the possibility of a "peaceful solution" and then did all they could to foster it. At Pskov the emperor did not even have the opportunity to send a telegram without Ruzsky's knowledge. All the information he received was relayed to him by the Northern Front commander. When at the emperor's request Voeikov tried to discuss the situation with Rodzianko by direct line, Ruzsky would not permit it. Without consulting the emperor, Ruzsky conferred with Stavka as to whether the imperial manifesto bearing the emperor's signature should be sent on. The emperor could not communicate with the outside world. Apparently he could not even leave Pskov without Ruzsky's permission. He was in effect a prisoner. Under those circumstances his consent to a "responsible ministry" after many hours of discussion with Ruzsky appears in a peculiar light. Every witness noticed that from that moment on an observable change—a feeling of despair—came over the emperor.

Having given his approval to the actual transfer of power to others, who in his opinion were incapable of exercising it, the emperor did not hesitate when Ruzsky informed him of the front commanders' responses to the question of abdication. The telegrams were received from Stavka at 2:30 p.m. By 3 o'clock Nicholas II had decided to abdicate. He never regarded power as an end in itself. To him it was a sacred obligation. Thus, having yielded power to others, he attached little importance to retaining the title of Tsar.

Accordingly, he addressed a telegram to Chief of Staff Alekseev: "In the interests of the welfare, tranquillity, and salvation of my deeply beloved Russia I am prepared to abdicate the throne in favor of my son. I request everyone to serve him faithfully and sincerely." In a second telegram to the chairman of the State Duma he wrote: "There is no sacrifice that I would not bear for the sake of the true welfare and salvation of our own Mother Russia . . . ." The emperor signed the two telegrams at 3 p.m. on 2 March. However, they were not transmitted, for at that moment came word that Guchkov and Shulgin had departed for Pskov on a mission for the Duma.

THE HOLLOW VICTORY OF THE DUMA BLOC

During the night of 1-2 March, the Tauride Palace served as the arena for a desperate struggle precipitated by Order No. 1. Because of it, Guchkov refused to participate in the government. On the other hand, the Executive Committee of the Soviet refused by a vote of 13-8 to participate in a government with "rightists." The radicals wanted a government completely subservient to them, but at the same time they refused to serve in or take any responsibility for it. The Soviet appeared to prefer the position of autocratic monarch, leaving it to the Committee of the Duma to play the role of a ministry. Meanwhile, bands of soldiers wandered through the streets of the city. Trucks continued to race about. Although the firing ceased, illegal activity spread alarmingly.[39] The imperial capital was draped in red banners.

The Duma committee, finally convinced by the Soviet to form a government, spent the morning of 2 March working out its program with the Executive Committee of the Soviet.[40] The program included the principal demand of the defected garrison, which otherwise had little interest in the composition of the cabinet or the formation of a government: "Those

military units which took part in the revolutionary movement shall be neither disarmed nor withdrawn from Petrograd." The "miracle" prayed for by 200,000 soldiers had
been granted: the new government solemnly promised that
the Petrograd garrison would not be sent to the front.

Around 4 p.m.—just after the emperor had decided to relinquish the throne—Miliukov addressed a crowd of several
thousand in the Catherine Hall of the Tauride Palace.[41] He
informed the mixed assembly that a new government had
been formed. "Who elected you?" they demanded. "We were
elected by the Russian revolution," he replied. Miliukov was
interrupted several times. There were objections to some
names—Prince Lvov and Guchkov, for example—while Tereshchenko's name provoked bewilderment and laughter.[42] The
announcement that Kerensky would become minister of justice, however, produced a great ovation. Then Miliukov declared: "The old despot who brought Russia to the brink of
ruin voluntarily will renounce the throne or he will be deposed. The power will be transferred to the regent, the Grand
Duke Michael Aleksandrovich. The heir will be Alexis." The
hall contained a considerable number of socialists who protested: "This is the old dynasty!"

"Yes," replied Miliukov, "this is the old dynasty, which
perhaps you do not like and which perhaps I do not like
either. But who likes what is beside the point right now . . . .
If we start arguing about [the form of government] instead
of reaching an immediate decision, Russia will find itself in a
state of civil war which can only revive the ruined regime."

PSKOV: THE LAST ACT

The representatives of the Committee of the Duma reached
Pskov late that evening. They hoped first to discuss the situation with General Ruzsky, but officials of the imperial suite
insisted that they proceed immediately to the tsar. Once together, Guchkov in a pompous tone began to speak of the
triumph of the revolution—the entire army was joining it,
even His Majesty's personal escort—resistance would be useless. For Guchkov that must have been his crowning moment,
the culmination of his long, overt and clandestine political
struggle. The tsar did not engage in conversation with the

М. П. С.

Центр. тел. ст.

5/3 191 г.

Служ отм

Телеграмма № 399

Изъ __Петрограда__ Центр. чис. сл. 100

Подана 4 " 13 ч. 46

Принялъ __Евстигнѣевъ__

военная.

Всѣмъ Н.

Объявите по линіи: Императоръ Николай второй отрекся 2 Марта отъ престола въ пользу Великаго Князя Михаила Александровича точка. Великій Князь 3 Марта отказался воспріять Верховную Власть до установленія образа Правленія учредительнымъ Собраніемъ созваннаго на осн въ всеобщаго прямого равнаго и тайнаго голосованія и обратился ко всѣмъ гражданамъ съ просьбой подчиниться Временному Правительству по почину Государственной Думы возникшему и облеченному всею полнотою власти до рѣшеній Учредительнаго Собранія объ образѣ правленія точка. Предсѣдателемъ Совѣта министровъ состоитъ Князь Львовъ Министромъ Путей Сообщенія Некрасовъ точка Актъ объ отреченіи сейчасъ разсылается точка. Спокойствіе въ Столицѣ полное.

Комиссаръ Государственной Думы

Членъ Ея Вубликовъ Добров скій.

вѣрно: Алекс

Тип. Николаевская М. А.

Сер. Тел. № 101 а.
Изд. № 527—1916 г. Врм. 54 ф. 1.оо и.

Bublikov's Telegram Announcing the Abdication of the Tsar

emissaries of his enemies. Calmly and stiffly he announced his decision.[43]

It is now too late to speculate as to whether the tsar should not have abdicated. The attitudes of Ruzsky and Alekseev precluded the possibility of resistance: his orders were not transmitted; loyalist telegrams were not delivered. Moreover, they could have announced his abdication without his consent—on 9 November 1918 Prince Max of Baden proclaimed the abdication of the German Emperor even though William II had done no such thing! The Russian Emperor at least retained the option of addressing his people in his own final words in his instrument of abdication.

Guchkov brought the draft of a manifesto with him, and Alekseev also sent a manifesto that had been composed at Stavka. The tsar left the coach and returned sometime later. "He extended a paper to Guchkov saying: 'Here is the text.' . . . How pitiful, I thought, is the draft that we brought," recalled Shulgin.

The Imperial Manifesto of 2 March 1917, signed by Nicholas in two copies, declared:

In the midst of our great struggle against a foreign enemy, who has been striving for nearly three years to enslave our native land, it has been God's will to visit upon Russia a grievous new ordeal. The popular disturbances that have arisen within our country threaten to have a calamitous effect on the successful continuation of our bitter struggle. The destiny of Russia, the honor of our heroic army, the welfare of our people, the entire future of our beloved fatherland demand that the war be carried to a victorious conclusion no matter what the cost. The cruel enemy is making his last effort, and the hour draws nigh when our valiant army, together with our glorious allies, will be able to crush him.

In these decisive days in the history of Russia We deem it Our duty as a matter of conscience to help Our people draw together and unite all their resources in order to hasten the day of victory. Therefore, in agreement with the State Duma, We have judged it best to abdicate the Throne of the Russian State and to lay down the Supreme Power.

Not wishing to be departed from Our Beloved Son, We convey Our Inheritance to Our Brother the Grand Duke Michael Aleksandrovich and give him Our Blessing on his accession to the Throne of the Russian State.

We enjoin Our Brother to administer the affairs of the State in union and harmony with the representatives of the people, according to the principles that they shall see fit to establish, and to take an inviolable oath to this effect.

In the name of Our dearly beloved native land, We call upon all true sons of the Fatherland to fulfill their sacred obligations to their country by obeying the Tsar in this hour of national stress and to help Him and the representatives of the people to lead the Russian State onto the path of victory, prosperity, and glory. May the Lord God help Russia!

NICHOLAS

The transfer of supreme power to Grand Duke Michael Aleksandrovich came as a shock to them, yet the Duma's emissaries could neither object nor argue. The sovereign had expressed his will: the only alternative was to obey. (Guchkov later declared: "We had to take what was offered.") Although the tsar signed the documents at twelve midnight, they were dated 3 p.m.—the hour at which he had decided to renounce the throne.[44]

The tsar had no confidence in the ability of his enemies to control the situation. That alone was why he tried to the very end to keep the helm of state in his own hands. When that became impossible—when it became clear that he was a virtual prisoner—he did all he could to make the task easier for his successors. He appointed General L.G. Kornilov, who was nominated by the Committee of the Duma, to the post of commander of the Petrograd military district. He also signed two ukazes, one appointing Prince Lvov chairman of the council of ministers, the other reappointing Grand Duke Nicholas Nikolaevich supreme commander in chief.[45] Finally, in his farewell message to the army the tsar called on his former troops to continue their struggle against the foreign enemy and to render faithful service to the new government.[46] He refused the new regime only one thing—his son. The tsar understood perfectly well that the young monarch, a minor, could not abdicate in his own behalf and therefore could be deposed only by other, bloody methods.

The tsar gave his enemies every advantage he could. Nevertheless they revealed themselves powerless to control events. They had torn the wheel out of the hands of the powerful "chauffeur"—and the car plunged into the abyss.

The tsar's diary under the date of the 2nd of March 1917 bears the inscription: "I am surrounded by treason, cowardice, and deception."

ONLY ONE MORE MONTH TO DAYBREAK

The most awesome achievement of Emperor Nicholas II—and the one most often ignored—was his magnificent struggle against impossible odds in leading Russia to the threshhold of victory. His enemies, however, prevented Russia from crossing that threshhold.

The strain that the emperor had to endure during the final months of his reign evokes, even more than the tribulations that followed the Japanese war, Pososhkov's tribute to the emperor's predecessor: "He has few helpers to his liking. He climbs the mountain and pulls ten with him, but millions pull downhill." Peter the Great needed nine years to transform the vanquished warriors of Narva into the victors of Poltava. The last Commander-in-Chief of the Imperial Russian Army accomplished the same monumental task in a year and a half. But, as General N.A. Lokhvitsky observed, his enemies also recognized the potential of his labors, and between the emperor, his army, and victory "they interposed the revolution." The greatest tribute, of all, however, was paid to the last tsar by Winston Churchill:[47]

"Surely to no nation has Fate been more malignant than to Russia. Her ship went down in sight of port. She had actually weathered the storm when all was cast away. Every sacrifice had been made; the toil was achieved. Despair and Treachery usurped command at the very moment when the task was done." The tsar ruled, the empire stood, the front was secure, victory was assured.

Now it has become fashionable to dismiss the imperial regime as "a purblind, corrupt, incompetent tyranny." But the record of its thirty months of bloody war allow us to gauge the strength of the empire "by the battering it had endured, by the disasters it had survived, by the inexhaustible forces it had developed, and by the recovery it had made." History inexorably summons to the bar the leader of the nation. Though the issue may be decided by the exertions of legions, "to the supreme responsible authority belongs the blame or credit for the result. Why should this stern test be denied to Nicholas II? . . . Should he reap no honour for decisions made "at the summit where all problems are reduced to Yea or Nay?" Does he earn no credit for the victories of his armies,

The Last Tsar

for their magnificent recovery from the horrors of their "munitionless retreat," for his indomitable character that had assured victory just at the moment he was struck down?

Exit Russia, less than a month before the United States entered the war, only a month before the dawn of a general victory. "Exit Czar. Deliver him and all he loved to wounds and death. Belittle his efforts, asperse his conduct, insult his memory; but pause then to tell us who else was found capable." Of contenders there was no want. "But none could answer the few plain questions on which the life and fame of Russia turned. With victory in her grasp she fell upon the earth, devoured alive, like Herod of old, by worms."

NOTES

CHAPTER EIGHTEEN

1. The historical debate on "war guilt"—the allocation of responsibility for World War I—is entering its seventh decade. The volumes of documents, books, and articles on the origins of the war are sufficient to form a respectable library. In summary the case against Russia rests primarily on the fact that Russia was the first great power to mobilize, or at least attempt to mobilize, against another great power, the Austro-Hungarian Empire. The basic case for Russia is that Vienna's unilateral attempt to deal with Serbia was a deliberate challenge and an intolerable affront to the Russian Empire. The British historian G.P. Gooch set the problem in perspective as well as anyone: "The same instinctive pride of a Great Power which prompted Vienna to throw down the glove compelled St. Petersburg to pick it up. It is true that, while Austria fought under the banner of self-preservation, Russia, whom nobody threatened, marched out to battle in the name of prestige. But in the accepted scale of national values, prestige, honour and security were motive factors of equal weight."

In general, the burden of the evidence clearly proves that no government deliberately planned a European war in 1914. It is equally convincing that only one country—Germany—had the power to prevent a general conflict. The German pledge of unqualified support for Austria in its quarrel with Serbia (the "blank check") meant that unless Russia accepted Serbia's humiliation and therefore its own, the great mechanism of European alliances would be set in motion.

Casual readers can recapture the atmosphere of the July Crisis in either of two eminently readable books: Barbara W. Tuchman, *The Guns of August* (Macmillan, 1962) and George Malcolm Thomson, *Twelve Days in July* (London, 1964). The latter depends mainly on Luigi Albertini's exhaustive documentary history, *The Origins of the War of 1914*, and in particular Vols. II and III. Other scholarly works and documents are mentioned in notes above and below and in the general list of works cited.

2. See above, Vol. I, p. 131. (Oldenburg's note) The tsar warned the Germans to respect Russia's historic interests in the Near East.

3. See above, Vol. III, pp. 167.

4. *Mezhdunarodnie otnosheniia*, ser. 3, Vol. 5 [?], p. 496. (Oldenburg's note)

5. Nicholas Nikolaevich Yanushkevich (1868-1918) became chief of the general staff in March 1914 from his post as professor and chief of the Nicholas Academy of the General Staff (1913-1914). Prior to that he had served for about a decade in various administrative capacities in the chancellery of the minister of war. He saw no action during the Russo-Japanese War and had little but bureaucratic experience to prepare him for his exalted position. During the crisis of July 1914 his cavalier behavior ill-served the tsar or the cause of peace.

6. Prewar military planning had proceeded from the reasonable assumption that Russia would be opposed by both Austria-Hungary and Germany. Therefore the Russian general staff planned only for simultaneous mobilization against both Central Powers. There was no plan for a "partial mobilization" although it was possible to put one together—to mobilize only against Austria—but to have done so would have made it practically impossible to mobilize later against Germany.

Russia therefore had but two viable options: to mobilize against both Austria and Germany or not to mobilize at all. Unfortunately, General Yanushkevich, who had been chief of staff for only five months, was not familiar with the details of the mobilization plan or he deliberately concealed the problem from Sazonov. At any rate, having discussed it with Yanushkevich, Sazonov recommended and the council of ministers on 11/24 July approved in principle the idea of a mobilization against Austria alone. On the following day, the tsar presided over a crown council which endorsed that recommendation and ordered pre-mobilization (the "period preparatory to war") to begin on 13/26 July.

The partial mobilization decided on by the crown council restricted mobilization to thirteen army corps and confined the concentrations to the four military districts of Kiev, Odessa, Moscow and Kazan. That form of mobilization would have upset completely the war plan of the general staff, for one of its provisions was to draw upon the reserves of the Warsaw district. However, Russia's strategy against Austria called for a two-pronged offensive westward from Kiev and southward from Warsaw. Moreover, the plan would have deprived the northern armies of adequate resources in the event that Germany entered the war.

On 15/28 July Yanushkevich finally informed Sazonov of these problems and asked whether he could make a "categoric assurance that war with Germany would be avoided." Sazonov could not, and the chief of staff therefore asked the foreign minister to acquaint the tsar with the dangers of the contemplated partial mobilization.

For details on the Russian mobilization and an analysis of it from the two principal points of view see Michael T. Florinsky, "The Russian Mobilization of 1914," *Political Science Quarterly*, 42 (June 1927): 203-27; and Alfred von Wegerer's reply, *ibid.*, 43 (June 1928): 201-28. For the relevant memoirs and principal monographs see the bibliographic note in Sidney Bradshaw Fay, *The Origins of the World War*, 2nd ed., revised (Macmillan, 1932), Vol. II, pp. 291-92.

7. Emperor Franz Josef signed the order for mobilization against Serbia on the evening of 12/25 July. Austria's mobilization began on the 28th, the same day as its declaration of war on Serbia. In an apparent rush to outdistance any diplomatic solution, the Austrian high command began to bombard Belgrade (just across the frontier) almost immediately, even though mobilization could not be completed and an invasion mounted until 12 August. Austria's mobilization against Serbia activated eight army corps, about half of its army. Although the Russian government knew this, it excused its own general mobilization by falsifying the record in its diplomatic correspondence with the assertion that Austria "was undertaking general mobilization" (i.e. against Russia as well). Russia's general mobilization in fact preceded Austria's general

mobilization by about twenty hours. However, the critical point is that even partial mobilization by Russia (which actually never took place, although the intention and threat were real) was *total with respect to Austria.*

In addition to the general diplomatic collections see in particular: Russia, Ministère des affaires étrangeres, *Recueil des documents diplomatiques. Negociations ayant précéde'la Guerre, 10/23 juillet-24 juillet/6 août 1914* [The Russian Orange Book] (Petrograd, 1914). That official explanation contains some 79 documents with numerous omissions and several forgeries which are itemized in G. von Romberg, *Falsifications of the Russian Orange Book* (London, 1923). More reliable documentation can be found in several articles in *Krasnyi arkhiv* and in *How the War began in 1914. Being the Diary of the Russian Foreign Office from the 3rd to the 20th of July, 1914* (London, 1925). Commonly known as Schilling's diary, this record covers the period 16 July to 1 August, New Style. Baron Schilling was Sazonov's confidential assistant. The diary was first published in *Krasnyi arkhiv* (4:1-62), and both officials have attested to its veracity. *Un livre noir. Diplomatie d'avant guerre d'après les documents des Archives Russes, 1910-1917*, ed. René Marchand, 3 vols. in 6 parts (Paris, 1922-1934). Marchand was for several years the St. Petersburg correspondent for the French paper *Figaro*. In 1918 he became a Communist and was one of the first investigators to make a systematic study of the Russian archives. He coordinated that material with Izvolsky's correspondence to produce the *Black Book*.

8. Because of the prospect of a two-front war and the military planning that proceeded from it, Germany was the only great power for whom mobilization meant war. For everyone else mobilization was a threat or bluff of the most desperate order, but nevertheless their mobilized forces could stand within their own frontiers. For Germany mobilization and war were inseparable: intricate railway timetables dictated that on the third day of mobilization the German army had to begin offensive operations—the invasion of neutral Belgium. Once set in motion, the mobilization could not be stopped without leaving German defenses in catastrophic disarray.

9. Having received news of the Austrian bombardment of Belgrade late in the afternoon of 16/29 July, the tsar gave permission for general mobilization to begin. Then in the evening he received a telegram from the kaiser urging him not to undertake military measures that threatened Austria and thereby jeopardized the kaiser's role as mediator. Nicholas immediately cancelled the order for general mobilization and instead ordered partial mobilization. That order went out around midnight.

At 11 a.m. on 17/30 July Sukhomlinov and Yanushkevich met with Sazonov and convinced him that partial mobilization was impossible. They urged him to phone the tsar and persuade him to reinstate the order for general mobilization. Nicholas refused but agreed to meet Sazonov at 3 p.m. Around 4 p.m. the tsar consented to general mobilization. Sazonov immediately telephoned Yanushkevich, and the machinery was set in motion. General mobilization began on the 18/31st. Since all reservists were granted one or two days to settle their personal affairs, there was no partial mobilization.

10. General-Adjutant Nicholas Yudovich Ivanov (1851-1918) served in the Russo-Japanese War and then in October 1905 led the suppression of the Kronstadt mutiny. From 1906 to 1908 he commanded the Imperial Guards and the St. Petersburg Military District as well as serving as governor of Kronstadt (November 1906-April 1907). He became commander of the Kiev Military District in 1908 and held that post until the outbreak of war when he assumed command of the Southwestern Front.

General Jacob Grigorovich Zhilinsky (1853-1917?) was a technical delegate to the First Hague Conference in 1899. From 1900 to 1903 he was quartermaster-general of the army and then served briefly in the war against Japan. He became commander of the Warsaw Military District in March 1914 and also governor-general of Warsaw.

General Nicholas Vladimirovich Ruzsky (1854-1918) commanded the Third Army at the beginning of the war. He later commanded the Sixth Army and then succeeded Zhilinsky as commander of the combined Northern and Northwestern Fronts.

11. "That too is a lie!" wrote the tsar on the report of the German note. (Oldenburg's note)

12. Kerensky, however, inserted a characteristic qualification: "We believe that on the fields of battle, in great sufferings, the brotherhood of all the nations of Russia will be consolidated and that there will be born a single will to liberate the country from its terrible political shackles." (Oldenburg's note)

13. Since the SDs walked out when the vote was taken, they were considered not to have voted and therefore the vote was recorded as unanimous. After this one-day session, the Duma was prorogued. It did not disperse, however, but continued to function unofficially as a provisional committee for the relief of war victims. Rodzianko, the chairman of the Duma, headed the committee, which included all deputies who lived or remained in the capital and which maintained close contact with the deputies in the provinces.

14. At the invitation of the Moscow zemstvo, representatives of 34 provincial zemstvos assembled in Moscow on 30 July to form the All-Russian Union of Zemstvos for the Relief of Sick and Wounded Soldiers. Only the notoriously reactionary Kursk zemstvo was not represented. During the Russo-Japanese War the zemstvos had formed a national organization under the chairmanship of Prince G.E. Lvov to assist the Russian Red Cross in the care of sick and wounded soldiers.

15. According to A.N. Yakhontov, assistant to the manager of the affairs of the council of ministers, by the end of 1914 the government had appropriated about 45 million rubles for use by the Unions. By 20 September 1916 the government's allocations had risen to 553,459,829 rubles. Those sums represented only the appropriations approved by the council of ministers after preliminary consideration by a war department board chaired by General Vedeniapin. In addition, the Unions received funds from the various military headquarters. *Vozrozhdenie* [Revival], No. 4038, 8 August 1936. (Oldenburg's note)

The Union of Municipalities, formed a few days after the Union of Zemstvos, worked closely with that organization and for essentially the same purposes. Michael Chelnokov (1863-) was elected president of the Union of Municipalities. He was the member of a wealthy industrial family and the owner of four brick factories. He had been active in zemstvo affairs since 1891 and was elected as a Kadet to the Second, Third, and Fourth Dumas. The interlocking directorate of the voluntary organizations was exemplified by Chelnokov who in addition to his mayorship and chairmanship of the Union of Municipalities also served on the central committee of the Union of Zemstvos and was deputy chairman of the Moscow War Industry Committee.

16. It dropped the proceedings against the lawyers who publicly protested the government's handling of the Beilis trial and the prosecution of V.V. Shulgin [also in connection with the Beilis affair]. (Oldenburg's note, from the text)

17. General Paul Rennenkampf played a prominent role in the conquest of Manchuria during the Boxer Rebellion and served with some distinction in the Russo-Japanese War. He conducted an aggressive campaign against mutinous troops in Manchuria after the war. In 1913 he became commander of the Vilna Military District and when the war broke out, he led the First Army in the field. His timidity in the first campaign of the war was mainly responsible for the destruction of Samsonov's forces and his own rout in the First Battle of the Masurian Lakes.

General Alexander Samsonov (1859-1914) was a cavalry officer, a graduate of the Cavalry School in St. Petersburg and the Nicholas Academy of the General Staff. He served in the Russo-Turkish War and later on the general staff. During the Russo-Japanese War he commanded the Ussuri Mounted Brigade and the Siberian Cossack Division. He was appointed Hetman of the Don Cossacks in 1907 and governor-general and commander of troops in Turkestan in 1909. He took command of the Second Army in August 1914.

18. At Tannenberg (Grünwald) [in 1410] a Polish-Lithuanian army inflicted a crushing defeat on the Order of Teutonic Knights. That was the battle which Grand Duke Nicholas Nikolaevich recalled in his appeal to the Poles. (Oldenburg's note)

German brilliance and Russian incompetence combined to produce a classic double envelopment in the Tannenberg campaign. The Russian Second Army was all but totally destroyed—the Germans captured 125,000 men and 500 guns at a cost to themselves of 10-15,000 men. There are no reliable figures on Russian casualties. For a synopsis of the East Prussian campaign in text and maps see *The West Point Atlas of American Wars*, ed. Colonel Vincent J. Esposito (New York, 1959), II: Maps 15-21. The tragedy forms the setting of Alexander Solzhenitsyn's novel *August 1914* (New York, 1972).

19. Field Marshal Paul von Hindenburg (1847-1934) was called out of retirement to assume command of the German forces in East Prussia. General Erich von Ludendorf (1865-1937) already was famous as the conqueror of the Belgian fortress of Liege. In 1916 Hindenburg became supreme commander of the armies of the Germanic empires, and Ludendorf continued to serve as his chief of staff and the actual director of German operations.

In the German army since the time of the elder Moltke and the Franco-Prussian War, the commander in chief made the broad basic decisions and his staff developed an over-all plan. The subordinate field commanders then fought the battle according to their best judgment and within the directives of the general plan. As the war progressed, however, Ludendorf began to exercise greater control over the actual conduct of operations on the battlefield.

20. In 28 days of fighting Rennenkampf lost 145,000 men and 200 guns. The only major history of the war on the Eastern Front in English is Winston S. Churchill, *The World Crisis*, Vol. VI: *The Unknown War: The Eastern Front* (New York, 1931, 1959). His account mainly reflects the German point of view. On the First Battle of the Masurian Lakes see pp. 215-27.

21. Sazonov wanted the British to adhere to the Franco-Russian Alliance, but Lord Grey preferred to retain more freedom of action. See C. Jay Smith, Jr., *The Russian Struggle for Power, 1914-1917* (Philosophical Library, 1956), pp. 43-45, a standard work on Russia's foreign policy during the war. The tripartite agreement of 5 September 1914 marked the first official application of the term "Allied Powers" as a designation of the Triple Entente.

22. In September 1914 Sazonov prepared a list of Russian war aims and presented it to the French and British ambassadors. Smith states that although they were modified somewhat, Sazonov's twelve points were comparable in 1914-1917 to Wilson's Fourteen Points in 1917-1918: 1) The Allies' "principal aim" was to destroy Germany's pretensions to military and political hegemony. 2) Territorial changes ought to be determined by the principle of nationality. 3) The lower course of the Nieman River and Eastern Galicia to be annexed by Russia; eastern Posen, Silesia, and western Galicia might be added to Poland. 4) Alsace-Lorraine to be returned to France and, if the French desired, also part of Rhenish Prussia and the Palatinate. 5) Belgium to receive "an important increase in territory." 6) Schleswig-Holstein to be restored to Denmark. 7) The Kingdom of Hanover to be restored. 8) Austria to be reconstituted as a tripartite monarchy: the Empire of Austria, the Kingdom of Bohemia, and the Kingdom of Hungary. The Austrian empire proper would include only "hereditary provinces." 9) Bosnia, Herzegovina, Dalmatia, and northern Albania to be added to Serbia. 10) Serbia to compensate Bulgaria with territory in Macedonia. 11) Greece to annex southern Albania, except Valona which would be given to Italy. 12) Germany's colonies to be partitioned by England, France, and Japan. Ibid., pp. 47-48.

23. The Battle of Lodz (11 November-6 December 1914) saw first a Russian and then a German army encircled. Mackensen's attack on the northern flank of the Russian front was designed to frustrate the Russian invasion of Silesia in the south. Between the 11th and 16th he forced a breach between the Russian First and Second Armies. Rennenkampf, still in command of the First, held the extreme northern end of the line. Repeating his dull performance in East Prussia, Rennenkampf allowed his army to be pushed away to the north. Mackensen then swung due south and encircled the Second Army around Lodz. At that

point, however, Stavka rushed in reinforcements and by the 21st they were encircling the Germans from the east. On the 23rd, however, the German 3rd Guard Division cut its way out of the trap and in the process demolished the crack 6th Siberian Division. The Battle of Lodz completely stopped the Russian invasion of Silesia. On 6 December the Russians evacuated Lodz and withdrew into positions around Warsaw. See *West Point Atlas*, Maps 24-25; Churchill, *Unknown War*, pp. 251-64.

24. Admiral Nicholas von Essen (1860-1915), a hero of the Russo-Japanese War (see above Chapter IX, note 52), served as commander of naval forces in the Baltic from 1908 until his death in 1915.

25. On 1 August 1914 the Turks concluded a secret military alliance with Germany and Austria and directed against Russia. The treaty called for the Turks to enter the war as soon as hostilities began between Russia and the Central Powers. With the approval of its allies, however, Turkey remained neutral until its military preparations were completed. General Liman von Sanders, who continued to head the German military mission in Turkey, urged the Turks to invade the Ukraine through Odessa and therefore possibly convince Rumania to enter the war against Russia. The Turks rejected that advice in favor of a campaign in the Caucasus.

26. Vorontsov-Dashkov, an old confidant of the tsar, served as viceroy of the Caucasus from 1905 to 1915.

Alexander Zachorovich Myshlaevsky (1856-) was army chief of staff in 1908-1909 and chief of the general staff from March to September 1909. He served as Dashkov's military deputy in 1913-1914.

Nicholas Nikolaevich Yudenich, a competent commander but poor politician, fought in the Russo-Japanese War, during which he was promoted to general. After the war he served on the general staff. He directed the Russian forces in the Causasus in 1914-1915 and again in 1917. After the Bolshevik revolution, Kolchak appointed him commander-in-chief of the White Army in the Baltic. When the Civil War ended, he fled to France.

27. In December 1914 savings deposited in savings banks totalled 29 million rubles compared to 700,000 rubles in December 1913; during the first two weeks of January 1915, deposits amounted to 15 million rubles as compared to 300,000 rubles in the same period a year earlier. (Oldenburg's note)

28. Lutz declared that "Germans who have lived in Russia always have considered her their mother and their homeland and they will, to the last man, lay down their lives for the dignity and honor of Great Russia." (Oldenburg's note)

29. The letters exchanged by the emperor and empress during the war were reprinted in 1970 as *The Nicky-Sunny Letters. Correspondence of the Tsar and Tsaritsa, 1914-1917* (Academic International Press). The AIP edition includes reprints of *The Letters of the Tsar to the Tsaritsa, 1914-1917*, trans. A.L. Hynes (London, 1929) and *The Letters of the Tsaritsa to the Tsar, 1914-1916* (London, 1923) from the Slovo edition first published in Berlin. (The empress's letters end shortly after the murder of Rasputin.) The letter quoted here was written on 25 September/8 October (*Letters of the Tsaritsa*, pp. 9-10).

The sovereigns always corresponded in English, though theirs was not always the "King's English." Moreover, it has suffered somewhat in transcription. Despite that, the letters are quoted here and below unedited and in the form that they reached the West.

30. Five Bolshevik deputies and [six] other individuals including the journalist L.B. Rosenfeld (Kamenev) were apprehended at a conference in Ozerki [a suburb of the capital] on 4 November 1914. An appeal to students adopted by the conference was undeniably defeatist in its message: "The grand ideas of Panslavism, of the liberation of peoples from the yoke of Germany and Austria and their subjugation to the authority of Russian *nagaikas* [whips], are patently scurrilous and loathsome. . . . Organize the masses, and prepare them for the revolution. Time marches on. The day draws nigh. Remember what happened after the Russo-Japanese War." Efforts to stage strikes to protest the trial of the SDs failed, and on 10 February they were sentenced to exile at hard labor. (Oldenburg's note)

Though arrested in a district of the capital under martial law and therefore subject to a court-martial and the death penalty (for conspiracy and treason), the Bolsheviks were tried before a civil court by order of the tsar. The five deputies were sentenced to exile at hard labor; five of the others received prison terms or exile, and one was released for lack of evidence. For the account of one of the deputies see Badmaev, *Bolsheviks in the Tsarist Duma*, pp. 204-42.

31. According to the head of the artillery department, state factories produced 600,000 rounds of shells per year, whereas the Stavka estimates in 1916 called for 42 million rounds. Although the war ministry underestimated its needs before the war (an error common to all countries), it also sought funds to increase its stores of ammunition. In 1912 the government appropriated 10 million rubles which increased the ammunition reserve for 3-inch guns by eight percent. At the beginning of the war the Russian army had about 1,000 rounds of ammunition for each 3-inch gun (the French had about 1,400 per gun.) Beside the enormous cost of increasing the stock of ammunition was the problem that ammunition stored for any length of time began to deteriorate. The fundamental problem, however, was that Russia lacked the industrial capacity to meet the unforeseen demands of the Great War.

General A.A. Manikovsky, *Boevoe snabzhenie russkoi armii v 1914-1918 g.g.* [The Armament and Ammunition Supply of the Russian Army in 1914-1918] (Moscow, 1922) cited in N.N. Golovin, *The Russian Army in World War I* (New Haven, 1931; reprint, 1969), pp. 38-41. See also B.E. Nolde, *Russia in the Economic War* (New Haven, 1928).

32. G.A. Bobrinsky, an aide-de-camp general, was an extreme right nationalist. The Russian persecution of Galicians actually was two-pronged. It was directed not only against the Ukrainian nationalists but also against the Uniates, who were forced to convert to Orthodoxy. The arrest of the widely-respected Uniate metropolitan did little to endear the conquerors to their new subjects.

33. Even after the revolution, reports in the press cast serious doubt on Miasoedov's guilt and implied that the entire affair was the result of a complex plot. See "Sud nad Miasoedovym (vpechatleniia ochevidtsa)" [The Miasoedov Trial (Impressions of a Witness)], *Arkhiv russkoi revoliutsii* [Archive of the Russian Revolution], XIV. Captain B., who had been a witness at the trial, maintained that no evidence of espionage was brought against Miasoedov but that he had been sentenced to death for looting. He had stolen two statuettes from an abandoned house in East Prussia. "But the crowd needed his death, just as the crowd in Moscow in 1812 needed the death of the son of the merchant Vereshchagin." (Oldenburg's note; and see above Chapter XVI, notes 13 and 14.)

34. Here the author refers to the Second Battle of the Masurian Lakes, also known as the Winter Battle of Masuria. The Austro-German strategy was a gigantic double envelopment of the Russian armies in Poland. The Austrians, stiffened by German troops, were to attack through the Carpathians while the Germans drove out of East Prussia. The Austrian offensive was a total failure. In the north, however, Hindenburg and Ludendorf enjoyed a measure of success. Their immediate objective was the Russian Tenth Army. The attack began on the 8th of February in a blinding snowstorm. The Russians were taken by surprise, forced back into the Forest of Augustow, and there nearly encircled. The Russian XX Corps was sacrificed so that the Tenth Army's other three corps could escape. The remnants of the XX Corps surrendered on 21 February. The Russians lost about 200,000 men, half of whom were captured. Despite its tactical success, the German assault produced only a slight strategic gain.

35. Italy declared war on Austria-Hungary on 23 May 1915 and on 21 August 1915 on Turkey. A year later (28 August 1916) Italy also declared war on Germany.

36. Golovin, *Russian Army* [pp. 220-21]. (Oldenburg's note)

37. Lavr Georgievich Kornilov (1870-1918), son of a minor government official (a former Cossack officer), rose from his obscure peasant origins to national fame and, after the February Revolution, to supreme command of the Russian armies. Kornilov was born in a Siberian garrison town. Largely through his own efforts he gained admission to the Siberian Cadet School and then to the Mikhailovsky Artillery School, where he earned his commission. After a tour of duty in Turkestan, he was recommended for appointment to the Nicholas Academy of the General Staff from which he emerged a captain in 1898. He returned to Turkestan and served with great distinction on the Afghan frontier. During the Russo-Japanese War he distinguished himself again at Mukden. From 1907 to 1911 he served as military attache in China. When the World War broke out, Kornilov was placed in command of a brigade on the Carpathian front. While covering the retreat of his division during the heavy fighting of 1915, he was wounded and captured. Imprisoned in Moldavia, he escaped in 1916 and as a result of his exploits became a national hero.

Because of his popularity and known sympathies for the revolution, he was given command of the Southwestern Front by the Provisional Government. Then from July to September 1917 he was commander of the Petrograd Military District and Commander in Chief of the Russian Army. After an alleged coup against the Kerensky regime, Kornilov was dismissed and imprisoned. Released in December 1917, he made his way to the south and with Alekseev and Kaledin organized the anti-Bolshevik Volunteer Army. He died on 13 April 1918 near Ekaterinodar when a shell blew up his headquarters. Richard Luckett, *The White Generals* (New York, 1971), pp. 61-64 ff.

38. Even the highest military circles were infected with the idea that some sort of "treachery" was responsible for the lack of ammunition. In a widely publicized speech in 1917, for example, General A.I. Denikin complained of the "rare thunder of my own artillery which treacherously had been deprived of ammunition." (Oldenburg's note)

Lieutenant-General Anton Ivanovich Denikin (1872-1947) was like Kornilov of common origins. His father, an emancipated serf, joined the army and eventually retired a major; his Polish mother was a housemaid. Denikin's only ambition was to be a soldier. When he came of age, he entered the army as a volunteer, earned a commission, and eventually attended the general staff college. He was totally dedicated to the army and the concept of service and utterly and unswervingly loyal to the ideal of the Russian Empire. His outspoken honesty frequently brought him into conflict with his superiors, particularly in the war ministry.

During the Civil War, Denikin succeeded Kornilov as commander of the Volunteer Army. After the defeat of his forces, he yielded his command to General Wrangel and left the country. He died in 1947 in Ann Arbor, Michigan. A.I. Denikin, *The White Army* (1930: reprint Academic International Press, 1973).

39. The Central War Industry Committee was to coordinate the work of War Industry Committees that were to be formed in every province. The central organization had the responsibility of determining the needs of the armed forces, establishing priorities, and directing the activities of the provincial committees. The Central War Industry Committee, the Union of Zemstvos, and the Union of Municipalities generally are referred to as the voluntary organizations.

40. In accepting the chairmanship of the Central War Industry Committee Guchkov did not conceal his concern that a major problem was to bring about political change. He had, he said, "a weakened and shaken confidence that our efforts might bear fruitful results . . . . Unless we manage to achieve certain goals, all our efforts, our sacrifices, our enthusiasm and devotion will fly up the chimney like smoke." (Oldenburg's note)

41. Miliukov indicated that the idea of a ministry of public confidence originated with the resolutions of the second congress of the Union of Zemstvos on 5 June: "Final victory can be assured only by a total exertion of all the national forces, given complete mutual trust between the government and the country." The congress urged "complete agreement of the people . . . [through] the Duma as the organ of the people's representatives, with the higher organs of State government." *Political Memoirs*, p. 322.

42. *Letters of the Tsar* (11/24 May 1915), p. 61.

43. The Statute on Field Administration, hastily adopted at the beginning of the war (29 July 1914), gave military authorities unlimited

control not only over the war zone but also over all military and related institutions in the rear. Thus all of western Russia including the capital came under military authority, as did Finland, Arkhangel, the Caucasus, and Vladivostok. The army was not responsible to any civil authority, including the ministers, and it was empowered to dismiss any local official regardless of whether he was locally elected or appointed by the central administration. The statute made no mention of the government. Only the ministers could communicate with and petition the military authorities, and the army generally preferred to operate without civilian interference. All the threads of this military dictatorship were concentrated in the hands of the chief of staff, Yanushkevich, who was peremptory and over-bearing in his dealings with the civil authorities.

44. Not to be confused with either A.P. or N.P. Ignatiev, Count Paul Nikolaevich Ignatiev (1870-1926) served as assistant minister of agriculture from 1912 to 1915 and as minister of education from January 1915 to December 1916.

45. Prince Nicholas Borisovich Shcherbatov (1868-1943), a moderate conservative, favored cooperation with the public as long as the leaders of public organizations did not press exorbitant demands. He was recommended for the post by Grand Duke Nicholas, who was impressed by Shcherbatov's abilities as director of the state stud farms (1913-1915).

46. Alexander Alekseevich Khvostov (1857-1922), a former associate of the prime minister, was Goremykin's nominee. Khvostov had served in the ministries of justice and interior since 1890. He was appointed to the Senate in 1906 and in 1912 to the State Council.

47. Alexander Dmitrievich Samarin (1869-1932), the scion of a famous Slavophile family, was deeply religious and strongly conservative. He had served as the elected marshal of the nobility of Moscow since 1908, as an appointed member of the State Council since 1912, and as a prominent Red Cross administrator since the beginning of the war. In 1906 Samarin had been offered but refused the post of director of the holy synod. One of his conditions of acceptance in 1915 seems to have been a guarantee that Rasputin would not interfere in the affairs of the church. At any rate, at the time of his appointment Rasputin left the capital for an extended visit to Siberia. Pares, *Fall of the Russian Monarchy*, pp. 247-48.

48. The appointment of General Alexis Andreevich Polivanov (1855-1922) to the head of the war ministry was urged by Grand Duke Nicholas and, as Oldenburg notes, it was a popular move. Although Polivanov was a competent administrator, his popularity stemmed in large part from his opposition to Sukhomlinov. Polivanov served as chief of the general staff in 1905-1906 and as assistant war minister from 1906 to 1912, when at Sukhomlinov's urging he was dismissed and appointed to the State Council. After the revolution, Polivanov remained in Russia as an advisor to the Red Army and as a military consultant to the Soviet government during the negotiations with Poland in 1920.

49. Golovin estimated that during the first year of the war the Russian army suffered 2,620,000 casualties (killed and wounded) and that 1,740,000 soldiers were captured—more than half of its losses during the entire war. The ratio of casualties to prisoners was about 3:2, a fact

which Golovin attributed to the war of movement (in contrast to the trench warfare that followed) and to the relatively inferior leadership of Yanushkevich compared to Alekseev. *Russian Army*, p. 98.

50. At the cabinet meeting of 6 August 1915 General Polivanov informed the ministers that "the commander of the Kovno fortress, General Grigoriev, frightened by the thunder of heavy German artillery, abandoned his post so rapidly and moved so far under the protection of our spaces that for the past few days he cannot be found anywhere. At the moment the gendarmes are searching for him in the rear, in order to deliver him to a court martial especially ordered by the Grand Duke . . . ." *Prologue to Revolution: Notes of A.N. Iakhontov on the Secret Meetings of the Council of Ministers, 1915*, ed. Michael Cherniavsky (Garden City, 1967), p. 76. Yakhontov's notes and summaries appeared originally in the *Arkhiv russkoi revoliutsii*, 17 (1926): 15-136.

51. Sergei Vasilievich Rukhlov (1853-1918) had served as minister of communications since 1909. One of the dark reactionaries of the old regime, he had been a member of the rightist bloc of the State Council since 1905. In 1908 Rukhlov founded the All-Russian National Union, a reactionary anti-semitic organization. In recognition of his services he was named His Majesty's State Secretary for 1912.

52. Cherniavsky's edition of Yakhontov's notes on the cabinet meetings (above, note 50) does not include the meeting of 16 July 1915, which Polivanov opened with the declaration that "the fatherland is in danger."

53. The cabinet meeting of 24 July 1915. [Yakhontov], *Prologue to Revolution*, p. 25.

54. Although the point was valid, Krivoshein made the statement earlier in July in connection with another matter. Like most of the other ministers he opposed the tsar's decision and joined them in trying to dissuade him.

55. General-Adjutant Michael Vasilievich Alekseev (1857-1918) was reputedly the army's best strategist, and Grand Duke Nicholas originally wanted him as his chief of staff. The tsar insisted, however, that the grand duke retain Sukhomlinov's nominee, Yanushkevich.

Alekseev was a graduate of the Nicholas Academy and a veteran of the Russo-Turkish War. During the Russo-Japanese War, he served as quartermaster general (operations chief) of the Third Army. In 1914-1915 as chief of staff of the Southwestern Front under N.Y. Ivanov, he directed the conquest of Galicia. The army welcomed his appointment as Stavka chief of staff, which meant that though nominally subordinate to the tsar he was the effective commander of the Russian armies. Modest, capable, and a tireless worker despite poor health (apparently cancer), Alekseev held the Eastern Front together for a year and a half.

In February 1917 the Provisional Government made Alekseev the commander in chief of the Russian armies, but unable to check the disintegration of the army or the front, he was replaced in May 1917. After the October Revolution, Alekseev formed the Volunteer Army. He died in southern Russia in October 1918.

56. Michael Katkov has analyzed the cabinet's illogical position in *Russia 1917*, pp. 198-217.

57. On 31 August 1914 the name of the capital was changed from the Germanic "Sankt-Peterburg" to the Russian "Petrograd."

58. Goremykin's reference to "influences" was in response to Prince Shcherbatov who argued that the tsar's decision would be attributed to "the influence of the notorious Rasputin." These remarks were recorded by Yakhontov during the cabinet meeting of 6 August 1915. *Prologue to Revolution*, pp. 77-82.

59. The different conceptions of loyalty within the cabinet were elaborated still more during the meeting of 21 August. Kharitonov tried to draw a distinction between service to the tsar and service to Russia, to which Goremykin replied: "In my conception, these ideas are inseparable. Here is the root of our discord." Sazonov then declared that "we can sacrifice everything for the Tsar except our conscience," and Samarin added: "The Russian Tsar requires the service of thinking men, not a slavish execution of orders. The Tsar can punish us, but we must tell him the truth. We could never forgive ourselves our silence at a time when the fate of the motherland is at stake."

Goremykin denied that it was a question of "slavish obedience. My opinion amounts to the fact that the will of the Tsar is the will of Russia . . . and that we owe obedience to this will . . . . In my understanding of the essence of the Russian monarchy, the will of the Tsar must be obeyed like commands of the Gospel."

In that case, Sazonov concluded, "the only alternative is to drown oneself."

60. On 18 June 1915 the government created "The Special Council to Coordinate Measures for National Defense," a blue-ribbon panel to coordinate the efforts of the government and unofficial organizations in provisioning the army. Its membership consisted of the minister of war (president), the chairman of the State Duma and nine deputies, the chairman of the State Council and nine councillors, seven other ministers (navy, commerce and industry, finance, interior, agriculture, transportation, and the state controller), heads of various departments in the war ministry, representatives of industry, and representatives of the Union of Zemstvos, the Union of Municipalities, and the Central War Industry Committee.

Following the pattern of the Special Council for National Defense, three other Special Councils were created at the same time: for Transportation (under the presidency of the minister of transportation), for Fuel (under the presidency of the minister of commerce and industry), and for Food Supply (under the presidency of the minister of agriculture). In order to coordinate the activities of these various councils, the law provided for the convening of special conferences to be chaired by the minister of war.

The creation of this cumbersome structure seemed a tacit admission of the inability of the government to cope with the demands of war and of the public's lack of confidence in the bureaucracy. Public participation in these quasi-governmental organizations exposed the nooks and crannies of much of the state administration to public scrutiny—a radical departure for any government.

The operations of the various special councils can be traced in several of the volumes of the Carnegie series, "The Economic and Social

History of the World War," all by Yale University Press: A.Y. Astrov, *The Municipal Government and the All-Russian Union of Towns* and P. Gronsky, *The Central Government*, both in the single volume titled *The War and the Russian Government* (1929); S.A. Zagorsky, *State Control of Industry in Russia during the War* (1928); T.J. Polner, Prince V.A. Obolensky, and S.P. Turin, *Russian Local Government During the War* (1930); and P.B. Struve, *Food Supply in Russia During the World War* (1930).

CHAPTER NINETEEN

1. General-Adjutant Alexis Ermolovich Evert (1857-1917) commanded the Western Front from August 1915 to April 1917. His previous service included a tour as chief of the army main staff (1906-1908), and when the war broke out he was serving as governor-general of Irkutsk.

2. The Russian delegation included the Bolsheviks Lenin and Zinoviev, the Mensheviks Martov and Axelrod, and the Socialist Revolutionaries Natanson and Chernov. Trotsky attended as a representative of the *Nashe slovo* group. The other Social Democrats were the Latvian Jan Berzin, Karl Radek who represented "Poland," and Christian Rakovsky representing "the Balkans." (Oldenburg's note)

3. A translation of the program of the Progressive Bloc can be found in Golder, *Documents*, pp. 34-36.

4. Goremykin told the council of ministers that "the tone and essence of the letter is so indecent that I have no intention of responding to it." The other ministers agreed. (Oldenburg's note)

5. The texts of the two resolutions appear in Golder, *Documents*, pp. 149-52.

6. Major-General Sir Alfred Knox (1870-) was the British military attache in Russia from 1911 to 1918. His experiences were recorded in *With the Russian Army, 1914-1917*, 2 vols. (New York, 1921).

7. In its article on the World War the *Encyclopaedia Britannica* (14th ed.) admitted that "the Allies did little to repay Russia for the sacrifices that she made for them in 1914." (Oldenburg's note)

8. An exact count of the refugees never was made, but estimates ran as high as six million. The Tatiana Committee (named for the grand duchess) registered 3,306,051 persons, but great numbers of refugees did not seek the committee's assistance and therefore were not counted. (Oldenburg's note)

9. Alexander Feodorovich Trepov (1862-1926), the younger brother of Dmitry and Vladimir, was generally respected as an honest conservative and capable administrator. A graduate of His Majesty's Corp of Pages, he entered the ministry of interior in 1899. In 1905-1906 he served on the special commission that drafted the plan of the State Duma. He was appointed to the Senate in 1906 and in 1914 to the State Council where he joined the group of rightists. He became the last minister of communications of the imperial government in November 1915.

10. Alexander Nikolaevich Volzhin (1862-) spent most of his career as an administrator in the western provinces. In 1913 he became governor

of Kholm and in the following year director of the department of general affairs of the ministry of interior. Volzhin, who was A.N. Khvostov's candidate, agreed to head the holy synod provided that he did not have to deal with Rasputin. Before long the empress was complaining about him, and in August 1916 he was retired to the State Council and replaced by one of Rasputin's lackeys.

11. Nicholas Nikolaevich Pokrovsky (1865-1930) spent most of his career in capable and honorable service in the ministry of finance. As an assistant minister since 1906, he had been a close associate of Kokovtsov. He held the post of state comptroller from January to November 1916, when he succeeded Sazonov as foreign minister. Pokrovsky was respected by liberals and conservatives, and even the empress described him as "a known Left—their nicest, luckily" (17 March 1916).

12. Nicholas Ivanovich Astrov, a prominent Moscow liberal, was a member of the Moscow municipal duma and the provincial zemstvo assembly.

13. The meetings of the Bloc have been reconstructed from the notes of Paul Miliukov published in *Krasnyi arkhiv*, vols. 50-51 and 52. (Oldenburg's note) See *KA* 50-51 (1932): 117-60; 52 (1932): 143-96: and 56 (1933): 80-135. The first segment (1932) lists the members of each faction of the Progressive Bloc.

14. The Austro-German attack on Serbia began on 6/19 September and Bulgarian mobilization was announced on 8/21 September. On 1/14 October Russia delivered an ultimatum to Bulgaria. It was rejected on 5/18 October, and Russia promptly severed diplomatic relations. The Bulgarians waited until they were certain of Austro-German assistance before attacking Serbia on 14/27 October. England and France declared war on Bulgaria on 15/28 and 16/29 October. The Russian declaration of war followed two days later. For details of the Balkan negotiations and the spread of the war see Smith, *Russian Struggle for Power*, pp. 282-340.

15. On 30 October 1915 Aristide Briand (1862-1932) became prime minister and minister of foreign affairs, succeeding Viviani and Delcassé. That was Briand's fifth ministry. During his entire public career he held 25 ministerial portfolios and headed eleven governments, the first in 1909 and the last in 1929.

16. Michael Katkov, whose more recent work has extended Oldenburg's general outline, attributed the alleged reactionary conspiracy to conclude a separate peace to liberal politicians in the Duma and the voluntary organizations. It became the central theme of their propaganda from the Moscow congresses of September 1915 to the revolution of February 1917. Russian liberals and radicals originally claimed that the government could not win the war without them. In 1915 they realized that they had stumbled into an awkward position, especially if the war did end in victory. Consequently, to maintain their pressure for a ministry of public confidence and to keep alive their goal of a liberal constitutional monarchy, they began to allege that reactionaries in the court and government were not working for victory but rather that they were secretly preparing to betray the Allies through a separate peace with Germany. Katkov noted that no evidence to appear since the war has

indicated any substance to the liberal allegations. Moreover, the Provisional Government's own inquest in 1917 clearly revealed "that great as the shortcomings, corruption and decrepitude of the regime may have been, there was no such thing as a German party or even a defeatist movement among the Tsarist bureaucracy, not even among the shady characters who were trying to push themselves into positions of favour and influence at court." *Russia 1917*, pp. 220-30; quoted, pp. 225-26.

17. Kuzma Antonovich Gvozdev (1883-), a Menshevik, subsequently became minister of labor in the Provisional Government (September-October 1917) and served in the Soviet administration after the revolution.

18. General Zhilinsky to General Alekseev, 8/21 December 1915, *Mezhdunarodnoe otnosheniia*, IX. (Oldenburg's note)

19. Stürmer's appointment came as a complete surprise (as the emperor intended) for even though he was well into his fifth decade of imperial service, his career had given little evidence of any capacity for leadership. But despite his lack of distinction, he was not unknown. As governor of Yaroslavl from 1896 to 1902, he had gained a reputation as a reactionary and as a less than honest administrator. He became Plehve's assistant in 1902, and as director of the interior ministry's department of general affairs he illegally disbanded the duly elected but liberal provincial zemstvo assembly of Tver. Following Plehve's assassination, Stürmer was appointed to the State Council, and he served there for more than a decade practically unnoticed as a member of the rightist group.

That Stürmer owed his appointment to Rasputin and the empress is beyond question. On 7 January 1916, for example, she urged the tsar that "Stürmer would do for a bit, & then later on if you ever want to find another you can change him . . . he very much values Gregory [Rasputin] wh. is a great thing." Stürmer took his orders from the empress and did not deal directly with Rasputin. His contact with the starets was through a thoroughly unscrupulous character, I.F. Manasevich-Manuilov, a former police spy and swindler who aspired to become Rasputin's sole agent for dealing with members of the government. (Manuilov prospered briefly in 1916 but was arrested in 1917 and executed by the Bolsheviks in 1918.) Rasputin once boasted: "I begat Pitirim [the metropolitan of Petrograd] and Pitirim begat Stürmer, but it was Manuilov who recommended Stürmer to Pitirim and brought them together."

Historians generally treat Stürmer's replacement of Goremykin as the beginning of the end.

20. In *Russian Local Government during the War and the Union of Zemstvos*. (Oldenburg's note; see above Chapter XVIII, note 60.)

21. The Zemgor—*Zemsko-Gorodskoi Soiuz*—was a joint committee of the Union of Zemstvos and the Union of Municipalities founded on 10 July 1915 to coordinate activities "for the supply of the army."

22. As of 1 January 1916 the Union of Zemstvos had received state subsidies in the amount of 115 million rubles; the Union of Municipalities received 32 million. Therefore, from January to August 1916 the government allocated an additional 317 million rubles (including 93 million rubles to the municipal dumas of Petrograd and Moscow). Stürmer's

government in other words generously supported the voluntary organizations. (Oldenburg's note)

23. According to Yakhontov's record, the Central War Industry Committee at the insistence of its chairman, Alexander Guchkov, obtained permission to add a surcharge of a maximum of one percent of the cost of defense orders which it placed and to apply those funds to its own needs. (Oldenburg's note)

24. Oldenburg originally assigned this survey to a footnote (Vol. II, pp. 193-95) but for the reader's convenience and because of its importance to the author's argument we have incorporated it into the text. The dates are those of the sovereigns' letters.

25. See, however, the empress's letter of 13 November 1915 and the postscript to her second letter of 15 November 1915.

26. Anna Aleksandrovna Vyrubova (1884-), confidante of the empress and a woman completely under the influence of Rasputin, gave a quite different version of the telegram in her memoirs: "Let Papa not plan war for with war will come the end of Russia and yourselves and you will lose to the last man." *Memories of the Russian Court* (New York, 1923), p. 104.

27. Khvostov dumped the job on Beletsky and his crony Kommissarov, probably with the idea of nailing the responsibility on them later. The two policemen knew that they were being set up, however, and tried to foist the job onto each other. Beletsky recounted their amusing efforts in testimony before the Provisional Government's investigating commission, and Pares has summarized them: S.P. Beletsky, *Padenie tsarskogo rezhima*, IV, pp. 335-420; A.N. Khvostov, ibid., I, pp. 7-51; and Pares, *Fall of the Russian Monarchy*, pp. 309-14.

28. In his history of the war on the Eastern Front Winston Churchill said this of Sukhomlinov: "For five years he had laboured to improve the Russian Army . . . . He was certainly the scapegoat of disaster. There is no doubt that the Russian Army of 1914 was incomparably superior to that which fought the Manchurian War." *The World Crisis*, VI, pp. 91-92. (Oldenburg's note)

29. The formal charges against Sukhomlinov cited him for malfeasance, corruption, and treason. Although he was indiscreet in his choice of associates and wont to babble confidential information, he clearly was not guilty of treason. And although he was an Olympian misfit, incompetence was never and nowhere a crime for public officials. The worst to be proved against the former war minister was that he used his position for private gain. A Russian bank closely tied to military contractors earned Sukhomlinov some 700,000 rubles in stock market speculations and then used that influence to obtain more lucrative government contracts. Sukhomlinov's wife had expensive tastes and habits.

Six months after the tsar's intercession, the liberals carried their charade to its conclusion. In April 1917 the Provisional Government rearrested Sukhomlinov, convicted him on charges of treason, and sentenced him to life imprisonment at hard labor. In 1918, however, the Bolsheviks provided the ironical anti-climax to the saga by releasing him. Sukhomlinov left the country and died a free man in Germany in 1926.

30. Édouard Herriot (1872-1957), a noted writer and statesman, was one of the principal leaders of the French Radical Socialists. Mayor of Lyons, he held posts in several governments and between 1924 and 1932 headed three ministries. He later served as president of the Chamber of Deputies and then (until 1954) of the National Assembly.

31. Alexis Alekseevich Brusilov (1853-1926), a general of cavalry, served in the Russo-Turkish War (1877-1878) but apparently not the Japanese War. In 1912-1913 he was troop commander in the Warsaw Military District, and from the outbreak of the war until March 1916 he commanded the Eighth Army (Southwestern Front) which formed the southern flank of the Russian front. In May 1917 the Provisional Government appointed him to succeed Alekseev as supreme commander in chief, but in July he gave way to Kornilov. Brusilov joined the Red Army in 1920 and took part in the Polish and Ukrainian campaigns of 1920 and 1921. He served as inspector of cavalry from 1923 to 1924, when he was appointed to the revolutionary military council.

32. The battle of Verdun, the first great struggle waged in the West under the desperate strategy of attrition, raged for six months from February to August 1916. Though it did not change the configuration of the front in any important way, Verdun succeeded nobly in its aim of slaughter: the French lost nearly 550,000 men and the Germans about 430,000. The Allied victory on the Somme—the reconquest of about 250 square miles of sacred French mud—was the worst conceived and most stupidly conducted campaign of the war. The Allies lost 600,000 men, about two-thirds of them British, including the cream of the Regular Army; German casualties numbered around 400,000.

Brusilov's victories were won mainly in June, when the Russians penetrated the Austrian front by as much as 60 miles. The Germans then sent reinforcements to prevent an Austrian collapse. Stavka, meanwhile, decided to allow Brusilov to make the main effort (a general offensive had been planned). Russia, however, lost the race to reinforce the front. Brusilov slugged away through August and September at great cost and to no avail. Finally on 7/20 September the Brusilov offensive—Russia's last major effort in the war—collapsed from exhaustion. Russian casualties, some 350,000 by July, mounted to over 1,000,000 by September. The Russians captured about 350,000 men, mostly Austrians, and Austro-German casualties numbered about 250,000.

33. Russian gold transfers to England during the war totaled about 700 million rubles. (Oldenburg's note)

34. Jacob H. Schiff (1847-1920) became head of the Wall Street investment banking firm of Kuhn, Loeb & Co. in 1885. During the Russo-Japanese War, he tried to enlist Jewish bankers to exert financial pressure on Russia in order to compel the imperial government to ease its restrictions on Jews. When that failed, he actively promoted the sale of Japanese bonds in America.

35. Actually the position of Jews in Russia improved considerably during the war. The government abolished all quotas for Jews who served in the war and their relatives, and general mobilization practically meant a complete revocation of the quota system. On 14 March 1916 Professor Levashov told the Duma that of 586 students enrolled

in their first year of medicine at Odessa University 340 were Jews. Jewish refugees, moreover, were permitted to settle outside the Jewish Pale. (Oldenburg's note)

36. Schiff and the senior J.P. Morgan (1837-1913) were old rivals. In 1901 Schiff and E.H. Harriman had engaged Morgan and J.J. Hill in a celebrated struggle for control of the Northern Pacific Railroad. John Pierpont Morgan II (1867-1943) succeeded on the death of his father to the head of the firm.

37. On 5 November 1916 the Central Powers formally proclaimed the "Kingdom of Poland" but limited its territory to the boundaries formerly held by Russia. Austria opposed the move but was by then without an independent voice in Germanic affairs. Berlin took the step in an unsuccessful attempt to raise a Polish army.

The French government meanwhile, in response to strong domestic pressure, was urging Russia to proclaim Poland's independence. The Russian position was that Poland did not constitute an international question. Russia was willing to allow France and England complete freedom to determine Germany's western frontiers in return for the same consideration in the East.

38. The author's account omits a few relevant details: The emperor summoned Sazonov to Mogilev on 28 June/11 July 1916 in order to discuss the disposition of Poland. Much to Stürmer's consternation, Nicholas approved Sazonov's plan for Polish autonomy and ordered him to prepare a manifesto. At that point the foreign minister went off to Finland for a few days' rest. Meanwhile the empress, prodded by Rasputin and Stürmer, both of whom opposed concessions to the Poles, began to intervene. On 3/16 July Stürmer went to Mogilev to urge Sazonov's dismissal and a reversal of the decision. On 7 July the empress herself journeyed to Stavka for a previously scheduled visit. Three days later Sazonov learned that he was fired. The projected manifesto was not issued, but on 28 July Nicholas assured the Russian Poles that he still intended to fulfill the promises of 1914. Less than two months later the tsar informed King George V that he intended to proclaim Poland's autonomy. Thus reasons other than policy seem to have determined Sazonov's downfall. For more on Oldenburg's treatment of Sazonov see below, note 50.

Stürmer, *Padenie tsarskogo rezhima*, V, p. 181; "Dnevnik Ministerstva inostrannykh del za 1915-1916 gg." [Diary of the Ministry of Foreign Affairs for 1915-1916], *Krasnyi arkhiv*, 31 (1929): 67-69; Sazonov, *Fateful Years*, pp. 312-14; and Maurice Paleologue, *La Russie des Tsars pendant la grand guerre*, 3 vols. (Paris, 1921), II, pp. 291-310.

39. For an account of the intrigues that apparently led to this turn of the ministerial carousel see Pares, *Fall of the Russian Monarchy*, pp. 341-43.

40. The Allied governments initially were fearful that the change of ministers foretold a new foreign policy receptive to a separate peace. Those misgivings soon were dispelled in foreign capitals but not, unfortunately, in Russia where the opposition believed or alleged that the German Stürmer was a pawn of the *nemka*, that "German woman"—the empress—and was working for a separate peace. The Allies quickly

found that Stürmer's ambition made him easier to deal with than Sazonov. Oldenburg's unjust characterization of Sazonov's alleged feeble defense of Russian interests was better suited to the vain and vacuous Stürmer. An anecdote recounted by Paleologue, the French ambassador, is illustrative: During one of his meetings in Stürmer's office, he noticed three pictures that had not been there before. They portrayed the three great European congresses of the nineteenth century—Vienna (1815), Paris (1856), and Berlin (1878). Pointing to a fourth place still empty, Stürmer said: "That is the place that I am reserving for the picture of the next congress which, if God listens to me, will be called the Congress of Moscow." *La Russie des Tsars,* III, p. 34. British ambassador Buchanan later wrote that Stürmer's appointment "first caused me to take a really serious view of the *internal* situation." *My Mission to Russia,* II, p. 18. See also Pares, *Fall of the Russian Monarchy,* pp. 345-47; and Smith, *Russian Struggle for Power,* pp. 405, 409-11.

41. Buchanan's dispatches indicate that he was more astute than to suspect a change in policy. Bulatsel was reprimanded because his article insulted the King of England by suggesting that he was a Freemason and thus by implication a revolutionary. Buchanan, *My Mission to Russia,* II, pp. 20-21.

42. Polivanov was dismissed on 13 March, the date of publication of a confidential report to the State Duma on a strike at the Putilov Works. The emperor believed that Polivanov had erred in granting permission for the report to be published. The emperor's letter to Polivanov also noted his displeasure at the close relations between the war minister and the war industry committees (headed by Guchkov): "The latter's activities do not inspire my confidence, and in my view your leadership in those matters has not been sufficiently authoritative." (Oldenburg's note)

43. By October 1916 Russia had mobilized 14,648,000 men. (Oldenburg's note) Golovin, the author's apparent source, reported that figure as of December 1916. *Russian Army,* p. 49.

44. Golovin, citing data from Mendeleyev's *K poznaniiu Rossii,* noted that only about 25 percent of Russia's population was productively employed. The average producer, therefore, supported nearly four (3.75) persons, including himself. The rural census of 1917 indicated little change in the ratio. In comparison about 40 percent of the German and French populations were productively employed. The military implication was that "the smaller the percentage of the population engaged in the productive work the greater is the economic disruption brought about by a mobilization in time of war." Ibid., pp. 15-17.

45. Protopopov was alleged to have discussed a separate peace with Warburg in Stockholm. Evidence available at the time indicated that the charge was untrue, and material available after the war confirmed its falsity. See Katkov, *Russia 1917,* pp. 108-19, and for a survey of works on the general question of a separate peace see the bibliographic note, pp. 579-81.

46. As of 1 November 1916 Russia held 1,737,000 Austrians, 159,000 Germans, and 65,000 Turks. There were, of course, practically no prisoners taken in 1917. (Oldenburg's note)

47. Those figures most likely were underestimated because they reflected only average monthly production. Golovin indicated that 3-inch shell production expanded from 50,000 per month before the war to two million per month, or 40 times as many. (Oldenburg's note)

48. *The World Crisis*, III (1), pp. 102-3.

49. With the Oletsk Railway, which was completed before the war, the Murmansk route was 1,440 kilometers [nearly 900 miles]. Oldenburg's note)

50. The Straits Agreement, ably negotiated by Sazonov in March-April 1915, was accepted definitively in a French note of 10 April (28 March) 1915. It seems quite improbable that the author erred by more than a year in dating a matter of such momentous concern to Russia. One must conclude that Oldenburg tampered with the chronology in order to minimize Sazonov's accomplishments and justify his dismissal by the tsar.

The Straits Agreement came into effect through an exchange of notes. In return for Russian sovereignty over Constantinople and the Straits, Russia promised England that the Straits would remain open to commerce and that a free port would be available at Constantinople. The city itself was to be governed by three civilian Allied high commissioners. The French, somewhat less forthcoming, held open the possibility of a future neutralization of the entire zone. To obtain this agreement Russia in effect yielded any possibility of absorbing Persia, and it consigned Syria, Palestine, and a substantial part of Armenia to French influence. The agreement remained secret until late 1916 for reasons discussed below in Chapter XX.

The course of the negotiation is summarized in Smith, *The Russian Struggle for Power*, pp. 217-38, with the principal documentation in Adamov, *Konstantinopol i prolivy*, I, pp. 251-85.

51. By 1 January 1917 domestic loans had raised a little over 10 billion rubles; foreign loans stood at slightly under 7 billion: 1 billion in France, 5.5 billion in England, and the rest in the United States, Japan, and Italy. (Oldenburg's note)

52. "One senses vague feelings of dissatisfaction everywhere, among the Parisian populace and in the Chambers," observed President Poincaré in November 1916. (Oldenburg's note, from the text)

53. Prince Vsevolod Nikolaevich Shakovskoy (1874-1954) entered the state administration in 1910 and served as minister of commerce and industry from February 1915 until the fall of the monarchy.

54. In January 1916 Stürmer applied for permission to change his name to Panin, an illustrious family in Russia's past. The emperor would not grant the petition unless the surviving Panins gave their consent, and they evidently refused. *Letters of the Tsar*, 5 January 1916.

CHAPTER TWENTY

1. From Guchkov's testimony before the supreme commission of inquiry of the Provisional Government, 2 August 1917. [*Padenie tsarskogo rezhima*, VI, pp. 248-79.] (Oldenburg's note)

2. Churchill, *World Crisis*, VI, pp. 376-77.

3. Further details appear in S.P. Melgunov's *Na putiakh k dvotsovomu perevorotu* [On the Roads to a Palace Revolution] (Paris, 1931), pp. 180-98. (Oldenburg's note) The existence of a Masonic plot forms the principal theme of Katkov's *Russia 1917.*

4. Miliukov specifically charged that Manuilov, arrested by order of A.A. Khvostov for accepting a bribe, had been freed by Stürmer acting in behalf of himself and other associates of Rasputin. At the time Manuilov was serving as Stürmer's personal secretary. Later, on 23 December 1916, the empress wrote to the tsar: "On Manuilov paper I beg you to write 'discontinue the case' and send it to Minister of Justice—an ugly story got up by others to harm Our Friend, Pitirim, etc." Four days after that the tsar sent the following message to the minister of justice: "I order you to discontinue the Manuilov case and not allow it to come to trial."

An expurgated version of Miliukov's speech of 1/14 November 1916 can be found in Golder, *Documents*, pp. 154-66; quoted, p. 157 n. 16.

5. One of the Duma's contributions to the war effort was to prohibit the use of the German language in its proceedings.

6. The remark subsequently was attributed to D.S. Shuvaev, the war minister. (Oldenburg's note)

7. Miliukov himself already had recognized the logic of that position. On 4 March 1916 he told the Duma: "I do not know whether the government will lead us to defeat . . . . But I do know for certain that a Russian revolution inevitably will sweep us to defeat . . . . If I were told that to organize Russia for victory meant to organize her for revolution, I would say: better then to leave her as she is—disorganized—for the duration of the war." (Oldenburg's note)

8. In an effort to bring Greece into the war the Entente, led by France, recognized a republican provisional government at Saloniki, which on 23 November 1916 declared war on Bulgaria and Germany. Meanwhile the Entente also demanded that the Greek government of King Constantine I expel the Central Powers' representatives from Athens and surrender all of its war material. When Athens refused, French and British forces landed at Piraeus; on 8 December Paris and London demanded the complete withdrawl of royalist forces from Thessaly, and a week later Constantine submitted.

Empress Alexandra Feodorovna meanwhile urged the tsar to save "Cousin Tino," and Russian representations in Paris led the French to withdraw their insistence on Constantine's abdication. In June 1917, however, without the protection of the Romanovs Constantine was forced to abdicate in favor of his second son, Alexander (1917-1920). In 1920 Constantine returned to the throne but in 1922 again was forced to abdicate, and he died in exile in the following year.

9. *Nachalo*, a Parisian emigre paper, wrote on 12 October 1916: "Since the Russian press is not subjected to the same censorship that daily mutilates the columns of *Nachalo*, the various editions of the Russian press that reach us afford some idea of what is going on in our homeland. We are, of course, not so audacious as to print in the pages

of our Paris edition the news and views of the Moscow, Samara, Kiev, or Tomsk press. What is permitted in the barbarous meridian of Tomsk is totally incompatible with the temperament of the censor here in the land of four revolutions and "The Rights of Man and the Citizen." (Oldenburg's note)

10. Miliukov, *Padenie tsarskogo rezhima*, VI, pp. 343-47. (Oldenburg's note)

11. The tsar also indicated that Stürmer was coming to Stavka on the following day "and I will give him leave for the present. As to the future, we shall see; we will talk it over when you come here."

12. The Straits agreements, concluded a year and a half earlier, had remained secret although their existence was suspected and had been hinted at (see above, Chapter XIX, note 49). The British and French urged Stürmer to make the announcement during the fall, but because of the Rumanian collapse the moment seemed inopportune. The German declaration of Polish independence in the first week of November made some response almost imperative. Finally it was decided that Stürmer should confound his critics by opening the Duma on 1/14 November with a simultaneous announcement of the Straits agreements and Polish autonomy. However, at the last moment he lost his nerve.

13. Purishkevich described himself as "the most extreme of the Rights." An abbreviated translation of his two-hour speech appears in Golder, *Documents*, pp. 166-75.

14. A.F. Kerensky, "Nichto o demagogii" [A Word on Demagoguery], *Severnye zapiski*, January 1917. (Oldenburg's note)

15. By way of explanation Markov declared that he deliberately berated Rodzianko, because the Duma's rostrum allowed speakers to insult high personnages with impunity. "Through the person of your chairman, who is partisan and dishonest, I intended to insult you," he shouted at the Duma majority. (Oldenburg's note)

16. Barclay de Tolly's Scottish ancestors settled in Russia in the seventeenth century, but during the Napoleonic invasion of 1812 the Russian nobility clamored for command of the army to be given to "a real Russian." Consequently, in August the tsar replaced Barclay with Michael Kutuzov. Kutuzov followed the original strategy of withdrawal before the French armies but under pressure made one bloody stand at Borodino. Barclay fought under Kutuzov and retained his post as war minister. When Kutuzov died in 1813, Barclay resumed command of the Russian army, which he led into Paris in 1815.

17. N.A. Maklakov, shot by the Bolsheviks in 1918, was one of the few former ministers who had the courage to defend the government before the Provisional Government's investigating commission. "Forgive me," he said, "but I do not understand how my views were in opposition to the people. It was my understanding that as long as the old system functioned properly the people were relatively well off . . . . I had no idea that Russia was collapsing until the very end, for on the contrary it was my impression that the country was progressing and thriving under the very system that existed until recently and is now changed. Never could I agree that that system dug a grave for Russia or her future." *Padenie tsarskogo rezhima*, III, p. 97. (Oldenburg's note)

18. See the text of the resolution in Golder, *Documents*, pp. 177-78.

19. On 16 December 1916 in the Duma Miliukov, assuming that Protopopov would be dismissed soon, turned to a discussion of Trepov: "Those people cannot talk to us—we have no common language . . . . Their phenomenal pomposity and their phenomenal ignorance place them outside of Russia . . . . Behind the desk of the chairman of the council of ministers sits that very Trepov who, with Stürmer, rejected Sazonov's plan for Poland." (Oldenburg's note)

20. The German peace overture of December 1916 was intended mainly to influence American opinion. The principal documentary source is: André Scherer and Jacques Grunewald, eds., *L'Allemagne et les problèmes de la paix pendant la premiere guerre mondiale. Documents extraits des archives de l'Office allemand des Affaires étrangeres*, Vol. I: *Des origines a la déclaration de la guerre sous-marine a outrance (août 1914-janvier 1917)* (Paris, 1962).

21. *Golos minuvshago* [Voice of the Past], 1926, No. 2, quoted M.A. Reiss (who as chairman of the "Political Red Cross" interviewed Protopopov shortly before his execution by a Bolshevik firing squad) to the effect that the former interior minister advised the emperor in December 1916 to notify the Allies that Russia could endure no more than a few more months of war and that that time should be devoted to the negotiation of a general peace. Except for Protopopov's own statement, no record of his advice has appeared in materials discovered and published by the Soviet regime. (Oldenburg's note)

22. A complete translation of the text of the tsar's address appears in Golder, *Documents*, pp. 51-53.

23. The "difficult days" referred apparently to the tsaritsa's successful battle to retain Protopopov. The tsar's letter, dated 4 December 1916, was written on the train returning him to Mogilev.

24. See, for example, the empress's letter of 13 December 1916, essentially a frenzied tirade against Trepov but also containing the revealing admonition: "Don't hide things from me—I am strong—but listen to me, wh. means our Friend & trust us through all—& beware of Trepov . . . ."

25. Prince Felix Feliksovich Yusupov (the younger) (1887-) was sole heir to the largest fortune in Russia. The wealth of the Yusupov's, estimated to be as much as half a billion dollars in 1913, exceeded that of the Romanov's. Young Prince Yusupov led a useless life of debauchery and was a frequent visitor to Rasputin's apartment. The elder Yusupovs, Prince Felix Feliksovich and Princess Zinaida, were convinced of the existence of a powerful German camarilla around the imperial family. Earlier in 1916 the empress had banished Zinaida from court, where once she had been a dazzling fixture.

The numerous descriptions of Rasputin's murder depend on the testimony of two of the principals: Prince Felix Youssoupoff, *Rasputin* (1927) and *Lost Splendor* (London, 1953) and Vladimir Pourichkevitch [Purishkevich], *Comme j'ai tué Raspoutine* (Paris, 1953). On the Yusupov's relations with the empress see Katkov, *Russia 1917*, pp. 273-80.

26. Rasputin was buried secretly on 21 December in one of the remote precincts of Tsarskoe Selo where Anna Vyrubova was building a

chapel. His mourners included the tsar's family and a few trusted friends. The body was entombed with an icon signed by the imperial family and a letter written by the empress beseeching his intercession. Shortly after the overthrow of the monarchy, the corpse was exhumed and apparently burned. An Associated Press correspondent who visited the site in March 1917 observed graffiti scrawled on the walls of the half-completed chapel. One item proclaimed: "Here lay Rasputin, the foulest of men, Shame of the Russian Church." Soldiers told the correspondent that someone had offered the guards a large sum to close the grave to prevent its further desecration.

27. Protopopov, it appears, took up Rasputin's custom of telephoning either the empress or Vyrubova at ten each morning. Frequently it was to report a nocturnal visit from the spirit of Rasputin and to relay his advice. Paleologue wrote that once during an interview with the empress Protopopov fell to his knees and exclaimed: "Oh, Your Majesty, I see Christ behind you!" The anecdote illustrated either the disposition of the empress and the route to favor or the malicious gossip that surrounded the imperial court and government.

28. The empress first encountered Golitsyn when he became vice-chairman of one of her charitable organizations. He presented every possible excuse to avoid the job but felt duty-bound to obey his sovereign's command.

29. Here the author listed the ministers who served in the last government of Nicholas II. A roster of all ministers for the entire reign is found in Appendix A.

30. Grand Duke Dmitry Pavlovich (1891-1942) was a cousin of the tsar and a favorite of the empress. His father was the youngest brother of Alexander III.

31. Grand Duke Cyril Vladimirovich (1876-1938), another cousin, became the claimant to the Russian throne after the death of the tsar's brother Michael in 1918. Cyril's son, Vladimir (1917-), the present head of the Romanov family, resides in Spain.

32. The author's account somewhat exaggerates the prospective role of the grand duke. Khatisov informed him that a coup was being planned in his behalf in Moscow and asked whether he would accept the crown when it was offered. According to Khatisov, the grand duke refused to be part of the conspiracy because he doubted whether the people would understand the need to overthrow the tsar and whether the army would be sympathetic to a coup. Cited by Katkov, *Russia 1917*, p. 296.

33. The name, revealed later, was that of General Krymov. (Oldenburg's note) General A.M. Krymov commanded the 3rd Cavalry Corps on the Northern Front. In September 1917 Krymov was involved in another abortive coup, the Kornilov affair, and committed suicide.

34. *Padenie tsarskogo rezhima*, VI, pp. 277-79. (Oldenburg's note)

35. The statement bore the signature of the provincial marshal, Prince L.I. Dondukov-Iziedinov. *Zemshchina*, 24 January 1917. (Oldenburg's note)

36. During the conference Russia made demands for war materials and strategic supplies that the Allies felt were exorbitant. The text of Milner's

note appears in V.P. Semennikov, *Monarkhiia pered khrusheniem* [The Monarchy before the Collapse] (Moscow-Leningrad, 1927), pp. 77-85.

37. "Another month," wrote Churchill, "and the accession of the United States to the cause of the Allies would have brought a flood of new energy, encouragement, and moral stimulus to Russian society . . . . Only another month and the world might have been spared the tribulations of the two most grievous years of the War." [*World Crisis*, VI, p. 377.] (Oldenburg's note) The United States declared war on Germany on 6 April 1917.

38. However, see Katkov's analysis of this move, which undoubtedly was a mistake on Protopopov's part. *Russia 1917*, pp. 317-25.

39. The quotation came from the version that appeared in *Rech* on 16 February 1917, but the censor apparently "softened" the text because Kerensky specifically mentioned not "the system" but "the tsar's power." (Oldenburg's note)

40. See above, note 4.

CHAPTER TWENTY-ONE

1. The levy of new recruits born in 1898 occurred on 7 February 1917, nearly three years earlier than normal; thus 18 and 19-year-old young men filled the barracks. The draft took place all over Russia without incident. (Oldenburg's note)

2. *Golos minuvshago*, 1926, No. 2. (Oldenburg's note)

3. Professor Rein's memoirs, *Iz perezhitago* (II, pp. 190-271), provide a detailed and exact account of events from 23 February to 1 March 1917; it is the only detailed account of events by a member of the last imperial government. (Oldenburg's note)

4. Znamensky Square was about two miles east of the Admiralty, which stands on the Neva River at the foot of Nevsky Prospekt. See Zenzinov's account of the riot in Robert Paul Browder and Alexander F. Kerensky, eds., *The Russian Provisional Government, 1917: Documents* (Stanford, 1961) I, pp. 31-32. This collection is cited below as Browder and Kerensky.

5. M.V. Rodzianko, "Gosudarstvennaia Duma i fevralskaia 1917 goda revoliutsiia" [The State Duma and the Revolution of February 1917], *Arkhiv russkoi revoliutsii*, 6 (1922):59; see also another major source of documents obviously consulted by the author: "Fevralskaia revoliutsiia 1917 goda" [The Revolution of February 1917], *Krasnyi arkhiv*, 21 (1927): 3-78; and 22 (1927): 3-70.

6. Shulgin, *Dni*, esp. pp. 153-70. Though not always the most accurate reporter of events, Shulgin's memoirs capture the atmosphere of February 1917 with an extraordinary detachment. After his first close encounter with a February mob, for example, he said to his colleague Shingarev, "I think our role is over."

7. A revolutionary witness of the Volynsky mutiny recorded that Colonel Lashkevich was killed "by a well-aimed stray bullet!" Quoted by Katkov, *Russia 1917*, p. 368.

8. Kutepov's sally, the "only serious attempt" by the military authorities in Petrograd to clear the capitol district, is described in some detail by Katkov, pp. 374-78. A.P. Kutepov (1882-1930?), a Preobrazhensky colonel on leave from the front, later served in the civil war as Wrangel's second in command. As an emigre he headed an association of White officers in Paris, where in 1930 he was kidnapped, presumably by Soviet agents.

9. The Tauride Palace was located in the Liteiny district about two and a half miles east of the Admiralty and Winter Palace.

10. The committee consisted of M.V. Rodzianko, P.N. Miliukov, V.N. Lvov, S.I. Shidlovsky, N.V. Nekrasov, V.V. Shulgin, D.I. Konovalov, A.F. Kerensky, N.S. Chkeidze, M.A. Karaulov, I.I. Dmitriukov, V.A. Rzhevsky, and B.A. Engelhardt.

11. Protopopov was so desirous of being helpful that reportedly he even offered to commit suicide. Minutes of the last meetings of the council of ministers never have been published or seen, and the testimony of the participants is contradictory.

12. Because of strikes, the Petrograd newspapers ceased publication on 26 February, and for about a week the capital was without its regular news sources. The citizens' only information came from a bulletin issued by a committee of Petrograd journalists accredited to the Duma and subsequently known as *Izvestiia revoliutsionnoi nedeli*—News of the Revolutionary Week. Ten issues appeared between 28 February and 5 March 1917. Oldenburg referred to the bulletin as the "*Izvestiia* of the Duma's Committee of Journalists." It published all formal statements of the Duma Committee as well as other correspondence that the committee wished to make public.

13. *Izvestiia Petrogradskogo Soveta Rabochikh Deputatov—Izvestiia* (News) of the Petrograd Soviet of Workers Deputies—appeared in two issues (28 February and 1 March). On the 2nd of March issue number 3, reflecting the expansion of the Soviet, appeared as the *Izvestiia* of the Petrograd Soviet of Workers and Soldiers Deputies. Several other agency changes were reflected in the title during the next year, but *Izvestiia* remained its principal rubric, and the paper continues today as the central organ of the Soviet government.

14. The author refers here to the first chaotic days of the Soviet; by the end of the month a 40-member executive committee had been elected with Chkeidze as president and Kerensky and Skobelev vice-presidents.

15. The grand duke's motive may have been somewhat more practical. As second in the line of succession, he was a likely candidate to become regent for the young tsarevich and even a possible candidate for the crown itself. Therefore he had no desire to see his name associated in the public mind with the suppression of the revolt.

16. Policemen and gendarmes stood in line to be arrested in the hope of being spared summary justice at the hands of the mob.

17. In his testimony before the investigating commission Miliukov admitted that the Duma's "dissolution" only incidentally coincided with the outbreak of the uprising. (Oldenburg's note)

18. The Northern Front designated the 67th and 68th Infantry Regiments and the 15th Uhlan Tatar and 3rd Ural Cossack Regiments; the

Western Front the 34th and 36th Infantry, the 2nd Pavlograd Hussars, and the 2nd Don Cossack Regiments; the Southwestern Front the Household Guard of the Preobrazhensky and the 3rd and 4th Guards Rifle Regiments. The movement of troops from the Northern and Western Fronts was scheduled to begin on 28 February and 1 March; the regiments of the Southwestern Front were to embark on 2-3 March. (Oldenburg's note)

19. Some of Alekseev's personal records were published in *Iz dnevnik M.V. Alekseeva* [From the Diary of M.V. Alekseev], ed. Jan Slavik (Prague, 1929).

20. Alekseev's principal contact in Petrograd was, of course, Rodzianko, but his "private" informant also may have been Bublikov, who had seized the ministry of communications and the telegraph system in the name of the Duma. However, General A.S. Lukomsky, who commanded the First Army Corps and was present at Stavka during the crisis, reported that Stavka on 28 February-1 March "received from Petrograd one telegram after another describing a revolutionary movement in full swing." "Dokumenty k 'Vospominaniiam'. A. Lukomskago" [Documents for the "Memoirs" of General A. Lukomsky], *Arkhiv russkoi revoliutsii*, 3 (1922): 21.

21. This message was addressed to General Ivanov with copies to all front commanders.

22. The inquiry was made in behalf of the commander, General Ruzsky.

23. The grand dukes' manifesto was written by Paul Aleksandrovich, who even invited the empress to sign it. She indignantly refused to be a part of Paul's "idiotic plan . . . to save us all." The manifesto was given to Miliukov, but he never saw fit to use it. *Krasnyi arkhiv*, 24 (1927): 208-10.

24. Katkov questions the provenance of the final version of the document. *Russia 1917*, pp. 492-94.

25. I.e. "Gosudarstvennaia Duma i fevralskaia revoliutsiia."

26. *Russkaia revoliutsiia* (New York, 1918).

27. Negotiations between the Temporary Committee of the Duma and the Executive Committee of the Soviet were then in progress (night of 1-2 March). An agreement was concluded only during the following day and announced on 3 March. The generals believed what Rodzianko wanted them to believe (and wanted to believe himself), but in the end the chairman of the Duma was shoved aside by Miliukov and the Kadets.

28. "Prebyvanie Gosudariia Imperatora v Pskove I i 2 marta 1917 goda, po rasskazu general-adiutanta N.V. Ruzskogo" [His Majesty the Emperor's Sojourn at Pskov on 1-2 March 1917, according to the account of General Adjutant N.V. Ruzsky], *Russkaia letopis*, 3 (1922): 161-87. There is another account: "Iz dnevnik V.A. Romanova" [From the Diary of V.A. Romanov], *Krasnyi arkhiv*, 26 (1928): 185-210.

29. Ruzsky indicated that Alekseev's telegrams were crucial; he also said that the tsar yielded because both he and Alekseev were unanimous on the need for the concession and, as Nicholas put it, they rarely agreed completely on anything.

30. In fact a train was kept ready for Rodzianko throughout the day—the same train that later carried Guchkov and Shulgin to Pskov. Later

in his direct wire conversation with Ruzsky, Rodzianko gave two reasons for failing to come: The troops sent to Petrograd had mutinied and were stopping all traffic (although in Rodzianko's version of events those troops were loyal to the Duma); and the unbridled mob in Petrograd required his presence, "since I remain the only one who is trusted and whose orders are carried out."

31. At 11:30 p.m. on 1 March Ruzsky's headquarters asked to speak to Rodzianko "on an extremely urgent and responsible matter." Colonel Engelhardt brought that message to the committee room where the Duma's committee was wrestling with the executive of the Soviet over the formation of the Provisional Government. Rodzianko was acting as chairman of the conference but was under no compulsion to remain. Rodzianko's unreliable memoirs have had an unfortunate effect on the interpretation of the February Revolution.

The scene described here by the author comes from Sukhanov's account: *Zapiski o revoliutsii* [Notes on the Revolution], 7 vols. (Berlin, 1922-23), of which a condensed version is *The Russian Revolution, 1917,* trans. Joel Carmichael (Oxford University Press, 1955). See especially Vol. I, pp. 146-57.

32. The conversation lasted four hours because of the complicated system of transmission; the text was reproduced by Vilchkovsky, *Russkaia letopis,* 3: 124-33; and by Lukomsky, *Arkhiv russkoi revoliutsii,* 3: 255-58. An incomplete version appears in Browder and Kerensky, I, pp. 92-93.

33. The conversation with Rodzianko did not entirely clarify the situation, for it still left Ruzsky with the impression that the Temporary Committee of the Duma led by Rodzianko remained the only potentially viable government in Petrograd. Having involved the high command in a constitutional struggle, Rodzianko continued his policy of deception: "I have immediately taken measures to free the tracks for the passage of His Majesty." (On the previous day he had tried to block the train at Bologoe and apparently considered going there to arrest the emperor.) The Duma and I, he lied, faced with growing anarchy had "no alternative but to take the movement into our hands and to lead it . . . ."

34. Alekseev's circular, from Lukomsky's documents, translated by Browder and Kerensky, I, pp. 94-95.

35. General Alekseev's misapprehension of the situation was apparently an honest mistake. General Lukomsky recorded that early on the 3rd of March Alekseev told him: "I shall never forgive myself for having trusted in the sincerity of certain people, for having followed them, and for having sent the telegram about the emperor's abdication to the commanders-in-chief."

Vilchkovsky, cited above [note 28], noted that General Ruzsky "quickly lost faith in the new government" and felt that "in his long interview with the emperor during the night of 1 March he had shaken the foundations of the throne, even though his intention had been to strengthen them. He bore a deep moral guilt until the end of his life and could not discuss the tragic days of March 1st and 2nd without great discomfort." (In October 1918 General Ruzsky, who had retired to the Caucasus, was shot by Bolsheviks.) (Oldenburg's note)

36. Lukomsky, "Dokumenty," 261-62; Browder and Kerensky, I, pp. 95-97.

37. Major-General Vladimir Nikolaevich Voeikov (1868-), son-in-law of Count Fredericks, the minister of the imperial court, became commandant of the imperial palace in 1913. In that capacity he accompanied the tsar wherever he went. His memoirs: *S Tsarem i bez Tsaria: Vospominaniia poslednego Dvortsovogo Komendanta Gosudaria Imperatora Nikolaia II* [With and Without the Tsar: Memoirs of the Last Palace Commandant of Emperor Nicholas II] (Helsingfors, 1936).

38. During that conversation, Lukomsky at the other end of the line advised Danilov: "According to information received, the Palace of Tsarskoe Selo has been occupied by [rebellious] troops.... If he does not agree [to abdicate] further excesses probably will take place, excesses that would endanger the imperial children." Lukomsky, "Dokumenty," 258-59.

39. The statistical department of the Petrograd municiapl duma estimated the number of casualties of the revolution—killed, wounded, and injured—at 1,315. The breakdown was: 587 citizens, 602 soldiers, 73 policemen, and 53 officers.

40. For the announcement of 3 March, which listed the new government and stated its guiding principles, see Browder and Kerensky, I, pp. 135-36. The first cabinet was headed by Prince G.E. Lvov, who also held the post of minister of interior. The others were: Miliukov (foreign affairs), Guchkov (war and navy), Nekrasov (communications), Konovalov (commerce and industry), Tereshchenko (finance), Manuilov (education), V.N. Lvov—no relation (holy synod), Shingarev (agriculture), and Kerensky (justice).

41. Miliukov's speech, ibid., pp. 129-33.

42. Michael Ivanovich Tereshchenko (1888-1958) was a young millionaire from Kiev who had directed the regional war industry committee.

43. Shulgin recorded: "His words were calm, simple, and precise. Only his accent was slightly alien, the accent of a guardsman: 'I have decided to abdicate the throne. Until 3 o:clock yesterday I thought that I could abdicate in favor of my son Alexis, but now I have changed my mind in favor of my brother Michael. I hope you will understand the feelings of a father.' The last sentence he pronounced more softly."

Ruzsky was more composed than Shulgin; his account was published within a week of the abdication and is probably a more accurate transcription of the emperor's words: "I have already signed the act of abdication in favor of my son but I have since come to the conclusion that my son is not of sound health, and I do not wish to be parted from him. Therefore I have decided to yield the throne to Michael Aleksandrovich."

The tsar's change of mind followed a discussion with the court physician who informed him that only a miracle could cure the tsarevich and that the boy's safety depended on close and constant care, supervision, and treatment. Nicholas could not bear the thought of entrusting that responsibility to others.

Five persons were present in the coach that served as the tsar's reception salon: Nicholas, Fredericks, Shulgin, Guchkov, and (eventually)

Ruzsky. Three of them left records: Shulgin, *Dni,* pp. 238-76; Guchkov, *Padenie tsarskogo rezhima,* VI, pp. 262-66; and Ruzsky, in *Russkaia volia,* No. 2 (7 March 1917): 3. The best historical accounts are: S.P. Melgunov, *Martovskie dni 1917 goda* [The March Days, 1917] (Paris, 1961), pp. 189-202; and Katkov, *Russia 1917,* pp. 445-75.

44. The documents were antedated to signify that the decision was made freely and not extorted by the representatives of the Duma. Two copies were drawn up: Guchkov took one to Petrograd, and the other was deposited with the chief of staff.

On 3 March 1917 Michael Aleksandrovich formally refused the crown until it might be offered by a duly elected Constituent Assembly. The call never came. On 10 July 1918, six days before the slaughter of his brother and his family, Bolsheviks murdered the grand duke at Perm.

45. Both decrees became a source of embarrassment to the Provisional Government since (in the view of the Soviet) they implied that the new regime had been ordained by the former tsar. Grand Duke Nicholas duly reported to Stavka only to learn that the government had nullified his appointment by a decree that prohibited the Romanovs from serving the new regime. Nicholas Nikolaevich promptly resigned, retired from public life, and settled in the Crimea. In April 1919 he was evacuated by the British Navy together with the tsar's mother, Empress Maria Feodorovna. Until his death in 1929 the grand duke was associated with General Wrangel in the World Organization of Russian War Veterans (ROVS), an organization that sought to maintain the cadre of the old imperial army, or its remnants, so that one day it again might fight Bolshevism.

46. Guchkov, the new minister of war, prohibited army commanders from reading it to their troops and newspapers from publishing it. For the text see Browder and Kerensky, I, pp. 105-6.

47. *World Crisis,* I, pp. 223-25; and VI, pp. 376-77; abridged and revised.

APPENDIX A

MINISTERS OF NICHOLAS II, 1894-1917

Chairman of the Committee of Ministers

Bunge, N.K.	1887-1895
Durnovo, I.N.	1895-1903
Witte, S.Yu.	1903-1905

Chairman of the Council of Ministers

Witte, S.Yu.	1905 Oct—Apr 1906
Goremykin, I.L.	1906 Apr—Jul
Stolypin, P.A.	1906 Jul—Sep 1911
Kokovtsov, V.N.	1911 Sep—Jan 1914
Goremykin, I.L.	1914 Jan—Jan 1916
Stürmer, B.V.	1916 Jan—Nov
Trepov, A.F.	1916 Nov—Dec
Golitsyn, N.D.	1916 Dec—Feb 1917

Minister of Internal Affairs

Durnovo, I.N.	1889—Oct 1895
Goremykin, I.L.	1895 Oct—Oct 1899
Sipiagin, D.S.	1899 Oct—Apr 1902
Plehve, V.K.	1902 Apr—Aug 1904
Sviatopolk-Mirsky, P.D.	1904 Aug—Jan 1905
Bulygin, A.G.	1905 Jan—Oct
Durnovo, P.N.	1905 Oct—Apr 1906
Stolypin, P.A.	1906 Apr—Sep 1911
Makarov, A.A.	1911 Sep—Dec 1912
Maklakov, N.A.	1912 Dec—Jul 1915
Shcherbatov, N.B.	1915 Jul—Sep
Khvostov, A.N.	1915 Sep—Mar 1916
Stürmer, B.V.	1916 Mar—Jul
Khvostov, A.A.	1916 Jul—Sep
Protopopov, A.D.	1916 Sep—Feb 1917

Minister of Finance

Witte, S.Yu.	1892—Aug 1903
Pleske, E.D.	1903 Aug—Feb 1904
Kokovtsov, V.N.	1904 Mar—Oct 1905
Shipov, I.P.	1905 Oct—Apr 1906
Kokovtsov, V.N.	1906 Apr—Jan 1914
Bark, P.L.	1914 Jan—Feb 1917

Minister of Foreign Affairs

Giers, N.K.	1882—Jan 1895
Lobanov-Rostovsky, A.B.	1895 Feb—Aug 1896
Muraviev, M.N.	1897 Jan—Jun 1900

Lamsdorf, V.N.	1900 Jul—Apr 1906
Izvolsky, A.P.	1906 Apr—Sep 1910
Sazonov, S.D.	1910 Sep—Jul 1916
Stürmer, B.V.	1916 Jul—Nov
Pokrovsky, N.N.	1916 Nov—Mar 1917

Minister of War

Vannovsky, P.S.	1881—Dec 1898
Kuropatkin, A.N.	1899 Jan—Feb 1904
Sakharov, V.V.	1904 Feb—Jun 1905
Rediger, A.F.	1905 Jun—Mar 1909
Sukhomlinov, V.A.	1909 Mar—Jun 1915
Polivanov, A.A.	1915 Jun—Mar 1916
Shuvaev, D.S.	1916 Mar—Jan 1917
Beliaev, M.A.	1917 Jan—Feb

Minister of Marine

Chikachev, N.M.	1888—1895
Tyrtov, P.P.	1896-1902
Avellan, F.K.	1903-1905
Birilev, A.A.	1906—1907
Dikov, I.M.	1908—1909
Voevodsky, S.A.	1910—1911
Grigorovich, I.K.	1911—Mar 1917

Minister of Justice

Muraviev, N.V.	1894 Jan—Jan 1905
Manukhin, S.S.	1905 Jan—Dec
Akimov, M.G.	1905 Dec—Apr 1906
Shcheglovitov, I.G.	1906 Apr—Jul 1915
Khvostov, A.A.	1915 Jul—Jul 1916
Makarov, A.A.	1916 Jul—Dec
Dobrovolsky, N.A.	1916 Dec—Feb 1917

Director-General of the Holy Synod

Pobedonostsev, C.P.	1880—Oct 1905
Obolensky, A.D.	1905 Oct—Apr 1906
Shirinsky-Shikhmatov, A.A.	1906 Apr—Jul
Izvolsky, P.P.	1906 Jul—Feb 1909
Lukianov, S.M.	1909 Feb—May 1911
Sabler, V.K.	1911 May—Jul 1915
Samarin, A.D.	1915 Jul—Sep
Volzhin, A.N.	1915 Oct—Aug 1916
Raev, N.P.	1916 Aug—Feb 1917

Minister of Commerce and Industry

Timiriazev, V.I.	1905 Oct—Feb 1906
Fedorov, M.M.	1906 Feb—Apr
Stoff, A.A.	1906 Apr—Jul
Filosofov, D.A.	1906 Jul—Jan 1907
vacant	1907 Jan—Dec
Shipov, I.P.	1908 Jan—Jan 1909

Timiriazev, V.I.	1909 Jan—Nov
Timashev, S.I.	1909 Nov—Feb 1915
Sakhovsky, V.N.	1915 Feb—Feb 1917

Minister (Director) of Agriculture

Ermolov, A.S.	1893—May 1905
Schwanebach, P.K.	1905 May—Oct
Kutler, N.N.	1905 Oct—Feb 1906
Nikolsky, A.P.	1906 Feb—Apr
Stishinsky, A.S.	1906 Apr—May
Vasilchikov, B.A.	1906 May—1908
Krivoshein, A.V.	1908—Oct 1915
Naumov, A.N.	1915 Nov—Jul 1916
Bobrinsky, V.A.	1916 Jul—Nov
Rittikh, A.A.	1916 Nov—Feb 1917

Minister of Public Education

Delianov, I.D.	1882—Dec 1897
Anichkov, N.M.	1897 Dec—Feb 1898
Bogolepov, N.P.	1898 Feb—Mar 1901
Vannovsky, P.S.	1901 Mar—Apr 1902
Zenger, G.E.	1902 Apr—Jan 1904
Glazov, V.G.	1904 Apr—Oct 1905
Tolstoy, I.I.	1905 Oct—Apr 1906
Kaufman, P.M.	1906 Apr—Jan 1908
Schwarz, A.N.	1908 Jan—Sep 1910
Kasso, L.A.	1910 Sep—Nov 1914
Kuzmin-Karavaev, V.D. (acting minister)	1914 Aug—Sep 1915
Ignatiev, P.N.	1915 Jan—Dec 1916
Kulchitsky, N.K.	1916 Dec—Feb 1917

Minister of Ways of Communication

Krivoshein, A.K.	1892—Dec 1894
Khilkov, M.I.	1895 Jan—Oct 1905
Nemeshaev, K.S.	1905 Oct—Apr 1906
Schaffhausen, N.K.	1906 Apr—1909
Rukhlov, S.V.	1909—Oct 1915
Trepov, A.F.	1915 Nov—Nov 1916
Voinovsky-Krieger, E.B.	1916 Dec—Feb 1917

State Comptroller

Filipov, T.I.	1889—Nov 1899
Lobko, P.L.	1899 Dec—Oct 1905
Filosofov, D.A.	1905 Oct—Apr 1906
Schwanebach, P.K.	1906 Apr—Jun 1907
Kharitonov, P.A.	1907 Sep—Jan 1916
Pokrovsky, N.N.	1916 Jan—Nov
Feodosev, S.G.	1916 Dec—Feb 1917

Minister of the Imperial Court

| Vorontsov-Dashkov, I.I. | 1881-1897 |
| Fredericks, V.B. | 1897-1917 |

Director, Main Administration of State Public Health

| Rein, G.E. | 1916 Sep—Jul 1917 |

APPENDIX B

DIRECTORY OF PERSONS MENTIONED

ABAZA, Alexis Mikhailovich (1853-?). Rear-Admiral; Manager of the Special Committee for Affairs of the Far East, 1903-5; a leading "Bezobrazovist."

ABDUL HAMID II. Sultan of Turkey, 1876-1909. Deposed by Young Turks, exiled to Saloniki, died 1918.

AERENTHAL, Baron Alois Lexa (1854-1912). Austrian foreign minister, 1906-12; architect of the Bosnian Crisis, 1908-9. Formerly Secretary of the Austro-Hungarian Embassy, St. Petersburg, 1878-83 and 1888-94; Minister to Bucharest, 1895-99; Ambassador to Russia, 1899-1906.

AIVAZOVSKY, Ivan Konstantinovich (1817-1900). Painter; marinist.

AKASHI Motojiro (1864-1919). Colonel, Japanese intelligence officer. Military Attache, St. Petersburg, 1903-4. European director of Japanese military intelligence during Russo-Japanese War; funded anti-Russian revolutionary and national movements.

AKHMATOVA (Gorenko), Anna Andreevna (1889-1966). Major acmeist poetess.

AKIMOV, Michael Grigorevich (1847-1914). Jurist, Minister, close advisor to Nicholas II. Assistant Director of District Courts, Vladimir, Moscow, and Kiev. Assistant Chairman, Kiev Court of Appeals, 1881-83. Chairman, District Court of Odessa, 1883-87, and Penza, 1887-91. Chairman, Court of Appeals of Moscow, 1891-94; of Odessa, 1894-99. Senate Court of Cassation for Criminal Affairs, 1899-1905. Minister of Justice, Dec 1905-Apr 1906. Appointed to State Council, 1906; President of the State Council, 1907-14. His Majesty's State Secretary in 1908.

ALEKSANDROVICH, Peter Aleksandrovich (-1918). Revolutionary; Left SR. Leader of the Petrograd Soviet, 1917. Vice-chairman, All-Russian CHEKA, 1918. Implicated in assassination of Mirback, executed by the Bolsheviks in July 1918.

ALEKSEENKO, Michael Martynovich (1847-1917). Professor of Economics, Kharkov University. Octobrist; elected to Third and Fourth Dumas; member of Octobrist Bureau. Chairman, Budget Commission, Fourth Duma.

ALEKSEEV, Eugene Ivanovich (1843-1909). Admiral. Began naval service in 1860; graduated Naval Cadet School, 1863. Naval Agent to France, 1883-88. Rear-Admiral, 1892; Chief, Main Naval Staff, 1892-95. Commander, Pacific Squadron, 1895-97; Black Sea Fleet, 1897-99; Kwantung Military District and Pacific Squadron, 1899-1903—directed capture of Tagu and Tienshan during the Boxer Rebellion. Supreme Commander, Far East, 28 Jan-12 Oct 1904. Retired, appointed to State Council, 1905. Supported an aggressive Far Eastern policy and was included among the "Bezobrazovists."

ALEKSEEV, Michael Vasilievich (1857-1918). General-Adjutant. Graduate of the Nicholas Academy of the General Staff. Veteran of Russo-Turkish War of 1877-78 and Russo-Japanese War (Chief of Operations, Third Army). Chief of Staff, Southwestern Front, 1914-15. Chief of Staff, Stavka, 1915-Mar 1917; instrumental in abdication of Nicholas II. Supreme Commander in Chief, Mar-May 1917. Founder of the Volunteer Army, 1918. Died 8 Oct 1918, of pneumonia.

ALEKSINSKY, Gregory Alekseevich (1879-). Social Democrat. Leading Bolshevik spokesman in Second Duma. Aligned with Mensheviks in 1917 in Plekhanov's Unity group; emigrated in 1918.

ALEXANDER. King of Greece, 1917-20. Second son of Constantine I.

ALEXANDER I PAVLOVICH (1777-1825). Emperor of Russia, 1801-25.

ALEXANDER II NIKOLAEVICH (1818-1881). Emperor of Russia, 1855-81.

ALEXANDER III ALEKSANDROVICH (1845-1894). Emperor of Russia, 1881-94.

ALEXANDER BATTENBERG (1857-1893). Prince of Bulgaria, 1879-86.

ALEXANDER MIKHAILOVICH, Grand Duke (1866-1933). Nephew of Alexander II, cousin of Nicholas II, husband of his eldest sister Xenia. Admiral of the Russian Navy. Head of the Main Administration of Commercial Navigation and Ports, 1902-5.

ALEXIS ALEKSANDROVICH, Grand Duke (1850-1908). Fourth son of Alexander II, uncle of Nicholas II. Directed the naval ministry as General-Admiral, 1882-1905.

ALEXIS NIKOLAEVICH, Grand Duke (1904-1918). The Tsarevich, son and heir of Nicholas II.

ALVENSLEBEN, Count Friedrich Johann von (1836-1913). German diplomat. Junior embassy posts, 1861-75, including St. Petersburg, 1872-75. General Consul, Bucharest, 1876-77. Ambassador: Darmstadt, 1877; The Hague, 1882; Washington, 1884; Brussels, 1886; and St. Petersburg, 1901-5.

ANDREEV, Leonid (1871-1919). Realist writer, nihilist. Successor in popularity and influence to Gorky after 1906 and with Gorky the leading representative of the Russian revolutionary realist tradition.

ANNA YAROSLAVNA, Princess. Daughter of Yaroslav, Grand Prince of Kiev, 1019-54, and wife of Henry I, King of France, 1031-60.

ANNENSKY, Innokenty Feodorovich (1856-1909). Classical scholar, translator, poet.

ANNENSKY, Nicholas Feodorovich (1843-1912). Statistician, journalist, and radical politician. Political exile, 1880-83. Headed statistical departments in the provincial zemstvos of Kazan, 1883-87, and Nizhni Novgorod, 1887-95. Chief, Central Statistical Office, St. Petersburg, 1895. A founder of the Union of Liberation. Chief editor, *Russkoe bogatstvo*, 1904. Founded the People's Socialist Party (chairman, 1906-12), which frequently aligned itself with the Kadets.

ANREP, Vasily Konstantinovich von (1852-). Professor of Forensic Medicine, Kharkov and St. Petersburg Universities. Director, Kharkov School District, 1899-1901; St. Petersburg, 1901-2. Director, State Medical Departments, 1902-7. Octobrist; member of the Octobrist Bureau. Elected to Third Duma; defeated for re-election in 1912.

ANTHONY (Antonius). Archbishop of Volynia.

ANTHONY (Vadkovsky). Metropolitan of St. Petersburg.

ANTOKOLSKY, Mark Matveevich (1843-1902). Sculptor, realist.

APUKHTIN, Alexis Nikolaevich (1840-1893). Poet, lyricist; early opponent of Russian "civic poetry."

ARCO-VALLEY, Count. German ambassador to Japan, 1901-6.

ARTSYBASHEV, Michael Petrovich (1878-1927). Realist writer; two sensational erotic novels, *Sanin* (1907) and *At the Brink* (1911-12). Expelled from the USSR in 1923.

ASQUITH, Herbert Henry (1852-1928). British statesman ("Liberal Imperialist"). Prime Minister, 1908-16, and Minister of War, 1914-16. Leader of the Liberal Opposition, 1916-26.

AUER, Leopold Semonovich (1845-1930). Violinist, teacher, and conductor; at the St. Petersburg Conservatory before the revolution; settled in the United States in 1918.

AURIC, Georges (1899-). French composer; associated with the Ballet Russe.

AVELLAN, Feodor Karlovich (1839-1916). Admiral. Chief of Main Naval Staff, 1896-1903. Director of the naval ministry, 1903-5.

AXELROD, Paul Borisovich (1850-1928). Revolutionary. Populist, 1872; in emigration in Switzerland after 1880. Founder with Plekhanov and others of first group of Russian Marxists and later of the RSDLP. Leading Menshevik ideologist and tactician; opponent of Lenin. Active in Second International. Supported Provisional Government in 1917, fled Russia after Bolshevik coup, died in Berlin.

AZEF, Evno Fishelevich (1869-1918). Notorious double agent; as head of Socialist Revolutionary Battle Organization organized the assassinations of Plehve (1904) and Grand Duke Sergei Aleksandrovich (1905). Imprisoned in Germany; died shortly after his release.

BACHE, Victor. French financier; brother of Jules and Leopold, founders of the American investment firm of Bache & Co. in 1892.

BADEN-POWELL, Lord Robert (1857-1941). Englishman; founder of the Boy Scouts.

BAKST, Leonid Samoilovich (1868-1924). Painter and decorator; internationally renowned as set designer for Diaghilev's Ballet Russe. Member of the *Mir iskusstva* movement.

BALANCHINE (Balanchivadze), George Melitonovich (1904-). Choreographer, with Ballet Russe, then Soviet State Dancers. Defected, 1924; with New York City Ballet in the 30s, revolutionized the American style of classical ballet.

BALASHOV, Nicholas Petrovich (1841-). Nationalist leader in State Council, 1906- . Member of one of the wealthiest landowning families in Russian Empire. Provincial marshal of nobility, Podolsk, 1874. Member, agricultural council of Main Administration of Land Organization, 1894; department of industry, science, and commerce of the State Council, 1905-6. Appointed to State Council, 1906.

BALASHOV, Peter Nikolaevich (1871-). Son of N.P. (above), elected to Third Duma from Podolia; moderate rightist. Organizer and chairman of the Russian National Union (Oct 1909), the Nationalist bloc in the Duma.

BALK, Alexander Pavlovich (1866-). General of Gendarmes. Chief of Police, Petrograd, 1916-Feb 1917.

BALMASHOV, Stefan Valerianovich (1882-1902). SR terrorist. Assassinated D.S. Sipiagin, Apr 1902; hanged in Schlusselburg Fortress, May 1902.

BALMONT, Constantine Dmitrievich (1867-1943). Symbolist poet. One of the first and most popular of the symbolists. Joined Social Democratic Party in 1905 and as a result forced to live abroad for a time; left Russia permanently after the October Revolution, died in poverty and obscurity in Paris.

BARCLAY de TOLLY, Prince Michael Bogdanovich (1761-1818). Field Marshal. Minister of War during the Napoleonic era; commander in chief of Russian Army, except Aug 1812-Apr 1813, when succeeded by Kutuzov. Resumed command upon Kutuzov's death and led the Russian invasion of Western Europe and France.

BARING, John (Lord Revelstoke) (1863-1929). Head of a prominent British banking house; member of British delegation to the Inter-Allied Conference in Petrograd, Jan 1917.

BARK, Peter Lvovich (1858-1937). Last imperial finance minister, Jan 1914-Feb 1917. In Ministry of Finance, 1892-1906: Manager, Petersburg branch, State Bank, 1905; Assistant Manager, State Bank, 1906. Manager, Volga-Kama Commercial Bank (private), 1906-11. Assistant Minister of Commerce and Industry, 1911-14. Appointed to State Council, 1915. Arrested, released by Provisional Government, 1917. Emigrated to England, manager of Anglo-International Bank of London, knighted by King George V, 1937.

BASHMAKOV, A.A. Conservative bureaucrat and publicist. In Peasant Section, Ministry of Interior, 1902-4. Member, Slavic Benevolent Society

(Pan-Slavist); charter member, right-wing Patriotic Union (1905). Editor, *Pravitelstvennyi vestnik.*

BASILY, Nicolas Aleksandrovich de (1883-1963). Diplomat. Graduate of the Imperial Alexander Lyceum, 1903; entered chancellery of the foreign ministry. Secretary of Embassy, Paris, 1908-11. Vice-director, Chancellery, Ministry of Foreign Affairs, 1911-14. Director, diplomatic chancellery, Stavka, 1914-17; drafted the act of abdication of Nicholas II.

BAUMAN, Nicholas Ernestovich (1873-1905). Bolshevik martyr; murdered by Black Hundred mob, 1905.

BEILIS, Menachem Mendel (1873-1934). Jewish brickmaker. Accused of ritual murder, 1911; acquitted 1913 in internationally famous trial. Emigrated to Palestine, 1914; to the United States, 1922.

BEKETOV, Nicholas Nikolaevich (1817-1911). Physical chemist; member of Imperial Academy of Sciences.

BELETSKY, Stefan Petrovich (1873-1918). Police official. In office of governor of Kiev, 1894-99, and Kovno, Vilna, Grodno, 1899-1907. Vice-governor of Samara, 1907-9. Assistant Director, Police Department, Ministry of Interior, 1910-12; Director, 1912-15. Senator, 1914. Assistant Minister of Interior, 1915-16. Arrested, Mar 1917, and subsequently executed by the Bolsheviks.

BELIAEV, Michael Alekseevich (1863-1918). General. Quartermaster-General of the General Staff, 1909-10. Assistant Minister of War, 1915-16. Minister of War, Dec 1916-Feb 1917.

BELINSKY, Vissarion Grigorievich (1811-1848). Major radical philosopher, critic, and writer of the early nineteenth century.

BELY, Andrei (pseud. of Boris Nikolaevich Bugaev) (1880-1934). Major symbolist writer and poet; the most original and probably the most influential symbolist; precursor of the futurists.

BENCKENDORFF, Count Alexander Konstantinovich (1849-1917). Diplomat. Counsellor to Embassy, Vienna, 1897. Minister to Copenhagen, 1897-1902. Ambassador to London, 1903-17.

BENOIS, Alexander Nikolaevich (1870-1960). Painter, art historian, and critic. Leader of the late nineteenth century renaissance of Russian art; one of the most gifted painters of the *Mir iskusstva* school. Author of a monumental *History of Painting.* Designed sets and wrote scenarios for several major ballets, including Stravinsky's *Petrouchka.*

BERDIAEV, Nicholas Aleksandrovich (1874-1948). Philosopher. Critic of Marxism and the formalism of Russian Orthodoxy.

BEREZOVSKY, Peter Vasilievich (1874-). Rightist deputy from Volynia in the Third Duma.

BERNHARDT, Sarah (Rosine Bernard) (1844-1923). World famous French actress.

BERNSTEIN, Eduard (1850-1932). German socialist. Founder and chief theoretician of revisionist (non-revolutionary) Marxism and the modern West European Social-Democratic movement.

BERNSTORFF, Count Johann Heinrich von (1862-1939). German diplomat. Charge d'affaires, Turkey, Serbia, Russia, England, and Egypt, 1889-1908. Ambassador: United States, 1908-17; Turkey, 1917. In foreign ministry, 1918-20. Elected to Reichstag, 1920; member of German delegation to League of Nations, 1924-28.

BERZIN, Jan Antonovich (1881-1941). Latvian revolutionary; Bolshevik since 1903. Secretary, Petersburg Bolshevik Committee, 1906-7. Abroad, 1908-17; participated in Zimmerwald Conference and formation of the "Zimmerwald Left." Elected to Central Committee, All-Russian Communist Party, 1917. Secretary, Comintern executive committee, 1918-19. Diplomat, 1921-27. Director, Central State Archives, 1932, and editor of *Krasnyi arkhiv*. Arrested during Great Purge, died in concentration camp, posthumously rehabilitated.

BETHMANN HOLLWEG, Theobald von (1856-1921). German chancellor, 1909-17.

BEZOBRAZOV, Alexander Mikhailovich (1855-1931). Financial speculator, confidante of Nicholas II, 1898-1904. Instigator behind the "East-Asiatic Company," formed 1898 to exploit timber concessions on the Yalu River and to promote Russian national interests in the Far East. Member, Special Committee for Affairs of the Far East, 1903-4.

BEZOBRAZOV, V.M. General. Commanded two corps of imperial guards during World War I; relieved for incompetence during the Brusilov offensive.

BIAZINGEN, A.S. Professor, Kharkov University; sponsor of conservative-nationalist student groups.

BILDERLING, General Baron A.A. Corps and army commander at Liaoyang, the Sha, and Mukden (Russo-Japanese War).

BIRILEV, Alexis Alekseevich (1844-1915). Admiral. Minister of Marine, 1905-7. Entered naval service, 1859. Commander, Mediterranean Squadron, 1900-3; Chief Flag Officer, Baltic Fleet, 1903-4; Commander, Baltic Fleet and Harbors, 1904-5; Commander, Pacific Fleet, May 1905. Appointed to State Council, 1907.

BISMARCK, Prince Otto von (1815-1898). Minister-President of Prussia, 1862-90; Chancellor of the German Empire, 1871-90.

BITSENKO, Anastasius. Terrorist; assassinated V.V. Sakharov, war minister, in Saratov, 1905.

BLOCH, Ivan G. (1836-1902). Russian-Polish financier and rail magnate; author of the prophetic *Future of War*.

BLOK, Alexander Aleksandrovich (1880-1921). Poet. Generally recognized as the greatest symbolist poet; remained, unhappily, in Soviet Russia after the revolution.

BOBRIKOV, Nicholas Ivanovich (1839-1904). General. Governor-General of Finland, 1898-1904; director of the disastrous policy of russification. Assassinated in Helsinki.

BOBRINSKAIA, Countess V.N. Philanthropist.

BOBRINSKY, Count Alexander Alekseevich (1823-1903). Statesman and genealogist. Governor of St. Petersburg, 1861-69. Petersburg provincial marshal of nobility, 1869-72. Member of State Council, 1896-1903.

BOBRINSKY, Count Alexis Aleksandrovich (1852-1927). Major landowner, sugar producer, archeologist, and conservative leader. District, then provincial marshal of nobility, St. Petersburg, 1875-98; also chairman, provincial zemstvo assembly. Director, Orphanages of Empress Maria Feodorovna, 1893-96. President, Imperial Archeological Commission for more than 30 years; Vice-president, Imperial Academy of Arts, 1889- . President, Free Economic Society, 1894. Member, Agricultural Committee, Main Administration of Land Organization, 1896- . Senator, 1896. Chairman, Union of Russian Nobility, 1905; member of the Union of Russian People. Elected to Third State Duma, 1907; defended the Stolypin reform against reactionary critics. Elected to State Council, 1912. Assistant Minister of Interior, 1916. Minister of Agriculture, July-Nov 1916. Fled Russia in 1918; died in Nice, France.

BOBRINSKY, Count Andrei Aleksandrovich (1860-). Brother of Alexis A.; also major sugar producer and public official. Director, Petersburg school district, 1906; member of the Council of the Ministry of Public Education, 1907. Founder and chairman of the Fatherland Union, a small conservative organization (1905-6); chairman, United Nobility, 1906. Member of rightist bloc in Third Duma and in State Council, 1912-17.

BOBRINSKY, Count G.A. General-Adjutant; rightist; briefly Governor of Galicia, 1915.

BOBRINSKY, Count Vladimir Alekseevich (1867-1927). Conservative zemstvo leader (Bogoroditsk district), 1892-95; chairman and district marshal of nobility, 1895-98. Leader of the moderate right in Second, Third, and Fourth Dumas; founder and vice-chairman of Nationalist Bloc in Fourth Duma.

BOGOLEPOV, Nicholas Pavlovich (1847-1901). Professor of Roman Law, Moscow University. Rector, 1883-95. Director, Moscow school district, 1895-98. Minister of Public Education, 1898-1901; assassinated by student terrorist—the first political murder since 1881.

BOGROV, Dmitry (1887-1911). Stolypin's assassin.

BOGUCHARSKY (Yakovlev), Vasily Yakovlevich (1861-1915). Liberal socialist; Legal Marxist during the 90s. One of the founders of the Union of Liberation. Historian of Russian Populism.

BOISDEFFRE, Raoul F.C.M. French general. Deputy Chief of French General Staff, 1890-94; Chief of Staff, 1894-99. Negotiator of the Franco-Russian Alliance.

BONCH-BRUYEVICH, Vladimir Dmitrievich (1873-1955). Bolshevik publicist, editor, and publisher; collaborated with Lenin on several journals. Authority on Russian religious sects. Secretary of Council of People's Commissars, 1917-20. Subsequently active as writer, historian, and Director of the Museum for the History of Religion and Atheism (1945-55).

BORIS VLADIMIROVICH, Grand Duke (1877-). Cousin of Nicholas II.

BORISHANSKY, Abram (1884-). Socialist Revolutionary terrorist; participated in the assassination of Plehve.

BOURGEOIS, Leon Victor Auguste (1851-1925). French politician and minister, 1889- . Prime minister, 1895-96. Member of French delegation to Hague Conference, 1899. President of Senate, 1902-4. Minister without portfolio and Minister of Labor, 1915-17. Delegate to League of Nations.

BRAHAM, Dudley Disraeli (1875-). British journalist; Petersburg correspondent for *The Times*, 1901-3. Expelled for slandering Russian government in connection with the Kishinev pogrom.

BRIAND, Aristide (1862-1932). French statesman; perennial minister, including prime minister and foreign minister, Oct 1915-Mar 1917.

BRIANSKY, V.D. Acting Mayor of Moscow, 1912-13.

BRISSON, Eugène-Henri (1835-1912). French statesman, Radical politician. President of Chamber of Deputies, 1881-85, 1894-98, and 1906-12. Prime Minister, 1885, 1898.

BRIUSSOV, Valery Yakovlevich (1873-1924). Major symbolist poet, first recognized in 1894-95. Joined Communist Party after the revolution and served in People's Commissariat of Education.

BRUNE de ST. HIPPOLYTE, Valentin Anatolovich (-1918). Senator. Chief of Police, 1914-15.

BRUSILOV, Alexis Alekseevich (1853-1926). General of Cavalry. Graduated His Majesty's Corps of Pages, began military service in 1872. Served with distinction in Russo-Turkish War of 1877-78. Commander, Warsaw Military District, 1912-13. In World War I commanded the Eighth Army, 1914-16, and the Southwestern Front, Mar 1916-May 1917; conducted last major offensive of imperial army in 1916. Supreme Commander in Chief, May-July 1917. Retired, 1917-20. Joined Red Army, served in war commissariat, participated in the Polish campaign of 1920 and in the Ukraine in 1921. Inspector of Cavalry, 1923-24. Appointed to the Revolutionary Military Council in 1924.

BUBLIKOV, Alexander Aleksandrovich (1875-). Engineer. Member of Fourth Duma (Progressive Party). Temporary Commissar for Railways for the Duma Committee in Feb 1917. Died in emigration.

BUCHANAN, Sir George William (1854-1924). British diplomat, since 1876. Minister to Sofia, 1904-8. Ambassador to St. Petersburg, 1910-18; to Rome, 1919-21.

BULAT, Andrei Andreevich (1873-). Lithuanian lawyer, prominent in political cases. Trudovik leader in Second and Third Dumas.

BULATSEL, Paul F. (1867-1919). Wealthy landowner and lawyer. Founder and leader of the Union of the Russian People; editor of its journal, *Russkoe znamia*.

BULGAKOV, Sergei Nikolaevich (1871-1944). Religious philosopher. One of the contributors to *Vekhi*.

BÜLOW, Prince Bernhard von (1849-1929). German diplomat and statesman; part of the aggressive German leadership of the early twentieth century. Secretary of Embassy, France, 1878-84; Russia, 1884-88. Minister to Rumania, 1888-94. Ambassador to Italy, 1894-97. Foreign minister, 1897-1900. Reich Chancellor and Minister-President of Prussia, 1900-9.

BULYGIN, Alexander Grigorievich (1851-1919). Provincial administrator and governor, 1871-93. Mayor of Moscow, 1893-1902, and assistant to the Governor-General (Sergei Aleksandrovich), 1902-5. Minister of Interior, Jan-Oct 1905. Member of State Council, 1905-17. His Majesty's State Secretary, 1913. Director, Fourth Section of H.I.M. Chancellery for Institutions of Empress Maria, 1913-17. Killed by revolutionaries, 1919.

BUNGE, Nicholas Khristianovich (1823-95). Minister of Finance, 1881-87. Chairman of the Committee of Ministers, 1887-95.

BUNIN, Ivan Alekseevich (1870-1953). Major poet and writer. Associated for a time with the *Znanie* school (realism) but during World War I passed over to naturalism and works reflecting pessimism and mystical resignation. Emigrated after revolution, published anti-Soviet works. In 1933 became the first Russian writer to win the Nobel Prize for Literature.

BURLIUK, David Davidovich (1882-1968). Futurist poet; organizer of Russian cubo-futurists. Emigrated to Japan, 1920; to United States, 1922.

BURTSEV, Vladimir Lvovich (1862-1942). Historian of the Russian revolutionary movement; editor of *Byloe*, 1900-4, 1908-12, a journal devoted to the history of revolutionary Russia. Exposed several double agents including Evno Azef and Roman Malinovsky.

BUTKOVSKY, Peter Mikhailovich (1842-1912). Jurist. Various positions in provincial judiciary, 1869-89. Director-General, Senate, 1889-92. Assistant Minister of Justice, 1892-1901. Member of State Council, 1901-12.

CAILLAUX, Joseph (1863-1944). French statesman; prime minister during the Agadir crisis, 1911.

CAMBON, Paul (1843-1924). French diplomat. Minister-Resident, Tunis, 1882-86; Ambassador: Spain, 1886-90; Turkey, 1890-98; Great Britain, 1898-1920. Advocate of Anglo-French cooperation.

CAMPBELL-BANNERMAN, Sir Henry (1836-1908). Leader of British Liberal Party. Member of Parliament, 1868-1908; Prime Minister, 1905-8.

CAPRIVI, Count Georg Leo von (1831-1899). German Chancellor, 1890-94; Minister-President of Prussia, 1890-92. Bismarck's immediate successor.

CARNOT, Sadi (1837-1894). President of France, 1887-94. Assassinated by an Italian anarchist.

CASIMIR-PERIER, Jean (1847-1907). President of France, 1894-95.

CATHERINE II ALEKSEEVNA, the Great (1729-1796). Empress of Russia, 1762-96. Born Sophia Augusta of Anhalt-Zerbst.

CHAIKOVSKY, Nicholas Vasilievich (1850-1925). Early populist leader; later a Socialist Revolutionary. Active mainly in emigration, principally England. Founder of the Society of Friends of Russian Freedom (London).

CHALIAPIN (Shalyapin), Feodor Ivanovich (1873-1938). World famous operatic bass.

CHAMBERLAIN, Joseph (1836-1914). British statesman, leader of the Liberal-Unionists. Colonial Secretary, 1895-1903.

CHANOINE, Jules (1835-1915). French general. Directed reorganization of Japanese army in 1867; served briefly as Minister of War in 1898.

CHAPLINSKY, N.D. Senator; State Prosecutor, Kiev Appellate Court. Principal instigator and chief prosecutor in the Beilis trial.

CHARLES I. Emperor of Austria and King of Hungary, 1916-18 (abdicated). Grandnephew, successor of Franz Joseph. Died 1922.

CHEKOV, Anton Pavlovich (1860-1904). Greatest Russian dramatist and writer of short stories. Associated with humanitarian and radical causes, especially after 1896.

CHELNOKOV, Michael Vasilievich (1863-). Moscow industrialist and public figure. Chairman, Moscow District Zemstvo Board, 1891-94, and subsequently member of the Moscow provincial zemstvo board and city duma. Participated in various zemstvo congresses. Elected as a Kadet to Second, Third, and Fourth Dumas. Mayor of Moscow, 1914-17. During World War I, President of the All-Russian Union of Municipalities, member of the central committee of the All-Russian Union of Zemstvos, and deputy chairman of the Moscow War Industry Committee.

CHELYSHEV, Michael Dmitrievich (1866-). Samaran millionaire. Temperance leader. Member of Third Duma; an Octobrist.

CHERNIAEV, Michael Grigorievich (1828-1898). General. Conqueror of Tashkent, 1865.

CHERNOV, Victor Mikhailovich (1873-1952). Founder, leader, and chief theoretician of the Socialist Revolutionary Party, 1902- . Minister of Agriculture in Provisional Government, May-Sept 1917. Chairman of the Constituent Assembly, Jan 1918.

CHERNYSHEVSKY, Nicholas Gavrilovich (1828-1889). Radical journalist, philosopher, and critic of the early nineteenth century.

CHICHERIN, Boris Nikolaevich (1828-1904). Historian, legal theorist, and liberal politician. Professor of Legal History, Moscow University until 1868; forced to resign for radical views. Mayor of Moscow, 1881-83; forced to resign. Regarded as one of the founders of modern Russian liberalism and a father of the Kadet Party.

CHICHINADZE (Kartvelov), N.G. Social Democrat (Menshevik) from the Caucasus.

CHIRIKOV, Eugene Nikolaevich (1864-1932). Minor writer; member of *Znanie* school of fiction.

CHKEIDZE, Nicholas Semonovich (1864-1926). Georgian Menshevik. Leader of Menshevik faction in Third and Fourth Dumas. First chairman of the Petrograd Soviet, May-Aug 1917. Chairman of Georgian Constituent Assembly. Emigrated after Soviet conquest of Georgia in 1921; died a suicide.

CHOLOKAEV, Prince Nicholas Nikolaevich (1830-). Elected to State Council by Tambov nobility, 1906. Earlier a provincial arbitrator (*mirovoi posrednik*) in implementing serf emancipation, 1861-68. Justice of the peace, Morshansk district, 1868-83 (chairman, 1871-83). Member of Morshansk board of peasant affairs, 1876-

CHRISTIAN IX. King of Denmark, 1863-1906. Father of Empress Maria Feodorovna, grandfather of Tsar Nicholas II.

CHUKNIN, Gregory Pavlovich (1848-1906). Vice-Admiral. Director, Naval Cadet Corps, 1902-4. Commander, Black Sea Fleet, 1904-6; responsible for suppression of the Sevastopol mutiny of Nov 1905. Assassinated by SR terrorists.

CHUPROV, Alexander Ivanovich (1842-1908). Professor of Political Economy and Statistics, Moscow University, 1874- . Associate of Witte. Member of study commissions on Russian railways and agricultural prices; author of a controversial study on grain production and prices (1897).

CLARETIE, Jule (1840-1913). French author; member of the French Academy. Director of the Comédie-Française.

CLEMENCEAU, Georges (1841-1929). French journalist and politician; wartime leader. Radical deputy, 1876-1902. Senator, 1902-6. Prime Minister, 1906-9, 1917-20. Retired from politics in 1920, devoted energies to writing; elected to the French Academy.

CONRAD von HOTZENDORF, Franz (1852-1925). Austrian Field Marshal. Chief of the General Staff, 1906-11, and 1912-18.

CONSTANS, Jean Antoine Ernest (1833-1913). French statesman and diplomat. Minister of Interior, 1880-81, 1889-90, 1890-92. Senator, 1889-98. Ambassador to Turkey, 1898-1907.

CONSTANTINE I. King of Greece, 1913-17 and 1920-22. The tsar's "Cousin Tino."

CONSTANTINE CONSTANTINOVICH, Grand Duke (1858-1915). Minor author; honorary member of the Imperial Academy of Sciences. Second cousin of Nicholas II.

COPPÉE, François (1842-1908). French poet.

CRISPI, Francesco (1819-1901). Italian statesman. Minister of Interior, 1877-78, 1887. Prime Minister, 1887-91, 1893-96.

CYON, see TSION

CYRIL VLADIMIROVICH, Grand Duke (1876-1938). Cousin of Nicholas II. Claimant to the Russian throne following the murder of the tsar and his brother Michael in 1918. The present head of the Romanov family and claimant is Cyril's son and heir, Vladimir Kirillovich (1917-), who currently resides in Spain.

DANIELSON, Nicholas Frantsevich (pseud. "Nikolay-on") (1844-1918). Populist ideologue and publicist.

DANILOV, (Yuri) George Nikiforovich (1866-1937). General. Known as "Black George." Quartermaster-General of the General Staff, 1909-14. Chief of Staff to General Ruzsky, 1915-17.

DANILOV, Vladimir Nikolaevich (1852-). Adjutant-General. Commander of the Corps of Imperial Guards, 1906-12.

DAVYDOV, L.F. Director of the Credit Chancellery, Ministry of Finance (?-1914); resigned with Kokovtsov, subsequently with Russian Foreign Trade Bank of St. Petersburg.

DEBUSSY, Claude (1862-1918). French composer; associated for a time with the Ballet Russe.

DELCASSÉ, Théophile (1852-1923). French statesman. Chief architect of the Franco-Italian rapprochement (1902-4), the *Entente cordiale* (1904), and the Triple Entente (1907). First elected to parliament, 1889. Minister of Colonies, 1894-96. Minister of Foreign Affairs, 1898-1905. Minister of Marine, 1911-12 (instrumental in Franco-Russian naval convention of 1912). Minister of Foreign Affairs, 1914-15.

DELIANOV, Count Ivan Davydovich (1818-1897). Minister of Public Education, 1882-97; identified, perhaps uncritically, with the "reactionary" educational policy of Alexander III.

DENIKIN, Anton Ivanovich (1872-1947). Lieutenant-General. Rose to command from common origins; graduate of Nicholas Academy of the General Staff. Served in Russo-Japanese War and as an army commander in World War I. Assistant Chief of Staff to Alekseev, Apr-June 1917; Commander in Chief, Western Front, Aug-Sept 1917. Participated in formation of the Volunteer Army during Civil War, succeeded Kornilov as its commander, 1918-20. Yielded command to Wrangel, Mar 1920, and emigrated. Died in the United States.

DÉROULÈDE, Paul (1846-1914). French poet and right-wing politician; leader of the extreme nationalist League of Patriots.

DERVIZ, Dmitry Grigorievich von (1830-). Jurist. Various posts in Ministry of Justice and Senate, 1850-66. Director-General, Senate Court of Cassation for Civil Affairs, 1866- ; State Council, 1884- .

DIAGHILEV, Sergei Pavlovich (1872-1929). Impresario, patron of the arts, and critic. A leader of the Russian artistic renaissance of the 1890s;

founder of *Mir iskusstva*. Founder of the Ballet Russe (Paris, 1909); for the next two decades he surrounded the Ballet with the most talented artists of Russia and Europe.

DIKOV, Ivan Mikhailovich (1835-). Admiral. Minister of Marine, 1907-9.

DILLON, E.J. (1854-1933). British journalist; Russian correspondent for the *Daily Telegraph*. Closely associated with Witte; critic of tsarist regime.

DISRAELI, Benjamin (Earl of Beaconsfield, 1876) (1804-1881). Leader of the British Conservative Party, 1848-81. Chancellor of the Exchequer, 1852, 1858-59; Prime Minister, 1868, 1874-80.

DMITRIUKOV, Ivan Ivanovich (1872-). Octobrist; member of Third and Fourth Dumas; Secretary of the Fourth Duma. Member of the Temporary Committee of the Duma, Feb-Mar 1917.

DMITRY PAVLOVICH, Grand Duke (1891-1942). Son of Paul Aleksandrovich, youngest son of Alexander II; cousin of Nicholas II; involved in the murder of Rasputin.

DMOWSKY, Roman (1864-1939). Polish leader. Founder and chairman of the Polish National Democratic Party; leader of the Polish Kolo in the Second Duma.

DOBROLIUBOV, Nicholas Aleksandrovich (1836-1861). Radical philosopher; intellectual father of Russian Populism.

DOBROVOLSKY, Nicholas Alekseevich (1854-1918). Senator; First Procurator of the Senate. Minister of Justice, Dec 1916-Feb 1917.

DOBUZHINSKY, Mstislav Valerianovich (1875-1957). Painter, set designer (Ballet Russe), etcher, and illustrator. Important figure in the *Mir iskusstva* movement. Active after the revolution mainly in Paris and New York (Metropolitan Opera).

DOLGORUKOV, Prince Peter Dmitrievich (1866-). Zemstvo figure and left-liberal politician. A founder of the Union of Liberation, the journal *Osvobozhdenie*, and the Kadet Party. Member of the zemstvo congresses of 1904-5. Vice-chairman of the First Duma; signed Vyborg manifesto and imprisoned, 1906. Rights restored, 1909; resumed zemstvo activities.

DOROSHEVICH, Vlas Mikhailovich (1864-1920). Journalist; editor of *Russkoe slovo*.

DOSTOEVSKY, Feodor Mikhailovich (1821-1881). Giant of Russian and world literature.

DOUMER, Paul (1857-1932). French statesman. President of France, 1931-32.

DOUMERGE, Gaston (1863-1937). French statesman. Prime Minister, 1913 and 1934. President of France, 1924-31.

DRAGOMIROV. Michael Ivanovich (1830-1905). General; military historian. Professor of Tactics, Nicholas Academy, 1879-98, and tutor to

Tsarevich Nicholas Mikhailovich. Distinguished record in the Russo-Turkish War of 1877-78. Governor of Kiev and Commander, Kiev Military District, 1898-1905. Appointed to State Council, 1903.

DUBASOV, Feodor Vasilievich (1845-1912). Admiral. Served in Russo-Turkish War of 1877-78. Commander, Pacific Squadron, 1897-99. Governor-General of Moscow and Commandant, Moscow Military District, Nov 1905-May 1906. Appointed to State Council, 1906.

DUBROVIN, Alexander Ivanovich (1855-1918). Reactionary politician and anti-semite. Member of the Russian Assembly and founder of the Union of the Russian People, 1905; founder and publisher of its journal, *Russkoe znamia*. Shot by the Bolsheviks in 1918.

DULEBOV, Egor Olimpievich (c.1883-). SR terrorist; assassin of Bogdanovich, 1903.

DUPUY, Charles Alexandre (1851-1923). French statesman. Republican deputy, 1885-; Prime Minister, 1893, 1894-95, and 1898-99.

DURNOVO, Ivan Nikolaevich (1830-1903). Minister of Interior, 1889-95. Chairman of the Committee of Ministers, 1895-1903. Previously Assistant Minister of Interior (1882-85) and State Secretary and Director of the Office for the Management of the Properties of H.I.H. Maria Feodorovna, 1886-89.

DURNOVO, Peter Nikolaevich (1844-1915). Jurist and minister; author of famous and prophetic memorandum urging reconciliation with Germany in the interest of preserving the monarchic principle. Naval officer, 1860-70; various military and civil judicial posts until 1881. Joined Police Department, 1881; Director, 1884-93. Appointed to Senate, 1893. Assistant Minister of Interior, 1900-5 (in charge of Posts and Telegraph, 1903-5); Minister of Interior, Oct 1905-Apr 1906. Appointed to State Council, 1905. His Majesty's State Secretary in 1906.

DURNOVO, Peter Pavlovich (1835-). Governor-General of Moscow, June-Nov 1905. Formerly Director, Department of Appanages of His Majesty's Chancellery, 1882-84.

DZHUNKOVSKY, see JUNKOVSKY.

EDWARD VII. King of England, 1901-10.

EFREMOV, Ivan Nikolaevich (1866-). Journalist. Member of First, Third, and Fourth Dumas; leader of the Progressive Party in Fourth Duma and member of the Progressive Bloc. Minister of Justice (Provisional Government), Aug-Sept 1917.

EISENSTEIN, Sergei Mikhailovich (1898-1948). Major Soviet film-maker.

ELIZABETH of Bavaria (1837-1898). Empress of Austria, 1848-98; assassinated by an anarchist.

ELIZABETH FEODOROVNA, Grand Duchess (1864-1918). Wife of Sergei Aleksandrovich; formerly Elizabeth of Hesse.

ELIZABETH PETROVNA (1709-1761). Empress of Russia, 1741-61; daughter of Peter the Great.

ELIZAROV, Mark Timofeevich (1862-1919). Revolutionary; one of the first Russian Marxists. Husband of Anna Ilynichna Ulianova (1864-1935), Lenin's sister.

ENGELHARDT, Boris Aleksandrovich. Colonel. Member of Fourth Duma (Centrist Party). Member of the Temporary Committee of the Duma and chairman of its military commission, Feb-Mar 1917.

ENVER PASHA (1879-1922). Leader of the Young Turks. War minister during World War I.

ERMOLOV, Alexis Sergeevich (1847-1917). Director, Main Administration of Agriculture and State Domains, 1894-1905. Member of the State Council, 1905-17. Began administrative career in the Ministry of Finance, 1871; Director, Department of Indirect Taxation, 1883-92; Assistant Minister of Finance, 1892; and head of the Department of State Domains, 1893.

ESSEN, Nicholas Ottovich von (1860-1915). Admiral. Hero of the Russo-Japanese War; commanded the cruiser *Novik* and later the battleship *Sevastopol*. Chief, Operations Department, Naval General Staff, 1908-15. Commander of the Baltic Fleet until his death (from pneumonia) in May 1915.

EULENBURG, Count Phillip von (1847-1921). German diplomat and close personal friend of Emperor William II. Prussian Secretary of Legation: Munich, 1881-87 and 1891-94; Oldenburg, 1888-90; Stuttgart, 1890-91. Ambassador to Vienna, 1894-1902. Frequently represented the foreign ministry in the kaiser's personal retinue.

EVERT, Alexis Ermolovich (1857-1917). General-Adjutant. Chief of Army Main Staff, 1906-8. Governor-General of Irkutsk, 1912-14. Commander of the Western Front, Aug 1915-Apr 1917.

EVLOGY, Bishop (1868-1945). Archbishop of Kholm and Lublin and in 1916-17 of Volynia. Moderate rightist deputy in Third Duma; member of the bureau of the Nationalist group. Noted for efforts to create a "Russian" province of Kholm in the Polish Kingdom.

FALLIÈRES, Armand (1841-1931). French statesman. Radical Republican deputy, 1876- ; held several ministerial posts, 1882-92. Senator, 1890-1906; President of the Senate, 1899-1906. President of the Republic, 1906-13.

FELKERSHAM (Felkerzam), Baron Gamilkar Evgenevich (1855-). Octobrist deputy in Third and Fourth Dumas. Member of the Baltic German aristocracy, elected from Kurland.

FEODOSIEV, Sergei Grigorievich (1880-). Assistant Minister of Finance, 1916. State Comptroller, Dec 1916-Feb 1917.

FERDINAND of Coburg (1861-1948). Prince (1887-1908) and King (Tsar) of Bulgaria, 1908-18.

FET (Shenshin), Afanasy Afanasievich (1820-1892). Major poet; a conservative idealist.

FILOSOFOV, Dmitry Aleksandrovich (1861-1907). One of Witte's close associates. Began career in 1886 in the Ministry of Public Education;

transferred to Imperial Chancellery in 1887: State Secretary, Section of State Economy, 1899-1900; Section of Industry, Science, and Commerce, 1900-1. Assistant State Comptroller, 1901-5; State Comptroller, Oct 1905-Apr 1906. Minister of Commerce and Industry, July 1906-Jan 1907. Appointed to State Council in 1906.

FISHER, Sir John (1841-1920). British Admiral. First Sea Lord, 1904— revolutionized naval architecture by directing construction of the first dreadnought.

FOCK, Alexander Viktorovich (1843-). Major-General. Commanded 4th East Siberian Rifle Division in Boxer Rebellion and early stages of Russo-Japanese War. Stessel's right-hand man during siege of Port Arthur; acquitted by court-martial but forced to resign commission, 1908. Served as volunteer in Bulgarian Army in First Balkan War. Earlier service in Corps of Gendarmes (1871-76), Russo-Turkish War, and various regimental commands.

FOFANOV, Constantine Mikhailovich (1862-1911). Lyric poet.

FOKINE, Michel Mikhailovich (1880-1942). Choreographer; father of modern ballet. With the Imperial Ballet (Mariinsky Theater) until 1908 when he joined Diaghilev's company in Paris.

FRANK, Simon Ludvigovich (1877-1950). Philosopher. Professor of Philosophy, Saratov University, Moscow University. Contributor to *Vekhi.*

FRANZ FERDINAND (1863-1914). Austrian Archduke (heir, 1896); assassinated at Sarajevo, Bosnia, 28 June 1914.

FRANZ JOSEPH (1830-1916). Emperor of Austria, 1848-1916, and King of Hungary, 1867-1916.

FREDERICKS, Baron Vladimir Borisovich (1838-1922?). General (aide-de-camp). Assistant Minister of the Imperial Court, 1893-97, and Minister, 1897-1917. Intimate of Nicholas II. Made a count, 1913. Arrested, 1917; allowed to retire to his estate in Finland in 1921.

FRENCH, Sir John Denton Pinkstone (1852-1925). British General. Inspector-General, 1907-11, 1914; Chief, Imperial General Staff, 1911-14. Promoted to Field Marshal, 1913. Commander, British Expeditionary Force, France, 1914-15. Viscount, 1915; 1st Earl of Ypres, 1921.

FRISCH, Edward Vasilievich (1833-1907). Jurist. Senate Court of Cassation for Criminal Affairs, 1860- ; Procurator, 1870. Assistant Minister of Justice, 1876-83. Appointed to State Council, 1883: Director of Codification Department, 1883-93; of Department for Civil and Ecclesiastical Affairs, 1897-99; of Legislative Department, 1900-6. Chairman of the State Council, May 1906-1907.

FROLOV, Ivan (-1906). Sailor; SR terrorist. Killed attempting to assassinate General Nepliuev in Sevastopol.

FULLON, Ivan Aleksandrovich (1844-1918). General-Adjutant and General of Infantry. Chief of Special Gendarme Corps, Poland. Governor of St. Petersburg, 1904-5 (backer of Father Gapon). Commander, Eleventh Army Corps, 1905-11.

GAPON, George Apollonovich (1870-1906). Priest; leader of the workers' march on the Winter Palace, 9/22 Jan 1905. Trained for priesthood, Poltava Seminary, 1893- , and Petersburg Spiritual Academy, 1898-1903. Became a Zubatov organizer in 1902; organized the Assembly of St. Petersburg Factory Workers, 1903-4. Fled abroad after Bloody Sunday; failed to unite revolutionary parties under his leadership. Returned to Russia and became secret agent for the Okhrana. Denounced as provocateur by Paul Rutenberg; "executed" by a revolutionary committee in March 1906.

GARSHIN, Vsevolod Mikhailovich (1855-1888). Popular novelist.

GEGECHKORY, Evgeny Petrovich (1879-1954). Georgian Menshevik; lawyer by profession. Menshevik leader in Third Duma. Member of the Presidium of the All-Russian Soviet, 1917. Minister of Foreign Affairs in Georgian Republic. President of the Transcaucasian Government. Emigrated after Soviet conquest of Georgia in 1921.

GEORGE ALEKSANDROVICH, Grand Duke (1871-1899). Brother of Nicholas II (second surviving son of Alexander III). Heir-apparent, 1894-99.

GERE, Vladimir Ivanovich (1837-1919). Professor of History; corresponding member of Academy of Sciences. Octobrist; appointed to State Council, 1907.

GERSHENZON, Michael Osipovich (1869-1925). Literary critic and historian. Author of several important works on Russian social thought; editor of *Vekhi*. After 1917, chairman of department of literature of the Academy of Arts and Sciences.

GERSHUNI, Gregory Andreevich (1870-1908). Founder and leader of the Socialist Revolutionary Party; member of its central executive committee, 1902-8. Organizer and leader of the SR Battle Organization, 1902-3.

GIERS, Michael Nikolaevich (1856-1924). Diplomat. Minister to Brazil, 1895-98; Peking, 1898-1901; Munich, 1901-2; Bucharest, 1902-12. Ambassador to Constantinople, 1912-14; to Rome, 1915-17.

GIERS, Nicholas Karlovich (1820-1895). Deputy foreign minister, 1875-82. Minister of Foreign Affairs, 1882-95.

GIOLITTI, Giovanni. Italian prime minister, 1891-93.

GIPPIUS, see HIPPIUS.

GLADSTONE, William Ewart (1809-1898). British statesman and Liberal Party leader. Colonial Secretary, 1845-46. Chancellor of the Exchequer, 1852-55, 1859-65, 1880-82. Prime Minister, 1868-74, 1880-85, 1886, and 1892-94.

GLAZOV, Vladimir Gavrilovich (1848-1916). General. Chief of the Nicholas Academy of the General Staff, 1901-4. Minister of Public Education, Oct 1904-Oct 1905.

GOBINEAU, Count Joseph Arthur de (1816-1882). French diplomat, but known mainly as a racial theorist.

GODNEV, Ivan Vasilievich (1856-). Economist. Member of Third and Fourth Dumas. Originally an Octobrist, later identified with center group. Member of the Progressive Bloc. State Comptroller (Provisional Government), Mar-Aug 1917.

GOGOL, Nicholas Vasilievich (1809-1852). Major writer; satirist.

GODUNOV, Boris Feodorovich (1551-1605). Successor to Ivan the Terrible: Regent, 1584-98. Tsar of Russia, 1598-1605.

GOLITSYN, Prince Nicholas Dmitrievich (1850-1925). Last Chairman of the Council of Ministers, Dec 1916-Feb 1917. No previous significant responsibilities.

GOLOVIN, Feodor Aleksandrovich (1867-). Liberal politician. Member, Moscow provincial zemstvo board, 1898- (chairman, 1904-6). A founder of the Union of Liberation, the congress of zemstvos, and the Kadet Party; organized and served as chairman of the Kadet Moscow committee. Chairman of the Second Duma. Elected to Third Duma, resigned 1910. Active in the Union of Municipalities during World War I. In the Provisional Government's administration, and after the second revolution in the Soviet administration.

GOLUCHKOWSKY, Count Agenor (1849-1921). Austrian statesman. Ambassador to Rumania, 1887-94. Minister of Foreign Affairs, 1894-1906; followed a policy of status quo with Russia in the Balkans.

GORCHAKOV, Prince Alexander Mikhailovich (1798-1883). Minister of Foreign Affairs, 1856-82. Chancellor, 1867-82.

GORDON, Charles George (1833-1885). British General. In China, 1860-64; Egypt, 1874-80. Killed by Mahdists at Khartum, 1884.

GOREMYKIN, Ivan Logginovich (1839-1917). Major conservative statesman. Chairman of the Council of Ministers, 1906 and 1914-16. Earlier service as Director-General, Second Department of the Senate, 1890-95; and Assistant Minister and Minister of Internal Affairs, 1895-99. An opponent of Witte.

GORKY, Maxim (pseud. of Alexis Maksimovich Peshkov) (1868-1936). Major realist writer of short stories, novels, and plays. Gained rapid fame in late 1890s. Led and supported a new school of radical realist writers grouped around his publishing house, *Znanie.* Provided active literary and financial support to the Bolsheviks; subsequently recognized in the USSR as the founder of "socialist realism" and the father of proletarian literature.

GOTZ, Michael Rafailovich (pseud. M. Rafailov) (1866-1906). Founder and early leader of the Socialist Revolutionary Party; member of the SR central executive committee in Geneva and co-editor of its journal.

GREDESKUL, Nicholas Andreevich (1864-). Professor of Law. Member of Kadet central committee. Second Vice Chairman of the First Duma. Resigned from Kadet Party in 1916.

GREY, Sir Edward (1862-1933). British Liberal statesman. Parliamentary Under-Secretary for Foreign Affairs, 1892-95; Foreign Secretary,

Dec 1905-Dec 1916. Instrumental in the Anglo-Russian rapprochement of 1907 and the strengthening of the Triple Entente.

GRIGORIEV, Boris (1886-). Impressionist painter; emigrated to Germany in 1918.

GRIGOROVICH, Dmitry Vasilievich (1822-1899). Novelist. A precursor of Turgenev as a realist who drew upon peasant life for his subjects, but most important for his role in the "discovery" of Dostoevsky and later of Chekov.

GRIGOROVICH, Ivan Konstantinovich (1853-1930). Admiral. Minister of Marine, 1911-17. Earlier, Commandant of Port Arthur (1904) and of Kronstadt (1908-9).

GRINGMUT, Vadim Andreevich (1851-1907). Conservative journalist. Editor of *Moskovskie vedomosti*, 1897-1907. Founder and chairman of the Russian Monarchist Party, 1906-7.

GRIPPENBERG, Oscar Kazmirov (1838-1916). General. Commander of the Vilna Military District, 1902-4. Commanded Second Manchurian Army, 1904-5. Inspector-General of Infantry, 1905-6.

GRODEKOV, Nicholas Ivanovich (1843-1914). General. Governor-General of the Amur and Commandant, Amur Military District, 1898-1902. Succeeded Linevich as Supreme Commander of Russian Army in the Far East, Feb 1906. Governor-General of Turkestan, 1906-7.

GROMAN, V.G. (1875-). Menshevik, economist. Head of food supply commission of Petrograd Soviet, 1917; subsequently directed Soviet State Planning Commission. Purged and convicted of "wrecking activities" in 1931.

GRUZENBERG, Oscar Osipovich (1865-1940). Leading Jewish attorney; involved in several major political cases, including the Beilis trial. Died in France.

GUCHKOV, Alexander Ivanovich (1862-1936). Wealthy industrialist; major political figure after 1905. Served with Boers as a volunteer in the Boer War; headed Russian Red Cross in Manchuria during Russo-Japanese War (captured). Founder and early leader of the Union of October 17. Dominant figure in the Third Duma (chairman, 1910-11); initially supported Stolypin. Elected from Moscow to State Council. Served during World War I as Chairman of the Russian Red Cross and then Chairman of the Central War Industries Committee. Member of the Progressive Bloc. Plotted military coup and overthrow of Nicholas II. Received the Tsar's act of abdication at Pskov. First Minister of War and of Marine in the Provisional Government, Mar-May 1917. In exile after October; died in Paris.

GUMILYOV, Nicholas Stepanovich (1886-1921). Acmeist poet; leader of Russian modernism. Executed in 1921.

GUREV, Alexander Nikolaevich (1864-). Close associate of Witte in Ministry of Finance; secretary and later a member of the ministry's scientific committee. Frequent contributor to journals on financial questions; editor of *Russkoe gosudarstvo*, a semi-official journal subsidized by the government during the Witte era.

GURKO, Joseph Vladimirovich (1828-1901). Field Marshal. Distinguished record in Russo-Turkish War, 1877-78. Commander, Odessa Military District, 1882-83. Governor-General of Warsaw and commander of Russian forces in Poland, 1883-94.

GURKO (Romeiko-Gurko), Vasily Ivanovich (1864-). Lieutenant-General. Acting Chief of Staff to the Supreme Commander in Chief, 1916-Feb 1917.

GURKO, Vladimir Iosifovich (1862-1927). Son of the field marshal; state official, agrarian expert. In the secretariat of the Imperial Chancellery, 1895-1902; Manager of the Peasant Section and later Assistant Minister of Interior, 1902-6. Played a major role in drafting what became Stolypin's agrarian reform. Retired from government service; active in Tver zemstvo, 1906-12. Elected to State Council, 1912. Helped draft the program of the Progressive Bloc, 1915. Joined anti-Bolshevik forces in Ukraine, 1917; emigrated, 1919, and died in Paris. Author of several works on agrarian problems and an important memoir.

GURLAND, Ilya Yakovlevich (1868-). Professor of Constitutional Law; official in the Ministry of Interior: Department of General Affairs, 1904-7; council of the ministry, 1907- . Editor of *Rossiia* (official publication), 1907-16; head of the government's press bureau, 1916-17. Emigrated after the February Revolution.

GVOZDEV, Kuzma Antonovich (1883-). Menshevik leader. Chairman of the Labor Group of the Central War Industries Committee, 1915-17. Minister of Labor (Provisional Government), Sept-Oct 1917. Subsequently in Soviet government in the People's Commissariat of Communications.

HANOTAUX, Gabriel (1853-1944). French Minister of Foreign Affairs, 1894-95, 1896-98.

HARDING, Warren G. (1865-1923). Twenty-ninth President of the United States (1921-23).

HARDINGE, Sir Charles (1858-1944). British diplomat. Junior diplomatic posts, 1881-98. Secretary of Embassy, St. Petersburg, 1898-1903. Assistant Under-Secretary for Foreign Affairs, 1903-4. Ambassador to St. Petersburg, 1904-6. Permanent Under-Secretary for Foreign Affairs, 1906-10, 1916-20. Viceroy of India, 1910-16. Ambassador to Paris, 1920-22.

HARRIMAN, Edward Henry (1848-1909). American financier.

HARTWIG, Nicholas Henrikovich (-1914). Diplomat. Assistant Director (1897-1900) and Director (1900-6), First Department of the Ministry of Foreign Affairs. Minister to Persia, 1906-9; to Serbia, 1909-14. Played major role in formation of the Balkan League.

HASENKAMPF, Michael Alekseevich (1843-1913). General. Commander of Troops, St. Petersburg Military District, 1905-13.

HATZFELDT, Count Paul Melchiorre (1831-1901). German diplomat. Ambassador to Turkey, 1879-81. State-Secretary for Foreign Affairs, 1881-85. Ambassador to Great Britain, 1885-1901.

HEARN, Lafcadio (1850-1904). American-Japanese writer.

HEIDEN, Count Feodor Logginovich (1821-1900). General-Adjutant and General of Infantry. Chief of Army Main Staff, 1866-77. Acting Minister of War, 1877-78. Governor-General of Finland and Commander of the Finnish Military District, 1881-97.

HEIFETZ, Yascha (1901-). Celebrated violinist. Pupil of Leopold Auer. Left Russia, 1917; U.S. citizen since 1925.

HENRY, Prince of Prussia (1862-1929). Brother of Kaiser William II. Naval career, 1878-1918: Vice-Admiral, 1895; Commander, Far Eastern Squadron (Kiaochow), 1898; Admiral, 1901; Grand Admiral, 1909.

HERMOGEN (-1918?). Bishop of Saratov; reactionary fanatic and anti-semite. Originally a supporter, then enemy of Rasputin; exiled. Bishop of Tobolsk, 1915; befriended the Emperor during his confinement there in 1917. Killed by the Bolsheviks.

HERRIOT, Édouard (1872-1957). French statesman; Radical Socialist leader. Served in several governments and headed three (1924-32). Important writer; member of the French Academy.

HERZEN, Alexander Ivanovich (1812-1870). Radical thinker; father of Russian socialism. Editor of the influential *Kolokol* (London, 1857-67).

HERZENSTEIN, Michael Yakovlevich (1859-1906). Economist and liberal politician. Professor, Moscow University, 1903. Elected to Moscow municipal duma, 1905; chairman of its finance committee; also member of the Moscow provincial zemstvo assembly. Elected as Kadet to First Duma; vocal critic of government's agrarian policy. Assassinated in Finland by Black Hundred terrorists organized by Dubrovin.

HILL, James J. (1836-1916). American financier.

HINDENBURG, Paul von Beneckendorf- (1847-1934). German Field Marshal. Commanded German forces in East Prussia and the Eastern Front, 1914-16. Supreme Commander, Armies of the Central Powers, 1916-18. President of the German Republic, 1925-33.

HIPPIUS, Vladimir Vasilievich (1876-1941). Writer.

HIPPIUS, Zinaida Nikolaevna (pseud. Anton Krainy) (1867?-1945). Symbolist poet and writer. Brilliant literary critic and social commentator; evinced great skill and power in poetry, less success in prose. Wife of D.S. Merezhkovsky.

HOFFMAN, Max von (1867-1927). German General. Served on Eastern Front throughout World War I as commander of Eighth Army, 1914-16, and Commander in Chief, Aug 1916-1918.

HOHENLOHE, Prince Ludwig Carl Victor (1819-1901). German statesman. Ambassador to France, 1874-85. Governor-General of Alsace-Lorraine, 1885-94. Reich Chancellor and Minister-President of Prussia, 1894-1900.

HOLSTEIN, Baron Friedrich August von (1837-1909). German statesman. Prussian diplomat, 1860-76. Counselor, Foreign Ministry, 1876-1909. Largely anonymous but basic influence on German foreign policy after 1890; convinced of inevitability of Russo-German conflict; sought closer ties with Austria and England.

HOROWITZ, Vladimir (1904-). Renowned pianist. Acquired world fame during European debut, 1924. Born Kiev, lived mainly in United States.

HSIEN-FENG. Emperor of China, 1851-61.

HUMBERT I (1844-1900). King of Italy, 1878-1900; assassinated by an anarchist.

HUNG HSIU-CHUAN (1814-1864). Founder and leader of the Taiping movement and rebellion, 1848-64.

IGNATIEV, Count Alexis Pavlovich (1842-1906). Lieutenant-General. In active service, 1859-85. Governor-General of Irkutsk, 1885-89; of Kiev, 1889-96. Appointed to State Council, 1896; chairman, Conference to Examine Special Regulations for Preservation of State Order, 1896; Special Conference on Religious Toleration, 1905. Assassinated in Kiev in 1906 by an SR terrorist.

IGNATIEV, Count Nicholas Pavlovich (1832-1908). Diplomat and statesman. Military attache, London, 1856; envoy to Khiva and Bokhara, 1858; to Peking, 1859—negotiated Treaty of Peking, 1860. Head of the Asiatic Department, Ministry of Foreign Affairs, 1861-64. Minister, then Ambassador to Turkey, 1864-77; major negotiator of Treaty of San Stefano, 1878. Governor of Nizhni Novgorod, 1877-81. Minister of Interior, 1881-82; helped set the conservative course of reign of Alexander III. Member of State Council, 1877-1908.

IGNATIEV, Count Paul Nikolaevich (1870-1926). Assistant Minister of Agriculture, 1912-15. Minister of Public Education, Jan 1915-Dec 1916.

IMERETINSKY, Prince Alexander Konstantinovich (1837-1900). General-Adjutant. Member of the State Council. Chief Military Procurator and Chairman, Supreme Military-Judicial Administration, 1881-91. Governor-General of Warsaw, 1897-99. Nicholas II's personal emissary to the German court, 1899.

IOLLOS, G.B. (1859-1907). Liberal editor of *Russkie vedomosti*, member of Kadet Party, deputy in First Duma. Assassinated by Black Hundred terrorists.

ITO Hirobumi, Marquis (1841-1909). Japanese statesman and diplomat. Prime Minister, 1886-89, 1894-96, 1898, 1900-1. President of the Privy Council, 1889, 1903. Resident-General, Korea, 1906-9; assassinated by a Korean nationalist. An advocate of compromise with Russia, a major figure in negotiations with the Russian government before the Russo-Japanese War.

IVAN IV VASILIEVICH (1530-1584). Ivan the Terrible, Tsar of All the Russias, 1533-84.

IVANOV, Nicholas Yudovich (1851-1918). General-Adjutant. Served in Russo-Japanese War; suppressed Kronstadt mutiny of Oct 1905 and then served as Governor of Kronstadt, Nov 1905-Apr 1907. Commander of the Imperial Guards and Commandant of St. Petersburg Military District, Jan 1906-Dec 1908. Commandant, Kiev Military District, 1908-14. Commander, Southwestern Front, 1914-Mar 1916. Sent by Nicholas II to restore order in Petrograd, Feb 1917, but his mission was interrupted by mutinies and the tsar's abdication.

IVANOV, Viacheslav Ivanovich (1866-). Major symbolist poet and prose writer; the dominant figure in Petersburg poetic circles, 1905-11. Compared to John Milton for his major work, *Cor Ardens* (1911). Professor of Greek, Azerbaijan State University (Baku), 1921-24; then emigrated to Italy.

IZGOEV (Lande), Alexander Solomonovich (1872-). Prominent *intelligents*, Kadet publicist. Regarded as an outstanding thinker until his participation in *Vekhi*.

IZVOLSKY, Alexander Petrovich (1856-1919). Diplomat and statesman. Minister to the Vatican, 1894-97; to Serbia, 1897; to Bayern (Munich), 1897-99; to Japan, 1899-1902; to Denmark, 1902-6. Minister of Foreign Affairs, Apr 1906-Sep 1910: followed a policy of stronger ties with France, rapprochement with England, and reconciliation with Japan; humiliated by Aerenthal in the Bosnian Crisis. Ambassador to France, 1910-May 1917.

JAGOW, Gottlieb von (1863-1935). German Secretary of State for Foreign Affairs, 1913-16.

JAURÈS, Jean (1859-1914). Leader of the French Socialist Party, 1885-1914; co-founder (with Briand) of *L'Humanité* (1904) and editor, 1904--14. Assassinated by a French nationalist, July 1914.

JOFFRE, Joseph Charles Cesaire (1852-1931). Marshal of France. Victor of the First Battle of the Marne, Sep 1914. Supreme Commander, Armies of France, 1914-16. Gained earlier fame in French colonial wars, including the conquest of Madagascar.

JUNKOVSKY, Vladimir Feodorovich (1865-1918). Assistant Minister of Interior and Commander of the Corps of Gendarmes, 1913-15.

KALIAEV, Ivan Platonovich (1877-1905). Socialist Revolutionary terrorist; chief assassin of Grand Duke Sergei Aleksandrovich (Moscow, 1905).

KAMENEV (Rosenfeld), Lev Borisovich (1883-1936). Bolshevik leader. Active in Russian revolutionary underground; Russian representative on the Bolshevik central committee, 1914-17. Prominent Soviet official, rival of Stalin. Purged 1935; a central figure in the first show trial, 1936, following which he was executed.

KAMENSKY, Peter Valerievich (1861-). Octobrist; member of the Third Duma.

KANKRIN, Count Egor Frantsevich (1774-1845). Minister of Finance, 1823-44.

KAPUSTIN, Michael Nikolaevich (1828-1899). Jurist. Professor of International Law, Moscow University. Tutor to Tsarevich Nicholas Aleksandrovich.

KAPUSTIN, Michael Yakovlevich (1847-). Professor of Medicine. Active in zemstvo medical and health programs. Member of the Octobrist Bureau and deputy in Third and Fourth Dumas.

KARABCHEVSKY, Nicholas Platonovich (1851-1925). Prominent attorney and author of legal studies. Defense attorney in the Beilis trial.

KARAMZIN, Nicholas Mikhailovich (1766-1820). Major historian of early nineteenth century; novelist, translator. Founder of *Vestnik evropy* (1802).

KARAULOV, Michael Aleksandrovich (1878-1917). Ataman of the Terek Cossacks. Member of Second and Fourth Dumas and of the Temporary Committee of the Duma, Feb-Mar 1917. Killed in December.

KARNEBEECK, Jonkheer Hermann van. Netherlands delegate to the First Hague Conference, 1899; President of its First Commission. Former Minister of Foreign Affairs.

KARPOV, Victor Ivanovich (1859-). Rightist. Elected to State Council, 1907. Member of the permanent committee of the United Nobility.

KARPOVICH, Peter Vladimirovich (1874-1917). Socialist Revolutionary terrorist; assassin of education minister N.P. Bogolepov in 1901.

KARSAVINA, Tamara (1885-). Prima ballerina with the Imperial Ballet, 1902- , and the Ballet Russe, 1909- . Married British diplomat Henry Bruce in 1915 and settled in England.

KARTSOV, Yuri S. A member of the Russian Assembly.

KASATKIN-ROSTOVSKY, Prince Nicholas Feodorovich (1848-1908). Leader of the Kursk nobility; prominent spokesman of the extreme right. Marshal of nobility, Povosolsk district, 1890-94. A founder of the United Nobility. Elected to the State Council, 1906.

KASPEROV, Vasily Ivanovich. Economist. Colleague of Witte; expert on grain prices and international grain trade; Manager of grain-trade section, Ministry of Commerce and Industry.

KASSO, Lev Aristidovich (1865-1914). Minister of Public Education, Sep 1910-Nov 1914.

KATKOV, Michael Nikiforovich (1818-1887). Influential conservative journalist; editor of *Moskovskie vedomosti*.

KAUFMAN, Constantine Petrovich (1818-1882). General. Directed conquest of much of Central Asia; Samarkand, 1868; Khiva, 1873; and Kokand, 1875-76. Governor-General of Turkestan, 1867-82.

KAULBARS, Baron Alexander Vasilievich von (1844-1929). General. Commander of Third and later of Second Siberian Army in the Russo-Japanese War. Governor of Odessa, 1905-9. Previous service in Central Asia (Khiva expedition, 1873) and in Russo-Turkish War of 1877-78. Held various garrison commands and served on Serbian Boundary Commission, 1882.

KELLER, Count F.A. General. Commander, Third Cavalry Corps, 1916-17.

KERENSKY, Alexander Feodorovich (1881-1968). Major socialist leader. Early prominence as a defense attorney in political cases. Originally a Socialist Revolutionary, then leader of the Trudovik faction in Third and Fourth Dumas. Vice President of Petrograd Soviet, 1917, and member of the Provisional Government: Minister of Justice, Mar-May; of War and Marine, May-Aug; Prime Minister, July-Oct. Emigrated and eventually settled in the United States.

KHABALOV, Sergei Semenovich (1858-1924). Lieutenant-General. Commandant, Petrograd Military District, 1916-Feb 1917.

KHARITONOV, Peter Alekseevich (1852?-1916). Bureaucrat. In Ministry of Justice, 1873-88. Codification Department of State Council, 1888-92. Director, State Printing Office, 1891-93. In Imperial Chancellery, 1893-1905: Assistant State Secretary, First (legislative) Section, 1893-97; Acting State Secretary, Second Section (civil and ecclesiastical affairs), 1897-1904; Assistant Imperial Secretary (director), 1904-5. Appointed to State Council, 1906. State Comptroller, Sep 1907-Jan 1916. In 1911 His Majesty's State Secretary.

KHARUZIN, Alexis Nikolaevich (1864-). Governor of Bessarabia, 1904-8. Director, Department for Ecclesiastical Affairs of Foreign Religions, 1908-11. Assistant Minister of Interior and Director of Department of General Affairs, 1911-13. Senator, 1913-17.

KHILKOV, Prince Michael Ivanovich (1834-1909). Railroad engineer and administrator. Head of the Bulgarian Ministries of Public Works, Communications, and Trade and Agriculture, 1882-85. Directed several Russian state railways, 1885-95. Minister of Ways and Communications, 1895-1905. Appointed to the State Council, 1905.

KHLEBNIKOV, Victor Vladimirovich (1885-1922). Poet; principal creator of Russian futurism.

KHODASEVICH, Vladislav (Wladyslaw Chodasiewicz) (1886-1939). Russian-Polish poet.

KHODSKY, Leonid Vladimirovich (1854-1919). Professor of Public Finance, St. Petersburg University, 1895- . Major critic of the Witte system. Editor and publisher of *Narodnoe khoziaistvo* (1900-5) and the Left-Kadet newspaper *Nasha zhizn* (1904-6).

KHOMIAKOV, Nicholas Alekseevich (1850?-1925). Conservative leader. Active in the zemstvo movement; also served in the Ministry of Agriculture. Member of Octobrist Party. Elected to State Council, 1906, and to the last three Dumas. Chairman of the Third Duma; resigned 1910. Member of the Progressive Bloc. Served in the Red Cross with Denikin during the Civil War; emigrated and died in Yugoslavia. Son of Alexis S. Khomiakov (1804-1860), a famous Slavophile ideologist, philosopher, and theologian.

KHRUSTALEV-NOSAR, George Stepanovich (1879-1918). Radical lawyer; Chairman of St. Petersburg Soviet of Workers Deputies, Oct-Nov 1905.

KHVOSTOV, Alexander Alekseevich (1857-1922). Jurist and minister. Graduated Imperial Alexander Lyceum; entered Ministry of Justice, 1890. In Ministry of Interior, 1895-1905: Chancellery, 1895-1900; Director, Department of Economy, 1900-5. Assistant Minister of Justice, 1905. Appointed to Senate, 1906; to State Council, 1912. Minister of Justice, July 1915-July 1916. Minister of Interior, July-Sep 1916. Arrested by Provisional Government; executed by the Bolsheviks. Sometimes known as "the uncle" (of A.N. Khvostov).

KHVOSTOV, Alexis Nikolaevich (1872-1918). Rightist leader and minister. Began administrative career in Ministry of Justice in early 1890s. Governor of Vologda, 1906-10; of Nizhni Novgorod, 1910-12. Elected to Fourth Duma, 1912, became chairman of the rightist faction. Member of Rasputin's clique; Minister of Interior, Sep 1915-Mar 1916. Arrested by Provisional Government, 1917; shot by the Bolsheviks, Aug 1918. "The nephew" (of A.A. Khvostov).

KIDERLEN-WAECHTER, Alfred von (1852-1912). German diplomat and minister. Secretary of Embassy, Petersburg, 1881-85; Paris, 1885-86; Constantinople, 1886-88. State Secretary for Balkan and Near Eastern Affairs, 1888-94. Minister, Hamburg, 1894-95; Copenhagen, 1895-99; Bucharest, 1899-1910. Acting State Secretary for Foreign Affairs, Nov 1908-Mar 1909 (during Bosnian Crisis). Imperial State Secretary, 1910-12.

KIREEV, Alexander Alekseevich (1833-1910). Lieut.-General. Prominent member of the Slavic Benevolent Society, an old Pan-Slavic organization; publicist and frequent spokesman for other conservative-nationalist organizations.

KISTIAKOVSKY, Bogdan A. (-1922?). Journalist and editor. Prominent figure in liberal intellectual and political circles; contributor to *Vekhi*. Editor of *Kriticheskoe obozrenie*.

KIZEVETTER, Alexander Aleksandrovich (1866-1933). Liberal historian and journalist. Member of the faculties of Moscow University and the Women's Higher Course (Moscow). Member of the Liberation movement, co-founder of the Kadet Party and a member of its executive committee. Elected to the Second Duma. Deported by Soviet government, 1922; settled in Prague as Professor of History at the Charles University and the Russian Emigre University.

KIZHNIAKOV, V.V. One of the founders of the Union of Liberation.

KLADO, Nicholas Lavrentevich (1862-). Captain (Imperial Navy). Critic of naval policy in the Russo-Japanese War; naval correspondent for *Novoe vremia*, 1904-5.

KLEIGELS (Clayhills), Nicholas Vasilievich (1850-1916). General-Adjutant. Chief of Police, Warsaw, 1888-95; St. Petersburg, 1895-1903. Governor-General of Kiev, 1903-5. Aide de camp to Nicholas II, 1903.

KLIUCHEVSKY, Vasily Osipovich (1841-1911). Distinguished historian; Professor of Russian History, Moscow University, 1881-1911.

KNOX, Sir Alfred (1870-). British Major-General. Military attache in Russia, 1911-18; at Stavka, 1914-17.

KNOX, Philander C. (1853-1921). U.S. Secretary of State, 1909-13.

KOBEKO, Dmitry Fomich (1837-). Functionary in the Ministry of Finance, c. 1856-1901. Director, Imperial Public Library, 1902- .

KODAMA Gentaro. Japanese General. Chief of Staff to Marshal Oyama during the Russo-Japanese War.

KOKOVTSOV, Count Vladimir Nikolaevich (1853-1943). Statesman. Graduated Imperial Alexander Lyceum, 1872. Served in Ministry of Justice, 1873-90 (mainly in penal administration). Assistant State Secretary, State Secretary, and Assistant Imperial Secretary of the Imperial Chancellery, 1890-96. Assistant Minister of Finance, 1896-1902. Imperial Secretary, 1902-4. Minister of Finance, 1904-14, and Chairman of the Council of Ministers, Sep 1911-Jan 1914. Titled and retired to State Council, 1914. Emigrated to France, 1918; ended active career as a banker.

KOLCHAK, Alexander Vasilievich (1873-1920). Admiral. Distinguished service in Russo-Japanese War. Initially commanded Baltic torpedo squadrons in World War I. Appointed Rear-Admiral in charge of mine-laying operations in Baltic and Black Seas, 1916. Unprecedented promotion to Vice-Admiral, July 1916; commander of the Black Sea Fleet. Admiral, 1917; resigned. Sent to USA as naval advisor by Provisional Government. Returned to Far East after October Revolution, became minister of war and marine in the Siberian government and in Nov 1918 "Supreme Ruler of All Russia." Led invasion of European Russia, 1919; defeated, captured, and shot by Bolsheviks at Irkutsk, Feb 1920.

KOMISSHARZHEVSKAIA, Vera Feodorovna (1864-1910). Actress and producer. Began career, 1894. Starred in the Aleksandriinsky Theater, Petersburg, 1896-1902. Organized her own Theater of Drama (St. Petersburg, 1904); produced and acted in plays by Gorky and Ibsen.

KOMURA Jutaro (1855-1911). Japanese diplomat. Foreign minister, 1904-4; negotiated the Treaty of Portsmouth. Out of office, 1906-8, because of Japanese resentment over the treaty. Foreign minister, 1908-11; cooperation with Russia to exclude the United States from Manchuria.

KONDRATENKO, Roman Isodorovich (1857-1904). Major-General. Commander, 7th East Siberian Rifle Division, 1904; killed at Port Arthur where he was known as "the soul" of the defense.

KONI, Anatole Feodorovich (1844-1927). Distinguished jurist and scholar. Prominent State Prosecutor, 1870-77. Chairman, St. Petersburg District Court, 1877-81 (presided at trial of Vera Zasulich); Chairman, Civil Department, St. Petersburg Court of Appeals, 1881-85. Director-General, Senate Court of Cassation for Criminal Affairs, 1885-91 and 1892-97. Senator, 1891-92. Honorary member of the Academy of Sciences, 1896. State Council, 1907-17. Professor of Law, St. Petersburg/Leningrad University, 1917-2?.

KONOPOLIANIKOVA, Zinaida (-1906). SR terrorist; assassinated General Min, Aug 1906.

KONOVALOV, Alexander Ivanovich (1875-1948). Industrialist and liberal politician. Vice President, Moscow Stock Exchange; member of the Council of Congresses of the Representatives of Trade and Industry. Member of the Fourth Duma (Progressist) and of the Progressive Bloc. Vice-chairman, Central War Industries Committee. Member of the Temporary Committee of the Duma, Feb 1917. Member of Provisional Government: Minister of Commerce and Industry, Mar-June; and Vice-chairman, Sep-Oct 1917. Died in emigration.

KORKUNOV, Nicholas Mikhailovich (1853-1904). Professor of Law, 1879-1904 (St. Petersburg University, Imperial Alexander Lyceum, Military Law Academy). Member of the Senate Section for the Codification of the Fundamental Laws of Finland, 1893-99.

KORNILOV, Lavr Georgevich (1870-1918). General. Cossack; graduate of Mikhailovsky Artillery School and Nicholas Academy. Served on Afghan frontier and in Russo-Japanese War. Military attache in China, 1907-11. Captured by Austrians during World War I; escaped, 1916—national hero. Appointed Commander of Southwestern Front by the Provisional Government, then Supreme Commander in Chief, July-Sep 1917. Imprisoned after alleged coup against Kerensky; released, Dec 1917. Helped organize the Volunteer Army in southern Russia; killed in action at Ekaterinodar, Apr 1918.

KOROLENKO, Vladimir Galaktinovich (1853-1921). Novelist, journalist, and editor; major Populist writer. Editor of *Russkoe bogatstvo* in late 1890s. Instrumental in the "discovery" of Gorky. Elected to Imperial Academy of Sciences, 1900; subsequently resigned in protest over the annulment of Gorky's election. Sometimes compared to Dickens for his sensitive and humorous characterization of common people.

KOROVIN, Constantine Alekseevich (1861-1939). Painter and set designer. Associated with *Mir isskustva* movement; originally a realist, turned to impressionism at end of nineteenth century. Dramatic sets noted for colorful pageantry intimately related to musical scores.

KOSATKIN-ROSTOVSKY, Prince N.F. Conservative spokesman; opposed majority in the zemstvo congress of July 1905.

KOTTEN, Michael Fridrikovich von (1870-1917). Major-General, Corps of Gendarmes.

KOVALEVSKY, Evgraf Petrovich (1865-). Educator. In Ministry of Public Education, 1890-1904. Octobrist; served in Third and Fourth Dumas.

KOVALEVSKY, Nicholas Nikolaevich (1858-). Zemstvo constitutionalist; a founding member of the Union of Liberation and the Kadet Party. Elected from Kharkov to First Duma.

KOVALEVSKY, Vladimir Ivanovich (1848?-). Agronomist. In Ministry of State Domains, then Ministry of Finance: Director, Department of Industry and Trade, 1892-1900; Assistant Minister (chiefly responsible for trade and industry), 1900-2. President, Imperial Russian Technical Society.

KRAINY, Anton, see HIPPIUS, Z.N.

KRAMÁŘ, Karl (1860-1937). Leader of the Czech Party in the Austrian Chamber of Deputies. Principal founder of the Neo-Slavist movement; organizer of the Prague Slav Congress, 1908.

KRAMSKOY, Ivan Nikolaevich (1837-1887). Realist painter.

KRASNOV, Peter Nikolaevich (1869-1947). Cossack officer. Noted mainly as an anti-Soviet leader. Elected Ataman of the Don Cossacks, May 1918. Active between wars in right-wing emigration in Germany; author of several novels. Fought with German Army in World War II; captured, hanged by Soviet government.

KRAVCHINSKY, Sergei Mikhailovich (pseud. S. Stepniak) (1851-1895). Populist terrorist; journalist.

KRIVOSHEIN, Alexander Vasilievich (1858-1923). Statesman. In Ministries of Justice and Interior, 1884-1905: Assistant Director (1896-1904) and Director (1904-5), Department of Peasant Colonization. Assistant Director, Main Administration of Land Organization and Agriculture, 1905-6. Appointed to State Council, 1906. Assistant Minister of Finance (for Nobles and Peasants Banks), 1905-8. His Majesty's State Secretary, 1910. Director (minister), Main Administration of Land Organization and Agriculture, 1908-15; supported Stolypin's agrarian reform. Active in anti-Bolshevik organizations after October 1917; member of Wrangel's government in southern Russia.

KRUPENSKY, Paul Nikolaevich (1863-). Wealthy Bessarabian landowner; prominent conservative (centrist) leader in Second, Third, and Fourth Dumas. Member of the Progressive Bloc.

KRUPSKAIA, Nadezhda Konstantinovna (1869-1939). Revolutionary; wife of Lenin, 1898- .

KRUSHEVAN, Pavolaki A. (1860-1909). Anti-semite. Publisher of the anti-semitic papers *Bessarabets* and *Drug*; instrumental in precipitating the Kishinev pogrom of 1903. Moved to St. Petersburg, became a central figure in the national campaign against Jews, radicals, and liberals; publisher of *Russkoe znamia*, the organ of the Union of the Russian People, 1905- . Elected to Second Duma as a URP representative. Articles on "The Program for the Conquest of the World by the Jews" in *Russkoe znamia* formed the core of material for the spurious *Protocols of the Learned Elders of Zion.*

KRYMOV, A.M. (-1917). General. As commander of the III Cavalry Corps, part of Guchkov's plot to force the abdication of Nicholas II. Later committed suicide.

KRYZHANOVSKY, Sergei Yefimovich (1862-1934). Functionary. In judiciary, 1885-96, and Ministry of Interior, 1896-1911: Assistant Minister, 1906-11; drafted several important pieces of legislation. Member and State Secretary of the State Council, 1911-17. His Majesty's Imperial Secretary, 1916.

KSCHESSINSKA, Mathilde (Princess Krassinska-Romanovska) (1872-196?). Ballerina of the Imperial Mariinsky Theater, St. Petersburg;

romantically involved with Tsarevich Nicholas Aleksandrovich in early 1890s.

KUANG-HSÜ. Emperor of China, 1875-1908. (See Tzu-hsi)

KULCHITSKY, Nicholas Konstantinovich (1856-1925). Director, Kazan school district, 1912-14; Petrograd, 1914-16. Minister of Public Education, Dec 1916-Feb 1917.

KULIABKO, N.N. Police Colonel. Okhrana chief in Kiev; dismissed for negligence in the assassination of Stolypin, 1911.

KULIKOVSKY, Peter Aleksandrovich. SR terrorist; assassinated P.P. Shuvalov, Mayor of Moscow, 1905.

KUPRIN, Alexander Ivanovich (1870-1938). Minor novelist of the *Znanie* school; a popular writer before World War I.

KURLOV (Komarov-Kurlov), Paul Grigorevich (1860-1923). Police official. Prosecutor in several district courts and Moscow Court of Appeals, 1889-1903. Vice-governor of Kursk, 1903-5. Governor of Minsk, 1905-6; dismissed for illegal activities, investigation suppressed. In Ministry of Interior: Council of the Ministry, 1906-7; Director, Police Department, 1907-9; Assistant Minister and Commandant, Corps of Gendarmes, 1909-11; dismissed for negligence in connection with Stolypin's assassination; prosecution stopped by order of the Tsar. Assistant for Civil Affairs, Vilna Military District, Sep-Nov 1914. Director of the Baltic governments, Nov 1914-Aug 1915. Intimate with Rasputin's associates. In 1916 public pressure prevented his reappointment as assistant interior minister and forced his dismissal from government service.

KUROKI Tametomo. Japanese General. Commanded First Army in Russo-Japanese War (Battle of the Yalu).

KUROPATKIN, Alexis Nikolaevich (1848-1925). General. Served in Central Asia and the Russo-Turkish War, 1866-83. Army Main Staff, 1883-90. Commandant, Trans-Caspian Region, 1890-98. Minister of War, 1898-1904. Assumed command of Manchurian Army and then Supreme Commander in Chief of Far Eastern forces, 1904-5. Appointed to State Council, 1906. In World War I: Commander, Northern Front, Feb-July 1916; Governor-General of Turkestan, 1916-17.

KUSKOVO (Yesipova), Ekaterina Dmitrievna (1869-1958). Journalist, liberal activist. Member of the first Russian Marxist group, then a Legal Marxist and author of the "Credo" of the "Economist" movement (1899). A co-founder of the Union of Liberation and of the Kadet Party; a major voice of the left-liberal intelligentsia. Expelled from the USSR in 1922. Wife of S.N. Prokopovich.

KUTEPOV, A.P. (1882-1930?). Colonel, Preobrazhensky Guards. In Petrograd, Feb-Mar 1917. Later second in command to General Wrangel. Kidnapped in Paris in 1930, presumably by Soviet agents.

KUTLER, Nicholas Nikolaevich (1859-1924). Lawyer, financial administrator. One of Witte's collaborators in the Ministry of Finance, 1882-1904: Assistant Director, 1892, and Director, 1899-1904, Department of Direct Taxation. Assistant Minister of Interior, 1904-5. Assistant Minister of Finance and Manager of the Nobles and Peasants Banks, 1905. Head of the Main Administration of Land Organization and Agriculture, Oct 1905-Feb 1906; forced to resign for advocating compulsory expropriation of private property in agrarian reform. Joined Kadet Party; elected to Third and Fourth Dumas. In the Soviet administration after 1917 in People's Commissariat of Finance; board of directors of Soviet State Bank, 1922-24.

KUTUZOV (Golenishchev-Kutuzov), Prince Michael Illarionovich (1745-1813). Field Marshal. Commander in Chief of the Russian Army, Aug 1812-Apr 1813 (Borodino, Moscow).

KUZMIN-KARAVAEV, Vladimir Dmitrievich (1859-1928). General, jurist, zemstvo leader. Professor of Jurisprudence, Military Law Academy, 1890-99; Nicholas Academy of the General Staff, 1899-1903; and St. Petersburg University, 1909-13. Active as a liberal constitutionalist in the zemstvo congresses of 1904-5; later a co-founder of the Party of Democratic Reforms. Member of the St. Petersburg municipal duma and the First and Second State Dumas. Barrister, St. Petersburg Court of Appeals, 1913-17. Member of Yudenich's Political Conference during the Civil War; died in emigration.

LAMSDORF, Count Vladimir Nikolaevich (1841-1907). Diplomat. Director, Chancellery of the Ministry of Foreign Affairs, 1880-85; Senior Advisor to the Foreign Minister, 1885-97; Assistant Minister, 1897-1900. Minister of Foreign Affairs, 1900-6; opposed aggressive Far Eastern policy.

LAUNITS, Vladimir Feodorovich Schmidt von der (1855-1907). General. Governor of St. Petersburg, 1906-7; assassinated.

LEER, Genrikh Antonovich (1829-1904). General. Tutor of Tsarevich Nicholas Aleksandrovich. Faculty of the General Staff Academy, 1858-98: Professor of Military Strategy, 1869-98; Director, 1889-98.

LEGRAS, Jules (1866-1939). French professor; author of several books on Russia.

LENIN (Ulianov), Vladimir Ilyich (1870-1924). Bolshevik leader.

LEO XIII. Pope, 1878-1903.

LEONTIEV, Constantine Nikolaevich (1831-1891). Conservative philosopher.

LERMONTOV, Michael Yurievich (1814-1841). Poet and writer. Usually ranked second to Pushkin as a lyricist. Major dramatist. His psychological novel, *A Hero of Our Times* (1840), was a landmark in the development of Russian prose. Exiled three times to the Caucasus; killed there in a duel with a fellow officer.

LEROY-BEAULIEU, Anatole (1843-1916). French economist and publicist. Popularized Russia in France; advocate of the Franco-Russian Alliance.

LESKOV, Nicholas Semonovich (1831-1895). Influential novelist.

LESSAR, Paul Mikhailovich (-1905). Engineer and diplomat. Political Agent for Asiatic Affairs, London, 1896-1900; Minister to China, 1901- .

LEVASHOV, S.V. Professor; prominent rightist in the Fourth Duma.

LI Hung-chang (1823-1901). Chinese General and statesman. Member of the Tsungli-Yamen (foreign ministry), 1895-96; Viceroy of Canton, 1899; Governor of Chili, 1900-1. Prominent negotiator with Europe and Russia.

LIDVAL, Egor. Corrupt official; assistant to V.I. Gurko in Ministry of Interior. Used position to embezzle state funds to speculate in grain purchased for famine relief in 1906; indicted but never punished.

LIMAN von SANDERS, Otto (1855-1929). German General. Headed German military mission to Turkey, 1913-18; commanded Turkish forces in World War I.

LINEVICH, Nicholas Petrovich (1838-1908). General of Infantry and General-Adjutant (1903). Early service in the Caucasus and Russo-Turkish War. Military governor of Southern Ussuri Region, 1895-1903; led Russian relief column to Peking in 1900. Commandant and Governor-General of the Amur Region, 1903-4. Commanded First Siberian Army, Nov 1904-Apr 1905 and succeeded Kuropatkin as Supreme Commander. Relieved Feb 1906 for insufficient vigor in suppression of revolutionary activity in Manchurian army.

LITVINOV, Maxim Maximovich (Meyer Wallach) (1876-1951). Revolutionary (1898); Bolshevik. Deputy People's Commissar for Foreign Affairs, 1921-30; Commissar, 1930-39. Again Deputy Commissar, 1941-46, and also Ambassador to the United States, 1941-43; and Minister to Cuba, 1942-43.

LLOYD GEORGE, David (1863-1945). Leader of British Liberal Party. Munitions minister during World War I; Prime Minister, 1918-22.

LOBKO, Paul Lvovich (1838-1905). General of Infantry. Graduated Nicholas Academy, 1861. Chancellery of the War Ministry, 1867-70. Professor, Nicholas Academy, 1870-98—tutor to Tsarevich Nicholas Aleksandrovich, 1885. Appointed to State Council, 1898. State Comptroller, 1899-Oct 1905.

LOMONOSOV, Michael Vasilievich (1711-1765). Eighteenth-century genius—scientist, writer, poet, historian.

LOPUKHIN, Alexis Aleksandrovich (1864-). Public prosecutor, Moscow and Kharkov, 1886-1902. Director, Police Department, 1902-5; responsible for directing Azef's activities. Confirmed Azef's double role in 1908; convicted and imprisoned for betraying official secrets; scapegoat for government's use of agents-provocateur.

LORIS-MELIKOV, Count Michael Tarelovich (1825-1888). General and statesman. Led conquest of Kars, 1877. Governor of Kharkov, 1879-80; Minister of Interior, 1880-81. Drafted "constitution" to allow public participation in legislative affairs as one means of counteracting revolutionary terror. Both he and the project were scrapped after the assassination of Alexander II, 1881.

LOUBET, Émile (1832-1929). French statesman. President of the Republic, 1899-1906.

LUDENDORF, Erich von (1865-1937). German General. Hindenburg's Chief of Staff, Eastern Front, 1914-16; and Supreme Commander, 1916-18.

LUKIANOV, Sergei Mikhailovich (1855-). Assistant Minister of Public Education, 1902-5. Director-General of the Holy Synod, 1909-11; dismissed for opposition to Rasputin and Illiodor.

LUNACHARSKY, Anatole Vasilievich (1875-1933). Literary critic and dramatist; Social Democrat since 1897. Split with Lenin after 1905; associated with Bogdanov, Gorky, and other "god-builders." Rejoined Bolsheviks in 1917; became People's Commissar for Education; removed by Stalin in 1929.

LUTZ, Baron Ludwig Gotlibovich. Kherson landowner. Assistant Prosecutor, Odessa Circuit Court. Octobrist, in last three Dumas.

LUXEMBURG, Rosa (1870?-1919). Major figure in the international socialist movement. Born in Russian Poland; leader of the Social Democratic Party of Poland and Lithuania, 1893-98. Mainly in Germany after 1898; leader of extreme left of German SDs (with Karl Liebknecht). A founder of the German Communist Party, 1919; murdered by *Freikorps* members.

LUZHENOVSKY, G.N. (1870-1906). Alleged Black Hundred organizer; directed suppression of peasant rebellion in Tambov, 1906. Assassinated by Spiridonova.

LVOV, Prince George Evgenevich (1861-1925). Liberal politician. In Ministry of Interior, 1886- : Special Board for Peasant Affairs (Epifan, Moscow, Tula). Member of the zemstvo assemblies of Epifan and Tula; chairman, Tula district zemstvo board, 1903-6. Chairman, All-Russian Union of Zemstvos, 1904-5 and 1914-17. Right-wing Kadet; elected to First Duma. Subsequently in Moscow provincial zemstvo assembly and Moscow municipal duma. Elected Mayor of Moscow, 1913, but not confirmed by the government. Prime Minister and Minister of Interior of the Provisional Government, Mar-June 1917. Arrested by the Bolsheviks, imprisoned at Ekaterinburg; escaped to France by way of Siberia and died in emigration.

LVOV, Nicholas Nikolaevich (1867-1944). Prominent Saratov landowner and public figure. Marshal of the Nobility, Saratov, 1893-1900; chairman, Saratov provincial zemstvo board, 1899. Participated in formation of the Union of Liberation and in the zemstvo congresses of 1904-5. Elected to First, Third and Fourth Dumas; originally a Kadet and one of Stolypin's links with that party. Withdrew in disagreement with Kadet agrarian policy and helped organize the Party of Peaceful Reconstruction. Vice-chairman of Fourth Duma. Joined anti-Bolshevik forces in the Ukraine after October 1917; subsequently emigrated and remained active in White organizations.

LVOV, Vladimir Nikolaevich (1872-). Chairman of the center faction in Third and Fourth Dumas. Director-General of the Holy Synod in the Provisional Government. Left Russia after October, but returned in 1922 and served in the Soviet administration.

LYKOSHIN, Alexander Ivanovich (1861-1918). Technical expert in Ministry of Justice, 1882-1907 (attached to Senate Court of Cassation for Civil Affairs). Member of the Council of the Ministry of Justice and also of the Ministry of Interior, 1904-14. Assistant Minister of Interior and Head of the Peasant Section, 1907-14 (active in drafting the Stolypin agrarian reform). Appointed to the Senate, 1911, and to the State Council, 1914.

MACKENSEN, August von (1849-1945). German Field Marshal. Army commander, Eastern Front, 1915-18; directed the Gorlice-Tarnow breakthrough in 1915.

MAIKOV, Apollon Nikolaevich (1821-1897). Poet. One of the "imagists" who flourished around mid-century; sought to reconcile poetry with science and positivism, without success. Admired by Dostoevsky.

MAIKOV, Leonid Nikolaevich (1839-1900). Realist poet and literary historian.

MAKAROV, Alexander Aleksandrovich (1857-1919). Prosecutor and judge in various district courts, c.1880-1906. Assistant Minister of Interior and Chief of Police, 1906-9. Imperial State Secretary, 1909-11. Minister of Interior, Sep 1911-Dec 1912. Appointed to State Council, 1912. Minister of Justice, July-Dec 1916.

MAKAROV, Stepan Osipovich (1848-1904). Admiral; outstanding naval leader—oceanographer, Arctic explorer, inventor, naval architect, tactician, theorist, and fleet commander. Distinguished service in Russo-Turkish War. Rear-Admiral, 1890. Chief Inspector of Naval Artillery, 1891-94. Commander, Mediterranean Squadron, 1894-95. Vice-Admiral, 1896. Chief of Fleet Training, 1895-99. Commandant of Kronstadt, 1899-1904. Commander, Pacific Fleet; killed in action, 1904.

MAKLAKOV, Nicholas Alekseevich (1871-1918). Reactionary bureaucrat. In Treasury, 1892-1908: Director, Tambov branch, 1906-8. Governor of Chernigov, 1909-11. Minister of Interior, Dec 1912-July 1915. Appointed to State Council, 1915. Shot by Bolsheviks, 1918.

MAKLAKOV, Vasily Alekseevich (1870-1959). Prominent lawyer; leader of Kadet right, and member of the last three Dumas. Chief defense counsel in the Beilis trial. Served as Ambassador to France for the Provisional Government; remained there after October and organized relief for Russian emigres. Brother of N.A. Maklakov.

MANASEIN, Nicholas Avksentevich (1835-1895). Minister of Justice, 1885-94.

MANASEVICH-MANUILOV, I.F. (1869-1918). Police agent, general scoundrel; power broker associated with Rasputin. Imprisoned, 1917; executed, 1918.

MANDELSHTAM, Osip Emilievich (1892-1940?). Major acmeist poet; died in Soviet concentration camp.

MANSUROV, Boris Pavlovich (1828-1910). Conservative statesman. State Secretary to His Imperial Highness, 1859. Appointed to Senate, 1865; to State Council, 1872. Active in Imperial Palestine Society.

MANUILOV, Alexander Apollonovich (1861-1929). Economist. Lecturer (1900), Assistant Rector and Rector, Moscow University, 1905-11. Member of the Moscow municipal duma and provincial zemstvo assembly. Kadet; elected to State Council, 1907-11. Editor of *Russkie vedomosti*. Minister of Education (Provisional Government), Mar-July 1917.

MANUKHIN, Sergei Sergeevich (1856-1921). Jurist. In Ministry of Justice, 1881-1905: First Department—acting director, 1884, and director, 1888; legal counsel, 1890-99. Also Assistant Chief Prosecutor, Senate Court of Cassation for Criminal Affairs from 1890. Assistant Minister of Justice and Director, First Department, 1900-4. Minister of Justice, Jan-Dec 1905. Appointed to State Council, 1906; headed official inquiry into the Lena goldfield massacre, 1912.

MARCHAND, Jean Baptiste (1863-1934). French officer; leader of the French expedition to Fashoda, 1896-98.

MARIA FEODOROVNA (1847-1928). Born Princess Dagmar of Denmark. Wife of Alexander III. Empress of Russia 1881-94; Dowager Empress, 1894- .

MARKOV, Nicholas Evgeneevich (1866-). (Markov II) Leader of the extreme right in Third and Fourth Dumas. Engineer by profession; associated with several private railways until 1908. Member of the Union of the Russian People; chairman, 1910-17.

MARTENS, Feodor Feodorovich (1845-1909). Jurist, diplomat, Professor of International Law, St. Petersburg University. Leading Russian authority on international law. Privy Councilor, Permanent Member of the Council of the Ministry of Foreign Affairs. Delegate to First and Second Hague Conferences. Permanent Member of the International Court of Arbitration, which he helped to create.

MARTOV, L. (Julius Osipovich Tsederbaum) (1873-1923). Menshevik leader. Originally a member of the Jewish Bund; co-founder with Lenin and others of the Union of Struggle for the Liberation of the Working Class. Co-editor of *Iskra* until 1903, when he broke with Lenin. Acknowledged leader of Mensheviks, 1905-7, but thereafter at odds with the party's policies. Opposed both Reds and Whites in 1917. Emigrated, 1920; settled in Berlin; founded and edited *Sotsialisticheskii vestnik* until his death.

MASSINE, Leonide (1894-). Dancer and choreographer. With Ballet Russe, 1913-21 and 1924-28. Emigrated to U.S.

MATISSE, Henri (1869-1954). French painter; post-impressionist.

MAYAKOVSKY, Vladimir Vladimirovich (1893-1930). Major futurist poet.

MAZEPA, Ivan Stepanovich (1644-1709). Hetman of the Ukraine, 1687-1709; allied with Charles XII of Sweden in unsuccessful effort to separate the Ukraine from the Russian Empire. Ukrainian nationalists were sometimes called "Mazeppists."

MELGUNOV, Sergei Petrovich (1879-1956). Historian. Authority on the fall of the Russian monarchy and early Soviet period.

MÉLINE, Félix Jules (1838-1925). French statesman. Prime Minister, 1896-98.

MELLER-ZAKOMELSKY, Baron Alexander Nikolaevich (1844-1928). General. Noted for suppression of the Sevastopol mutiny (Nov 1905) and ruthless punitive expedition along the Great Siberian Railway to Chita in Jan 1906. In 1863 he took part in the suppression of the Polish revolt. Attended Nicholas Academy, 1866-68; served in Russo-Turkish War and held several important commands, 1878-1905. Governor of Kurland, 1906-9. Retired, appointed to State Council, 1909. One of the organizers of the Progressive Bloc in 1915.

MENDELEYEV, Dmitry Ivanovich (1834-1907). World-famous chemist; creator of the periodic table of elements. Professor of Chemistry, St. Petersburg Institute of Applied Technology, 1864-90. Director, Bureau of Weights and Measures, Ministry of Finance, 1893- .

MENDELSOHN-BARTHOLDY, Ernst. Head of Mendelsohn and Co., a German banking firm; one of Witte's German associates.

MENSHIKOV, M.S. (1859-1919). Prominent journalist.

MEREZHKOVSKY, Dmitry Sergeevich (1866-1941). Novelist, critic; symbolist. Founder, with Diaghilev and Benois, of the journal *Mir iskusstva*, 1899. Largely responsible with V.V. Rozanov for organizing the religious-philosophical assemblies of 1901-3.

MESHCHERSKY, Prince Vladimir Petrovich (1839-1914). Reactionary journalist; intimate of Alexander III. Editor and publisher of *Grazhdanin*.

MEYENDORF, Baron Alexander Feliksovich (1869-). Privat-docent of Law, St. Petersburg University. Octobrist; Vice Chairman of the Third Duma.

MEYER, George von Lengerke (1858-1918). U.S. Ambassador to Russia; prominent in negotiations between St. Petersburg and Washington before and during the Portsmouth Peace Conference.

MEYERHOLD, Vsevolod Emilievich (1874-1942). Avant-garde dramatic director.

MIASOEDOV, S.N. (1867-1915). Gendarme Colonel; counter-intelligence officer. Hanged as German spy, 1915.

MICHAEL ALEKSANDROVICH, Grand Duke (1878-1918). Brother of Nicholas II (third surviving son of Alexander III). Heir-apparent, 1899-1904. Murdered at Perm by Bolsheviks, 10 July 1918.

MICKIEWICZ, Adam (1798-1855). National poet of Poland.

MIKHAILOVSKY, Nicholas Konstantinovich (1842-1904). Radical journalist, philosopher, sociologist, and literary critic.

MILAN (OBRENOVICH) (1854-1901). Prince of Serbia, 1868-82; King, 1882-89.

MILIUKOV, Paul Nikolaevich (1859-1943). Historian, liberal leader, and statesman. Foremost student of P.N. Vinogradoff and V.O. Kliuchevsky. Professor of History, Moscow University, 1886-95; fired and exiled from Moscow for two years for "harmful influence on students" followed by two years' exile abroad. At Sofia University, Belgrade, 1897-99. Six months' imprisonment and six-month exile in 1900 for political activities in Russia. Studied and lectured in England, Western Europe, and the United States, 1901-5; founding member of Union of Liberation, Paris, 1904; of Union of Unions and Kadet Party, 1905. Principal leader and spokesman of Kadets and Kadet left in First, Third, and Fourth Dumas. Member and leader of the Progressive Bloc. Member of the Temporary Committee of the Duma and Minister of Foreign Affairs in the Provisional Government, Mar-May 1917. With Kornilov and Denikin in southern Russia after October 1917 and then active in the Russian emigration, settling eventually in Paris.

MILNER, Alfred Viscount (1854-1925). British statesman. Prominent member of Lloyd George's war cabinet; responsible for food supply.

MILSTEIN, Nathan (1904-). Celebrated violinist; student of Leopold Auer. Born in Odessa, emigrated to U.S.A., 1925.

MIN Chii-rok (1848-1895). Queen of Korea, 1873-95. Murdered by the Japanese.

MIN, George Aleksandrovich (1855-1906). General. Commander of the Semenovsky Guards, 1904-6, which he led in crushing the Moscow uprising of Dec 1905. Assassinated by an SR terrorist.

MINSKY (Vilenkin), Nicholas Maksimovich (1855-1937). Poet, playwright, essayist, and translator.

MIQUEL, Johannes von. German diplomat. Charge d'affaires, St. Petersburg, 1906-8.

MIRSKY, see SVIATOPOLK-MIRSKY

MOHRENHEIM, Baron Arthur Pavlovich (1824-1907). Diplomat. Department of Domestic Affairs of foreign ministry, 1845-51. Second Secretary of Embassy, Vienna, 1851-56; Junior Counselor, foreign ministry, 1856-58; Counselor to Mission to Prussia, 1858-67. Minister to Denmark, 1867-82. Ambassador, Great Britain, 1882-84; and France, 1884-97. Retired and appointed to State Council, 1897.

MOLTKE, Helmuth Johannes Ludwig von (1848-1916). General. Chief of the German General Staff, 1906-14; nephew of the real Moltke (1800-91).

MONET, Claude (1840-1926). One of the original French impressionist painters.

MONTEBELLO, Count Gustav Louis (1838-1907). French diplomat. Ambassador to Turkey, 1886-91; to Russia, 1891-1903.

MORGAN, John Pierpont (1837-1913) and John Pierpont II (1867-1943). American financiers.

MOROZOV, Savva Timofeevich (1862-1905). Textile magnate, grandson of a serf, heir to one of the country's greatest fortunes. Substantial contributor to revolutionary organizations. Committee suicide at Cannes, France.

MROZOVSKY, Joseph Ivanovich (1857-). General. Commander of the Corps of Grenadiers, 1912-15. Commandant, Moscow Military District, 1915-Mar 1917.

MUNSTER, Prince Georg Herbert (1820-1902). German diplomat. Hanoverian Minister to St. Petersburg, 1856-64. German Ambassador to London, 1873-85; to Paris, 1885-1900. Formerly Count; became Prince Munster-Derneburg in 1899.

MURAVIEV (MURAVIEV-AMURSKY), Count Nicholas Nikolaevich (1809-1881). Governor-General of Eastern Siberia, 1847-61; responsible for final phase of Russian expansion to the Pacific (Treaty of Aigun, 1858).

MURAVIEV, Michael Nikolaevich (1845-1900). Diplomat. Entered the diplomatic service in 1864. Ambassador to Copenhagen, 1893-96. Minister of Foreign Affairs, Jan 1897-June 1900.

MURAVIEV, Nicholas Valerianovich (1850-1908). Jurist and diplomat. Lecturer in Criminal Law, Moscow University. Procurator, St. Petersburg Court of Appeals, 1879-84; Moscow Court of Appeals, 1884-90; Imperial Secretary, 1892-93. Minister of Justice, 1894-1905. Ambassador to Italy, 1905-8. (Nephew of Muraviev-Amursky.)

MUROMSTEV, Sergei Andreevich (1850-1910). Professor of Roman Law, Moscow University; editor of *Iuridicheskii vestnik*, 1879-92. Active in the zemstvo movement since early 1890s; a founder and early leader of the Kadet Party, member of its central committee. Chairman of the First Duma, Apr-July 1906; signed the Vyborg manifesto. Lectured at Shaniavsky University, 1908-10.

MUTSUHITO (1852-1912). Emperor of Japan, 1867-1912. Presided over Japan's modernization. Father of Emperor Hirohito, the reigning sovereign.

MYSHLAEVSKY, Alexander Zachorovich (1856-). General. Army chief of staff, 1908-9; and Chief of the General Staff, Mar-Sep 1909. Military assistant to the Viceroy of the Caucasus, 1913-14.

NABOKOV, Vladimir Dmitrievich (1869-1922). Founder and leader of the Kadet Party; member of the First Duma; signed the Vyborg manifesto. Executive Secretary of the Provisional Government. Served in Wrangel's government. Murdered in Berlin.

NADSON, Semyon Yakovlevich (1862-1887). Lyric poet.

NANSEN, Fridtjof (1861-1930). Norwegian Polar explorer.

NAPRAVNIK, Edward Frantsevich (1839-1916). Composer and conductor.

NATANSON, Mark Andreevich (1850-1919). Populist and Socialist Revolutionary leader. A founder of the Land and Freedom movement and the People's Right Party in the 1870s; frequently imprisoned or exiled. One of the original founders of the SR Party, member of its central committee. Member of the Left-SRs in 1917-18 in alliance with the Bolsheviks. Emigrated 1919 and died in Switzerland.

NAUMOV, Alexander Nikolaevich (1868-1937). Prominent conservative. Publisher of *Golos samary* and provincial official (Samara): zemsky nachalnik, 1893-97; Stavropol district zemstvo assembly, 1894-97; acting chairman, provincial zemstvo board, 1897-1902; marshal of Stavropol district nobility, 1902; of provincial nobility, 1905. An organizer and leader of the United Nobility, 1906. Elected from Samara to the State Council, 1909, 1912, 1915. Minister of Agriculture, Nov 1915-July 1916. Appointed to State Council, 1916.

NEBOGATOV, Nicholas Ivanovich (1849-1912). Rear-Admiral. Commanded Third Pacific Squadron under Rozhestvensky at Tsushima; surrendered remnant of fleet on second day. Court-martialled 1906, sentenced to death (later reduced to ten years' imprisonment, deprivation of rank, and dismissal from the service).

NEIDHARDT, Baron Alexis Borisovich (1863-). Graduated His Majesty's Corps of Pages, served three years in Preobrazhensky Guards. Active for 25 years in province of Nizhni Novgorod: justice of the peace, chairman of provincial zemstvo board, and marshal of nobility. Governor of Ekaterinoslav, 1904-5. Member of State Council (elected 1906, 1909, 1912); organized and led the moderate rightists.

NEKRASOV, Nicholas Vissarionovich (1879-1940?). Professor, Tomsk Technical Institute. Left-Kadet; elected to Third and Fourth Dumas. Member of the Progressive Bloc and its bureau. Minister in the Provisional Government, 1917: Communications, Mar-July; Finance, Aug-Sep. Served in the Soviet administration. Tried and convicted of sabotage, 1930.

NELIDOV, Alexander Ivanovich (1835-1910). Diplomat. Junior positions in missions in Europe, 1856-73. Ambassador: Turkey, 1873-96; Italy, 1897-1903; and France, 1903-10. Staunch proponent of the Franco-Russian Alliance and of an anti-German orientation in Russian policy; in 1896 proposed Russian seizure of the Straits.

NEMESHAEV, Klavdy Semenovich (1849-). Engineer. Manager of the Southwestern Railway, 1896-1905. Witte's choice as Minister of Communications, Oct 1905-Apr 1906.

NERATOV, Anatole Anatolovich (1863-1928). Assistant Minister of Foreign Affairs, 1910-17; acting minister during the Agadir Crisis, 1911.

NESTEROV, Michael Vasilievich (1862-1942). Realist painter.

NICHOLAS MIKHAILOVICH, Grand Duke (1859-1919). Historian. Grandson of Nicholas I. Shot by Bolsheviks in Petrograd, 28 Jan 1919.

NICHOLAS NIKOLAEVICH, Grand Duke (1856-1929). Uncle of the Tsar. Supreme Commander in Chief, 1914-Aug 1915. Commander of the Caucasus Front, Aug 1915-Mar 1917. Emigrated to France.

NICHOLAS I PAVLOVICH (1796-1855). Emperor of Russia, 1815-55.

NICHOLAS (NEGOSH) (1841-1921). Prince of Montenegro, 1860-1919.

NICOLSON, Sir Arthur (1849-1928). British diplomat and minister. Entered diplomatic service in 1870. Ambassador to Madrid, 1904-5; to St. Petersburg, 1906-10. Under-Secretary of State for Foreign Affairs, 1910-16. Generally worked for a strong Anglo-French-Russian combination against Germany.

NIJINSKA, Bronislava (1891-). Polish dancer and choreographer. With the Ballet Russe, 1909-14 and 1921-24, and then with various French companies. Resident of U.S. since 1938.

NIJINSKY, Vaslav (1890-1950). Famed dancer with the Ballet Russe; brother of Nijinska.

"NIKOLAY-ON"—pseudonym of N.F. Danielson.

NIKOLSKY, Boris V. Professor, St. Petersburg University. Organized conservative students under the aegis of the Russian Assembly. Member of the Russian Club and also active in the Union of the Russian People.

NOETZLIN, Eduard. French banker; director of *Banque de Paris et des Pays Bas.* Witte's chief foreign negotiator; head of the syndicate that raised the great Russian loan of 1906.

NOGI Maresuke. Japanese General; commanded the Third Army, which besieged and captured Port Arthur, 1904.

NOVIKOVA, Olga Kireeva (1840-1925) Russian lobbyist in England; advocate of Anglo-Russian entente.

NOVOSELOV, M.A. Prominent religious layman. Editor and publisher of *Religiozno-filosofskaia biblioteka.* Expert on religious sects; lecturer at the Religious Academy of the Trinity and St. Sergius. Campaigned against Rasputin.

NOZU Michitsura. Japanese General. Commanded the Fourth Army in the Russo-Japanese War.

OBOLENSKY, Prince Alexis Dmitrievich (1855-1933). Bureaucrat; associate of Witte. Various provincial posts, 1881-94. Manager of the Nobles and Peasant Banks, 1894-97 and briefly in 1905. Assistant Minister of Interior, 1897-1901. Senator, 1901. Assistant Minister and Director, Department of Taxation, Ministry of Finance, 1902-5; member of the Special Conference on the Needs of Agricultural Industry, 1903. Appointed to State Council, 1905. Director-General of the Holy Synod, Oct 1905-Apr 1906. Drafted the Manifesto of October 17th (1905).

OBOLENSKY, Prince Ivan Mikhailovich (1853-1910) General. As Governor of Kharkov the object of an unsuccessful SR assassination in July 1902. Governor-General of Finland, 1904-5.

OBRAZISOV, Vasily Afanaseevich (1857-). Religious instructor and missionary. Member of the Union of the Russian People. Elected from Ekaterinoslav to Third Duma; member of rightist bloc.

OBRUCHEV, Nicholas Nikolaevich (1830-1904). General. Chief of the Army Main Staff, 1881-98.

OKU Yasukata. Japanese General. Commanded the Second Army in the Russo-Japanese War (Battles of Nanshan, Telissu).

OLENINA-d'ALHEIM, Marie (1869-). Soprano. Outstanding interpreter of Russian songs, especially Mussorgsky's. Born near Riazin; emigrated to France.

OLGA KONSTANTINOVNA, Queen (1851-1926). Granddaughter of Nicholas I, Consort of George I of Greece; Queen of the Greeks, 1867.

OLGA NIKOLAEVNA, Grand Duchess (1895-1918). Eldest daughter of Nicholas II.

OLSUFIEV, Prince Dmitry Adamovich (1862-). Prominent landowner of Moscow and Saratov; elected member of the State Council since 1906. Octobrist. Also Saratov marshal of the nobility, 1894- ; and chairman of the provincial zemstvo board, 1902-4.

ORLOV, Prince Vladimir Nikolaevich (1868-1927). Courtier. Chief of His Imperial Majesty's Chancellery, 1906-15. Dismissed for opposition to Rasputin, appointed Assistant for Civil Affairs to the Viceroy of the Caucasus, 1915-17.

OSTEN-SACKEN, Count Nicholas Dmitrievich (1831-1912). Diplomat. Minister of Bavaria, 1880-82, 1884-95. Ambassador to Germany, 1895-1912.

OYAMA Iwao. Japanese Field Marshal. Supreme Commander of the Imperial Armies in Manchuria, 1904-5.

OZEROV, Ivan Khristoforovich (1869-). Professor of Economics, Moscow University.

OZOL, Ivan Petrovich (1878-), Social Democrat. Elected to Second Duma from Riga. Major figure in alleged military conspiracy.

PAHLEN, Count Constantine Ivanovich (1833-1912). Member of the State Council, 1878-1912. Previously served in the Council's Chancellery, 1855-67, and as Assistant Minister of Justice, 1867-78.

PALITSYN, Feodor Feodorovich (1851-). General. Chief of the General Staff, 1905-8.

PANTALEEV, Alexander Ilyich (1838-). General. Director of the Imperial School of Law, 1890-96. Commander of the Corps of Gendarmes, 1896-1900. Governor-General of Eastern Siberia, 1900-3. In 1905 directed the suppression of the peasant revolt in Tambov.

PASIC, Nicholas (1845?-1926). Serbian nationalist. Prime Minister and Minister of Foreign Affairs, 1906-18.

PAVLOV, Nicholas Aleksandrovich. Saratov landowner; conservative publicist. Leader of the Union of Landowners.

PAVLOV, Platon Petrovich (1834-1904). General; military engineer. Chief of Staff of Army of the Caucasus during the Crimean War, served under Skobelev in Central Asia, and in the Russo-Turkish War. Commander, VI Army Corps, 1883-89; VII Army Corps, 1889-91. Deputy Commandant, Warsaw Military District, 1891-94. On the General Staff, 1894-1902. Appointed to the State Council, 1902.

PAVLOV, V.P. (-1906). Lieutenant-General. Chief Military Prosecutor; assassinated Dec 1906.

PAVLOVA, Anna Pavlovna (1881-1931). Greatest ballerina of the early twentieth century. With St. Petersburg Imperial Ballet, 1899-1913 (and the Diaghilev Ballet in 1909). Formed her own company in 1914 and toured widely (except Russia, to which she never returned) until her death.

PERTSOV, Peter Petrovich (1868-1947). Journalist. Editor of *Novyi put*; correspondent for *Novoe vremia*.

PESHEKHONOV, Alexis Vasilievich (1867-1933). Economist, journalist. Associated with the SR Party, contributor to its journal, *Revoliutsionnaia Rossiia*. An editor of *Russkoe bogatstvo* from 1904. A leader of the "third element" in the Union of Liberation. Minister of Food Supply (Provisional Government), May-Sep 1917.

PETER NIKOLAEVICH, Grand Duke (1864-1931). Cousin of Nicholas II. Inspector-General of the Department of Military Engineering, 1904-8. Married to Militsa Nikolaevna (1866-), daughter of Nicholas of Montenegro.

PETRAZHITSKY, Lev Iosifovich (1867-). Internationally recognized authority on civil law and legal philosophy; Professor, St. Petersburg University. Member of the Kadet Party and the First Duma. Collaborator on the liberal journals *Pravo* and *Vestnik prava*. Emigrated to Poland after the revolution and joined the faculty of Warsaw University (1917).

PETRUNKEVICH, Ivan Ilyich (1844-1928). Early and prominent zemstvo leader and constitutionalist. Banished for organizing the Moscow Zemstvo Congress of 1879; banished again, 1886 and 1894, for similar constitutional activities. Finally allowed to resume public activities after the death of Plehve (1904). A founder of the Union of Liberation and the Kadet Party. Kadet floor leader in the First Duma. Signed the Vyborg manifesto; imprisoned 1906-7. Published *Rech* and *Sovremennyi mir*, 1908-17. Emigrated in 1920.

PICHON, Stephen (1857-1933). French statesman and diplomat. Radical deputy, 1885-93. Ambassador: Haiti, 1894; Brazil, 1896; and China, 1898-1900. Resident-General, Tunis, 1901-6. Senator, 1906-24. Minister of Foreign Affairs, Oct 1906-Feb 1911 and Nov 1917-Jan 1920.

PIKHNO, Dmitry Ivanovich (1853-1913). Professor of Political Economy and Statistics, Kiev University, 1877- . Editor of the reactionary newspaper, *Kievlianin*, 1879-1913; leader of the Kiev section of the Union of the Russian People. Member of the State Council from 1907.

PILSUDSKI, Joseph (1867-1935). Polish political and military leader. A founder of the Polish Socialist Party, 1892. Inveterate enemy of Russia; led Polish Legion (Austrian Army) in World War I and commanded Polish forces in the Russo-Polish War of 1920-21. Led right-wing coup, 1926; headed dictatorship until his death.

PISAREV, Dmitry Ivanovich (1840-1868). Radical thinker; a founder of the nihilistic ethnic in Russia.

PISEMSKY, Alexis Feofilaktovich (1821-1881). Conservative realist writer; novelist and playwright.

PITIRIM. Churchman. Archbishop of Kursk, of Samara. Through Rasputin's influence became Exarch of Georgia (1914) and Metropolitan of Petrograd, Nov 1915.

PLATON, Bishop (P.F. Rozhdestvensky) (1866-). Rightist deputy, Second Duma; elected from Kiev.

PLATONOV, Sergei Feodorovich (1860-1933). Historian and public figure. Student of Bestuzhev-Riumin; succeeded him as Professor of Russian History, St. Petersburg University (1887). Corresponding member, 1908, and member, 1920-31, of the Academy of Sciences. Chairman, Historical-Archeological Commission, 1918-29. Purged, 1930; died in exile in Samara.

PLEHVE, Viacheslav Konstantinovich von (1846-1904). Reactionary policeman and minister. Director, Police Department, 1881-84; Assistant Minister of Interior and Senator, 1884-94. Imperial State Secretary, 1894-1902. State Secretary for Finland, 1899-1902. Minister of Internal Affairs, 1902-4. Known as a ruthless agent of repression, russification, and anti-semitism. Directed suppression of peasant revolts in Kharkov and Poltava provinces, 1902; an alleged accessory to the Kishinev pogrom, 1903. Bitter opponent of Witte, whom he replaced. Assassinated by SR terrorists.

PLEKHANOV, George Valentinovich (1856-1918). Marxist theoretician ("father of Russian Marxism") and one of the founders of the Russian Social Democratic Party. Returned to Russia in 1917 after nearly 40 years in exile in Switzerland; opposed Bolsheviks. Died in Finland.

POBEDONOSTSEV, Constantine Petrovich (1827-1907). Ultraconservative statesman. Professor of Civil Law, Moscow University, 1859-65. Tutor of the future Emperors Alexander III and Nicholas II, 1865- ; major advisor in reign of Alexander III and early years of the reign of Nicholas II. Member of the State Council, 1872-1905. Director-General of the Holy Synod, 1880-1905.

POINCARÉ, Raymond (1860-1934). French statesman. President of the Republic, 1913-20. Prime Minister, 1912, 1922-24, and 1926-29.

POKROVSKY, Nicholas Nikolaevich (1865-1930). Financial administrator. Began career in Ministry of Finance, 1889. In the Chancellery of the Committee of Ministers, 1893-99. Assistant Director, 1899, and Director, 1904, of the Department of Direct Taxation. Assistant Minister of Finance, 1906-15. Appointed to State Council, 1914. State Comptroller, Jan-Nov 1916. Minister of Foreign Affairs, Nov 1916-Feb 1917. Died in emigration.

POLIVANOV, Alexis Andreevich (1855-1922). General. Served in Russo-Turkish War. Editor, *Voennyi sbornik* and *Russkii invalid*, 1899-1904. On General Staff: Second Quartermaster General, 1905; Chief, 1905-6. Assistant Minister of War, 1906-12; established close relations with Guchkov and Duma circles; dismissed on Sukhomlinov's recommendation and appointed to State Council. Minister of War, June 1915-Mar

1916; appointed to appease the Progressive Bloc. Served after the revolution as an advisor to the Red Army and as military expert in Soviet-Polish negotiations of 1920.

POLONSKY, Jacob Petrovich (1819-1898). Poet; an "imagist."

POLOVTSEV, Alexander Aleksandrovich (1832-1909). Administrator. In the Senate, 1851-83: Acting State Councillor, 1865-67; Director, First Department, 1867-73. Senator, 1873-83. Secretary of the State Council, 1883-92; appointed to State Council, 1892. Member of the Special Commission on Needs of Agricultural Industry, 1902-5; participated in the major conferences that drafted legislation establishing the State Duma, 1905-6. Conceived and became a co-founder of the Imperial Historical Society (1866); president, 1879-1909. A major diarist for the period 1877-1908.

POSNIKOV, Alexander Sergeevich (1846-). Economist. Professor of Economics, Novorossiisk University, 1876-82. Served in the Smolensk zemstvo, then on the editorial staff of *Russkie vedomosti*, 1886-97. Dean, Faculty of Economics, St. Petersburg Technical Institute, 1902- . Co-author with A.I. Chuprov of a controversial study on grain prices, 1897.

POSOSHKOV, Ivan Tikhonovich (1652-1726). Administrator in the reign of Peter the Great; self-educated peasant, author of *A Book on Poverty and Wealth*.

POTEKHIN, Alexis Antipovich (1829-1908). Novelist and dramatist; honorary member of the Academy of Sciences.

POTEMKIN, Prince Gregory Aleksandrovich (1739-1791). Statesman, diplomat, field marshal, and favorite of Catherine the Great.

POURTALES, Count Friedrich (1853-1928). German diplomat. Ambassador to The Hague, 1899-1902. Prussian Minister to Munich, 1902-7. Ambassador to St. Petersburg, 1907-14. Counselor to the German Foreign Office, 1914-18.

PREYER, Wilhelm Dietrich (1877-). German economist.

PROKOFIEV, Sergei Sergeevich (1891-1953). Composer and conductor.

PROKOPE (Procope), Victor Napoleon (1839-1906). Assistant State Secretary for Finland, 1891-1900; Acting State Secretary for Finland, 1898-99. Solicitous of Finnish sensibilities; dismissed to pave way for policy of russification directed by N.I. Bobrikov.

PROKOPOVICH, Sergei Nikolaevich (1871-1955). Liberal politician and economist; pioneered study of Russian national income. Legal Marxist and one of the ideologists of "Economism." Charter member of the Union of Liberation. Served in Provisional Government, 1917: Chairman, National Economic Council and Minister of Commerce and Industry, Aug-Sep; Minister of Food Supply, Sep-Oct. Professor of National Economy, Moscow University, 1919-22; helped organize famine relief in 1921. Expelled 1922; resumed professional activities in Czechoslovakia.

PROTOPOPOV, Alexander Dmitrievich (1866-1918). Wealthy Simbirsk landowner. Left-Octobrist in Third and Fourth Dumas; member of the Progressive Bloc and Vice-chairman of the Duma, 1914-16. Minister of Interior, Sep 1916-Feb 1917 (partly through the influence of Rasputin). Regarded as turncoat by former colleagues; suspected of favoring separate peace and of progressive insanity. Arrested by Provisional Government; shot by the Bolsheviks.

PROTOPOPOV, Dmitry Dmitrievich (1856-). Served on Nikolaevsk district zemstvo board and in Samara provincial zemstvo assembly. Member of Kadet Party, elected to First Duma, signed the Vyborg manifesto.

PU-I. Last Emperor of China, 1908-12, under the regency of his father, Prince Chun. Born 1906.

PUGACHEV, Yemelian Ivanovich (1742-1775). Leader of Russia's greatest serf revolt, 1773-75.

PURISHKEVICH, Vladimir Mitrofanovich (1870-1920). Reactionary fanatic and anti-semite. Co-founder of the Union of the Russian People and vice-president; broke away in 1908 to form the rival Union of the Archangel Michael. Elected to Second, Third, and Fourth Dumas. Coconspirator in the assassination of Rasputin, Dec 1916. Fought for restoration of the monarchy; died in the Caucasus.

PUSHKIN, Alexander Sergeevich (1799-1837). Russia's greatest poet; also a major dramatist and master of prose fiction.

RAABEN von. Lieutenant-General (retired); Governor of Bessarabia during the Kishinev pogrom of 1903.

RACHMANINOV, Sergei Vasilievich (1873-1943). Pianist, composer and conductor.

RADOLIN (Radolinsky), Prince Hugo Leszczyc (1841-1917). German diplomat. Ambassador to Turkey, 1892-95; Russia, 1895-1900; France, 1900-10.

RADEK, Karl Bernhardovich (Sobelsohn) (1885-194?). International socialist. Born in Lvov (Austrian Galicia) and active in Polish and German Social Democratic Parties before World War I. Participant in the Zimmerwald Conference. Came to Russia with Lenin in 1917; joined the Bolsheviks. Imprisoned in Germany for revolutionary activities, 1918. Secretary of the Comintern, 1921. Expelled from Communist Party and exiled, 1927; reinstated 1928. Purged, 1937; presumably died in a concentration camp during World War II.

RAKOVSKY, Christian Georgevich (1873-). Rumanian socialist. Imprisoned in Russia, 1916; joined Bolsheviks, 1917. Headed Soviet Government of the Ukraine during Civil War. Ambassador to Great Britain, 1923-27. Expelled from Communist Party in 1927; exiled; recanted, 1934. Tried for high treason, 1938; sentenced to 20 years' hard labor and presumed to have died in a labor camp.

RASPUTIN, Gregory Efimovich (1872-1916). "Friend" of the Russian Empress and Emperor.

RASTRELLI, Bartholomew (1700-1771). Architect. Designed several major buildings, primarily in the reign of Elizabeth Petrovna: Petrodvorets (Peterhof), the Catherine Palace at Tsarskoe Selo, the Winter Palace, Smolny, etc.

RATAEV, L. Police official. Head of the Okhrana in 1903 and its foreign section, 1903-5; supervisor of Evno Azef, the double agent.

RAZIN, Stepan (Stenka) Timofeevich (-1671). Leader of a major peasant rebellion, 1667-71.

REDIGER, Alexander Feodorovich (1853-1920). General of Infantry. Minister of War, July 1905-March 1909. A graduate of His Majesty's Corp of Pages and the Nicholas Academy of the General Staff. Served in the Russo-Turkish War. Assistant Minister and Minister of War of the Bulgarian Government (under Russian auspices), 1882-83. Professor, Nicholas Academy, 1883- . Director, Chancellery of the War Ministry, 1898-1905; Acting Director of the War Ministry, June-July 1905. Appointed to the State Council in 1905.

REIN, George Ermolovich (1854-1942). Professor of Medicine. Director, Main Administration of State Public Health, Sep 1916-Mar 1917.

RENAN, Joseph Ernest (1823-1892). French philosopher.

RENNENKAMPF, Paul Karlovich Edler von (1854-1918). General. Led Russian conquest of Manchuria, 1900-1; prominent in the suppression of revolutionary manifestations in Manchuria in 1905-6. Commandant, Vilna Military District, 1907. Commander, First Army; routed in East Prussia in 1914 in the First Battle of the Masurian Lakes.

REPIN, Ilya Yefimovich (1844-1930). Leading painter of the naturalist school.

REVELSTOKE, see Baring.

REX, Count von. German charge d'affaires, St. Petersburg, 1893-94; Minister in Teheran, 1898-1906, and Peking, 1906-11.

RIBOT, Alexandre (1842-1923). French statesman; served in and headed several ministries.

RIMSKY-KORSAKOV, Nicholas Andreevich (1844-1908). World famous composer and conductor.

RICHARD, Cardinal François Marie Benjamin (1819-1908). Archbishop of Paris, 1886-1908.

RIMAN, N.K. (1864-1917). Military officer; commanded punitive expedition along the Moscow-Kazan Railway late in 1905.

RITTIKH, Alexander Aleksandrovich (1868-1930). Official in the Main Administration of Land Organization and Agriculture, 1905-16: Director, Department of State Domains, and Manager of the Committee for Land Organization, 1905-12; Assistant Director of the Main Administration, 1912-16; Director (Nov 1916) and then Minister (Jan 1917) of the Ministry of Agriculture.

RITTIKH, Alexander Feodorovich (1831-). Lieutenant-General (retired 1894), cartographer, and writer. Author of several collections of ethnographic maps; frequently contributed articles on nationality questions to the conservative press.

RODICHEV, Feodor Izmailovich (1854-1933). Liberal leader. Member of a wealthy gentry family, province of Tver. District marshal of nobility (Vesegon), 1877-90; election as chairman of Tver Provincial Zemstvo Board, 1891, nullified by Ministry of Interior. Deprived of electoral rights as an instigator of the Tver Zemstvo's address to the tsar, 1894; exiled, 1901-4. Member of the Union of Liberation and one of the founders of the Kadet Party; member of its central committee and one of its leading speakers. Member of all four State Dumas, of the Provisional Committee of the Duma and Provisional Government (Commissar for Finland). Emigrated after the October Revolution.

RODZIANKO, Michael Vladimirovich (1859-1924). Member of an old noble family, educated in the aristocratic Corps of Pages, served in Her Majesty's Regiment of the Cavalry of the Guard (1877-82), and appointed court chamberlain. Appointed marshal of the nobility and in 1900 elected chairman of the Ekaterinoslav Provincial Zemstvo. Elected to the State Council, 1906. Joined the Octobrists, elected to Third and Fourth Dumas, succeeded Guchkov as Chairman of the State Duma in 1911 (re-elected 1912). Chairman of the Temporary Committee of the Duma, 1917, and a central figure in the abdication of Nicholas II. Associated with Denikin during the Civil War; emigrated to Serbia where he died in great poverty.

ROOP, Christopher Khristoforovich (1831-). General. Governor-General and Commandant of the Odessa Military District, 1883-90.

ROOSEVELT, Theodore (1858-1919). President of the United States, 1901-9.

ROSEBERY, Lord Archibald Philip Primrose (5th Earl) (1847-1929). British Liberal leader; Foreign Secretary, 1886, 1892-94; Prime Minister, 1894-95.

ROSEN, Baron Roman Romanovich (1849-1922). Russian diplomat. Began career in Ministry of Justice, 1868; transferred to Asiatic Department of Foreign Ministry, 1872. Vice-Consul, Yokohama, 1875; Secretary of Mission, Tokyo, 1884. Consul-General, New York, 1884-90. Minister: Mexico City, 1890-95; Belgrade, 1895-97; Tokyo, 1897-99; Munich, 1900-1; Athens, 1901-4; Tokyo, 1904; Washington, 1905-11. Second Plenipotentiary at the Portsmouth Peace Conference, 1905. Member of the State Council, 1911-17.

ROSTOVSKY, A.A. Russian diplomat. Consul, Bitol (Macedonia), murdered July 1903.

ROTHSCHILD, Baron Nathan Meyer (1840-1915). International financier.

ROUVIER, Maurice (1842-1911). French political leader, frequently President of the Council of Ministers.

ROZANOV, Vasily Vasilievich (1856-1919). Major conservative author, literary commentator (especially on Dostoevsky), and publicist. Rozanov's thought and style were regarded as the epitomy of mysticism and intuitive naturalistic spiritualism.

ROZHESTVENSKY (Rozhdestvensky), Zinovi Petrovich (1848-1909). Vice-Admiral (1904). Chief of the Naval General Staff, 1903-5. Commander (Aug 1904) of the Second Pacific Squadron, destroyed at Tsushima, May 1905.

RUKHLOV, Sergei Vasilievich (1853-1918). Conservative bureaucrat. Early career in Ministry of Interior and Imperial Chancellery (State Secretary, Section on State Economy). Assistant Manager, Main Administration of Navigation and Ports, 1903-5. Appointed to State Council, 1905; member of the Rightist bloc. Founder (1908) and first president, All-Russian National Union, a reactionary anti-semitic organization. Minister of Ways and Communications, 1909-Oct 1915. His Majesty's State Secretary, 1912.

RUTENBERG, Peter Moiseevich (1874-). Socialist Revolutionary. Closely associated with Father Gapon, 1904-5; condemned and executed him in 1906. Civil governor of Petrograd briefly in 1917; subsequently emigrated to Palestine.

RUZSKY, Nicholas Vladimirovich (1854-1918). Gen.-Adjutant. Served during World War I as commander of the Third Army, Sixth Army, and Kiev Military District; then succeeded Zhilinsky as Commander of the Northern Front and later of the combined Northern and Northwestern Fronts. Ruzsky and his headquarters at Pskov formed the principal link between the high command and the Duma during the abdication crisis. Murdered by Red sailors at Kislovodsk, 1918.

RYKACHEV, Andrei Mikhailovich (1876-1914). Economist and publicist.

RZHEVSKY, V.A. Member of the Fourth Duma (Progressive Party) and of the Temporary Committee of the Duma, 1917.

SABLER (Desiatovsky), Vladimir Karlovich (1845?-1923?) Reputed crony of Rasputin. Early career in Ministry of Justice and Imperial Chancellery (1873-81). Holy Synod, 1881-95: Director of synodal chancellery, 1883-85; Assistant Director-General, 1892-95. Senate, 1896-1905. State Council, 1905-11. Director-General of Holy Synod, May 1911-July 1915. Changed name after dismissal in 1915.

SABUROV, Andrei Aleksandrovich (1838-1916). Served in chancellery of Committee of Ministers, 1857-59, and Ministry of Justice, 1859-64, then held various administrative positions in the Senate, 1864-72, before returning to Ministry of Justice as member of its advisory board, 1872-75. Supervisor, Dorpat Education District, 1875-80. His Majesty's State Secretary, 1880, and Director of Ministry of Education, 1880-81. Appointed to Senate, 1881; to State Council, 1899; became chairman, First Department, State Council, 1906.

SADOVSKY, Boris Aleksandrovich (1881-1952). Symbolist poet.

SAINT SERAPHIM of SAROV (1759-1833). Holy man canonized in 1903 by order of Nicholas II.

SAKHAROV, Victor Viktorovich (1848-1905). Lieutenant-General. Minister of War, Feb 1904-June 1905. Killed in Saratov province while directing the suppression of a peasant rebellion. Graduate of the Nicholas Academy; served in Russo-Turkish War, 1877-78. Various staff positions thereafter, including Chief of the Army Main Staff, 1898-1904.

SAKHAROV, Victor Viktorovich (1853-). Commander of the Rumanian Front, Aug 1916-Apr 1917.

SALISBURY, Robert Arthur Talbot Gascoyne-Cecil (Third Marquess of) (1830-1903). British statesman. Secretary of State for India, 1866-67, 1874-78. Foreign Secretary, 1878-80, 1885-86, 1887-92, 1895-1900. Prime Minister, 1885-86, 1886-92, and 1895-1902.

SALTYKOV-SHCHEDRIN, Michael Evgrafovich (1826-89). Satirist.

SAMARIN, Alexander Dmitrievich (1869-1932). Member of famous slavophile family; leader of Moscow provincial nobility. Military service, 1891-93. Province of Moscow: *zemsky nachalnik* (Bronnitsky district). 1899-1908; provincial marshal of nobility, 1908-15. Appointed to State Council, 1912. Prominent leader of Russian Red Cross, 1914-17. Director-General of the Holy Synod, July-Sept 1915.

SAMARIN, Feodor Dmitrievich (1858-1908). Brother of A.D. Samarin; also active in Moscow provincial affairs: member of Moscow Provincial Assembly, 1881-84; marshal of nobility (Bogorodsk district), 1884-91; chairman, Bogorodsk district zemstvo, 1886; chairman, Moscow Provincial Zemstvo Assembly, 1886-1903. Justice of the Peace for the city of Moscow and the Bogorodsk district. Elected to the State Council, 1906.

SAMSONOV, Alexander Vasilievich (1859-1914). General. Commander of the Second Army, August 1914, destroyed and routed at Soldau (Tannenberg), after which Samsonov shot himself. Earlier service: Russo-Turkish War, 1877-78; Army Main Staff, 1884; Commandant of Elizavetgrad Cavalry School, 1896-1904 (promoted to general, 1902). Commanded the Ussuri Mounted Brigade and the Siberian Cossack Division in the Russo-Japanese War. Hetman of the Don Cossacks, 1907-9. Governor-General and Commander of Troops, Turkestan, 1909-14.

SÄNGER, G.E., see Zenger

SATIE, Erik (1866-1925). French composer, associated with the Ballet Russe.

SAVENKO, Anatole Ivanovich. Leader of the Progressive-Nationalist group in the Fourth Duma.

SAVICH, Nikanor Vasilievich (1870-). Octobrist; member of the land-owning gentry of Kharkov province. Served in Third and Fourth Dumas. Member of the Octobrist Bureau and the Duma's committee on imperial defense; member of the Progressive Bloc.

SAVINKOV, Boris Viktorovich (1879-1925). SR terrorist, headed the Battle Organization groups which assassinated Plehve and Grand Duke Sergei Aleksandrovich. Assistant Minister of War in the Provisional Government, then active in the struggle against the Bolsheviks. Returned secretly to Soviet Russia in 1924; arrested, imprisoned, and allegedly committed suicide in 1925.

SAZONOV, E.S., see Sozonov.

SAZONOV, Sergei Dmitrievich (1860-1927). Diplomat and foreign minister. Began service in the chancellery of the foreign ministry in 1883; subsequently served as counselor of the embassy in London and Washington and as head of the legation to the Vatican. Summoned from Rome in 1909 to become Assistant Minister of Foreign Affairs under Izvolsky, whom he succeeded in 1910. Resigned July 1916; appointed Ambassador to London, but the revolution intervened. Represented various White organizations in Paris, 1918-20, and remained there until his death.

SCHAUMANN, Eugen. Finnish nationalist, assassin of N.I. Bobrikov, June 1904.

SCHIFF, Jacob Henry (1847-1920). Jewish-American financier, head of Kuhn, Loeb & Co. (1885). Active in promoting sale of Japanese bonds in the United States during the Russo-Japanese War.

SCHMIDT, Peter Petrovich (1867-1906). Naval lieutenant. Led rebellion to free *Potemkin* mutineers, Oct 1905; arrested but released under popular pressure and dishonorably discharged. Assumed leadership of Sevastopol mutiny, Nov 1905; arrested, court-martialled, and executed in March 1906.

SCHWANEBACH, Peter Khristianovich (1846-1908). Financial administrator, Ministry of Finance. Then Assistant Director of Agriculture and State Domains, 1903-5; and Director, Main Administration of Land Organization and Agriculture, 1905. Appointed to State Council, 1906, and also State Comptroller, Apr 1906-June 1907.

SCHWARTZ, Alexander Nikolaevich (1848-1915). Professor of Classical Philology, educational administrator, and minister: Director, Constantine Institute of Surveying, 1897-1900; Head of the Dorpat School District, 1900-2; Warsaw, 1902-5; and Moscow, June-Nov 1905. Minister of Public Education, Jan 1908-Sept 1910.

SCHWARTZKOPPEN, Maximilian. German military attache, Paris, 1891-97. Aide-de-camp of Kaiser William II, 1896.

SCHWARZHOFF, Gross von. Colonel. German Army technical delegate to the First Hague Conference, 1899. Killed in China during the Boxer Rebellion.

SCHWEIZER, Maximilian Ilyich (1881-1905). SR terrorist, killed accidentally by a bomb explosion (Feb 1905) while preparing to assassinate Grand Duke Vladimir Aleksandrovich.

SCRIABIN, Alexander Nikolaevich (1871-1915). Noted composer.

SERAPHIM of SAROV, see Saint Seraphim.

SERGEEVICH, Vasily Ivanovich (1835-1911). Professor of History, noted authority on ancient Russian law. Rector of St. Petersburg University during the student riots of 1899-1900.

SERGEI ALEKSANDROVICH, Grand Duke (1857-1905). Sixth (fourth surviving) son of Alexander II, uncle of Nicholas II. Husband (1884) of Elizabeth Feodorovna (1864-1918), elder sister of Empress Alexandra Feodorovna. Served in the Russo-Turkish War, 1877-78; commanded Preobrazhensky Guards Regiment, 1887-91; Governor-General of Moscow, 1891-1905, and Commander of the Moscow Military District, 1896-1905. Widely recognized symbol of reaction, religious fanaticism, and anti-semitism. Murdered 4 Feb 1905 by the SR terrorist Ivan Kaliaev.

SEROV, Valentin Aleksandrovich (1865-1911). Painter, master portraitist; associated with *Mir iskusstva*. Portraits included the family of Alexander III and many prominent figures in the reign of Nicholas II, including the tsar. In later life Serov turned to modern art and to antiquity, historical subjects, and illustrating.

SEVERIANIN (Lotarev), Igor Vasilievich (1887-1942). Poet, founder of "ego-futurism."

SEYMOUR, Sir Edward Hobart (1840-1929). British admiral (1889), commanded Royal Navy's Pacific Squadron, 1897-1901; led unsuccessful effort to relieve Peking in 1900 during Boxer Rebellion. Admiral of the Fleet, 1905; retired, 1910.

SHAKOVSKOY, Prince Dmitry Ivanovich (1861-). Liberal politician and zemstvo leader (province of Yaroslavl). Participated in founding of the Union of Liberation and the zemstvo congresses of 1904-5; co-founder of the Kadet Party, member of its central committee; identified with the left-Kadets. Vice-President of the First Duma. Minister of Social Welfare (May-July 1917) in the Provisional Government. Worked in Soviet cooperative organizations following the October Revolution.

SHAKOVSKOY, Prince Vsevolod Nikolaevich (1874-1954). Minister of Commerce and Industry, Feb 1915-Feb 1917.

SHARAPOV, Sergei F. (1855-1911). Small industrialist (farm machinery), editor and publisher. Vocal opponent of Witte's fiscal and economic policies. Member of the Russian Assembly. Founder, Nov 1905, of the Russian People's Party, from which he soon separated; associated with other Black Hundred activity in Moscow. Editor and publisher, with alleged government subsidies, of *Russkoe delo* and *Pakhar*, 1905-10.

SHCHEGLOVITOV, Ivan Grigorevich (1861-1918). Jurist and statesman. Various positions in the Senate and Ministry of Justice, 1890-1905; then Assistant Minister (Jan-Apr 1906) and Minister of Justice, Apr 1906-July 1915. Appointed member of State Council, 1907-17 (President, Jan-Feb 1917). His Majesty's State Secretary, 1911. As Minister of Justice, Shcheglovitov was a principal conspirator in the fabrication of the Beilis case. He was arrested by the Provisional Government in 1917 and executed by the Bolsheviks in August 1918.

SHCHERBATOV, Prince Alexis Grigorevich. Scion of an ancient princely family that traced its lineage to Rurik. Chairman of the Moscow Agricultural Society, 1890- ; member of the Special Commission on the Needs of Agricultural Industry, 1902-4. A leader of the Union of Russian Men. An associate of S.F. Sharapov and co-founder in 1905 of the Russian People's Party.

SHCHERBATOV, Prince Nicholas Borisovich (1868-1943). Marshal of the Nobility of Poltava, 1907- . Director, Main Administration of State Stud Farms, 1913-15. Elected to the State Council, 1915. Minister of Interior, June-Sept 1915.

SHCHERBINA, Feodor Andreevich (1849-1936). Statistician. Elected to Second Duma as a Popular Socialist from the Kuban Oblast. One of the founders of Russian budgetary statistics. In exile after 1917; Professor of Statistics at Prague University.

SHCHERBINA, G.S. Russian diplomat. Consul, Mitrovits (Macedonia); murdered, March 1903.

SHECHKOV, Gregory Alekseevich (1856-). Kursk landowner; district marshal of nobility. Rightist deputy in Third and Fourth Dumas.

SHEREMETEV, Count Sergei Dmitrievich (1844-1918). Historian, archaeologist, and antiquarian. Honorary member of the Academy of Sciences. Chairman, Imperial Archaeological Commission, 1900-17, and also of the Society of Lovers of Old Russian Letters and Promoters of Russian Historical Knowledge in Memory of Emperor Alexander III. Member of the State Council.

SHIDLOVSKY, Nicholas Vladimirovich (1843-1907). State Secretary, Imperial Chancellery, 1865-92. Member of the Senate and State Council, where he served on the finance committee of the Codification Department and in 1905 chaired a committee to investigate workers' needs.

SHIDLOVSKY, Sergei Illiodorovich (1861-1922). Prominent landowner and zemstvo leader (Voronezh). Served on the board of the Peasants Bank, 1899-1905, and then in the Main Administration of Land Organization and Agriculture. A left-Octobrist, Shidlovsky was the Octobrists' principal agrarian expert. He was elected Vice-President of the Third Duma and was an important leader of the Progressive Bloc in the Fourth. In 1917 he was a member of the Temporary Committee of the Duma and of the Pre-Parliament. He emigrated in 1920.

SHINGAREV, Andrei Ivanovich (1869-1918). Physician, zemstvo leader. Member of the Kadet Party and its central committee. Elected to Second, Third, and Fourth Dumas. Minister of Agriculture, Mar-May 1917, and Minister of Finance, May-June 1917, in the Provisional Government. Murdered by Bolshevik sailors in January 1918 while in a hospital under arrest.

SHIPOV, Dmitry Nikolaevich (1851-1920). Right-Octobrist. Active in zemstvo and public affairs, 1877- ; co-founder of the Union of 17

October (1905) and later of the Party of Peaceful Reconstruction. Elected to the State Council, 1907. Arrested by the Bolsheviks, died in Butyrskaia Prison, 1920.

SHIPOV, Ivan Pavlovich (1865-1920). One of Witte's proteges; various positions, 1887-97, then Director of the General Office (Ministry of Finance), 1897-1902; Secretary of the Special Commission on the Needs of Agricultural Industry, 1902-3; Director, Department of the State Treasury, 1902-4. Accompanied Witte to Portsmouth in 1905. Minister of Finance in Witte's cabinet, Oct 1905-Apr 1906. Sent on special mission to study economic problems in the Far East (Manchuria, China, Japan) in 1907. Minister of Trade and Industry, Jan 1908-Jan 1909. State Council, 1909-17, and Director of the State Bank, 1914-17.

SHIRINSKY-SHIKHMATOV, Prince Alexis Aleksandrovich (1862-1930). Reactionary bureaucrat. In Ministry of Interior, 1884-1900, and Holy Synod, 1900-3 (in charge of arrangements for the canonization of St. Seraphim). Governor of Tver, 1903. First Department of the Senate, 1904. Assistant Director-General, 1905, and Director-General of the Holy Synod, Apr-July 1906. Appointed to the State Council, 1906. Acting Governor of Saratov, 1913. Council of the Ministry of Interior, 1915. Prominent supporter of the Black Hundreds.

SHISHKIN, Nicholas Pavlovich (1830-1902). Diplomat. Deputy Minister of Foreign Affairs, 1891-96, and Acting Minister, 1896-97. State Council, 1897-1902. Previous service: Asiatic Department, 1852-57; attached to Embassy in Paris, 1857-61; Consul, Adrianople, 1861-63; Consul-General, Belgrade, 1863-75; Minister to U.S., 1875-80, to Greece, 1880-84; and to Royal Court of Sweden and Norway, 1884-91.

SHMAKOV, A.S. Moscow attorney, professional anti-semite; served with the prosecution in the Beilis trial.

SHOEN, Baron William E. von. German diplomat. Minister to Copenhagen, 1900-5. Ambassador to St. Petersburg, 1905-7. State Secretary for Foreign Affairs, 1907-10.

SHUBINSKY, Nicholas Petrovich (1853-). Noble landowner from Tver province; right-Octobrist in Third and Fourth Dumas.

SHULGIN, Vasily Vitalievich (1878-1945?). Volynian landowner, conservative nationalist. Associated with rightists but not an anti-semite. Editor of *Kievlianin*, 1911- . Member of Second, Third, and Fourth Dumas and of the Progressive Bloc. With Guchkov he represented the Duma in securing the abdication of Nicholas II. Subsequently served with Denikin during the Civil War and then emigrated. Visited the USSR in 1926 (arrangements, unknown to him, were made by the secret police) and subsequently wrote a favorable report on conditions (*Three Capitals*, 1927). Captured by the Red Army in Yugoslavia in 1945, and was either killed or imprisoned. Some accounts speculate that Shulgin survived ten years in concentration camps and was then freed to reside in the USSR.

SHUVAEV, Dmitry Savelovich (1854-). General. Head of the war ministry's quartermaster and supply department, 1909-16; Minister of War, Mar 1916-Jan 1917.

SHUVALOV, Paul Andreevich (1830-98). General-Adjutant. Served in Crimean and Russo-Turkish Wars; retired from military service in 1885. Ambassador to Germany, 1885-94. Governor-General of Warsaw, 1894-96.

SHUVALOV, Paul Petrovich (1858-1905?). Apparently the Mayor of Moscow assassinated, June 1905, by the SR terrorist Kulikovsky. Aide-de-camp to Grand Duke Sergei Aleksandrovich, c. 1890- .

SIKORSKY, Schimel-Leiba Vulfovich. SR terrorist; participated in the assassination of Plehve; sentenced to twenty-years' imprisonment.

SIPIAGIN, Dmitry Sergeevich (1853-1902). Acting Minister (1902) and Minister of Internal Affairs, 1900-2; assassinated. Previously provincial marshal of nobility, Moscow, 1884-85; Vice Governor of Kharkov, 1886-87; Governor of Kurland, 1888-91, and of Moscow, 1891-94. Assistant Minister of State Domains, 1893-94; Assistant Minister of Internal Affairs, 1894-95; and Head of His Majesty's Private Chancellery to Receive Petitions, 1895-99.

SKOBELEV, Michael Dmitrievich (1843-82). General. Popular hero of the Russo-Turkish War, 1877-78; outspoken Panslavist.

SKOBELEV, Michael Ivanovich (1885-1939). Menshevik. Member of the Fourth Duma. Vice President of the Executive Committee of the Petrograd Soviet, 1917, and Minister of Labor in the Provisional Government, May-Sept 1917. Emigrated after October; returned in 1922, joined Communist Party, and served in the Soviet administration.

SKRYDLOV, Nicholas Illarion (1844-). Vice-Admiral. Commander of the Pacific Squadron, 1904: appointed to succeed Makarov but was unable to reach Port Arthur and spent the war at Vladivostok. Commander of Fleet and Harbors, 1906-7.

SKVORTSOV, Ivan Ivanovich (1870-1928). Bolshevik. Economist and journalist. Editor of *Kolokol*, of *Izvestiia*, 1917-18; and Assistant Editor of *Pravda*, 1924.

SMIRNOV, Constantine Nikolaevich. Lt.-General; commander of Fortress Port Arthur, 1904.

SOLOGUB, Feodor (pseud. of Feodor Kuzmich Teterinkov) (1863-1927). Symbolist poet and writer. Both prose and poetry recognized as among the finest in Russian literature; widely held to be Russia's best novelist after Dostoevsky.

SOLOVIEV, Sergei Mikhailovich (1820-79). Foremost Russian historian; founder of the "statist" or "institutional" school and author of a monumental *History of Russia*. Professor of History, Moscow University, 1847-79.

SOLOVIEV, Vladimir Sergeevich (1853-1900). Philosopher and poet. Critic of official Orthodoxy and russification, advocate of a universal "free theocracy" and a synthesis of eastern and western social and spiritual values. Enjoyed a wide following among Russian intellectuals, although most of his religious works were published outside of Russia.

SOLSKY, Count Dmitry Martynovich (1833-1910). Conservative states-man and councilor. Assistant Director, Second Section (codification of laws) of His Majesty's Private Chancellery, 1852-67; Imperial Secretary, 1867-73; State Comptroller, 1873-89. State Council, 1889-1910: Chair-man, Legislative Department, 1889-93; Chairman, Department of State Economy, 1893-1902; Chairman of the State Council, 1904-6. Count, 1902.

SOMOV, Constantine Andreevich (1869-1909). Painter and illustrator. Student of Repin, 1888-96, and member of the *Mir isskustva* school. Widely exhibited and acclaimed in Russia and abroad after 1894.

SOZONOV, Egor Sergeevich (1879-1910). SR terrorist, chief assassin of V.K. Plehve (July 1904). Expelled from Moscow University, 1901; joined Socialist Revolutionary Party. Arrested, exiled (July 1903) to Eastern Siberia for five years. Escaped, joined Battle Organization, and became a member of the team that undertook the murder of Plehve. Sentenced to life imprisonment, Sozonov committed suicide in 1910.

SOZONOVICH, Ivan Petrovich. Professor, rightist deputy from Mogilev and Secretary of the Third State Duma.

SPIRIDONOVA, Maria Aleksandrovna (1884-1941). Terrorist and Left-SR leader. Assassinated a government official in 1905; imprisoned until 1917. Member of Left-SR central committee in 1917-18; imprisoned by the Bolsheviks. Amnestied around 1930 and died in the USSR.

STAAL, Baron Egor Egorovich (1824-1907). Russian diplomat. Minis-ter to Wurttemberg, 1871-84; Ambassador to England, 1884-1902. Pres-ident of the First Hague Conference, 1889.

STACKELBERG, Baron G.K. Lieutenant-General, commander of the First Siberian Army Corps, 1904-5.

STAKHOVICH, Michael Aleksandrovich (1861-1923). Prominent land-owner and public figure; co-founder of the Octobrist Party. Marshal of Nobility, Orel Province, 1895-97; active as a publicist and participant in various official and public conferences and commissions. Served Witte as intermediary with zemstvo leaders and as unofficial advisor on pro-vincial conditions. Chief representative of the detachment of nobility in Manchuria during the Russo-Japanese War. Helped organize the Union of October 17, and served in First and Second Dumas, eventually leav-ing the Octobrists to form the Party of Peaceful Reconstruction. Elected to the State Council, 1907, 1912. One of the organizers of the Progres-sive Bloc, 1915. Briefly held the post of Governor-General of Finland in the Provisional Government.

STALIN, Joseph (Joseph Vissarionovich Dzugashvili) (1879-1953). Ac-tive revolutionary, 1898- ; Bolshevik, 1903- ; Soviet leader, 1917- ; and master of the USSR, 1926-53.

STAMBULOV, Stefan (1854-95). Bulgarian politician. Headed the Re-gency, 1886-87; Prime Minister and Minister of Interior, 1887-94. Major opponent of Russia in Bulgarian affairs.

STANISLAVSKY, Constantine Sergeevich (1863-1938). Actor and di-rector. Founder with V.I. Nemirovich-Danchenko of the Moscow Art

Theater, 1897; creator of the "Stanislavsky method." People's Artist of the USSR.

STEAD, W.T. (1849-1912). British correspondent for *The Times* (London).

STEER, Andrew Pavlovich. Naval officer; commander of the destroyer *Novik* in Battle of the Yellow Sea, 1904.

STEKLOV (Nakhamkes), Yuri Mikhailovich (1873-193?). Bolshevik since 1903; several times arrested and exiled. Member of the Executive Committee of the Petrograd Soviet, 1917. Original editor of *Izvestiia*. Subsequently a member of the Central Executive Committee of the Soviet government. Disappeared, presumably purged, in the 1930s.

STEPANOV, Alexander Vasilievich (1865-). Senator; Assistant Minister of Interior, 1916.

STEPNIAK, see Kravchinsky, S.M.

STESSEL, Baron Anatole Mikhailovich (1848-1915). Lieutenant-General (1901); self-styled "hero of Port Arthur." Commandant of Fortress Port Arthur, Aug 1903-Jan 1904; Commander, Third Siberian Corps, Jan-Dec 1904; Chief, Kwantung Military District, Mar-Dec 1904. Court-martialled 1908 for violation of regulations in surrender of Port Arthur; death sentence commuted to ten years' imprisonment. Pardoned by Nicholas II and released, April 1909.

STISHINSKY, Alexander Semenovich (1852-1920). Administrator. In Ministry of Interior, 1872-73, and Imperial Chancellery, 1873-86 (Assistant State Secretary, 1882-86). Returned to Interior, 1886: Head of Peasant Section, 1893-96; Assistant Imperial Secretary, 1896-99; Assistant Minister, 1899-1904. Appointed to State Council, 1904. Head of Main Administration of Land Organization and Agriculture in Goremykin's cabinet, Apr-June 1906. Chairman of the Committee to Fight German Domination, 1916.

STOESSEL, see Stessel.

STOLYPIN, Alexander Arkadeevich (1863-). Journalist. Editor, *Peterburzhskie vedomosti* until 1903 when Plehve forced his resignation; subsequently joined editorial staff of *Novoe vremia*. Active member of the Union of October 17th.

STOLYPIN, Peter Arkadeevich (1862-1911). Statesman. Led government's struggle against upheaval with a policy of repression and reform, 1906-11. Began official career as Marshal of Nobility, Kovno province, 1887-1902. Then Governor of Grodno, 1902-3, and of Saratov, 1903-6. Appointed Minister of Interior, April 1906, and Chairman of the Council of Ministers in July 1906. Held both posts until September 1911 when he was assassinated in Kiev by a double-agent.

STRAVINSKY, Igor Feodorovich (1882-1971). World-famous composer and conductor.

STREMOUKHOV, Peter Petrovich. Governor of Saratov, 1906-11.

STRUKOV, Baron Anany Petrovich (1851-). Conservative politician. Served in Imperial Chancellery in early 70s and in the Russo-Turkish War of 1877-78. Returned to state administration in 1883 (Ministry of Interior) and then Marshal of Nobility of Ekaterinoslav province, 1886-1906. A founder and leader of the United Nobility. Elected member of State Council, 1906-12; appointed member, 1912-17.

STRUVE, Peter Berngardovich (1870-1944). Economist and politician. A founder and theoretician of Legal Marxism in 1890s; subsequently a Liberationist and Kadet. Grew politically more conservative as Russian politics became increasingly more radical.

STRUVE, Vasily Berngardovich (1854-1912). Engineer. Director of the Konstantinovsky Survey Institute, 1900-12.

STÜRMER, Boris Vladimirovich (1848-1917). Administrator and war-time leader of the government. Appointed Chairman of the Council of Ministers, January 1916 (widely held to be a syncophant of the Empress, Rasputin, and the "German clique" of the imperial court). Held that post until November 1916. Also Minister of Interior, Mar-July 1916, and Minister of Foreign Affairs, July-Nov 1916. Earlier career included service in the Senate (First Department), 1872-75; in the Ministry of Justice, 1875-78; and in the Senate's Department of Heraldry and the Ceremonial Office of the Ministry of the Imperial Court, 1878-1892. Chairman, Tver provincial zemstvo, 1892-94. Governor of Novgorod, 1894-96, and of Yaroslavl, 1896-1902. Director, Department of General Affairs, Ministry of Interior, 1902-4. Appointed to the State Council in 1904.

SUKHANOV (Gimmer), Nicholas Nikolaevich (1882-). Revolutionary. Originally a follower of Tolstoy, then an SR (1903), then a Menshevik (1909). Editor of *Sovremennik*, 1914, and of *Novaia zhizn* (with Gorky), 1918. Member of the Executive Committee of the Petrograd Soviet, 1917. Renounced the Mensheviks in the early 20s and served as an economist in the Soviet administration. Arrested in 1931 for sabotage, sentenced to ten years' imprisonment, and never reappeared.

SUKHOMLINOV, Vladimir Aleksandrovich (1848-1926). General and wartime War Minister. Graduate of the Nicholas Academy of the Army Main Staff; served on Skobelev's staff during the war with Turkey, 1877-78. Promoted to General in 1890. Troop commander and then Governor-General of Kiev, 1904-8. Chief of the General Staff, 1908. Minister of War, 1909-June 1915. Charged with treason and imprisoned, April 1916; placed under house arrest by order of the tsar, October 1916. Rearrested, convicted of treason, and sentenced to life imprisonment at hard labor by the Provisional Government, April 1917. Released by the Bolsheviks, 1918. Died in Germany.

SUKHOTIN, N.N. General. Commandant of the Siberian Military District in 1905.

SUKOVKIN, N.I. Governor of Kiev in 1914.

SULLY-PRUDHOMME, René François Armand (1839-1907). French poet. Member of Academie Française and recipient of the Nobel Prize for Literature in 1901.

SURIKOV, Vasily Ivanovich (1848-1916). Painter—historical realism; a *peredvizhnik*.

SUSANIN, Ivan (d. 1613). Peasant hero who saved Tsar Michael, the first Romanov ruler, from death at the hands of the Poles.

SUVORIN, Alexis Sergeevich (1834-1912). Major publisher. Editor of the moderate newspaper, *Novoe vremia*.

SUVOROV, Alexander Vasilievich (1730-1800). General-Field Marshal. Imperial Russia's greatest commander (reigns of Catherine II and Paul). Order of Suvorov created by Soviet government in 1942.

SVIATOPOLK-MIRSKY, Prince Peter Dmitrievich (1857-1914). Statesman. Served in Russo-Turkish War and thereafter as Governor of Penza and then Ekaterinoslav. Assistant Minister of Interior and Commander of the Gendarme Corps, 1900-2. Governor-General of the Northwest Territory, 1902-4. Minister of Interior, Aug 1904-Jan 1905. As minister, Mirsky attempted but failed to liberalize government policy.

TAGANSTSEV, Nicholas Stepanovich (1843-1923). Authority on criminology and penology. Professor of Law at St. Petersburg University and the Imperial Alexander Lyceum, 1868- . Editor, *Journal of Civil and Criminal Law*, 1873-78. Appointed to the Senate in 1887: chairman of the commission to study new legislation for Finland, 1890; chairman of the criminal law division and of the commission to study Russian legislation, 1894; principal author of the Russian penal code of 1903. Appointed to the State Council in 1906.

TANTSOV, Alexander Zakharovich. Right-Octobrist deputy from Smolensk to Second, Third, and Fourth State Dumas. Editor of the *Smolenskie gazety*.

TATAROV, Nicholas Yurievich (c.1870-1906). Agent-provocateur;"executed" by SRs for betrayal of revolutionaries, March 1906.

TATISHCHEV, Count Sergei Sergeevich (1872-1915). Governor of Saratov, ?-1911; Chief of the Main Administration for Press Affairs, 1912-15.

TAUBE, Baron Michael Aleksandrovich de (1869-1961). Jurist, Professor of Law, genealogist. Legal advisor to the Ministry of Foreign Affairs; Assistant Minister of Public Education, 1911-15. Important memoirist.

TERESHCHENKO, Michael Ivanovich (1888-1958). Millionaire industrialist. Chairman of the Kiev War Industry Committee, 1915-17. Minister in the Provisional Government: Finance, Mar-May, and Foreign Affairs, May-Oct 1917.

THÉRY, Edmund. Editor of the *Economist Europien*.

TIKHOMIROV, Lev Aleksandrovich (1852-1923). Populist revolutionary and later a staunch monarchist. Member of the Land and Freedom movement of the 1870s and a leader of The People's Will, 1879-88. Recanted, 1888, pardoned, and returned to Russia. Edited *Moskovskie vedomosti*, 1909-13; retired from public life in 1917.

TIMASHEV, Sergei Ivanovich (1858-1920). Director of the State Bank, 1903-9. Minister of Trade and Industry, Nov 1909-Feb 1915. His Majesty's State Secretary, 1915.

TIMIRIAZEV, Vasily Ivanovich (1849-1919). In Ministry of Finance, 1873-1905, rising to Assistant Minister and Head of the Department of Industry, Science, and Commerce (1902-5). Minister of Trade and Industry, 1905-6. Entered private business, appointed to State Council, 1906. Reappointed Minister of Trade and Industry, January 1909; resigned in November.

TITTONI, Tommaso (1855-1931). Italian statesman. Foreign minister, 1903-9 and 1919. Ambassador to France, 1910-16. Strived before the war to lead Italy out of the Triple Alliance and into a rapprochement with France; after the outbreak of the World War, Tittoni was instrumental in Italy's adherence to the side of the Entente.

TIUTCHEV, Feodor Ivanovich (1803-1873). Romantic poet.

TOGO Heihachiro (1847-1934). Vice-Admiral, commander of the Imperial Japanese Combined Fleet in the Russo-Japanese War; victor over the Russians at Tsushima. Subsequently Chief of the Naval Staff.

TOLSTOY, Alexis Konstantinovich (1817-1875). Author, poet and dramatist. One of the most versatile and popular writers of the mid-nineteenth century. Creator with his two cousins, the brothers Zhemchuznikov, of the famous pseudonym "Kuzma Prutkov," whose satirical, humorous, and nonsense verse and prose created a Russian tradition. Also a major historical dramatist (*Death of Ivan the Terrible, Tsar Feodor,* and *Tsar Boris*).

TOLSTOY, Count Alexis Nikolaevich (1883-1945). Novelist, poet, and dramatist. Although established as a writer before the revolution, A.N. Tolstoy's major works appeared during the Soviet and especially the Stalinist period. A popular writer, his works won three Stalin Prizes.

TOLSTOY, Dmitry Andreevich (1823-1889). Director-General of the Holy Synod and Minister of Education, 1866-80; Minister of Interior, 1882-89. One of the major reactionary figures of the reign of Alexander III.

TOLSTOY, Ivan Ivanovich (1858-1916). Archeologist and writer; minister in Witte's cabinet. Member of the Imperial Archeological Commission (1886-): Secretary, 1886-90; Vice-President, 1899. Imperial Academy of Fine Arts: Secretary, 1889-93; Vice-President (acting director), 1893-1905. Chairman of the Russian Society of the Art of Printing, 1900- . Minister of Public Education, Oct 1905-Apr 1906.

TOLSTOY, Count Leo Nikolaevich (1828-1910). Giant of Russian Literature, author of *War and Peace,* etc.

TREPOV, Alexander Feodorovich (1862-1926). Second of the three Trepov brothers who were major figures in the reign of Nicholas II.

Graduate of His Majesty's Corps of Pages, entered Ministry of Interior in 1889. Marshal of Nobility, Pereiaslavl district, 1892-95. Assistant State Secretary, 1899. Member of the special commission to draft the plan for the State Duma, 1905-6. Senator, 1906; appointed to the State Council, 1914 (member of the rightist group). Minister of Communications, Nov 1915-Jan 1917; and Chairman of the Council of Ministers, Nov 1916-Jan 1917. Died in France.

TREPOV, Dmitry Feodorovich (1855-1906). Police official. Chief of Moscow Police, 1896-1905. Governor-General of St. Petersburg, Jan-Oct 1905. Assistant Minister of Interior and Chief of Police, May-Oct 1905. Commandant of the Palace, Oct 1905-1906. One of the Emperor's closest advisors during the revolutionary upheavals of 1905-6.

TREPOV, Vladimir Feodorovich (1860-1918). Assistant Director and then Director of the Department of General Affairs, Ministry of Interior, 1899-1902. Governor of the Tauride, 1902-5. Senator, 1905-7; member of the State Council, 1908-11 (resigned after being disciplined for his role in the western zemstvo crisis). Became a director of the St. Petersburg International Bank of Commerce, 1911-17. Arrested and shot by the Bolsheviks in 1918.

TROTSKY, Leon (Lev Davidovich Bronstein) (1879-1940). Marxist revolutionary. Opponent of Lenin, 1903-17, but joined Bolsheviks after the February Revolution; played a decisive role in the Bolshevik coup of October and also in securing Soviet power during the Civil War. Considered to be Lenin's likely successor but lost out in the power struggle with Stalin and others. Expelled from the Communist Party in 1927 and banished from the USSR in 1929. Abroad, Trotsky campaigned against Stalinism until murdered by a Soviet agent in Mexico City in August 1940.

TRUBETSKOY, Prince Eugene Nikolaevich (1863-1920). Professor of Legal Philosophy and History, Kiev University, 1894-1906; Moscow University, 1906- . Member of the Kadet Party, 1905-6, and then a founder of the Party of Peaceful Reconstruction.

TRUBETSKOY, Prince Peter Nikolaevich (1858-1911). Elder brother of Eugene and Sergei and, like them, an aristocratic liberal. Provincial Marshal of Nobility, Moscow, 1893-1906. Elected to the State Council in 1906, where he led the centrist bloc and served as chairman of the land committee.

TRUBETSKOY, Prince Sergei Nikolaevich (1862-1905). Lecturer and Professor of Philosophy, Moscow University, 1888-1905, and first Rector of the university. Champion of liberal reform.

TRUSEVICH, Maximilian Ivanovich (1863-1916?). Director of Police, 1906-9. Senator; headed the inquiry into the assassination of Stolypin.

TSCHIRSKY, Heinrich von. German diplomat. First Secretary of the German Embassy in Russia, 1894-1900. State Secretary for Foreign Affairs, 1906-7. Ambassador to Austria-Hungary, 1907-16.

TSEDERBAUM, see Martov.

TSERETELLI, Irakly Georgevich (1882-1960). Georgian Menshevik leader. Major Social Democratic figure in Second Duma; ultimately arrested, sentenced to imprisonment at hard labor and exile. Returned to Petrograd in 1917 and became a leader of the Petrograd Soviet; also served as Minister of Communications (May-Aug) and Minister of Interior (July-Aug) in the Provisional Government. Returned to the Caucasus after the Bolshevik coup; joined the government of the Georgian Republic, which the Bolsheviks ultimately crushed. Emigrated to France and in 1940 to the United States.

TSERTELEV, Prince Dmitry Nikolaevich (1852-). Philosopher and poet. Frequent contributor to conservative periodicals and newspapers.

TSION (Cyon), Ilya Faddeich (1842-1912). Critic of Russian economic and financial policy. Served 1880-91 as agent in Paris for the Ministry of Finance; quit in disagreement with the policies of Vishnegradsky and Witte and persistently berated the latter from Paris while refusing to heed summons to return to Russia. Earlier, Tsion held the post of Professor of Physiology at St. Petersburg University (1870-75).

TSVETAEVA, Marina Ivanovna (1892-1941). Poet and essayist.

TUGAN-BARANOVSKY, Michael Ivanovich (1865-1919). Economist. One of the original proponents of Legal Marxism in the 1890s; joined the Kadet Party in 1906. Major theorist and advocate of the Russian cooperative movement.

TUNG-CHIH. Emperor of China, 1861-75.

TURGENEV, Ivan Sergeevich (1818-1883). Major writer.

TZU-AN. Empress of China, 1851-61; Dowager and Regent, 1861-81.

TZU-HSI (c.1835-1908). The "Iron Empress"—actual ruler of China from 1861 to 1908; unsuccessfully attempted to preserve Manchu (Ching) authority in China. Imperial concubine, 1851-61; Regent, 1861-81; and Dowager Empress, 1881-1908.

UKHTOMSKY, Prince Esper Esperovich (1861-1921). Poet, publicist, and orientalogist. Authority on Buddhism; served in Ministry of Interior's Department of Ecclesiastical Affairs of Foreign Religions. Confidante of Nicholas II; encouraged his Great Asian policy. President of the Russo-Chinese Bank and the Chinese Eastern Railway. Publisher and editor of *Sankt-Peterburgskie vedomosti* since 1896.

UKHTOMSKY, Prince Paul Petrovich. Rear-Admiral; second-in-command of the Russian Pacific Squadron, 1903-4.

ULYANOV, Alexander Ilyich (1866-1887). Terrorist; hanged for his role in the attempted assassination of Alexander III.

ULYANOV, Vladimir Ilyich—see Lenin.

UNTERBERGER, Paul Feodorovich (1842-1921). General. Governor of Nizhni Novgorod, 1905. Governor-General of the Amur (Eastern Siberia), 1905-10.

URITSKY, Moisei Solomonovich (1873-1918). Revolutionist. Identified with Trotsky between 1905 and 1917; joined Bolsheviks in July

1917. Member of the Military Revolutionary Committee of the Petrograd Soviet, instrumental in the October coup d'etat. Headed Petrograd CHEKA (Extraordinary Commission for the Suppression of Counterrevolution and Sabotage) until his assassination by an SR terrorist in August 1918.

URUSOV, Prince D.D. Vice President of the Fourth Duma; member of the Progressive Bloc.

URUSOV, Prince Sergei Dmitrievich (1862-). Administrator and liberal aristocrat. Held several posts in his native province of Kaluga and served in the Ministry of Interior, 1900-2. Vice-Governor of Tambov, 1903. Governor of Bessarabia, 1903-4, following the Kishinev pogrom. Governor of Tver, 1904. Assistant Minister of Interior, 1905-6. Elected to First Duma as a Kadet; imprisoned May-Aug 1908 for signing the Vyborg manifesto. Assistant Minister of Interior in the Provisional Government, 1917.

URYU Stokichi. Rear-Admiral; commander of Second (cruiser) Division, Japanese Second Fleet, in 1904-5.

USPENSKY, Gleb Ivanovich (1843-1902). Major author, journalist.

UVAROV, Count Alexis Alekseevich (1859-). Saratov landowner. Employed by the Ministry of Interior since 1884; specialist in zemstvo and urban affairs and economy. Member of the Saratov provincial zemstvo assembly. Elected to Third Duma as an Octobrist; joined the Progressists in 1908.

VANNOVSKY, Peter Semenovich (1822-1904). General. Minister of War, 1881-98. Minister of Public Education, 1901-2.

VASNETSOV, Victor Mikhailovich (1848-1926). Realist painter, noted especially for his epic works.

VELOPOLSKY (Wielopolsky), Count Sigismund Iosifovich (1863-). Master of the Imperial Preserves in Poland. Elected from Poland to the State Council, 1909, 1912.

VERESHCHAGIN, Vasily Vasilievich (1842-1904). Painter, batalist. Killed on the *Petropavlovsk* off Port Arthur.

VICTOR EMMANUEL III (1869-1947). King of Italy, 1900-46; succeeded his assassinated father, Humbert I. Abdicated after World War II and died in exile.

VILBUSHEVICH, Mania. Jewish labor leader; the most prominent of the Zubatov leaders in the Pale of Settlement; emigrated to Palestine.

VILKITSKY, B.A. Naval officer; Arctic explorer.

VINAVER, Maxim Moiseevich (1863-1926). Liberal politician. One of the founders of the Kadet Party, played a prominent role in the First Duma. Convicted, imprisoned 1908 for signing the Vyborg manifesto. Active in Jewish affairs. Served as foreign minister in the anti-Bolshevik regime in the Crimea, 1918. Emigrated and subsequently edited the journal *Zveno* [The Link].

VINOGRADOV, Paul Gavrilovich (1854-1925). Historian. Professor of History, Moscow University, 1884-1902 and 1908-17; Oxford University, 1903-8 and 1918-25. Resigned from Moscow University in 1902 in protest against the policies of Vannovsky; resumed his post in 1908. Authority on medieval Europe, particularly English institutions. Produced several major works and edited the Oxford Studies in Social and Legal History from 1909 until his death.

VITGEFT, see Witgeft.

VIVIANI, Rene (1863-1925). French politician; Prime Minister in 1914.

VOEIKOV, Vladimir Nikolaevich (1868-). Major-General. Member of the Emperor's suite. Commander, Imperial Hussars Regiment (Tsarskoe Selo), 1907-13. Commandant of the Imperial Palace, 1913-March 1917.

VOGAK, Constantine Ippolitovich. Major-General. Russian military attache in the Far East (Peking, Tokyo). A "Bezobrazovist."

VOINOVSKY-KRIEGER, Eduard Bronislavovich (1862-1933). Second Assistant Minister of Communications, 1916, and Minister, Dec 1916-Feb 1917.

VOLKONSKY, Prince Nicholas Sergeevich (1848-1910). Landowner from Riazin. Active in zemstvo affairs: chairman of the provincial zemstvo board, 1897- ; and a member of the various zemstvo congresses. Elected to the State Council in 1906 but resigned in order to stand for election to the Duma. Served in First and Third Dumas as an Octobrist. Sometimes identified as Volkonsky-I.

VOLKONSKY, Prince Vladimir Mikhailovich (1868-). Tambov landowner. Served as a cavalry officer before being appointed provincial marshal of nobility. Member of the tsar's suite. One of the founders of the United Nobility (1906). Elected to the Third Duma; member of the rightist bloc and Vice President of the Duma. Known as Volkonsky-IV.

VOLZHIN, Alexander Nikolaevich (1862-). Administrator. Provincial marshal of nobility, Podolsk, 1897-1904; Sedlets, 1904- . Governor of Kholm, 1913-14. Director of the Department of General Affairs, Ministry of Interior, 1914-15. Director-General of the Holy Synod, Oct 1915-Aug 1916. Appointed to the State Council, 1916.

VONLIARLIARSKY, Vladimir Mikhailovich (1852-). Colonel, speculator and promoter. Associated with Bezobrazov and others in the ill-fated Yalu River concession.

VORONTSOV-DASHKOV, Count Illarion Ivanovich (1837-1916). Major figure in the reigns of Alexander III and Nicholas II. Distinguished military service in the Caucasus, Turkestan, and the Russo-Turkish War of 1877-78. Minister of the Imperial Court, 1881-97. One of the enthusiastic promoters of the Yalu River concession (1898-1903). Viceroy of the Caucasus and Commander of the Caucasus Military District, 1905-15.

VOSKRESENSKY, Alexander Petrovich (1854-). Zemstvo physician; wrote extensively on rural public health.

VYRUBOVA, Anna Aleksandrovna (1884-). Closest friend and confidante of Empress Alexandra Feodorovna; totally under the influence of Rasputin.

VYSHNEGRADSKY, Ivan Alekseevich (1831-1895). Minister of Finance, 1886-92.

WAHL, Victor-Karl-Konrad-William von (1840-1915). General of Police. Chief of Police, St. Petersburg, 1892-95. Governor of Vilna, 1901-2 (target of an unsuccessful assassin). Assistant Minister of Interior and Commandant of the Corps of Gendarmes, 1902-3. Appointed to the State Council, 1903.

WALDECK-ROUSSEAU, Pierre Marie Rene (1846-1904). French politician; Prime Minister, 1899-1902.

WALDERSEE, Count Alfred von (1832-1904). German General, Field Marshal. Chief of the German General Staff, 1888-91. Commander of German forces in the Far East, 1900-1, and supreme commander of the international relief column to Peking during the Boxer Rebellion.

WALLACE, Donald MacKenzie (1841-1919). British journalist. Correspondent and writer for *The Times*, 1878- . One of the early western writers on Russia.

WARBURG, Fritz. German industrialist; erroneously alleged to have been involved in negotiations for a separate peace during World War I.

WERDER, Bernhard Franz William von (1823-1907). German officer and diplomat. General of Infantry; military attache to the tsar (military plenipotentiary), 1869-86. Governor of Berlin, 1886-88. Ambassador to Russia, 1892-95.

WILLIAM II (1859-1941). King of Prussia and Emperor of Germany, 1888-1918. The tsar's "Cousin Willy."

WINDISCHGRÄTZ, Prince Alfred. Austrian Minister-President, 1893-95.

WIREN, Robert Nikolaevich (1856-1917). Admiral. Commander of Ships and Harbors, 1907-8. Commandant, Kronstadt Naval Base, 1909-17; murdered during the mutiny of February 1917.

WITGEFT, William Karlovich (1847-1904). Rear-Admiral. Chief of Staff of the Pacific Squadron, 1899-1904; acting commander, Mar-July 1904. Killed aboard his flagship *Tsesarevich* in the Battle of the Yellow Sea.

WITTE, Sergei Yulievich (1849-1915). Count (1905). Chief architect of Russian policy during the first decade of the reign of Nicholas II. Director of Railways, 1889-92. Minister of Communications, 1892. Minister of Finance, 1892-1903. Chairman of the Committee of Ministers, 1903-5, and President of the Council of Ministers, Oct 1905-Apr 1906. Witte directed Russian industrialization and carried out the financial reform which placed Russia on the gold standard in 1898. Negotiated the Treaty of Portsmouth (1905) and laid the foundation for the desperately needed French loan of 1906. Had a major role in drafting the Had a major role in drafting the October Manifesto and the Fundamental

Goremykin on the eve of the opening of the First Duma and spent an embittered decade in forced retirement.

XENIA ALEKSANDROVNA, Grand Duchess (1875-1960). Sister of Nicholas II.

YANUSHKEVICH, Nicholas Nikolaevich (1868-1919). General. Chief of the General Staff (later Supreme High Command—Stavka), Mar 1914-July 1915. Then Assistant Viceroy of the Caucasus and Assistant Commander of the Caucasus Military District (under Grand Duke Nicholas Nikolaevich), 1915-17. Earlier career: Chief, Legislative Section, Chancellery of the War Minister, 1905-11; Professor, Nicholas Academy of the General Staff, 1910-11; Assistant Manager, Chancellery of the War Minister, 1911-13; and Professor and Chief of the Nicholas Academy, 1913-14.

YERMOLOV, see Ermolov.

YI KOJONG 9born 1852). King of Korea, 1864-1907 (regency, 1864-73). Deposed by the Japanese.

YUDENICH, Nicholas Nikolaevich (1862-1933). General. Served in the Russo-Japanese War and later on the General Staff. Commanded Russian forces in the Caucasus, 1914-15 and 1917. Commanded a White Army in the Baltic during the Civil War. Died in France.

ZAGRUDNY, A.S. Defense counsel for Mendel Beilis (1913).

ZAITSEV, Boris Konstantinovich (1881-1972). Major "impressionist" writer; emigrated in 1922.

ZAMENHOF, Louis Lazarus. Polish philologist; inventor of Esperanto.

ZAMYSLOVSKY, Egor Egorovich (1841-1896). Professor of History and Philology, St. Petersburg University, 1871-96. Tutor of Nicholas II.

ZAMYSLOVSKY, Georgy Georgievich (1872-). Assistant prosecutor of the Vilna Circuit Court; served with the prosecution in the Beilis trial. Elected to the Third and Fourth Dumas; served as assistant secretary and was noted even among the rightist bloc as an extreme reactionary and anti-semite.

ZANKEVICH, M.I. (1882-). Major-General. Acting chief of staff to General Khabalov, Commandant of Petrograd in 1917.

ZASULICH, Michael Ivanovich. Lieutenant-General. Commandant, Warsaw Military District, 1900(?)-1904. Commander of the Far Eastern Detachment; defeated at the Yalu River, Apr-May 1904. Brother of the noted revolutionary, Vera Zasulich.

ZASULICH, Vera Ivanovna (1849-1919). Populist and later Marxist revolutionary leader. Member of the Land and Freedom movement since 1869, then the terrorist organization, The People's Will. Emigrated to Switzerland in 1880 and soon joined Plekhanov in the first group of Russian Marxists. Member of the editorial board of Iskra; supported the Mensheviks after 1903. Returned to Russia in 1905, followed Plekhanov's leadership in 1917, and died in Russia, an opponent of Lenin and the Bolsheviks.

ZENGER, Gregory Edwardovich (1853-1919). Philologist (corresponding member of the Academy of Sciences); Minister of Public Education, 1902-4.

ZHEMCHUZNIKOV, Alexis Mikhailovich (1821-1908). Satirist and poet. Creator, with his cousin A.K. Tolstoy, of the pseudonymous "Kuzma Prutkov" and a tradition of nonsense poetry.

ZHILINSKY, Jacob Grigorovich (1853-1917?). General. Technical Delegate to the First Hague Conference, 1899. Quartermaster-General, 1900-3. Served briefly in the Russo-Japanese War. Commander of the Warsaw Military District, Mar-July 1914, and Governor-General of Warsaw, Mar-Sept 1914. As Commander of the Northwestern Front in 1914-15, Zhilinsky presided over the disastrous East Prussian campaigns.

ZHILINSKY, Sergei Grigorovich. General. Russian representative at the Chantilly conference, December 1915.

ZHILKIN, Ivan Vasilievich (1874-). Journalist. Elected from Saratov to the First Duma—a Trudovik. Correspondent for *Nedeli* (1898-) and *Vestnik evropy* (1910-).

ZHITOMIRSKY, Jacob. Police spy, close to Lenin.

ZHUKOVSKY, Vasily Andreevich (1783-1852). Romantic poet; a precursor of Pushkin.

ZILLIACUS, Konni (1855-1924). Finnish nationalist and revolutionary leader.

ZIMBALIST, Ephrem (1889-). Violinist and composer. Born in Rostov-on-the-Don, emigrated to the United States in 1911. Student of Leopold Auer (1901-7) at the St. Petersburg Conservatory. Retired, 1968.

ZINOVIEV, Gregory Evseevich (Evsei Aronovich Radomyslsky) (1883-1936). Bolshevik. Active revolutionary since 1901. Member of the Bolshevik committee in Petersburg and Kronstadt during the 1905 Revolution. Member of the Bolshevik Central Committee, 1907-27. Attended the Zimmerwald and Kienthal conferences during the war. Executive Director of the Third International (Comintern), 1919-26. Expelled from the party by Stalin in 1927; reinstated, 1928; again expelled, 1932. Sentenced to ten years' imprisonment in 1935 for "moral complicity" in the assassination of Kirov. Retried in the first show trial of the Great Purge and executed (1936).

ZUBATOV, Sergei Vasilievich (1864-1917). Assistant Chief (1889-96) and Chief (1896-1902) of the Moscow Okhrana. Named in 1902 to head a special section of police charged with organizing and directing "police unions" in order to divert workers from the revolutionary movement. The Zubatov plan culminated in the mass march on the Winter Palace in January 1905 and the "Bloody Sunday" massacre. Zubatov, meanwhile, had been retired. He committed suicide in 1917 to avoid arrest.

ZURABOV, Arshak Gerasimovich (1873-). Armenian Social Democrat. Imprisoned and exiled several times. Vocal leader of the SD fraction in the Second Duma.

WORKS MENTIONED

Nicholas II: Correspondence and Papers

Dnevnik Imperatora Nikolaia II. Edited by S.P. Melgunov. Berlin, 1923. French edition: *Journal Intime.* Translated by A. Pierre. Paris, 1925.

"Iz perepiski Nikolaia II i Marii Feodorovni, 1907-1910 gg." *Krasnyi arkhiv*, 50-51 (1932): 161-93.

"Iz perepiski P.A. Stolypina s Nikolaem Romanovym." *Krasnyi arkhiv*, 30 (1928): 80-88.

Letters from the Kaiser to the Czar. Edited by Isaac Don Levine. New York, 1920. Also: *Correspondance entre Guillaume II et Nicolas II, 1894-1914.* Translated by Marc Semenoff. 9th ed. Paris, 1924.

The Nicky-Sunny Letters: Correspondence of the Tsar and Tsaritsa, 1914-1917. Academic International Press, 1970. Includes: *The Letters of the Tsar to the Tsaritsa, 1914-1917.* Edited by C.E. Vulliamy. New York, 1929. *The Letters of the Tsaritsa to the Tsar, 1914-1916.* Introduction by Sir Bernard Pares. London, 1923.

"Nikolai Romanov ob ubiistve Stolypina." *Krasnyi arkhiv*, 35 (1929): 209-11.

"Perepiska N.A. Romanova i P.A. Stolypina." *Krasnyi arkhiv*, 5 (1924): 102-28.

The Secret Letters of the Last Tsar. Being the Confidential Correspondence between Nicholas II and His Mother, Dowager Empress Maria Feodorovna. Edited by Edward J. Bing. London, 1938.

Semennikov, V.P. *Monarkhiia pered khrusheniem 1914-1917 gg. Bumagi Nikolaia II i drugie dokumenty.* Moscow-Leningrad, 1927.

—————. *Nikolai II i Velikie kniazia.* Moscow-Leningrad, 1925.

Documentary Records and Materials

Adamov, E.A., ed. *Konstantinopol i prolivy po sekretnym dokumentam byvshego Ministerstva inostrannykh del.* 2 vols. Moscow, 1915. French edition: *Constantinople et les détroits . . . .* Paris, 1930-32.

Akademiia nauk SSSR. Institut istorii. *Revoliutsiia 1905-1907 gg. v Rossii: Dokumenty i materialy.* 15 vols. Moscow, 1955-63.

"Anglo-russkaia konventsiia 1907 g. i razdel Afganistana." *Krasnyi arkhiv*, 10 (1925): 54-66.

Browder, Robert Paul, and Kerensky, Alexander F., eds. *The Russian Provisional Government, 1917: Documents.* 3 vols. Stanford, 1961.

Carnegie Endowment for International Peace. Division of International Law. *Manchuria: Treaties and Agreements.* Washington, 1921.

Conférence Internationale de la Paix. La Haye, 18 mai-29 juillet, 1899. 4 Parts in 1 Volume. La Haye, 1899.

Correspondance secrète de Bulow et de Guillaume II. Translated by Gil-Lenoir. Paris, 1931.

"Dnevnik Ministerstva inostrannykh del za 1915-1916 gg." *Krasnyi arkhiv, 31 (1929): 3-87.*

"Fevralskaia revoliutsiia 1917 goda." *Krasnyi arkhiv,* 21 (1927): 3-78; and 22 (1927): 3-70.

France. Ministère des affaires étrangères. *Documents diplomatiques L' Alliance Franco-Russe.* Paris, 1918.

————. *Documents diplomatiques française, 1871-1914.* 42 vols. Paris, 1929-59.

Germany. General Staff. Historical Section. *The Russo-Japanese War.* Translated by Karl von Donat. 9 vols. London, 1909.

————. *Die Grosse Politik der europaischen Kabinette, 1871-1914.* Edited by Johannes Lepsius, Albrecht Mendelssohn, and Friedrich Thimme. 40 vols. in 54. Berlin, 1922-26.

Golder, Frank A., ed. *Documents of Russian History, 1914-1917.* Translated by Emanuel Aronsberg. Century, 1927; Peter Smith, 1964.

Great Britain. Admiralty War Staff (trans.). *Japanese Official Naval History of the Russo-Japanese War.* 2 vols. London, 1913-14.

————. *British Documents on the Origins of the War, 1898-1913.* Edited by G.P. Gooch and H.W.V. Temperley. 11 vols. London, 1926-38.

————. Committee of Imperial Defence. Historical Section. *Official History, Naval and Military, of the Russo-Japanese War.* 3 vols. and 3 vols. of Maps and Appendices. London, 1910-20.

How the War Began in 1914. Being the Diary of the Russian Foreign Office from the 3rd to the 20th of July 1914. Foreword by S.D. Sazonov. Introduction by Baron Schilling. London, 1915.

"K istorii Potsdamskogo soglasheniia 1911 g." *Krasnyi arkhiv,* 58 (1933): 46-57.

Kalinychev, F.I., ed. *Gosudarstvennaia duma v Rossii v dokumentakh i materialakh.* Moscow, 1957.

Un livre noire. Diplomatie d'avant guerre d'après les documents des Archives Russes 1910-1917. René Marchand, ed. 3 vols. Paris, 1922-34.

Lvov, N.N., and Stakhovich, A.A., comps. *Nuzhdy derevni po rabotam komitetov selskokhoziaistvennoi promyshlennosti.* St. Petersburg, 1904.

MacMurray, John V.A., ed. *Treaties and Agreements with and concerning China, 1894-1919.* 2 vols. Oxford Univ Press, 1919.

"Okonchatelyni tekst proekta manifesta Goremykina-Budberga." *Krasnyi arkhiv,* 11-12 (1925): 94-97.

Pashukanis, K., ed. "K istorii anglo-russkogo soglashenia 1907 g." *Krasnyi arkhiv,* 69-70 (1935): 3-39.

"Pervye shagi russkogo imperializma na Dalnem Vostoke (1888-1903 gg.)." *Krasnyi arkhiv,* 52 (1932): 34-124.

Pokrovsky, M.N., ed. *1905. Materialy i Dokumenty.* 8 vols. Moscow, 1925-28.

Polenov, A.D., comp. *Izsledovanie ekonomicheskago polozheniia tsentralno-chernozemnykh gubernii. Trudy osobago soveshchaniia 1899-1901 gg.* Moscow, 1901.

Pribram, Alfred Francis. *The Secret Treaties of Austria-Hungary, 1878-1914.* English edition by Archibald Cary Coolidge. 2 vols. Harvard Univ Press, 1920-21.

"Protsess Beilisa v otsenke departmenta politsii." *Krasnyi arkhiv,* 44 (1930): 85-125.

Raffalovich, A. *L'Abominable vénalité de la presse française . . . d'après les documents des archives russes (1897-1917).* Paris, 1931.

Romberg, Baron G. von. *Falsifications of the Russian Orange Book.* London, 1923.

Russia. Chrezvychainaia sledstvennaia komissia. *Padenie tsarskogo rezhima. Stenograficheskie otchety doprovosov i pokazanii dannykh v 1917 g. v Chrezvychainoi sledstvennoi komissii Vremennogo pravitelstva.* 7 vols. Moscow-Leningrad, 1924-27.

_____. Gosudarstvennaia Duma. *Stenograficheskie otchety.* 32 vols. St. Petersburg/Petrograd, 1906-16. See Chapter XII, note 10.

_____. Ministère des affaires étrangères. *Recueil des documents diplomatiques. Negociations ayant précédé la Guerre, 10/23 juillet-24 juillet/6 août 1914.* Petrograd, 1914. [Russian Orange Book]

_____. Ministerstvo inostrannykh del. *Mezhdunarodnie otnosheniia v epokhu imperializma.* 14 vols. Moscow-Leningrad, 1931- . German edition: *Die internationalen Beziehungen im Zeitalter des Imperialismus. Edited by Otto Hoetzsch. 16 vols.* Berlin, 1933- .

_____. *Sbornik dogovorov Rossii s drugimi gosudarstvami, 1856-1917 gg.* Moscow, 1952.

_____. Morskii generalnyi shtab. *Voenno-istoricheskaia komissiia po opisaniiu deistvii flota v voinu 1904-05 gg. Russko-iaponskaia voina 1904-05 gg.* 7 vols. St. Petersburg, 1912-18.

_____. *Polnoe sobranie zakonov rossiskoi imperii. Sobranie tretie.* 34 vols. St. Petersburg, 1885-1916.

_____. Tsentralnyi statisticheskii komitet. *Obshchii svod po Imperii rezultatov razrabotki dannykh pervoi vesobshchei perepisi naseleniia.* 2 vols. St. Petersburg, 1905.

_____. *Pervaia vesobshchaia perepis naseleniia Rossiskoi Imperii, 1897 g.* Edited by N.A. Troinitsky. 89 vols. in 24. St. Petersburg, 1899-1905.

_____. *Voenno-istoricheskaia komissiia po opisaniiu rossko-iaponskoi voiny. Russko-iaponskaia voina, 1904-05 gg.* 9 vols. St. Petersburg, 1910.

"Russko-germanskii dogovor 1905 goda." *Krasnyi arkhiv,* 5 (1924): 1-49.

Scherer, André, and Grunewald, Jacques, eds. *L'Allemagne et les problémes de la paix pendant la premiére guerre mondiale. Documents extraits des archives de l'Office allemand des Affaires étrangéres.* Vol. I: *Des origines á la declaration de la guerre sous-marine á outrance (août 1914-janvier 1917).* Paris, 1962.

Shilovsky, P. *Akty otnosiashchiesia k politicheskomu polozheniiu Finlandii.* St. Petersburg, 1903.

Soiuz russkogo naroda: po materialam sledstvennoi komissii Vremennogo pravitelstva 1917 g. Moscow, 1929.

Teleshev, L., ed. "K istorii pervoi Gaagskoi konferentsii." *Krasnyi arkhiv,* 50-51 (1932): 64-96.

_____. "Novie materiali o Gaagskoi mirnoi konferentsii, 1899 g." *Krasnyi arkhiv,* 54-55 (1932): 49-79.

"Tsarskoe pravitelstvo i protsess Beilisa." *Krasnyi arkhiv,* 55 (1932): 162-204.

"Tsarskoselskie soveshchaniia: Protokoly sekretnago soveshchaniia v aprele 1906 goda pod presedatelstvom byvshago imperatora po peresmotru osnovnykh zakonov." *Byloe,* 4 (26) (October 1917): 183-245.

"Tsarskoselskie soveshchaniia: Protokoly sekretnago soveshchaniia v fevrale 1906 goda pod presedatelstvom byvshago imperatora po vyrabotke Uchrezhdenii Gosudarstvennoi Dumy i Gosudarstvennago Soveta." *Byloe,* 5-6 (27-28) (Nov-Dec 1917): 289-318.

"V tserkovnikh hrugakh pered revoliutsiei." *Krasnyi arkhiv,* 31 (1928): 204-13.

Witte, S.Yu. *Po povodu neprelozhnosti zakonov gosudarstvennoi zhizni.* St. Petersburg, 1914.

_____. *Samoderzhavie i zemstvo. Konfidentsialnaia zapiska Ministra Finansov, stats-sekretaria S.Yu. Vitte (1899 g.).* Stuttgart, 1899.

_____. *Zapiska po krestianskomu delu predsedatelia vysochaishe uchrezhdennago osobago soveshchaniia o nuzhdakh selsko-khoziaistvennoi promyshlennosti, stats-sekretaria Vitte.* St. Petersburg, 1904.

_____. "Zapiska Vitte ot 9 oktiabria." *Krasnyi arkhiv,* 11-12 (1925): 51-57.

[Yakhontov]. *Prologue to Revolution: Notes of A.N. Iakhontov on the Secret Meetings of the Council of Ministers, 1915.* Edited by Michael Cherniavsky. New York, 1967.

Bibliography, Historiography, and Reference

American Association for the Advancement of Slavic Studies. *The American Bibliography of Slavic and East European Studies* (annual), 1957- .

Boiovich, M.M. *Chleny Gosudarstvennoi dumy. (Portrety i Biografii).* 4 vols. St. Petersburg, 1906-13.

"Chleny Gosudarstvennoi dumy pervogo, vtorogo i tretego sozyva." *Entsiklopedicheskii slovar Granat,* XVII.

Curtiss, John Shelton, ed. *Essays in Russian and Soviet History.* New York, 1963.

Derenkovsky, G.M. *Pervaia russkaia revoliutsiia, 1905-1907 gg. Annotirovannyi ukazatel' literatury.* Moscow, 1965.

————— and Vartanian, A.D. "Dokumentalnie izdaniia po istorii pervoi russkoi revoliutsii." *Istoricheskii arkhiv,* 6 (1956): 185-97.

Diplomaticheskii slovar. Edited by A.A. Gromyko *et al.* Moscow, 1971.

Dmytryshyn, Basil. *Imperial Russia: A Source Book, 1700-1917.* 2nd edition. Dryden, 1974.

Encyclopaedia Brittanica. 11th edition.

Encyclopaedia of Religion and Ethics.

Florinsky, Michael T., ed. *McGraw-Hill Encyclopedia of Russia and the Soviet Union.* New York, 1961.

Gindin, I.F. "Problemy istorii fevralskoi revoliutsii i ee sotsialno-ekonomicheskikh predposylok." *Istorii SSSR* (1967), No. 4: 30-49.

Grigorev, A.L. *Pervaia russkaia revoliutsiia 1905-1907 gg. i zarubezhnaia literatura.* Leningrad, 1956.

A History of the All-Union Communist Party (Bolshevik): A Short Course. Moscow, 1938; English edition, 1948.

History of the Communist Party of the Soviet Union. Second revised edition. Moscow, 1960.

McNeal, R.H., ed. *Russia in Transition, 1905-1914.* New York, 1970.

Mendel, Arthur P. "On Interpreting the Fate of Imperial Russia." In *Russia Under the Last Tsar,* pp. 13-41. Edited by T.G. Stavrou. Minneapolis, 1969.

The Modern Encyclopedia of Russian and Soviet History. Edited by Joseph L. Wieczynski. Academic International Press, 1976- (multivolume reference work in progress).

The Modern Encyclopedia of Russian and Soviet Literature. Edited by Harry B. Weber. Academic International Press, 1977- (in progress).

Morrison, John A. "Russia and Warm Water: A Fallacious Generalization and Its Consequences." U.S. Naval Institute *Proceedings,* 78(1952): 1169-79.

Pushkarev, Sergei G., comp. *Dictionary of Russian Historical Terms from the Eleventh Century to 1917.* Edited by George Vernadsky and Ralph T. Fisher, Jr., New Haven, 1970.

Rollins, Patrick J. "Russia's Fictitious Naval Tradition." U.S. Naval Institute *Proceedings,* 99 (1973): 65-71.

Sovetskaia istoricheskaia entsiklopediia. 15 vols. (in progress). Moscow, 1961- .

Spravochniki po istorii dorevoliutsionnoi Rossii. Edited by P.A. Zaionchkovsky. Moscow, 1971.

Szeftel, Marc. "The Historical Limits of the Question of Russia and the West." In *The Development of the USSR,* pp. 378-85. Edited by Donald W. Treadgold. Seattle, 1964.

Walsh, Warren B., comp. and ed. *Readings in Russian History*. Vol. 3: *The Revolutionary Era and the Soviet Period*. 4th revised ed. Syracuse, 1963.

————. "The Romanov Papers: A Bibliographic Note." *The Historian*, 31 (1969): 163-72.

The West Point Atlas of American Wars. Edited by Colonel Vincent J. Esposito. New York, 1959.

Diaries, Memoirs, and Autobiographies

Alekseev. *Iz dnevnik M.V. Alekseeva*. Edited by Jan Slavik. Prague, 1929.

Alexander, Grand Duke of Russia. *Once a Grand Duke*. New York, 1932.

Badayev, A. *The Bolsheviks in the Tsarist Duma*. New York, 1929.

Baring, Maurice. *The Mainsprings of Russia*. London, 1914.

Benckendorff. *Graf Benckendorffs diplomatischer Schriftwechsel*. Edited by B. de Siebert. Revised ed. 3 vols. Berlin, Leipzig, 1928.

Benois, Alexandre. *Reminiscences of the Russian Ballet*. London, 1941.

Bobrinsky. "Dnevnik A.A. Bobrinskiia 1910-1911 gg." *Krasnyi arkhiv*, 26 (1928): 127-50.

Bock, Maria Petrovna von. *Reminiscences of My Father, Peter A. Stolypin*. Translated and edited by Margaret Patoski. Scarecrow Press, 1970.

Bublikov, A.A. *Russkaia revoliutsiia (ee nachalo, arest Tsaria, perspektivy)*. New York, 1918.

Buchanan, Sir George. *My Mission to Russia*. 2 vols. London, New York, 1923.

Bülow, Prince Bernhard H.M.K. von. *Memoirs*. Translated by Geoffrey Dunlop and F.A. Voight. 4 vols. London, 1931-32.

Cambon, Paul. *Correspondance, 1870-1924*. Paris, 1940.

Conrad von Hötzendorf, F. *Aus meiner Dienstzeit*. 5 vols. Vienna, 1921-25.

Danilov, G.N. [Yuri]. *La Russie dans la guerre mondiale 1914-1917*. Paris, 1927. Russian edition: *Uchastie Rossii v mirovoi voine*.

Gapon, George. *The Story of My Life*. London, 1905. Also serialized in *The Strand Magazine*, 30 (1905): 3-33, 169-80, 304-17, 363-77, and 483-96.

Gilliard, Pierre. *Thirteen Years at the Russian Court*. New York, 1921.

Grey of Fallodon [Sir Edward Grey]. *Twenty-five Years, 1892-1916*. 2 vols. London, 1915.

Guchkov, "Iz vospominaniia A.I. Guchkova." *Poslednie novosti*, 1936.

Gurko, V.I. *Features and Figures of the Past: Government and Opinion in the Reign of Nicholas II*. Edited by J.E. Wallace Sterlin, Xenia Joukoff Eudin, and H.H. Fisher. Translated by Laura Matveev. Stanford, 1939.

Izvolsky, A.P. *The Memoirs of Alexander Iswolsky*. Academic International Press, 1974 [1920].

_____. *Au service de la Russie . . . Correspondance diplomatique,* 1906-*1911*. 2 vols. Paris, 1937.

Karsavina, Tamara. *Theatre Street: The Reminiscences of Tamara Karsavina.* London, 1930, 1905.

Kerensky, Alexander F. *The Crucifixion of Liberty.* New York, 1934.

Knox, Major-General Sir Alfred. *With the Russian Army, 1914-1917.* 2 vols. New York, 1921.

Kokovtsov, Vladimir N. *Iz moego proshlago: Vospominaniia, 1903-1919.* 2 vols. Paris, 1933. English edition: *The Memoirs of Count Kokovtsov: Out of My Past.* Edited by H.H. Fisher. Stanford, 1935.

Korostovetz, Ivan Iakovlevich. *Prewar Diplomacy, the Russo-Japanese Problem, Treaty signed at Portsmouth, USA, 1905; Diary of J.J. Korostovetz.* London, 1920. The same in *Byloe* (1918) and *Stranitsa iz istorii russkoi diplomatii* (Peking, 1923).

Kovalevsky, Maxime. *La crise russe; notes et impressions d'un temoin.* Paris, 1906.

Kryzhanovsky, S.Ye. *Vospominaniia.* Berlin, 1938.

Kschessinska, Mathilde. *Dancing in Petersburg.* Translated by Arnold Haskell. New York, 1961.

Kurlov, P.G. *Der Zusammenburch des kaiserlichen Russlands.* Berlin, 1929.

Kuropatkin. "Dnevnik A.N. Kuropatkina." *Krasnyi arkhiv,* 2 (1922): 9-112.

_____. *Zapiska generala Kuropatkina o russko-iaponskoi voine.* 2 vols. Berlin, 1909. English edition: *The Russian Army and the Japanese War.* Edited by Major E.D. Swinton. Translated by Captain A.B. Lindsay. 2 vols. London, 1909.

Lenin, V.I. *Sochineniia.* 2nd ed. 30 vols. Moscow-Leningrad, 1929-32. English edition: *Collected Works.* 38 vols. Moscow, 1960-61.

Lopukhin, A.A. *Vospominaniia.* Moscow, 1923.

Lukomsky. "Dokumenty k 'Vospominaniiam' gen. A. Lukomskago." *Arkhiv russkoi revoliutsii,* 3 (1922): 247-71.

Makarov, S.O. *"Vitiaz" i Tikhii okean.* 2 vols. St. Petersburg, 1894.

Maklakov, V.A. *Vlast i obshchestvennost na zakate staroi Rossii: Vospominaniia sovremennika.* Paris, 1939.

Martov, L. *Annals of a Social Democrat.* Berlin, 1922.

Meshchersky, V.P. *Moi vospominaniia.* St. Petersburg, 1912.

Meyendorf, Baron Alexander. *The Background of the Russian Revolution.* New York, 1928.

Miliukov, Paul. *Political Memoirs, 1905-1917.* Edited by Arthur P. Mendel. Translated by Carl Goldberg. Ann Arbor, 1967.

_____. "Rokovye gody." *Russkie zapiski,* 1938-39.

_____. *Russia and Its Crisis.* Chicago, 1905.

_____. *Tri popytki: k istorii russkogo lzhekonstitutionalizma.* Paris, 1921.

_____. *Vospominaniia, 1895-1917 gg.* Edited by M. Karpovich and B. Elkin. 2 vols. Paris, 1955.

Nekliudov, A.V. *Diplomatic Reminiscences before and during the World War, 1911-1917.* London, 1920.

Novikoff-Priboy, A. *Tsushima, Grave of a Floating City.* Translated by Eden and Cedar Paul. New York, 1937.

Paleologue, Maurice. *La Russie des Tsars pendant la grand guerre.* 3 vols. Paris, 1921.

Pobedonostsev, C.P. *Moskovskii sbornik.* Moscow, 1896. English edition: *Reflections of a Russian Statesman.* Translated by R.C. Long. London, 1898; Ann Arbor, 1965.

Poincaré, Raymond. *Au service de la France.* 5 vols. Paris, 1926-28.

Politovsky, E.S. *From Libau to Tsushima: A Narrative of the Voyage of Admiral Rojestvensky's Fleet to Eastern Seas.* Translated by Major F.R. Godfrey. London, 1906.

Polovtsev, A.A. "Dnevnik A.A. Polovtseva." *Krasnyi arkhiv,* 4 (1923): 63-128.

_____. *Dnevnik gosudarstvennogo sekretaria A.A. Polovtsova, 1883-1892.* Edited by P.A. Zaionchkovsky. 2 vols. Moscow, 1966.

Purishkevich, V.M. *Comme j'ai tué Raspoutine.* Paris, 1923.

_____. *Dnevnik chlena Gosudarstvennoi dumy V.M. Purishkevicha.* Riga, 1924.

Rein, G.E. *Iz perezhitogo, 1907-1917 gg.* 2 vols. Berlin, 1935.

Rodzianko, M.V. "Gosudarstvennaia Duma i fevralskaia 1917 goda revoliutsiia." *Arkhiv russkoi revoliutsii,* 6 (1922): 5-80.

_____. *The Reign of Rasputin.* Academic International Press, 1973 [1927]

Romanov, V.A. "Iz dnevnik V.A. Romanova." *Krasnyi arkhiv,* 26 (1928): 185-210.

Rosen, Baron [Roman Romanovich]. *Forty Years of Diplomacy.* 2 vols. New York, 1922.

Savinkov, Boris. *Memoirs of a Terrorist.* Translated by Joseph Shaplan, with a foreword and epilogue. New York, 1931, 1972.

Sazonov, Sergei. *Fateful Years, 1909-1916.* London, New York, 1928.

Semenov, V.I. *The Battle of Tsushima.* Translated by Captain Lendery. London, 1906.

_____. *Rasplata (The Reckoning): His diary during the blockade of Port Arthur and the voyage of Admiral Rojestvensky's Fleet.* Translated by L.A.B. London, 1909.

Shidlovsky, S.I. "The Imperial Duma and Land Settlement." *Russian Review* [London], (1912): 18-26.

_____. *Vospominaniia.* 2 vols. Berlin, 1923.

Shipov, D.N. *Vospominaniia i dumy o perezhitom.* Mosocw, 1918.

Shulgin, *Dni.* Belgrade, 1925.

Sozonov, E.S. *E. Sozonov: Materialy dlia biografii.* Moscow, 1919.

_____. *Pisma E. Sozonova, 1895-1910 gg.* Moscow, 1925.

Steer, A.P. *The "Novik" and the Part She Played in the Russo-Japanese War*. London, 1913.

Stolypin. *Sbornik rechei P.A. Stolypina (1906-1911 gg.)*. Edited by V. V. Logachev. St. Petersburg, 1911.

Sukhanov, N.N. *Zapiski o revoliutsii*. 7 vols. Berlin, 1922-23. Abridged English edition: *The Russian Revolution, 1917*. Translated by Joel Carmichael. 2 vols. Oxford, 1955.

Tagantsev, N.S. *Perezhitoe*. Petrograd, 1919.

Taube, Baron M. de. *La Politique russe d'avant Guerre et la Fin de l'Empire des Tsars (1904-1917)*. Paris, 1928. Enlarged German edition: *Der grossen Katastrophe entgegen: Die russische Politik der Vorkriegszeit und das Ende des Zarenreiches (1904-1917)*. Berlin-Leipzig, 1929.

Tikhomirov, L.A. "25 let nazad (iz dnevnikov L. Tikhomirova." *Krasnyi arkhiv*, 38 (1930): 20-69; 39 (1930): 47-75; 40 (1930): 59-96; and 41 (1930): 103-47.

————. *Vospominaniia*. Moscow-Leningrad, 1927.

Ukhtomsky, Prince [E.E.]. *Travels in the East of His Majesty, Tsar Nicholas II of Russia*. Translated by Richard Goodlet. 2 vols. London, 1896.

Urusov, S.D. *Zapiski gubernatora*. St. Petersburg, 1907. Authorized English edition: *Memoirs of a Russian Governor, Prince Serge Dmitriyevich Urussov*. Translated by Herman Rosenthal. New York, 1908, 1952.

Varnashev, N. "Ot nachala do kontsa s Gaponovskoi organizatiei (vospominaniia)." *Istoriko-revoliutsionnyi sbornik*, 1 (1924): 177-208.

Vilchkovsky, S.N. "Prebyvanie Gosudariia Imperatora v Pskove 1 i 2 marta 1917 goda, po rasskazu general-adiutanta N.V. Ruzskogo." *Russkaia letopis*, 3 (1922): 161-87.

Voeikov, V.N. *S Tsarem i bez Tsaria. Vospominaniia poslednego Dvortsovogo Komendanta Gosudaria Imperatora Nikolaia II*. Helsingfors, 1936.

Witte, S.Yu. *The Memoirs of Count Witte*. Edited by Abraham Yarmolinsky. New York, 1921. Complete Russian edition: *Vospominaniia*. Edited by A.L. Sidorov. 3 vols. Moscow, 1960.

Woytinsky, W.S. *Stormy Passage: A Personal History through Two Russian Revolutions to Democracy and Freedom, 1905-1960*. New York, 1961.

Yusupov (Youssoupoff), Prince Felix. *Lost Splendor*. London, 1953.

————. *Rasputin: His Malignant Influence and His Assassination*. Dial, 1927.

Biographies

Ascher, Abraham. *Pavel Axelrod and the Development of Menshevism*. Harvard Univ Press, 1973.

Baron, Samuel H. *Plekhanov: The Father of Russian Marxism*. Stanford, 1963.

Beletsky, S.P. *Grigorii Rasputin*. Petrograd, 1923.

Berdiaev, Nicholas. *Leontiev*. London, 1940; Academic International Press, 1968.

Byrnes, Robert F. *Pobedonostsev: His Life and Thought*. Indiana Univ Press, 1968.

Deutscher, Isaac. *The Prophet Armed: Trotsky, 1879-1921. The Prophet Unarmed: Trotsky, 1921-1929*. Oxford, 1954-1959.

Essad-Bey, Mohammed [pseud.]. *Nicholas II: Prisoner of the Purple*. Translated by P.M. and Elsa Branden. New York, 1937.

Fülöp-Miller, Rene. *Rasputin, the Holy Devil*. Translated by F. Flint and D. Tait. New York, 1928.

Garvin, J.L. *The Life of Joseph Chamberlain*. Vol. 3: *Empire and World Policy, 1895-1900*. New York, 1934.

Getzler, Israel. *Martov: A Political Biography of a Russian Social Democrat*. Cambridge, 1967.

Gould, George M. *Concerning Lafcadio Hearn*. With a bibliography by Laura Stedman. London, Philadelphia, 1908.

Gummerus, Herman. *Konni Zilliacus*. Helsingfors, 1933.

Howe, M.A. DeWolfe. *George von Lengerke Meyer: His Life and Public Services*. New York, 1919.

Kantorovich. V. "Khrustalev-Nosar." *Byloe*, 4 (32) (1925): 117-53.

Kaun, Alexander. *Maxim Gorky and His Russia*. London, 1931.

Komori Tokuji. *Akashi Motojiro*. 2 vols. Tokyo, 1928.

Marco [Bozin Simic]. "Nikolaus Hartwig." *Kriegsschuldfrage-Berliner Monatshefte*, 6 (1928): 745-69.

Massie, Robert K. *Nicholas and Alexandra*. New York, 1967.

Mitchell, Donald W. "Admiral Makarov." U.S. Naval Institute *Proceedings*, 91 (1965): 57-67.

Nicolson, Harold. *Portrait of a Diplomatist: Being the Life of Sir Arthur Nicolson, First Lord Carnock*. London, 1930.

Nikolaevsky, Boris. *Azef, the Spy*. New York, 1934; Academic International Press, 1970.

Ogasawara Nagayo. *The Life of Admiral Togo*. Tokyo, 1934.

Ostrovsky, B.G. *Stepan Osipovich Makarov, 1848-1904*. Leningrad, 1951.

Rasputin, Maria. *My Father*. London, 1934.

Semanov, S.N. *Makarov*. Moscow, 1972.

Stead, W.T. *An M.P. for Russia*. 2 vols. London, 1909. [Olga Kireeva Novikov]

Steinberg, Isaac. *Spiridonovna, Revolutionary Terrorist*. Translated and edited by Gwenda David and Eric Mosbacher. London, 1935.

Stieve, Friedrich. *Isvolsky and the World War*. London, 1926.

Sverchkov, D. *Georgy Gapon*. Moscow, 1930.

Trevelyan, G.M. *Grey of Fallodon*. London, 1937.

Trufanoff, Sergei [Illiodor]. *The Mad Monk of Russia*. New York, 1918.

_____. *Sviatoi chort*. Moscow, 1917.

Tucker, Robert C. *Stalin as Revolutionary, 1879-1929: A Study in History and Personality*. New York, 1974.

Monographs and Other Materials

Ahmad, Feroz. *The Young Turks*. Oxford, 1969.

Albertini, Luigi. *The Origins of the War of 1914*. 3 vols. Oxford, 1952-57.

Alston, Patrick L. *Education and the State in Tsarist Russia*. Stanford, 1969.

Alzona, Encarnacion. *Some French Contemporary Opinions of the Russian Revolution of 1905*. Columbia Univ Press, 1921.

Amalrik, Andrei S. "K voprosu o chislennosti i geograficheskom razmeshchenii stachechnikov v evropeiskoi Rossii v 1905 g." *Istoricheskie zapiski*, 52 (1955): 142-85.

Amburger, Erik. *Geschichte der Behördenorganisation Russlands vom Peter dem Grossen bis 1917*. Brill, 1966.

Ananich, B.V. "Vneshnie zaimy tsarizma i dumskii vopros v 1906-07 gg." *Istoricheskie zapiski*, 81 (1968): 172-98.

Andrew, Christopher. *Theophile Delcasse and the Making of the Entente Cordiale: A Reappraisal of French Foreign Policy, 1898-1905*. New York 1968.

Anweiler, Oskar. *Die Ratebewegung in Russland 1905-1921*. Brill, 1958. English edition: *The Soviets: The Russian Workers, Peasants, and Soldiers Councils, 1905-1921*. Translated by Ruth Hein. New York, 1974.

Arendt, Hannah. *On Violence*. New York, 1970.

Artsybashev, M.P. *Sanine*. Translated by Percy Pinkerton. World, 1932.

Askew, William C. *Europe and Italy's Acquisition of Libya, 1911-1912*. Durham, 1942.

Astrov, A.Y. *The Municipal Government and the All-Russian Union of Towns* in *The War and the Russian Government*. New Haven, 1929.

Avrekh, A.Ya. *Stolypin i tretia duma*. Moscow, 1968.

Ballard, Admiral A.G. *The Influence of the Sea on the Political History of Japan*. London, 1921.

Becker, Seymour. *Russia's Central Asian Protectorates: Bukhara and Khiva, 1865-1924*. Harvard Univ Press, 1968.

Block, Jan [Ivan]. *The Future of War in Its Technical, Economic, and Political Relations*. Translated by R.C. Long. Garland, 1972 [1899].

Blum, Jerome. *Lord and Peasant in Russia from the Ninth to the Nineteenth Century*. Princeton, 1961.

Busch, Briton Cooper. *Britain and the Persian Gulf, 1894-1914*. Berkeley, 1967.

Cecil, Lamar J.R. "Coal for the Fleet that had to Die." *American Historical Review*, 69 (1964): 990-1005.

Chermensky, E.D. *Burzhuaziia i tsarizm v revoliutsii 1905-07 gg.* Moscow, 1939.

_____. "Russkaia burzhuaziia oseniu 1905 goda." *Voprosy istorii* (1966), No. 6: 56-72.

_____. "Vybory v 4-uiu Gosudarstvennuiu Dumu." *Voprosy istorii* (1947), No. 4: 21-40.

Chmielewski, Edward. *The Polish Question in the Russian State Duma.* Knoxville, 1970.

_____. "Stolypin's Last Crisis." *California Slavic Studies,* 3 (1964): 95-126.

Chuprov, A.I., and Posnikov, A.S. *Vliianie urozhaev i khlebnykh tsen na nekotoryia storony russkago narodnago khoziaistva.* St. Petersburg, 1897.

Churchill, Winston S. *The World Crisis.* 6 vols. London, 1931.

Crisp, Olga. "The Russian Liberals and the 1906 Anglo-French Loan to Russia." *Slavonic and East European Review,* 39 (1961): 497-511.

Curtiss, John Shelton. *Church and State in Russia: The Last Years of the Empire, 1900-1917.* Columbia Univ Press, 1940.

Dennett, Tyler. *Roosevelt and the Russo-Japanese War.* New York, 1925; reprint, 1959.

Diakin, V.S. *Russkaia burzhuasiia i tsarizm v gody pervoi mirovoi voiny.* Leningrad, 1967.

Dillon, E.J. *The Eclipse of Russia.* London, 1918.

Dubnow, S.M. *History of the Jews in Russia and Poland from the Earliest Times until the Present Day.* Translated by I. Friedlaender. 3 vols. Philadelphia, 1920.

_____. *History of the Jews.* Vol. 10: *From the Anti-Semitic Reaction of 1881 through the Rise of Nazi Germany.* Translated by Moshe Spiegel. New York, 1973.

Dubrovsky, S.M. *Stolypinskaia zemelnaia reforma.* Moscow, 1963.

Edwards, E.W. "The Japanese Alliance and the Anglo-French Agreement of 1904." *History,* 42 (1957): 19-27.

Fay, Sidney Bradshaw. *The Origins of the World War.* 2 vols. Second ed., revised. New York, 1932.

Feuer, Lewis S. *The Conflict of Generations: The Character and Significance of Student Movements.* New York, 1969.

Fisher, J.R. *Finland and the Tsars, 1809-1899.* Second ed., London, 1901.

Fischer, George. *Russian Liberalism from Gentry to Intelligentsia.* Harvard Univ Press, 1958.

Florinsky, Michael T. *The End of the Russian Empire.* New Haven, 1931.

_____. "The Russian Mobilization of 1914." *Political Science Quarterly,* 42 (1927): 203-27.

Futrell, Michael. *Northern Underground: Episodes of Russian Revolutionary Transport and Communications through Scandanavia and Finland, 1863-1917.* London, 1963.

Geshov, Ivan. *The Balkan League*. London, 1915.

Girault, René. *Emprunts russes et investissements français en Russie, 1887-1914*. Paris, 1973.

————. "Sur quelques aspects financiers de l'alliance franco-russe." *Revue d'histoire moderne et contemporaine*, 8 (1961): 67-76.

Golder, Frank A. *Russian Expansion on the Pacific, 1641-1850*. New York, 1914.

Golovin, N.N. *The Russian Army in World War I*. New Haven, 1931; reprint, 1969.

Golubinsky, E.E. *Istoriia kanonizatsii sviatykh v russkoi tserkvi*. Moscow, 1903.

Gorky, M. et al., eds. *The History of the Great Civil War in the USSR*. Vol. 1: *The Prelude of the Great Proletarian Revolution*. London, 1937; Academic International Press, 1974.

Grey, Camilla. *The Great Experiment: Russian Art, 1863-1922*. New York, 1962.

Grigoriev, S.L. *The Diaghilev Ballet, 1909-1929*. London, 1953.

Gronsky, P. *The Central Government* in *The War and the Russian Government*. New Haven, 1929.

Haimson, Leopold. "The Problem of Social Stability in Urban Russia, 1905-1917." *Slavic Review*, 23 (1964): 619-42; and 24 (1965): 1-22.

Hans, Nicholas. *History of Russian Educational Policy (1701-1917)*. New York, 1931; reprint 1964.

Harcave, Sidney. *First Blood: The Russian Revolution of 1905*. New York, 1964.

Harper, Samuel N. *The New Electoral Law for the Russian Empire*. Chicago, 1908.

Harris, N.D. *Europe and the East*. New York, 1926.

Hearn, Lafcadio. "After the War." *Atlantic Monthly*, November 1895, 599-604.

Helffrich, Karl. *Das Geld im russisch-japanischen Krieg*. Berlin, 1905.

Helmreich, Ernst C. *The Diplomacy of the Balkan Wars, 1912-1913*. Harvard Univ Press, 1938.

Hodgson, J.H. "Finland's Position in the Russian Empire, 1905-10." *Journal of Central European Affairs*, 20 (1960): 158-73.

Hoetzsch, Otto. *Russland. Eine Einfuhrung auf Grund seiner Geschichte vom japanischen bis zum Weltkrieg*. Berlin, 1917.

Hosking, Geoffrey A. *The Russian Constitutional Experiment: Government and Duma, 1907-1914*. Cambridge, 1973.

Hough, Richard. *Dreadnought: A History of the Modern Battleship*. New York, 1964, 1975.

————. *The Fleet that had to Die*. New York, 1958.

————. *The Potemkin Mutiny*. New York, 1961.

Hsü, Immanuel C.Y. *The Rise of Modern China*. Oxford, 1970.

Intelligentsia v Rossii. Edited by I.I. Petrunkevich. St. Petersburg, 1909. [Liberal reply to *Vekhi*]

Jelavich, Barbara. *A Century of Russian Foreign Policy, 1814-1914.* New York, *1964.*

Johnson, William H.E. *Russia's Educational Heritage.* Carnegie Press, 1950; reprint, 1969.

Jutikkala, Eino, with Kauko Pirinen. *A History of Finland.* Translated by Paul Sjöblom. New York, 1962.

Katkov, George. *Russia 1917: The February Revolution.* London, 1967; Fontana, 1969.

Kazemzadeh, Firuz. *Russia and Britain in Persia, 1864-1914.* New Haven, 1964.

Keep, J.H.L. *The Rise of Social Democracy in Russia.* Oxford, 1963.

Kennan, George. *Siberia and the Exile System.* 2 vols. New York, 1891.

Kennan, George F. "The Breakdown of the Tsarist Autocracy." In *Revolutionary Russia*, pp. 1-19. Edited by Richard Pipes. New York, 1969.

Kerner, Robert J. "The Mission of Liman von Sanders." *Slavonic Review*, 6 (1927-28): 12-27, 344-63, 543-60; and 7 (1928-29): 90-112.

King, V. "The Liberal Movement in Russia, 1904-1905." *Slavonic and East European Review*, 14 (1935): 124-37.

Klado, Captain N.L. *The Battle of the Sea of Japan.* Translated by L.J. H. Dickinson. London, 1906.

————. *The Russian Navy in the Russo-Japanese War.* Translated by L.J.H. Dickinson. London, 1905.

Kochan, Lionel *Russia in Revolution, 1890-1918.* London, 1966.

Langer, William L. *The Diplomacy of Imperialism.* 2 vols. Second ed. New York, 1956.

————. "Russia, the Straits Question, and the European Powers, 1904-1908." *English Historical Review*, 44 (1929): 59-85.

————. "Russia, the Straits Question, and the Origins of the Balkan League." *Political Science Quarterly*, 43 (1928): 321-63.

Lapradelle, Albert Geouffre de. *La question du desarmement et la seconde circulaire du tsar.* Paris, 1899.

————. *Les conferences de la paix de La Haye de 1899 et 1907.* 2 vols. Paris, 1909.

Lederer, Ivo J., ed. *Russian Foreign Policy: Essays in Historical Perspective.* New Haven, 1962.

Lee, Dwight E. *Europe's Crucial Years: The Diplomatic Background of World War I, 1902-1914.* Univ Press of New England, 1974.

Legras, Jules. *Au pays russe.* Paris, 1895.

Leroy-Beaulieu, Anatole. *L'Empire des tsars.* Paris, 1890 English edition: *The Empire of the Tsars and the Russians.* 3 vols. New York, 1898.

Levin, Alfred. "Peter Arkad'evich Stolypin: a Political Reappraisal." *Journal of Modern History*, 37 (1965): 445-63.

————. *The Second Duma: A Study of the Social Democratic Party and the Russian Constitutional Experiment.* Second edition. Archon, 1966.

_____. *The Third Duma, Election and Profile*. Archon, 1973.

Lewitter, L.R. "Ivan Tikhonovich Posohkov (1652-1726) and 'The Spirit of Capitalism.'" *Slavonic and East European Review*, 51 (1973): 524-53.

Li, Dun J. *The Ageless Chinese: A History*. Second edition. New York, 1971.

Lensen, George A. *The Russian Push toward Japan: Russo-Japanese Relations, 1697-1875*. Princeton, 1959.

Luckett, Richard. *The White Generals: An Account of the White Movement and the Russian Civil War*. New York, 1971.

Manikovsky, A.A. *Boevoe snabzhenie russkoi armii v 1914-1918 gg.* Moscow, 1922.

Markov, Vladimir. *Russian Futurism: A History*. Berkeley, 1968.

Mehlinger, Howard D., and Thompson, John M. *Count Witte and the Tsarist Government in the 1905 Revolution*. Bloomington, 1972.

Melgunov, S.P. *Martovskie dni 1917 goda*. Paris, 1961.

_____. *Na putiakh k dvortsovomu perevorotu*. Paris, 1931.

Mendel, Arthur P. "Peasant and Worker on the Eve of the First World War." *Slavic Review*, 24 (1965): 23-33.

Mendelsohn, Ezra. *Class Struggle in the Pale: The Formative Years of the Jewish Workers' Movement in Tsarist Russia*. Cambridge, 1970.

Miller, Margaret. *The Economic Development of Russia, 1905-1914, with Special Reference to Trade, Industry, and Finance*. Second edition. London, 1967; reprint, 1967.

Mirsky, D.S. *A History of Russian Literature*. Revised edition. Edited by Francis J. Whitfield. New York, 1966.

Mitchell, Donald W. *A History of Russian and Soviet Sea Power*. New York, 1974.

Mitelman, M. *et al. Istoriia Putilovskogo zavoda*. Second edition. Moscow, 1941.

Monger, George. *The End of Isolation: British Foreign Policy, 1900-1907*. T. Nelson, 1963.

Mosely, Philip. "Russian Policy in 1911-1912." *Journal of Modern History*, 12 (1940): 69-86.

Mosse, W.E. "Stolypin's Villages." *Slavonic and East European Review*, 43 (1964-65): 257-74.

Muratov, Kh. *Revoliutsionnoe dvizhenie v russkoi armii v 1905-1907 gg.* Moscow, 1955.

Naida, S.F. *Revoliutsionnoe dvizhenie v tsarskom flote, 1825-1917*. Moscow, 1948.

Nazansky, V.I. *Krushenie Velikoi Rossii i Doma Romanovikh*. Paris, 1930.

Nolde, B.E. *Russia in the Economic War*. New Haven, 1928.

Owen, Launcelot. *The Russian Peasant Movement, 1906-1917*. London, 1937.

Pares, Sir Bernard. *The Fall of the Russian Monarchy*. New York, 1939, 1961.

Patrick, George Z. *Popular Poetry in Soviet Russia*. Berkeley, 1929.

Pavlovsky, G.P. *Agricultural Russia on the Eve of the Revolution*. London, 1930.

Petrov, M.A. *Podgotovka Rossii k mirovoi voine po more*. Moscow, 1926.

Petrov, V.A. *Ocherki po istorii revoliutsionnogo dvizhenie v russkoi armii v 1905 g*. Moscow-Leningrad, 1964.

Piaskovsky, A.V. *Revoliutsiia 1905-1907 gg. v Rossii*. Moscow, 1966.

Pierce, Richard A. *Russian Central Asia, 1867-1917: A Study in Colonial Rule*. Berkeley, 1960.

Pipes, Richard. *Russia under the Old Regime*. New York, 1974.

Poggenpohl, M. *Ocherk vozniknoveniia i diatelnosti Dobrovolnago flota*. St. Petersburg, 1903.

Polner, T.J., Obolensky, Prince V.A., and Turin, S.P. *Russian Local Government During the War*. New Haven, 1930.

Preobrazhensky, E.A., ed. *Russkie finansy i evropeiskaia birzha v 1904-1906 gg*. Moscow-Leningrad, 1926.

Preyer, W.D. *Die russische Agrarreform*. Jena, 1914.

Robinson, Geroid Tanquary. *Rural Russia under the Old Regime: A History of the Landlord-Peasant World and a Prologue to the Peasant Revolution of 1917*. Third edition. New York, 1957.

Rogger, Hans G. "The Beilis Case: Anti-Semitism and Politics in the Reign of Nicholas II." *Slavic Review*, 25 (1966): 615-29.

_____. "The Formation of the Russian Right, 1900 to 1906." *California Slavic Studies*, 3 (1964): 66-94.

_____. "Russia in 1914." *Journal of Contemporary History*, 1 (1966): 95-119.

_____. "Was There a Russian Fascism?" *Journal of Modern History*, 36 (1964): 398-415.

Rolo, P.J.V. *Entente Cordiale: The Origins and Negotiation of the Anglo-French Agreement of 8 April 1904*. New York, 1969.

Romanov, B.A. *Russia in Manchuria (1892-1906)*. Translated by Susan Wilbur Jones. Ann Arbor, 1952.

Rotshtein, F.A. *Mezhdunarodnie otnosheniia v kontse XIX veka*. Moscow-Leningrad, 1960.

Samuel, Maurice. *Blood Accusation: The Strange History of the Beiliss Case*. New York, 1966.

Schapiro, Leonard. *The Communist Party of the Soviet Union*. New York, 1960.

_____. "The Vekhi Group and the Mystique of Revolution." *Slavonic and East European Review*, 34 (1955): 56-76.

Schmitt, Bernadotte E. *The Annexation of Bosnia, 1908-1909*. Cambridge, 1937.

Schwarz, Solomon M. *The Russian Revolution of 1905: The Workers' Movement and the Formation of Bolshevism and Menshevism.* Translated by Gertrude Vakar. Chicago, 1967.

Shatsillo, K.F. *Russkii imperializm i razvitie flota.* Moscow, 1968.

Shumpei Okamoto. *The Japanese Oligarchy and the Russo-Japanese War.* Columbia Univ Press, 1970.

Sidelnikov, S.M. *Obrazovanie i deiatelnost pervoi Gosudarstvennoi dumy.* Moscow, 1962.

Sidorov, A.L., ed. *Istorii SSSR.* Tom 2: *Period kapitalizma, 1861-1917.* Second edition. Moscow, 1965.

————. "Denezhnoe obrashchenie i finansovoe polozhenie Rossii (1904-07 gg.)." *Istoricheskii arkhiv,* 3 (1956): 88-123.

————. "Finansovoe polozhenie tsarskogo samoderzhaviia v period russko-iaponskoi voiny i pervoi russkoi revoliutsii." *Istoricheskii arkhiv,* 2 (1955): 121-49.

Siebert, B. de, trans., and Schreiner, George Abel, ed. *Entente Diplomacy and the World, 1909-1914.* London, New York, 1921.

Slonim, Marc L. *The Epic of Russian Literature from Its Origins through Tolstoy.* Oxford, 1949.

————. *Modern Russian Literature from Chekov to the Present.* Oxford, 1953.

Smith, C. Jay Jr. *The Russian Struggle for Power, 1914-1917: A Study of Russian Foreign Policy during the First World War.* Philosophical Library, 1956.

————. "The Russian Third State Duma: An Analytical Profile." *Russian Review,* 17 (1958): 201-10.

Smolitsch, Igor. *Geschichte der russischen Kirche.* Leiden, 1964.

Solzhenitsyn, Alexander. *August 1914.* Translated by Michael Glenny. New York, 1972.

Sontag, John P. "Tsarist Debts and Tsarist Foreign Policy." *Slavic Review,* 27 (1968): 529-41.

Stavrianos, L.S. *Balkan Federation: A History of the Movement toward Balkan Unity in Modern Times.* Smith College, 1944.

————. *The Balkans since 1453.* New York, 1958.

Stone, Norman. "Moltke-Conrad: Relations between the Austro-Hungarian and German General Staffs, 1909-1914." *Historical Journal,* 9 (1966): 201-28.

Strakhovsky, Leonid I. *Craftsmen of the Word* [Acmeism]. Harvard Univ Press, 1949.

————. "The Statesmanship of Peter Stolypin." *Slavonic and East European Review,* 37 (1959): 348-70.

Struve, P.B. *Food Supply in Russia during the World War.* New Haven, 1930.

Sumner, B.H. *Russia and the Balkans, 1870-1880.* Oxford, 1937.

Tager, A.S. *Decay of Tsarism: The Beiliss Trial.* Jewish Publication Society of America, 1935.

Thaden, Edward C. "Charykov and Russian Foreign Policy at Constantinople in 1911." *Journal of Central European History*, 16 (1956): 25-44.

_____. *Russia and the Balkan Alliances of 1912*. Penn State Univ Press, 1965.

Théry, Edmond. *La transformation economique de la Russie*. Paris, 1914.

Thiess, Frank. *The Voyage of Forgotten Men (Tsushima)*. Translated by Fritz Sallagar. Bobbs-Merrill, 1937.

Thomson, George Malcolm. *Twelve Days in July*. New York, 1964.

Togo Kichitaro. *Naval Battles of the Russo-Japanese War*. Tokyo, 1907.

Totomiants, V. *Kooperatsiia v Rossii*. Prague, 1922.

Treadgold, Donald W. *The Great Siberian Migration: Government and Peasant in Resettlement from Emancipation to the First World War*. Princeton, 1957.

_____. *Lenin and His Rivals, 1898-1906*. New York, 1955.

_____. *The West in Russia and China*. Vol. 1: *Russia, 1472-1917*. Cambridge, 1973.

Trotsky, L.B. *Die russische Revolution 1905*. Berlin, 1923.

Tuchman, Barbara. *The Guns of August*. New York, 1962.

_____. *The Proud Tower: A Portrait of the World before the War, 1890-1914*. New York, 1966.

Tyler, Sidney. *The Japan-Russia War*. Philadelphia, [1905].

"*Vekhi* (Signposts): A Collection of Articles on the Russian Intelligentsia." Translated and edited by Marshall Schatz and Judith Zimmerman. *Canadian Slavic Studies*, 2 (1968): 151-74, 291-310, 447-63; 3 (1969): 1-21; 4 (1970): 36-59, 183-98; and 5 (1971): 327-61.

Venturi, Franco. *Roots of Revolution: A History of the Populist and Socialist Movements in Nineteenth Century Russia*. Translated by Francis Haskell. New York, 1960.

Volin, Lazar. *A Century of Russian Agriculture: From Alexander II to Krushchev*. Harvard Univ Press, 1970.

Von Laue, Theodore H. "The Chances for Liberal Constitutionalism." *Slavic Review*, 24 (1965): 34-46.

_____. *The Global City: Freedom, Power, and Necessity in the Age of World Revolutions*. New York, 1969.

_____. "Problems of Industrialization." In *Russia Under the Last Tsar*, pp. 117-53. Edited by T.G. Stavrou. Minneapolis, 1969.

_____. *Sergei Witte and the Industrialization of Russia*. Columbia Univ Press, 1963; Atheneum, 1969.

_____. *Why Lenin? Why Stalin? A Reappraisal of the Russian Revolution, 1900-1930*. New York, 1964.

Walder, David. *The Short Victorious War*. New York, 1974.

Walkin, Jacob. *The Rise of Democracy in Pre-Revolutionary Russia*. New York, 1962.

Wallace, Donald MacKenzie. *Russia*. London, 1877.

Walsh, Warren B. "Political Parties in the Russian Dumas." *Journal of Modern History*, 22 (1950): 144-50

Warner, Denis and Peggy. *The Tide at Sunrise: A History of the Russo-Japanese War, 1904-1905*. New York, 1974.

Wegerer, Alfred von. "The Russian Mobilization of 1914." *Political Science Quarterly*, 43 (1928): 201-28.

Weigh, Ken Shen. *Russo-Chinese Diplomacy, 1689-1924*. Second edition. University Prints and Reprints, 1967 [1928].

Westwood, John. *The Illustrated History of the Russo-Japanese War*. Chicago, 1974.

————. *Witnesses of Tsushima*. Tokyo, 1970.

White, J.A. *The Diplomacy of the Russo-Japanese War*. Princeton, 1964.

Wilkinson, H.R. *Maps and Politics: A Review of the Ethnographic Cartography of Macedonia*. Liverpool, 1951.

Wilson, Herbert W. *Battleships in Action*. London, 1926.

Wolf, John B. *The Diplomatic History of the Bagdad Railroad*. Univ of Missouri Press, 1936.

Wolfe, Bertram D. *Three Who Made a Revolution*. New York, 1948; Boston, 1955.

Woodward, David. *The Russians at Sea*. London, 1965.

Yakhontoff, Victor A. *Russia and the Soviet Union in the Far East*. New York, 1931.

Yakovlev, N.N. *Vooruzhennye vosstaniia v dekabre 1905 g*. Moscow, 1957.

Yaney, George L. "The Concept of the Stolypin Land Reform. *Slavic Review*, 23 (1964): 275-93.

————. "Social Stability in Prerevolutionary Russia." *Slavic Review*, 24 (1965): 520-27.

————. *The Systematization of Russian Government: Social Evolution in the Domestic Evolution of Imperial Russia, 1711-1905*. Univ of Illinois Press, 1973.

Yarmolinsky, Avrahm. *Road to Revolution: A Century of Russian Radicalism*. New York, 1962.

————, ed. *A Treasury of Russian Verse*. New York, 1949.

Zagorsky, S.A. *State Control of Industry in Russia during the War*. New York, 1928.

Zaionchkovsky, A.M. *Podgotovka Rossii k imperialisticheskoi voine*. Moscow, 1926.

Zaionchkovsky, P.A. *The Russian Autocracy under Alexander III*. Ed. and trans. by David R. Jones. Gulf Breeze; Academic International Press, 1976.

Zavalishin, Vyacheslav. *Early Soviet Writers*. New York, 1958.

Zilliacus, Konni. *The Russian Revolutionary Movement*. London, 1905.

Volume numbers are followed by slashes; pages within volumes are separated by commas and enclosed by semi-colons. The entry "1/12, 39, 164; 3/68, 188n" refers to Volume 1, pages 12, 39, and 164; and to Volume 3, page 68 and a note on page 188. "Biog" refers to supplementary biographical information.

For their invaluable assistance in preparing this Index the editor thanks Professor Richard A. Skinner, Director, and the staff of the Computer-Based Laboratory for Instruction and Analysis, School of Arts and Letters, Old Dominion University. The editor also gratefully acknowledges the continued support of the Old Dominion University Research Foundation.

2/206; biog, 2/307n, 4/233

Nachalo [The Beginning], 1/202n, 4/183-84n; on obshchina, 2/9, 10-11; supports SPB Soviet, 2/170; on revolution, 2/175

Nadson, S.Ya. 1/22, 4/233

Nansen, Fridtjof, 3/165, 4/233

Nanshan, battle of, 2/79, 266n, 267n

Napoleon I, 1/71

Napoleon III, 1/67, 71

Napoleonic Code, in Poland, 1/8

Napravnik, E.F., 3/84, 4/233

Narev River, 4/27, 29

Naroch, Lake, 4/75

Narodnaia svoboda [The People's Freedom], 2/181

Narodnaia volia—see People's Will

Narodnik movement, origins in westernism, 1/31, 194n; see Populism

Narodnyi vestnik [The People's Messenger], 2/308n

Narva, battle of (1700), analogies drawn, 2/95, 272n; 4/159

Nasha zhizn [Our Life], 3/6, 180n; begins publication, 2/99; on concessions to Japan, 2/139; on revolution, 2/175; supports SPB Soviet, 2/170

Nashe slovo [Our Word], 4/11, 175n

Nashi dni [Our Days], on fall of Port Arthur, 2/103

Natanson, M.A., 2/95, 272-73nn; 4/175n; biog, 4/233

National Union, 4/173n

Nationalism, in electoral pattern, 3/84-85; growth of, 3/85-86ff, 105-6; in teachers congress, 3/149; unleashed by war, 4/21-22, 30-31

Nationalists, support Stolypin land reform, 3/41; as major element in Duma, 3/76; and Finnish autonomy, 3/87; in western zemstvo crisis, 3/94;

and Stolypin's assassination, 3/117-18, 209-10n; and Beilis affair, 3/131; spurn Progressive Bloc, 4/47; see also Progressive Nationalists

Naumov, A.N., 4/195; organizes United Nobility, 2/308n; heads ministry of agriculture, 4/55; dismissed, 4/80; biog, 4/234

Naval commission (Duma), 4/43, 64, 105

Naval staffs crisis, 3/76; origins, 3/21, 42, 57-59, 182n; tsar vetoes bill, 3/60-61; consequences of, 3/61-62; jurisdictions defined, 3/71

Navarin (cruiser), 3/218n

Navarino (battleship), 2/96

Navy, 1/206n; 3/208-9n; in 1894, 1/16; program of 1898, 1/100; in occupation of Port Arthur, 1/126, 127; in Boxer Rebellion, 1/133, 136; before Russo-Japanese War, 2/57, 62; in Russo-Japanese War, 2/74-77, 87-88, 96-98, 101, 123-26, 262-65nn, 266-67n, 270n, 273-75nn, 276n, 283-85nn; and revolutionary movement, 2/169, 170, 297n; appropriations and Duma, 3/72, 113, 195n; Franco-Russian naval convention, 3/120, 211-12n; on eve of Great War, 3/145, 218n; unpreparedness of, 3/216n; in Great War, 4/18-19; construction (1914-17), 4/89;

Navy—see also Merchant fleet, Mutiny, Naval staffs crisis, Pacific Squadron, Port Arthur, Tsushima, Vladivostok

Nazerevsky, V.P., 2/32

Nebogatov, N.I., leads Third Squadron, 2/124, 125, 126, 284n; court-martial of, 3/22; biog, 4/234

Neidhardt, A.B., 2/50; biog, 4/234

Nekrasov, N.V., 4/188n, 191n; defends war committees, 4/63; biog, 4/234

Nelidov, A.I., 2/153, 3/68; plan to seize Straits, 1/76; biog, 4/234